# Hard-Core Delinquents

## Reaching Out Through the Miami Experiment

Seymour Gelber

**Foreword by F. Lee Bailey**

**The University of Alabama Press**
Tuscaloosa and London

Library of Congress Cataloging-in-Publication Data

Gelber, Seymour.
    Hard-core delinquents : reaching out through the Miami experiment /
Seymour Gelber ; with a foreword by F. Lee Bailey.
    p    cm.
    Includes index.
    ISBN 0-8173-0399-5
    1. Rehabilitation of juvenile delinquents—Florida—Miami—Case
studies.  2. Juvenile justice, Administration of—Florida—Miami—Case
studies.  3. Juvenile courts—Florida—Miami—Case studies.  4. Social
work    with    delinquents    and    criminals—Florida—Miami—Case
studies.  I. Title.
HV9106.M45G45 1988
364.6—dc19                                                    88-10665
                                                                  CIP


British Library Cataloguing-in-Publication Data is available.

To my wife, Edith, for listening
patiently and sympathetically at
dinnertime as I recounted the
continuing saga of these troubled
youngsters. And for helping me
put it all down on paper.

# Contents

# Contents

# Foreword

## F. Lee Bailey

I don't pretend to be an expert on the juvenile court. Contending with the perversities and uncertainties of the adult court provides enough trouble for me. I have often thought that, if I were to come back in another life, I might like to be a juvenile court Judge. True, defense lawyers thrive on the exciting contest to save an innocent man; yet, there's a certain purity about the juvenile court, a challenge in meeting the unknown that is appealing. It reminds me of the days when I was a young Marine pilot flying Sabre jets. Even though my senses warned me that the sky was full of surprises and peril, I was still in control. There was a coolness up there, a feeling that the world belonged to me. Judging in juvenile court must be like that, a feeling that you can still change a young person's life. Point him in the right direction; see the metamorphosis from a vile little wretch to a decent young person; realize that at any moment Humpty Dumpty can come tumbling down.

Those who know judges personally will tell you that their darkest moments come when duty requires them to punish another human being: the worst is execution, the second worst is prison, and the third worst is some lesser alternative. All of our breeding, education, and adult sense is liberty-oriented. To impinge upon that liberty is at least unpleasant, and at worst abhorrent, to any thinking, caring, sensitive judge. In my long experience, the vast majority of such judges are all of the above.

But, painful as it is to deal with adults who must feel the wrath of the law, this is a mere picnic compared to facing the same circumstances with juveniles. Some adult offenders are repetitive losers who have proved over and over that they must be segregated from society for so long as is possible, simply to protect society. For those transgressors in the twilight zone between adolescence and adulthood, the judgments are of necessity a lot more complex. A juvenile judge almost always faces this dilemma: "From my very limited choices, how can I best help steer this young person back to the track of reality?" The choices are poor.

An undisciplined youth given probationary freedom believes that he has "beaten the system," and peer pressure often steers him to resume his anti-social ways. If he is put in a prison—any prison, no matter how it is labeled—the likelihood that he will come out of that experience as a better citizen is near zero. Prisons make bitter, anti-social people out of almost any material dumped into them, and every thinking judge knows that.

Judge Seymour Gelber is a thinking judge, and much more than that. He searches for a better way with the intensity that prodded Demosthenes to seek out an "honest man." He is, in Florida, and beyond its borders, the model of what a Juvenile Judge ought to be: Unhappy with the system, searching for new and better ways, innovating always where others have all but thrown up their hands. Most important, he understands acutely the agony and helplessness of parents—both rich and poor—who are baffled by the anti-social conduct of their progeny, and ill-equipped to deal with it.

The springboard of this book is an experiment involving youthful offenders—six of them, all "tough cases"—who are given the "maximum treatment" that a benevolent and non-budgeted society could offer. They were given direct, continuous, and intense supervision and guidance from a "Master Counselor," a person uniquely qualified to deal with such problem cases. One would like to say that Judge Gelber's foray into enemy terrain was an overwhelming victory. Unfortunately, that was not the result. Some showed marked movement toward acceptable, "normal" behavior, and others did not.

The message sent by these six, each of whom has violated our turf repeatedly is that you had better help us in order to help yourself. This is not a message the public wants to hear. Most people want punishment to be the focus, not rehabilitation. Model it after the adult court, they insist—an idea deserving an early demise. Imposing a bankrupt system on one that still shows signs of vitality is senseless.

The depth of this book is Judge Gelber's profound experience of nearly thirty years in hands-on dealing with these most frustrating problems. Simply put, "What the hell do we do with our kids when they behave in a way we never taught, cannot condone, and do not understand?" He tells us authoritatively, and in a thoroughly documented and expert way, what we might do if we would but face up to the problems instead of sticking our heads in the sand, unpleasant though those problems might be. Juvenile judges may be blessed with the wisdom of Solomon in some cases, but they cannot take terminal cases and somehow give them again the gift of life simply because they wear robes and are sensitive and caring. They need help, much help, long before the youngsters are brought before them. They need the help of parents, sociologists, psychologists, police, and all who can prevent juvenile misconduct rather than face the problem after it is too late.

In short, Judge Gelber is calling for a complete overhaul of the juvenile justice system. I cannot imagine that any lawyer who has had to represent juveniles—and frankly, we all recoil from this responsibility because we have so few answers—would take serious exception to what he proposes. He shows dramatically that it is not working, has not worked, and probably won't work in the future unless substantial changes are made. For what it is worth, I agree with virtually all that he says.

As to the business of juvenile justice, I claim some credentials, mostly on my mother's side. When I was nine, World War II was in progress and I used to get up early to cook porridge for the hordes of young children who would arrive at my mother's "war nursery school" so that their mothers could be free to work in defense factories while their fathers were serving in uniform. That same mother who had her teaching degree in the 1920s went on to get her bachelor's degree in 1954, her master's degree in 1963, and her Ph.D. in 1979 at the age of seventy. She is one of the nation's leading authorities on the education of youngsters, their personality formation, and where they are likely to "go wrong" because of lack of affection, or abuse, or treatment, or worse. I predict with confidence that she will give this book to her many friends with a polite "I told you so . . ."

This is an important book about a problem that affects more Americans than almost any other problem in our culture. One only has to represent one juvenile in a career of practicing law to appreciate the abject agony etched into a baffled parent's face when a child's misdeeds are spread across a cold court record for all the public to see. Those who undertake the awesome responsibility of guiding a young person through the perils and temptations of life until that person is equipped to make judgments individually will vastly improve their chances of success if they will but absorb the tireless wisdom of the pages within.

# Preface

The ultimate belief of social-work practitioners is that under ideal conditions every delinquent child can be saved. The experiment described in this book tests that concept. Take a handful of recently convicted hard-core delinquents, who all have long rap sheets and don't give a damn about society. Sentence them to the harshest punishment in the juvenile system, namely, putting them on the next bus to the state reformatory. Meanwhile, obtain the best streetwise counselor; have him pull these young toughs off the bus. Tell them that not only are they free, but also that every need of theirs and their families will be attended to in the coming year. Jobs, schooling, counseling, housing, and clothing will be provided through the auspices of a Master Counselor.

Selected for this position is Cornelius Foster, from Liberty City's ghetto streets, a former liquor store holdup specialist who has five years of hard time in Raiford State Prison to his credit. Throw in a college-trained supervisor who follows the book and knows all the bureaucratic ropes to assist Master Counselor Foster. Add an idealistic judge who will open doors, guaranteeing everything they are entitled to, and more. Mix these ingredients with recalcitrant, selfish, unyielding, unappreciative clients and the hypothesis for the social experiment is created: providing the highest quality staff, available twenty-four hours a day seven days a week, without limitations on time or cost, utilizing every worthwhile resource in the community, cajoling, directing, and nurturing. Then, at the end of a year, according to the theory, each of these alienated youths will have made remarkable progress toward becoming an accepted and contributing member of society. Finding: It ain't necessarily so.

This volume is about the new breed of hard-core delinquent. Numbering only a few, they are the youths who have made an adjustment to crime. They have adapted to it and adopted it, easily and casually. Fifty years ago, even twenty years ago, the juvenile court focused on minor offenses: incorrigibility, runaways, shoplifting, and occasionally a burglary. Inner-city streets had a few youth gangs and some violence occurred, but these situations were not pervasive. Family, school, and church were relied on in those days for moral indoctrination.

Today, the inordinate concern over crime has created an atmosphere of frustration and fear. A host of studies and antidotes for treating persistent youthful criminals has surfaced. The finger points toward juvenile delinquency as the incubator, and the hard-core, repetitive offender is emphasized. The public attitude has hardened toward the treatment of juveniles, but public fear is still present.

Over a two-year period, this book follows six hard-cores and describes the interaction among them and the various professionals who guide them. The "system," in its own plodding way, provides everything that is available. The families, in dire straits, seem to be impervious to all efforts. The delinquents, long gone from the mainstream, are indifferent to it all. Numbering four at first and later six, these youths are not the kind whose horrible crimes are recounted on the front page. They are run-of-the-mill hard-core and are not pathologically violent. Friendly on the basketball court, they are a threat in a dark alley. Regulars in the "system," they run from crime to crime and through program after program.

More than any empirical study, this volume exposes the muscle and flab of the "system." The bureaucracy crawls along where speed is essential, then rushes blindly where long-term action is needed. The experts—psychologists, psychiatrists, judges, and others—flail about, hoping that the wheel-of-fortune falls on the winning numbers. This book is about young people rejecting community values and the struggle to make those values important to them. More than determining success or failure of an effort to save six kids, the experiment demonstrates how slow, drawn out, and uncertain the effort is, no matter what the resources. The issues of the day stand out clearly: the clamor for safe streets, the failure to improve ghetto life, the weakness of the family, the ineffectiveness of the school. All these embody what ails delinquent youth in America.

Some broad questions are examined in this book. What does the social-work system really deliver? Are the bad kids beyond repair doomed to crime and prison? How much can teams of social workers, psychiatrists, and other specialists contribute to the solution? Are we deluding ourselves with false hopes? The Master Counselor experiment to determine how effective an all-out effort can be touches only the surface.

No matter what the outcome with these six youths, the same questions will be raised for the next six and the six thereafter. In each case, all the layers need to be peeled away to find what makes the Laurences and the Marcos tick. These youngsters, hell-bent on self-destruction, don't pause for reflection. Too often, neither does the community, angry and impatient with recalcitrant youth. Somewhere and somehow, a path must be found that both can follow together.

Selection criteria required subjects with at least ten delinquency and dependency cases, including several felony arrests. The six averaged twelve arrests each and many neglect reports. Excluded were individuals over their sixteenth birthday, psychotics, and those considered beyond assistance. To be eligible, participants also had to be detained in lockup, waiting transportation to the state reformatory. Master Counselor Cornelius Foster interviewed each of the likely subjects and originally accepted four who were deemed suitable for the program; he rejected three candidates. Initial plans called for him to carry a caseload of four for one year, but these figures were later increased to six for two years.

# The Major Characters

**CORNELIUS FOSTER** - Vietnam veteran. Returned to Miami, unable to adjust, went on crime spree. Sentenced to two fifteen-year terms for liquor-store robberies. While serving five years at Raiford State Prison, attended junior-college classes and upon release won a degree from Florida A & M University. Employed for eight years as field counselor with juvenile delinquents. Tough-outside, soft-inside type. Doesn't give up on kids, and plays whatever cards are dealt him with resigned humor. Growing up in the streets of Liberty City makes him ideal Master Counselor for young toughs. Comfortable on their street corners, he knows their language and has their respect.

**FRANK MANNING** - Foster's supervisor. Graduate of social-work school. Sensitive, well-spoken young man, twenty-nine years of age, working his way up the ladder of the bureaucracy. Certain to head a major social-work agency someday. Calm and cool, can be counted on for reasoned approach. Adept at the conference table, knows who can do what. Good Catholic upbringing, wants to do all the right things. Heavy set, six feet, five inches tall, compared to Foster, who is a foot shorter and compact. They look like the odd couple, but get along well together.

**SEYMOUR GELBER** - Veteran jurist, former prosecutor, thirty years in the criminal-justice system. Cynical, wry sense of humor. Sometimes boosts potential of juvenile system; other times bemoans unbroken, unchanging cycle. Credits highly motivated individuals as key, rather than content of program. Sees community expectations as totally unrealistic.

**LESTER BURROWS** (The Runner) - Black male, fifteen. Last conviction: burglary. Twelve arrests plus innumerable neglect charges. Discarded by mother at early age. Literally grew up in the streets. Placed in more than twenty shelter homes; ran away from them all. Able to survive living off the streets, hustling homosexuals. Breaks into homes, steals cars. Anything to make a buck. Not a thrill seeker or macho; crime just a necessary act. Illiterate due to rarely attending school. Pleasant, likable, devious young man. Rejects help from state agencies, the courts, or any authority group.

**MARCO ZARGULA** (The Charmer) - Latin male, fifteen. Last conviction: armed robbery. Twelve arrests. Follows housing project gang into drugs, burglary, and robbery for the excitement. Has potential and is easy learner, but defies all efforts to be socialized. Envisions himself as desperado, modeled after Al Pacino role in *Scarface*. Father disappeared, stepfather serving jail sentence in New Jersey for robbery. Mother, distraught over poor family situation and problem siblings, is living on welfare. Marco, small for his age, handsome, immature, cries when locked up. Goes on drug binge immediately upon release. Charms all who come into contact with him. Thrives within institutions, but cannot survive on outside.

**DWIGHT ANDERSON** (The Migrant) - Youngest in group. Black male, twelve. Fifteen arrests. Comes from large family of migrant workers who breed generations of illiteracy, poverty, and ignorance. Thinks nothing wrong with taking other person's property. Low IQ. Indifferent to threat of punishment. Avoids school and any outside influence. Will not ride on special school bus with his problem-classmates because he hates "retards." Glum, little to say, aggressive, always fighting and in trouble. Lives in overcrowded hovel with countless relatives. No one in charge. No one cares. Mother prefers sleeping all day, staying on welfare.

**LAURENCE SAMUEL** (The Fighter) - Black male, fifteen. Eighteen arrests, eleven involving violence. Tough, aggressive, powerfully built, six feet four, strikes out at all in his way, particularly school teachers or anyone in authority. No apparent reason for assaultive behavior. Introverted, indifferent to others, acts as if world owes him a living. No scruples about committing crime to obtain what he wants. Mother and stepfather provide good home, but family members fearful of Laurence's outbursts. Very little school progress. Has potential, but it may be too late.

**ANDY SILLS** (The Drinker) - White male, fifteen. Eight arrests plus nine neglect charges. Comes from broken family. Father is alcoholic, mother has experienced similar problem, as has Andy. Mother has moved from city to city, trailer to trailer, from man to man trying to make ends meet. Andy gets drunk, commits burglary, acts remorseful after sobering up. Always claims he will reform, but never does. Lies profusely, lacks character. Long arrest record and lack of motivation suggest he is likely candidate for life in prison. Has ability to succeed, but cannot discipline himself to study or work.

**JAMIE FOREST** (The Nuisance) - Black male, fifteen. Eighteen arrests, mostly burglaries. A follower, not a planner of crimes. Slightly retarded, probably from early spinal meningitis. Amiable, funny, and warm, until provoked. Then becomes assaultive, using any weapon available. Constantly challenges older, bigger boys, but is ignored. Education primitive and at a standstill. No father around, but very caring mother, unable to control him. Spends time fantasizing about being rich. Psychologists and counselors see him as always being a drain on society. Served time in juvenile rehabilitation programs but no progress made. Believes shortcuts outside the law are the way to make it. Has no qualms about participating in crime. Will probably become more violent as he grows older.

NOTE: *The names of all juveniles and their families referred to in this volume have been changed to protect their identities. Where direct excerpts from assessment reports are used, the full names of counselors, psychologists, and psychiatrists are replaced by initials. All other individuals are identified by their correct names.*

# Hard-Core
## Delinquents

# 1

---

# Taking Bad Dudes
# Off the Bus
# to State School
# Is Good for the Soul

**Friday, March 30, 1984**

Our Master Counselor wasn't quite what I had anticipated, but it's hard to tell who has the magic formula. When Jay Kassack and I set up the Master Counselor Program, we had a super counselor in mind, the best in the field, who by dint of supreme effort and extraordinary empathy with children, would turn the worst ones around. No counselors rushed to volunteer for this great experiment. Although it represented an imposing challenge, many of those proposed for the assignment declined: some, because the salary structure didn't provide additional compensation; others, already in a higher pay grade, faced a pay cut. Most preferred the anonymity of their 35–50 caseload, realizing that only four juveniles in the proposed caseload for the new Master Counselor Program would spotlight their results. Although Jay Kassack, as district administrator, is top man in Dade County for the Florida Health and Rehabilitative Services (HRS), he can't offer a more significant inducement to his counselors.

From three recommendations made by Kassack's staff, Juvenile Court Administrator George LaMont selected Cornelius Foster, an eight-year veteran HRS counselor. Through the years, Foster had earned a reputation as a no-nonsense individual, who was more comfortable in the streets taking care of his kids than arguing in court with lawyers. I felt comfortable with him, but some lingering doubts remained in my mind about his ability to rise above a routine approach in handling really tough cases. Court Administrator La-Mont, with many years of experience in the field as a probation officer, cautioned me to quit looking for some ideal: "This project will need a lot of legwork and patience. It's going to be a long haul. Foster is a diligent, serious guy who won't be satisfied to conduct his business by telephone. Foster will turn up wherever these young-sters are—at home, in school, street corners, or anyplace else. He'll be there when those kids need him."

We will see. I'll make every effort to motivate Foster. At our first meeting I laid it right out for him:

> This is a great opportunity. It is the ultimate test to determine whether the social-work delivery system can actually deliver. The Master Counselor will have a caseload of four tough, hard youngsters with long records of juvenile crimes, each literally taken off the bus en route to State School. He will be available twenty-four hours a day, seven days a week, covering every aspect of the child's life: social, educational, religious, and vocational, including the family of the child. Jobs and parenting skills for the mother and father will also be a concern of the counselor.

Foster stood there respectful but impassive. This wasn't the first "hot" program sold to him. I continued assuring him: "The judge will be there opening doors and meeting regularly with the child and family. For the next twelve months, your four clients and their fami-lies will have top priority, with anything and everything in the com-munity available."

Ending on a resolute note, I predicted this experiment would exert a significant impact on the juvenile-delinquency field because it would show that, when enough resources were available, even the worst delinquents could be saved. Foster hesitated a moment, then asked: "Suppose there's a family with eleven children, do I take responsibility for all of them, monitoring their school attendance and curfew?" Ignoring his question, I assured him that he would find satisfaction in meeting these challenges, and let it go at that. This noble experiment of mine was just another tough job to him. He was concerned about pragmatic matters, not some grand philosophy. No emotion. No vision of glory. Whatever the purpose of the Master Counselor Program, he was going to take it in stride.

2

"Here's your first case," I announced. It was a fifteen-year-old black kid who had appeared in court this morning. Perfect for this program, he had been kicked around all his life; nobody cared about him and he distrusted the world. I told Foster that Lester Burrows (The Runner) was a loser and he would be assigned only losers. None would be psychotics or desperately involved in drug problems, but all would have lengthy arrest records and a long laundry list of failures. In each, there had to be some ray of hope I wanted him to ignite.

That morning, I had ordered Burrows returned to State School. He was now waiting for the bus. I directed Foster to go down to the lockup, interview him, and report back whether or not he was salvageable. Foster's supervisor, Frank Manning, sitting there absorbed in thought, expressed concern that the child had been hospitalized in the past: "Is this some permanent disability requiring medical treatment?" I shrugged a quick "no," looking toward Foster. He had no questions, only stating he would look at the case, then turning abruptly, not waiting to be excused, departed with Supervisor Manning in his wake. They made an odd pair: Manning, 6'5" and weighing 270 pounds, circumspect, follow-the-rules bureaucrat, son of a Catholic Services Bureau child-adoption worker; Foster, a foot shorter, black, rugged, a laid-back college graduate who had learned about life in the streets. There's no telling what they thought. Foster probably just wanted to get away from the chatter to work with his new client, and Manning was probably concerned that now he will have to cater to the judge's latest experiment.

Neither Foster's past performance in court nor his response to my outline of the project evinced a gung ho driving force, but his quiet air of self-assurance suggested more than appeared on the surface.

## Thursday, April 5, 1984

Reading the Burrows file made it easy to see why he needed a Master Counselor. Now fifteen years old, he has been in the court system as both a delinquent and dependent child since age eleven. Court records indicate that he started as a dependent in 1980, running away from home with such regularity that his mother sought help from the state. Four dependency cases were filed during the next two years. Constantly a truant, he lived in the streets, retreating to his grandmother's house whenever hunger or the elements became too severe. Often brought to court by the police, he was placed in shelters or foster homes, only to renew the cycle by fleeing again.

The first of many criminal charges appeared a year later at age twelve and they increased in number thereafter. His was the typical sequence of crimes committed by delinquents who were wending their way up the ladder of crime. Initially, two arrests were made for shoplifting, the entry crime for beginners, usually committed for excitement and recreation. They were followed by an arrest for loitering and prowling, the prelude to house burglaries. Sure enough, the next three entries showed burglary arrests that earned him a six-month sentence to State School, hopefully to give him the opportunity to get his act together. Not at all. Upon return, after being ordered to attend school regularly and keep in weekly contact with his counselor, he promptly disappeared. Running true to form, young Lester was rearrested shortly thereafter, charged with a new offense, grand larceny, and ordered returned to State School. At this juncture, the Master Counselor Program intervened, and he was chosen to be "saved."

Foster's plan for Lester covers all the traditional social-work bases and more. For the past five days, he has spent several hours each day in Lester's detention cell, carefully outlining the steps to be taken. The youth will be placed in the best foster home available. A team of public-school counselors will determine how to bring him back into the educational process. Our Mental Health Clinic will recommend the kind of counseling and therapy needed. In addition, Foster persuaded the grandmother to allow Lester weekend visits in order to provide some semblance of family life again. The counselor also contacted a YMCA near the foster home to make recreational opportunities available with, as he puts it, "positive thinking peers." Further, he intends to find part-time employment for his client and personally provide transportation to all the programs and activities. It was a workmanlike effort, accomplished without any judicial assistance. Obviously not awed by working with a judge, Foster intends to take over. A good sign.

I'll wait a week or two until Lester settles into all these activities before sitting down with him for a personal conference in chambers. I'd like to know what makes a kid like this tick. Why does he keep running away? Who does he really trust? What was his reaction to being placed in the Master Counselor Program? Does he have any ambitions in life other than daily survival? What motivates him to crime? Is he too far gone for love and affection? That should be a fascinating interview.

4

## Friday, April 6, 1984

At 9:00 A.M. Foster called, advising that Lester had gone from detention cell to new foster home, stayed there exactly thirty minutes . . . and disappeared. Considering his past behavior, this news shouldn't have been unexpected, but in truth I was taken aback. After being fortunate enough to be selected for the program, how could he completely reject the benefits?

On my 2:00 P.M. calendar, Foster was first in line for a Pickup Order to hold Lester in secure detention after the police locate him. I so ordered. Foster sounded strained rather than embarrassed by what had happened. I tried to lighten his responsibility with some humor, suggesting he write down all the techniques used to influence Lester so that a permanent record existed of how *not* to handle a youngster in trouble. Foster, ignoring my heavy-handed attempt at humor, said he'd camp out at grandmother's house and have him back shortly.

I don't know what Foster has in mind for Lester Burrows when we get him back. If we give up and ship him straight to State School, he will, at the most, be out of circulation about a year. When released, he's likely to be a bigger problem for the community. Is it worth the effort to try again? Will we be wasting one of the four spots available in the Master Counselor Program?

## Monday, April 9, 1984

No word on Lester yet. Foster reported no action at his grandmother's house, though a telephone call from an unidentified source disclosed that Lester usually "shacks up with homosexuals" to make a few bucks for living expenses. "Why didn't the psychologists recognize he was a homosexual?" I asked Foster.

"He's not a homosexual," Foster commented dryly. "He just bunks in with those guys." Foster had to be in another court, so I couldn't pursue this new angle. I suppose Foster means he's not a full-time gay and that selling a little sex is a normal diversion for youngsters living in the street. We'll have to talk about that some more.

## Tuesday, April 10, 1984

Still no sign of Lester. I pulled his files again to see what made him run. In 1980, when Lester was eleven, a social worker, asking him

5

why he continues to run away from home, received this response: "I'm not running away. My mother just leaves me in the street everyday. Nobody ever tells me when to come home. No one is ever home. Since nobody cooks regular meals in the house, I go wherever somebody will feed me. My mother doesn't care if I come home." When confronted by the social worker, his mother defended her indifference, saying he was out of control and she was afraid of what she might do to him.

The next year, a psychotherapist described him as an emotionally disturbed youngster who has responded to his deficits by becoming distrustful, by decreasing verbal communication and by increasing use of fantasy. The therapist concluded that Lester was seeking a warm and trusting relationship with an adult. In 1982 another psychologist found him to be personable and bright beyond the 93 IQ score shown in testing and concluded that he does what he has to in order to survive the abandonments and deprivations of his early childhood. In 1983 a teacher at State School described him as disruptive, totally lacking in motivation, and performing poorly in class.

Other assessments in his files confirmed that the juvenile system had made a reasonable effort to reach him. All the assessors agreed on his need for attention. Before going to State School in 1983, he had run away from fourteen foster homes. At age fifteen, he's already had a squad of psychologists and psychiatrists work him over without making a dent.

## Wednesday, April 11, 1984

Reports have Lester spotted roaming Liberty City but successfully evading the police. Foster, still smarting from what appeared to be a failure on his part, seemed hesitant at my suggestion that we try again when Lester is picked up. This doubt was reinforced after he learned from other counselors that the boy had actually fled from twenty placements in foster homes and shelters in the years they had been dealing with him. None foresaw much hope for him. Apparently, he trusted no one and, no matter how good the intentions, nothing made an impact on him. One of his earlier counselors recalled an aunt who rejected him when he became too intimate with her young daughters. Another counselor reported that his great-grandmother, though old and infirm, wanted him, but, when an expensive diamond ring disappeared, she, too, decided he couldn't be handled any longer. Foster's uncertainty is understandable: the decision will be his.

Reflecting back on the many hours of earnest discussion with Lester, Foster realized he had been duped. Lester had only been biding his time. Foster had carefully selected the best foster home available. The Latin parents had two young children of their own, plus two foster boys, both black, about the same age as Lester. The foster father, a long-distance truck driver, often took the two foster boys along as helpers to earn some money and enjoy seeing other parts of the country. Lester needed a stable family that paid attention to one another, and, because of the two other boys his own age, Foster sensed he could fit in easily.

The new foster mother had introduced her small children, asked Lester what he'd like for dinner, then went to the kitchen. Lester had assured Foster that everything was o.k., said he didn't like little kids hanging around, and requested money to buy a soda. Foster, the good sport, had given him four dollars and a pat on the back. "Can I go for a soda now?" an obviously uncomfortable Lester had asked. "Sure," replied Foster, and that was the last seen of Lester Burrows or Cornelius Foster's four dollars.

## Thursday, April 12, 1984

Foster was more optimistic talking about Dwight Anderson (The Migrant), the new twelve-year-old referral, who had been arrested for thirteen burglaries and grand larcenies during a ten-day spree. Looking at his arrest record, I immediately announced from the bench that he was the new record-holder, scarcely able to catch his breath between crimes. Foster described the family thusly: "This is a family of migrant workers who have worked their way up to living in a shack on the outskirts of town. For generations they lived in trucks, traveling from state to state picking crops. Now they have a permanent place, with eleven sleeping on floor space no larger than my living room. All cousins, sisters, brothers, uncles, aunts, and whatever."

Five years ago, the family had applied for public housing and were still waiting for the first response. "Do you have any influence with the Housing Authority?" Foster wanted to know. I told him we'd sure find out. As he went on with plans for the brood, I wondered how he could maintain any enthusiasm working with a family like this.

I suggested he sort out all their needs, catalogue Dwight's problems and then prioritize them. In the past, when social workers talked in terms of "prioritizing needs," it always upset me, sounding

7

so calculating and lacking any personal feeling. Sensing how difficult this youngster and his family may turn out to be, it was apparent that some order in our approach was required. So off we go to prioritizing needs.

I couldn't resist reminding Foster about his uncertainty last week when the possibility of facing a family of eleven arose: "You weren't sure then, but now you are raring to go." For the first time since this project began, he gave me a big smile. "Don't worry about me. I can handle this job." As he started out the door, he added that he was ready for another referral. Smiling back, I told him he'd have one soon and, feigning seriousness, cautioned him about spending four dollars of his money for a soda when a dollar was more than enough. The four dollars told me a lot about Cornelius Foster I didn't know before.

## Monday, April 16, 1984

Another likely candidate for the program was scratched. He was Rudy Lander, a fourteen-year-old, charged in two cases of strong-arm robbery, knocking down several women, and stealing their purses. Our hearing was to determine if he should be "waived" over for trial in the adult court. Despite four witnesses identifying him, he maintained his innocence, claiming he was home at a barbeque during the hours the crimes were committed. His mother was his alibi. She was the same lady who had caused a commotion two weeks earlier during his trial for loitering and prowling. At that trial, she had angrily refused Court Administrator LaMont's direction to sit in the outer room awaiting her turn to testify. Even though the case was dismissed, she stomped out in a fury.

Back, once more, certain the justice system was out to get her son, she was determined to protect him regardless of the circumstances. Barely restraining herself, she jumped up and down, shaking her head vigorously as each witness identified him. Several times, I had to caution her to sit quietly. On the stand, she conceded he had once stolen a car, but other than that it had been total harassment.

Despite her aggressiveness, harnessing the mother's energy might turn this kid around. During a recess, I mentioned this to LaMont, who warned, "This lady is primed to fight every 'whitey' in sight." As the hearing progressed, it became clear that her only goal was to protect her son from outside intervention. There was no Master Counselor or judge with whom she would willingly cooperate. Regrettably, I decided Rudy was inappropriate for our program and sent the case to adult court. Bringing Foster together with that mean kid and his overaggressive mother had seemed promising, but it wasn't in the offing. Almost every court case involves absent parents. Here, finally, we have a vigorous mother, willing to battle for her son; unfortunately, her efforts are not likely to benefit him. Too bad.

Only several days had passed since Dwight Anderson's admission to the program, and Foster was back reporting a new arrest: assaulting a cell mate in the detention center. Although only twelve years old and scheduled for State School, Dwight seems indifferent to the prospect of punishment. Foster was somewhat perplexed. "I know you want me to save Dwight from going to State School by taking him off the bus. But if he doesn't care about what happens and gets arrested again and again, how am I helping him? Are we going to let him do whatever he wants to do?"

I hesitated a moment before replying: "There's some risk in what we are doing. And we are not giving out licenses to commit crime. However, we are committed to staying with these kids through all their problems and giving them total support—something they have never had before."

"Judge, tell me what you want. Shall I give him individual counseling, set up group sessions, or what?"

"You do what has to be done. If it's counseling, then counsel. If it's fishing, then fish. Use whatever abilities you have, as if these are your own kids. Then, also use whatever else is available in the community."

In a "you-are-the-boss" manner, Foster departed, noting he was on his way to the detention center to give Dwight some of the support I was talking about.

## Tuesday, April 17, 1984

The drive to the Broward County Courthouse with George LaMont gave me time to reflect upon our program. Although it had only been operational for two weeks, one—a street waif—had already deserted; the other, from an unstable migrant family, was indifferent to the law; and two more unknowns were yet to be selected. Hardly an auspicious beginning. Considering that this is a "by chance" selection, what else is in store?

I had been assigned to try a burglary case involving the son of a Broward County legislator—all the judges in that county had declined to hear the case. It was a first offense, but something about the case bothered me. In this instance, instead of fighting the system in the manner of the hostile Mrs. Lander, these parents were using it. Their battery of lawyers was filing every conceivable motion to avoid prosecution. When the legal maneuvers failed, in came psychologists and psychiatrists to persuade me that locking up the juvenile wasn't in his best interest. It turned out that Marlon Jameson had a high IQ, but for years had been under treatment for a learning disability. He had made little progress in school, dropping out before graduation. The neighbors were frightened, suspecting him of assorted crimes, fearful he was part of a gang that was terrorizing the neighborhood. During the trial, he sat detached and sullen while his mother and father had that air of anxiety that often tells more about the child than all the evidence.

Listening to the psychologist expound so glibly on his success with learning-disabled children but knowing only too well the frustrations of fifteen-year-olds who are unable to read or write, I hoped Marlon's parents recognized the long, difficult road ahead. I had seen too many intellectually endowed youngsters from high-achiever families paying a heavy price for dyslexia and other learning impediments.

When the psychiatrist said that Marlon's perception of life needed to be altered by a system of reward as well as punishment, I had trouble restraining myself. This kid damn well knew all about reward and punishment. My guess was that he'd had plenty of other scrapes, always rescued by his parents. Everyone assured me he would straighten out. I placed him on probation, ordered counseling, some community service hours, and curfew. Marlon doesn't qualify for our Master Counselor Program, but he bears further watching. Lacking the hard-core criminal record of Dwight and never concerned about the absence of a meal or bed, Marlon, as well as his family, may still find the problems just as severe. The good things in life—a supportive family, special schooling, job opportunities—are not guarantees of success. In a sense, the very resources readily available to Marlon are the precise ones the Master Counselor Program will attempt to provide our four hard-core clients. Why would it work for disadvantaged ghetto youths, when it hasn't been enough for some kids who have it all?

## Friday, April 20, 1984

The shuttle from Boston had been delayed and, after waiting three hours in the doctor's office, I was relieved to finally arrive in New

10

York for the meeting of the American Bar Association (ABA) Task Force on Crime at the Ritz-Carlton Hotel. Because the hotel rates start at $125 a night, I stayed at sister-in-law Irene's East 69th Street apartment while she was visiting in Miami. I had decided to combine the ABA meeting with a quick trip to my doctor in Boston, who told me I'd need another operation, this time on my left hip, following two earlier ones on my right hip. Although not unexpected, the doctor's verdict didn't exactly leave me brimming with joy.

Once I was inside the apartment, the TV reported that twenty-two youngsters, ages thirteen to twenty, had gone on a subway mugging spree. After robbing and assaulting twenty passengers on a train ride from Queens to Brooklyn, they had finally been intercepted by twenty-five transit police. The group was described as a rat-pack that was terrorizing citizens until the police posse came to the rescue.

The next news item showed the funeral of eight children, executed in what police thought was a drug-revenge scenario. I closed the upper and lower dead bolts on the door, put on the latch, and called Miami to tell my wife, Edith, that her sister's apartment was secure for the night. Welcome to the Big Apple!

## Saturday, April 21, 1984

En route to the Ritz-Carlton, the cab driver absentmindedly forgot to put up the meter flag and could only charge one dollar for what obviously was a three- or four-dollar trip. Magnanimously, I paid the fare, tipped him a dollar, and felt great, coming out ahead of a New York cabbie. Horse-driven carriages were cloppety-clopping along the streets, and itinerant artists were setting up their stands on its Central Park side. At the entrance to the hotel, three doormen were escorting people into the building. The sun was shining, and any moment I expected a band to strike up "New York, New York."

We were there to tidy up an earlier report issued in response to Chief Justice Warren Burger's complaint several years ago that lawyers weren't doing enough in response to the crime situation in America. Ours was an ad hoc task force whose recommendations had to run a gauntlet of committees and sections before earning the ABA House of Delegates' approval. After that, it would be even harder to carry out the proposals unless the top ABA brass was really supportive.

We were a cross section of practitioners, judges, and law professors, the best known being F. Lee Bailey, the noted criminal de-

**11**

fense lawyer. Richard Gerstein, chairman of the task force, an old hand at criminal-justice politics, knew just how far the ABA would go. He had been the prosecuting attorney for Dade County (Miami) for twenty-five years before going into private practice. For fifteen of those years, I had worked for him, serving as his administrative assistant. Entertaining no illusions about the difficulty of persuading the House of Delegates, he concentrated on practical approaches that these conservative, impatient lawyers would tolerate. Occasionally, in the past, he had enjoyed some success in striking a liberal vein: he persuaded the House of Delegates to support gun control; he also convinced them, over the opposition of the U.S. Justice Department, to lift somewhat the veil of secrecy under which grand juries function.

Only five of the committee members were present for the 10:00 A.M. roll call. Gerstein wasted little time going through the agenda. F. Lee Bailey, though absent, had asked that we consider the problems of delays in the appeal process. According to him, too often new trials are ordered as a result of the trial judge appointing inexperienced and often incompetent lawyers for indigents, particularly in murder cases. We agreed, referring the matter to a standing ABA committee that was already working on this issue.

Sylvia Bacon, a Washington, D.C., judge, telephoned a request that we support the position recently taken by the ABA opposing capital punishment for juveniles. Gerstein had somehow managed to obtain the House of Delegates' approval, leaving many prosecutors miffed; they now were threatening to revive the issue. None of us saw it as an important public matter until some state chose to electrocute a fourteen-year-old. Usually a juvenile murderer sits on death row for several years, and, when electrocuted at about twenty, nobody notices or cares that he was a juvenile at the time he committed a horrible atrocity.

A former Boston prosecutor asked for a report on what was happening in the juvenile-justice area. Gerstein eyed me with a message requesting I avoid my usual long-winded Kiwanis Club speech. I cut it short, but couldn't resist pointing out that there was little leadership in the field, each interest group focusing on its own concern. Whoever was in political power at the moment played his tune. Because the Reagan administration was only funding programs involving hard-core violent offenders, everyone had joined that chorus. I let it go at that, and Gerstein looked relieved.

A law professor from North Carolina suggested we support an

increase in the number of law-education programs that teach grade-school students to better understand and appreciate the legal system. I shot back, "These are 'Boy Scout' programs for white, middle-class kids who don't need much reaching. The kid that needs these programs is already a dropout, a truant who unfortunately learns the legal system, the hard way, in the street."

The law professor was a little taken aback by my intensity. He had been in the U.S. Justice Department during the 1960s when the federal government, under President Lyndon Johnson, made the first movement toward aiding the local anticrime effort. "A lot of these helping programs worked then," he said.

"Those were the salad days, the days of innocence," I rejoined. "The public isn't buying goodness anymore." Gerstein smiled indulgently, certain I'd manage one of those outbursts before the day was done. We discussed a few more items, determined our agenda was completed, had lunch, and went off to our respective destinations—me to the airport and back to Miami.

The meeting had been rather casual. One would hardly expect a task force representing the lawyers of America to treat the crime crisis as if it were planning the company's annual picnic. The message was clear: crime is here to stay; relax, we'll do whatever we can, but don't raise your hopes too high.

## Tuesday, April 24, 1984

Lester had been visiting his grandmother's house for food, always avoiding the police. Yesterday, they arrived there seconds after he had called Foster, offering to surrender if placed in a better foster home. How's that for gall? When recaptured, it's back to the lockup and then State School for a long spell of contemplation.

Foster is beginning to assume the role expected of him. In a letter requesting $100 from our Children's Fund to purchase clothing for Dwight Anderson, he wrote "I, Cornelius Foster, Master Counselor, is requesting $100.00. . . ." His grammar may be wanting, but more importantly he realizes that in this role he is someone special who can accomplish everything needed for his charges. "I, Cornelius Foster, Master Counselor. . . ." It has a ring to it.

Today is the regular Tuesday morning meeting with top staff members of the juvenile-court Mental Health Clinic and our School Support Program. At the request of the judges, they provide psychological evaluations and school-progress assessments. Working close-ly together, they make certain that a full appraisal of a youngster is available to the court. This morning, Ed Tutty, administrator of the Mental Health Clinic, reported disproportionate numbers of Puerto Ricans among the referrals as well as a large number of clients under twelve years of age. I suggested he gather this information in a more empirical fashion so that the data can be more useful.

His counterpart with the School Support Program, Johnny Steph-erson, reported progress in establishing a format for transferring de-linquents back to the public schools after a term at a state institu-tion. In the past, students advanced as many as two school grades at State School only to have the public school refuse to accept those credits on their return. Now Stepherson's program not only provides for a procedure for accepting credits, but special counselors in each of the schools are also paid a bonus for the added responsibility of easing the transition of returning delinquents to the school system.

While I was describing the Master Counselor Program to the group, one of Tutty's colleagues interrupted me to recommend a fifteen-year-old Latin who, I was assured, would make Cornelius Foster earn his stripes.

## Wednesday, April 25, 1984

According to the statements made by Dwight Anderson to the po-lice, social workers, and psychologists, this twelve-year-old commit-ted ten burglaries and grand larcenies, two auto thefts, and one assault and battery—all in a period of two weeks. Prior to that two-week period, there had been no contact with the police, though Dwight had been transferred to J. R. Lee Opportunity School follow-ing disruptive behavior and habitual truancy in school. What caused this outbreak of school disorder followed by a two-week crime spree?

The police, called to a burglary in progress, arrested Dwight and an older juvenile departing the scene on a bicycle. Both quickly confessed, taking the police to other sites in Homestead where they had committed burglaries. Property loss and damage came to several thousand dollars in each house. Although monetary restitution is considered in these kinds of cases, prospects of collection are usu-ally dim because too often the culprit has no earning capacity and his parents are impoverished.

Each of the several psychological examinations paints a drab picture. Using the Revised Wechsler Intelligence Scale for Children, a school psychologist placed Dwight at the upper limits of the mildly retarded and said he demonstrated a particular weakness in both long- and short-term memory. Neurological screening indicated he had significant perceptual and motor impairment as well as a learning disorder. In his recommendation, the psychologist saw little hope unless Dwight was removed from the influence of his migrant-worker family. On an earlier occasion, a school counselor visiting the one-bedroom apartment had described it as overcrowded, lacking electricity, smelling of urine, unsanitary, unkempt, and uninhabitable.

Our juvenile-court clinic psychologist added other dimensions. Projective testing confirmed the earlier findings but indicates that Dwight is not experiencing a major psychological disturbance in terms of a formal psychosis or affective disorder. He found the twelve-year-old able to perceive the world in a conventional manner, given his intellectual limitations of being unable to read and functioning at the level of a first-grade student. According to the clinic psychologist, Dwight thinks logically as well as orderly and understands the difference between right and wrong at an elementary level, but lacks sufficient ability to predict fully the consequences of his action. All in all, a mess, but still workable.

Like many other delinquents, Dwight lies a lot, claiming, among other things, to be a seventh-grader, attending classes regularly. He has created a "father" who is employed in a vegetable packing plant and gives him ten to fifteen dollars weekly for doing household chores. Not only is all of this untrue, but he uses it to excuse his behavior: "This money isn't enough, that's why I'm always broke and get into trouble." Exposed to negative peers on the streets, he has begun to adopt criminal behavior as a viable life-style, referring to burglary as if it were a respectable vocation, a way to "make money." The clinic psychologist agreed with earlier examiners that, unless moved from his present environment, the youth can be expected to become an habitual criminal.

The profiles of Dwight Anderson, whose family is rootless, and Lester Burrows, totally abandoned to the streets, are typical of those of thousands of other children who are surviving in the ghetto, aimlessly bouncing around, ignoring the dictates of authority, and creating a life-style that shuts out traditional standards. Dwight, at age twelve, and Lester, at fifteen, are already cast in concrete. It is unlikely that a state training institution will result in chipping away sufficiently to restructure them. Although some risk to the community is involved in allowing Dwight to stay in that dismal household, the acid test ultimately is how he does in his own environment. The Master Counselor Program is the way to find out. With Lester the problem is even more complex, but first we have to catch him.

## Thursday, April 26, 1984

Waiting in my chambers for Dwight Anderson and his family, I thought about the strange dream I had last night. The elusive Lester Burrows telephoned, agreeing to surrender to me personally if I would "retire" his street corner. I'd like to retire his number, but his street corner? The program is not even a month old and the kids are beginning to get to me. Some analyst can probably do wonders with that one.

They sat around the long conference table in my chambers, comfortable and relaxed, as if meeting with the judge were an everyday social event. Dwight, his mother, grandmother, and Foster were present for an informal discussion. Mother and grandmother were fairly talkative, but Dwight limited himself to nods of the head and some guttural comments that were barely responsive. Expecting him to be withdrawn, I did not seriously pursue any dialogue. After being in the program longer and more at ease in my presence, he may be more open.

The mother, pregnant with her ninth child, is part of a large extended family that came here years ago as migrant workers and remained to live in the city of Homestead, in a rural part of Dade County, where they occasionally work picking vegetables. The grandmother, a woman in her fifties who has only a few teeth remaining in her mouth, is attired in colorful dress, and is wearing large silver rings on each of her fingers, emphasized that Dwight had never been in trouble during those early years living with her. She stated matter-of-factly that, of the eighteen children produced by her two daughters, eleven have been removed from their households by state authorities. Dwight's mother interrupted, taking exception, noting that two of her children had been returned. The family included many other relatives living nearby, staying in each other's residences, particularly Dwight, who moved freely among them. His father, in and out of jail for the past fourteen years, never sent him money, and was not employed, as claimed, in a vegetable packing plant.

**16**

Dwight minimized his role in the burglaries, saying he was only the lookout, received no share of the loot, and actually committed far fewer crimes than attributed to him by the police. This is par for the course. In ten years on the bench, all I've ever heard is "The other dude did it." He said the scrapes in school were related to gangs of older boys constantly shaking him down for money. When I pointed out that he and two others had been recently charged with assaulting a cell mate whose sneakers they wanted, he offered the unlikely story that he was only helping the victim up from the floor.

I tried to probe the cause of his behavior in that two-week crime spree. Family conflict? Was Dwight angry over some incident? Had he heard from his father? Some school problems? Mother smiled, "No, only this bad friend." Grandmother shrugged "I dunno," and Dwight just shrugged. All three took the conference in stride. This wasn't a family voicing appreciation for Dwight's second chance. They'd been through many second and third chances before—whatever happened wouldn't make much difference.

Although I hadn't expected this icebreaker to turn into a revealing session, I had hoped for more progress than was made. This was an apathetic family whose life-style far exceeded my understanding. Dwight, guarded with authority figures, distrustful, emotionally taut, was not able or willing to express himself. Penetrating those layers is a lifetime pursuit for a psychotherapist. Perhaps Cornelius Foster speaks their language, but this family may be too much even for him.

## Friday, April 27, 1984

The fifteen-year-old recommended by the Mental Health Clinic psychologist is Marco Zargula. Because he's not one of my court cases, I checked him out with Herman Perry, his field counselor. Perry didn't waste any words: "This kid is impossible to deal with, pays no attention to direction, and will waste our time." I told him that sounded good to me, exactly the qualities sought by the Master Counselor Program. Perry, lacking much sense of humor, just looked confused.

When I reported this conversation to Foster, he smiled and said he'd handle it. Later in the day, he called back. After talking to Perry, examining all the court records, and interviewing Marco in detention, he was ready to take him on. What about Perry's reservations, I asked. "Piece of cake, piece of cake," Foster repeated and hung up.

## Monday, April 30, 1984

Pressing ahead to aid the migrant family of Dwight Anderson, Foster contacted the Housing Authority (HUD) about a new place for them. Mrs. Anderson had applied for a three-bedroom apartment in 1979, but HUD was still handling 1976 applicants.

Dwight, released from the detention center, has been enrolled at Cutler Ridge Junior High School for placement in a Special Education Program for Slow Learners. A daily progress report plus three visits a week by Foster will start things rolling at school. Other agenda items were a trip to Jackson Memorial Hospital (JMH) for a dental examination, a new outfit of clothing, a 9:00 P.M. curfew, and orders to keep in daily contact with Master Counselor Cornelius Foster. Starting Dwight on the right foot will be a lot easier than stabilizing the family situation.

## Tuesday, May 1, 1984

Both father and mother took responsibility for their son's present condition. They were alcoholics and so was he. Andy Sills, at sixteen, had been in trouble since the age of nine. After finding him guilty of attempted burglary, I told both parents he would probably be assigned to the Master Counselor Program. Neither one approved. The father, in town for the trial from Boston, where he was completing an alcohol rehabilitation program, wanted Andy to live with his grandparents in a small upstate New York town. Mrs. Sills, now remarried and apprehensive about the prospect of Andy living at home with her, preferred a local residential program.

Andy was sixteen, looked fourteen, and acted twelve. When ordered back into the lockup, he rushed in tears to his mother's arms sobbing, "I don't want to be in detention. I'll be good." A glance at his record showed him to be a habitual offender who had a serious drinking problem.

He and a friend had helped an old man fix a flat tire, followed him home, and then at 6:00 A.M. were spotted pulling jalousies out of his back door. When the police arrived, Andy explained that they were there to mow the man's lawn, apparently unaware that what appeared to be grass was an asphalt lawn painted green. They obviously were too drunk to know the difference.

Looking at Andy's file, Court Administrator George LaMont remarked that Foster was no miracle worker. I nodded in agreement.

Andy's lack of resolution as well as his air of weakness and defeat suggested he'd go bad the minute someone no longer stood over him. Foster will have his hands full with this one. Maybe it was only intuition, but I could sense a loser here.

In the midst of my diet lunch of an apple and yogurt, Foster walked in with Marco Zargula, just released from detention. Marco, swarthy, slim, and handsome, looked like a lead from central casting. Uncertain as to what was going on, he knew for sure it was better than the earlier plans. Yesterday, Judge Bill Gladstone had ordered him to a long stay at State School. Today, hair slicked back, he was nonchalantly strolling out, on the way home. In designing this program, the concept of releasing juveniles from incarceration seemed sensible and dramatic; now, facing reality, it seems risky and questionable. It's a Jekyll-Hyde situation. Arrest records portray our charges as terrors, and yet in friendlier atmospheres they look and act like normal teenagers. I hope we know what we are doing, releasing Marco.

## Wednesday, May 2, 1984

Foster agreed that getting Dwight Anderson back into school wasn't enough. Unless some dramatic changes occurred in his life, his former bad habits were likely to recur. The plan of action called for shoring him up by reuniting him with his father, making certain of appropriate school placement, enrolling him in a neighborhood after-school recreation program, and then sending him to a private summer camp. A battery of medical, dental, and psychological examinations will be interspersed, periodically. In addition, a team of social workers will try to establish some new behavior patterns for the family. Once these things are under way, Dwight's progress will be measurable.

## Thursday, May 3, 1984

The Mental Health Clinic case staff presentation scheduled for noon looked interesting enough to forgo lunch. These sessions enable the entire staff to critique one specially selected case. This one involved a thirteen-year-old white youth who had shot his abusive father to death. As the story unfolded, it was both bizarre and frightening. Not a prospect for the Master Counselor Program, Clark Carden

**19**

typified the class of delinquents who religiously follow the rules until one day something happens and the mind snaps.

He'd been in detention for weeks, awaiting trial in adult court after the grand jury indicted him for first-degree murder. Before pulling the trigger, he had written two notes, the first a confession: "I, Clark Oden Carden, have shot and killed my father in cold blood because he deserved to die because of the way he treated me and mother. The time was 8:00 A.M. I killed him." The second note merely stated, "Go to sleep Daddy." The boy's statement to the police was clear: "I don't think I'm innocent and I don't think I am guilty. What I did, I had to do. I don't think I'm insane, and I don't think I should go home. I did it for a good reason: to protect my mother and myself."

The father, a burly, tough security guard, was all macho, collecting knives, guns, swords, and brass knuckles. Unrelenting, fixated cruelty marked his behavior. For the slightest provocation, sometimes invented, he beat his wife for sheer pleasure. She left on several occasions always returning. Often he brought a prostitute home and forced his wife to watch, while Clark, in the next room, could hear what was going on. Never allowed outside alone, Clark spent most of his time viewing TV. Although often abused in the past by his father, the child had no recent abrasions on his body. What he did had been brewing for a long time. He needed no current reminder.

On the day of the shooting, his father planned to visit school to discuss a teacher's complaint about Clark's disruptive behavior. Informed that he was in danger of flunking a course, Clark had burst into a rage, calling his teacher a bitch and stating that only his mother disciplined him. The teacher's letter to his father made the boy anxious and apprehensive, causing him to skip school the rest of the week. On that fateful morning, he made certain his father was asleep, wrote the notes, removed his shoes, put on ear protectors, and took a gun from the rack. The first bullet missed, waking his father, who looked startled as his son calmly readjusted his ear protectors, resighted the gun, and summarily killed him with the next bullet.

Objecting to the state prosecuting in adult court, the public defender declared that this was a family situation caused by continued, severe abuse of both the mother and the child. "He's not a danger to anybody," asserted the defense lawyer. "We are certainly not talking about the kind of child who would commit a violent crime like a robbery or take some violent action against a stranger."

The dozen psychologists, psychiatrists, and social workers sitting in administrator Ed Tutty's office around a tableful of Rorschach inkblots and drawings weren't so sure. The slide presentation was revealing. Asked to draw his family, Clark had first sketched three figures, representing himself, his mother, and father. They were poorly drawn, lacking in form, and were devoid of expression; no background was provided in the drawing. He then drew lines through his mother, which were interpreted as meaning he was fearful of losing her. On the other side of the paper, he again pictured the family, this time without the father. The features were now sharply drawn as well as smiling and the sun shone on a fancy car alongside a nice house, all obviously implying a new, ideal life. However, the inkblots indicated a frightened youngster who was out of control. His statements were unemotional, insistent that he had not shot his father—he had executed him.

Asked for a clinical assessment, one of the examining psychologists said the child was "straight out crazy." All those present at the staff in-training session agreed that he was seriously deteriorating in detention and needed immediate long-term residential treatment to remediate the severe damage. "Would he commit violence again?"

"Yes," was the answer. "The next time he faces a situation that he cannot otherwise resolve, he may kill again in the same methodical manner." Looking at Clark, I suddenly saw the problems of Dwight, Marco, and Andy as a lot more manageable.

## Sunday, May 6, 1984

The longer I listened to the young lawyer denounce the state training schools in Florida, the more I was certain the Master Counselor Program was the right course. We were at a meeting of the Juvenile Section of the Florida Circuit Judges Conference and he was describing his lawsuit in federal court to close down the several state correctional institutions for juveniles known as State Schools.

"These so-called schools," he said, "collect a grab bag of juveniles: dangerous psychopaths, emotionally disturbed, mentally retarded, repeat as well as first offenders, truants, and those inadvertently committed. Without any effort at classification, they are placed in the care of an indifferent staff for a period of time dependent solely upon the availability of space." It was obvious that our ratio of one counselor to four delinquents has a good chance, while the State School ratio of one to forty is doomed to fail.

My mind wandered off to the Master Couselor Program again as the second speaker described a research program, disclosing that both the public school and the juvenile court were ignoring runaways and incorrigibles until they were rearrested for serious offenses. It occurred to me that each one in Foster's caseload had started that way, moving up the ladder to qualify for the very State Schools that were about to be closed. Maybe if we responded to early warnings, fewer problems would be encountered later.

## Monday, May 7, 1984

Last night, nine detainees tore up the detention center, and this morning the media are pestering me for an explanation. No one hurt, one escaped, and, other than damage to a few cells, everything is normal for now. I took advantage of the situation to complain about the poverty wage scale for the child-care workers at the detention center, bemoaning their situation as underpaid, understaffed, and undertrained. It won't help much with this session of the legislature, but maybe next year.

## Tuesday, May 8, 1984

On the surface, Marco Zargula (The Charmer), our fifteen-year-old Latin "druggie" and burglar, looks easy to reach. Every counselor has been optimistic, describing him as charming, outgoing, and amenable to direction. In each program, he promptly rises to a leadership position, marking him immediately as a successful conversion. This has happened half a dozen times. As soon as he is released, he's back to drugs and is rearrested for breaking into a house or stealing a car.

The Zargulas came from Cuba, settled in Detroit, the birthplace of Marco, then moved to New York City and finally to Miami. After the parents divorced, the family came to Miami, ironically to escape New York City crime. Unfortunately, the Larchmont Gardens Housing Project, a marketplace for drugs and crime, became home. Inevitably, Marco hooked up with older, more experienced Latin boys who quickly taught him how to break into houses.

Testing showed that Marco was able to hold his own in school at his age level, but, due to truancy, he had flunked both the seventh and eighth grades. The clinical psychologist found good contact with conventional reality, but little tolerance for interpersonal conflict. However, the boy was not suffering any major psychological disorders and responded to appropriate supervision.

Marco has reenrolled as a ninth-grade student at Edison Senior High, impressing Foster that he can handle tough courses such as biology, English and algebra. "Registering for the courses and completing them are two different matters," I reminded Foster.

This family has problems galore. The stepfather, presumably a body-and-fender repairman, has glaucoma, but sees well enough to follow his real pursuit: robbing banks in New Jersey. After each such excursion, he usually hides out in Miami, occasionally joining Marco and his accomplices, lending expertise to their local burglaries. Both the stepfather and older brother provide structure for Marco in the form of old-fashioned discipline. Recently, reacting to a harsh beating by his stepfather, Marco, according to Foster, "dropped a dime" on him, notifying the FBI of his whereabouts. As a result of the phone call, the stepfather is now in jail awaiting trial for bank robbery and also as a suspect in a murder case. Older brother Newton, angry at Marco for coming home "high," stealing cars, and for the phone call, blackened his eye, gave him a fat lip, bruised his ribs, impressed a few cigarette burns on his arm, and then made certain he'd stay home by tying him with cord.

Although several of the nine assorted relatives in the family group are occasionally employed, the Zargulas depend mainly on Aid to Families with Dependent Children (AFDC) and food stamps. Father's whereabouts is unknown; Newton is unemployed. Both sisters work at Burger King; the older one, being married soon, will bring her new husband home to the Zargulas's small three-room apartment. Because Marco's mother recently lost her job and she is concerned over his drug usage, she is simply overwhelmed by the difficulties confronting her. The clinical psychologist found her unable to cope with the everyday tensions of life, recommending that she receive treatment at a local community mental-health clinic. Living in Larchmont Garden, a high-crime government housing project, amid all these strained relationships, is certainly not conducive to Marco's rehabilitation.

He enjoys his peers, but keeps a distance from his family, whose influence on him is negligible. His sisters have little time for him, and he carefully avoids his brother and stepfather. Mother is loved, but is ineffective and ignored. A small, bright, friendly youngster,

## Off the Bus to State School

Marco is a bit of a con man, lacking in self-discipline, relying on his wits to avoid trouble. Along with his friendly approach, he manifests a layer of wariness, not easy to fathom. He starts a smile, but it quickly turns cold and distant. I'm not sure what he's thinking. In his mind, the intervention of the Master Counselor Program may be just another of a long series of "victories" enabling him to avoid punishment. The events this past month certainly support this view. First, he was saved when Judge William Gladstone decided not to send him to adult court, where he faced a long prison term, instead ruling that he go to State School. Then, good fortune in the name of the clinical psychologist who recommended him for this program saved him from State School. Now he is receiving all this attention from Foster and a judge.

He appears pliable, but like a chameleon he changes to conform to whatever situation he faces. After it's over, he's back to square one. Unless Foster stays on him, he'll be shooting up and into the next parked car he sees, or worse. His only success has been in surviving the system, and we've contributed more to that than he has.

Yesterday was movie day with Marco and Dwight as Foster's guests. At 9:00 P.M.—curfew time—he tucked them in safely at home. Today, they go to Jackson Memorial Hospital (JMH), Marco for a hearing test and Dwight to complete work on his teeth.

Dwight Anderson is reacting favorably, albeit unenthusiastically. The novelty of having someone like Foster involved in his life has had an impact. Dwight has been enrolled in a special school program for the emotionally handicapped and participates in the Explorers program of the Homestead Police Department. Although sources indicate his father is in prison, nobody knows where. Foster was also pleased that he had rejected a joint burglary venture that was proposed by some of his former accomplices. This provoked a fight, requiring Dwight's older brother Derrick to come to his rescue.

Foster seems sanguine about his charges, wondering out loud if the juveniles selected are sufficiently hard-core. I suggested he wait a few more innings before claiming victory. Each has his own particular problems. Dwight, the youngest, is dull, glum, indifferent, burdened with an illiterate family of migrant workers, untouched by the world outside. Marco is bright, alive to the excitement of crime, drugs, and whatever his crowd is willing to chance. Andy Sills, our newest charge, drinks beer, whimpers, has no ambition, engages in an occasional burglary. He's white, yet he is no better prospect than the most deprived black ghetto youngster. Other than Lester running off, things are going as expected.

## Thursday, May 10, 1984

Perseverance is Foster's strength. He starts optimistically with each new charge, and, even when the bloom begins to fade, continues to find positive factors in their behavior, often downplaying or explaining away their misbehavior. When I suggest he not play the role of defense counsel, he merely smiles.

Although Foster somehow is an excellent communicator with his clients, he comes across less clearly to me. He talks in spurts, so fast that I keep slowing him down, asking him to repeat each statement. It's almost as if he's in a hurry to finish his report to me so that he can get back out in the street. No matter what his style, it's more important he impress the kids than me. So long as he goes beyond the bureaucratic response of generating boiler-plate reports and working from a checklist, I should be grateful. He gets along fine with his supervisor, Frank Manning, who has agreed to serve as a resource for finding special services and, in addition, to keep records documenting this experiment. Foster is to be the outside man, reaching the kids at their own level; Manning, the inside man, taking care of the books. I'll do what I can. Four was to be the caseload, but Foster, feeling some guilt over the abrupt departure of Lester, asked for a fifth participant to replace him.

## Friday, May 11, 1984

Foster introduced his new prospect in court today: fifteen-year-old Laurence Samuel (The Fighter), fresh out of State School, facing two new charges of aggravated assault. Six feet, four inches tall, with gangling arms and legs as well as sturdy shoulders, Laurence looked ready to play basketball for the New York Knicks. School records revealed a poor student who was not living up to his potential.

His mother and stepfather, also in court, joined us in chambers. The mother, an aide at the Veterans' Hospital, and the stepfather, employed by the Marriott-In-Flight Food Service, sounded like concerned, caring parents who hadn't given up on their son. Both agreed his conduct had improved since returning from State School, but they found him still combative, always ready to strike out at anyone displeasing him. His natural father lived in Miami, but no regular contact occurred nor was financial support provided. Laurence sat quietly and alertly, nodding in agreement that this was his last chance.

**25**

Off the Bus to State School

After they left, Foster reported the bad news from the JMH Outpatient Clinic. Marco's hearing impairment was serious enough to warrant further attention. Although expressing concern, the JMH doctor provided no medication, recommended no hearing aid, and did not suggest possible surgery. He only prescribed sitting up front in class and avoiding loud music. Next stop for Marco is a more attentive hearing specialist.

### Wednesday, May 16, 1984

He was an itinerant youth of sixteen, continuously moving from state to state, school to school, trailer park to trailer park, and detention cell to rehabilitation program. He drank too much, used drugs, and lied. It was the latter that bothered Foster most. When Andy Sills (The Drinker) said he didn't drink or use drugs, Foster rose, slammed the cell door shut, and told the youth he'd return in a couple of weeks to hear the truth.

Nothing had ever gone right in Andy's family. Alcohol wasn't the only problem. His mother, a neglected child herself, left home at fourteen, moved in with Mr. Sills, beginning a long, stormy relationship. No sooner had he departed, taking the youngest of their three daughters, than she found a twenty-year-old security guard to replace him. Her own erratic life-style apparently has created guilt feelings; she blamed herself for Andy's misdeeds. She couldn't wait to tell counselors how she had failed, meanwhile lauding Andy as cooperative as well as helpful at home and minimizing each new act of criminal behavior as something of the past.

Andy's first psychological examination, done in our juvenile-court mental health clinic, gave us an insight into his behavior: ". . . in the low average range of intelligence with ability to make accurate judgments regarding the consequence of behavior. No psychosis or thought disorder present. Though immature and prone to act on impulse, he is neither aggressive nor hostile. He has not developed a social conscience, and shows no remorse. His criminal behavior may be attributed to alcohol abuse." His rap sheet consisted of seventeen entries: seven years of grand larceny, burglary, shoplifting, truancy, and neglect.

We intend to use as many clinicians as are necessary to obtain a full range of psychological and medical assessments of Andy as well as the others. Properly putting Humpty Dumpty together again means no loose pieces in the puzzle.

26

## Thursday, May 17, 1984

Foster, in court today for Andy, had twelve-year-old Dwight Anderson (The Migrant) in tow for a visit to JMH for more dental work. They stopped by my chambers, and I tried again to engage Dwight in a dialogue. The last time, he had been nervous, under pressure, tight as a clam. Today more relaxed, he dutifully followed three paces behind Foster, still miles from me. I tried my best, jollying him with light banter, complimenting him on his progress, but he responded only enough not to appear rude to the judge.

Court Administrator George LaMont overheard Foster and Andy in deep conversation in the waiting room. Foster had enrolled the sixteen-year-old in vocational school, and apparently the boy had missed class yesterday because Foster hadn't been there to transport him. Foster was clear and direct: "You better get your ass on the bus and get to school if I'm not available." Tears welled in Andy's eyes, as he assured Foster it wouldn't happen again. As Foster walked away, Mrs. Sills cautioned her son to obey Foster or he'd be in trouble. Andy snapped back, ordering her to leave him alone, and she immediately desisted. LaMont concluded from this scenario that Andy probably ruled the roost at home and, unless Foster strongly interceded, hard times were ahead.

Mrs. Sills and son Andy listened quietly to my declaration that this was his last chance in the juvenile system. Both quickly indicated their cooperation, Andy claiming beer a thing of the past. Mrs. Sills assured me her new husband brought stability to the household and further assured me that jobs were at hand—she, returning to work as a store clerk, and Andy as a dishwasher. How many times in the past had someone listened to the Sillses' unlikely assurances? Could she stay with this new husband, fifteen years her junior? Would she and Andy really keep their jobs? How long would he avoid getting drunk and stay out of trouble? Soap operas thrive on this kind of material.

## Friday, May 18, 1984

It was my best Knute Rockne speech, about winning one for the Gipper. I would be gone for two months, for hip surgery and recuperation, and in my most compelling manner urged Foster and Manning to give it their all, fully documenting their activities in my absence. Manning assured me it was thumbs up, but Foster, perhaps less impressed with my oratory, quickly switched the discussion to a recent newspaper story describing my teenage behavior as a member of a Brooklyn gang. It came from a Sunday feature story that made better reading by overplaying a youthful indiscretion of mine that had casually been mentioned to a reporter. In truth, I had been somewhat overprotected as a child and, other than one or two minor larcenies, had been more of a goody-goody than a neighborhood menace. Foster, obviously intrigued that we might have similar backgrounds, asked, "Do you know of my record as a convicted felon?"

His academic background had seemed sparse, but never once had I considered a possible criminal background. And what a background! It included two fifteen-year sentences for armed robbery, serving five years in Raiford State Prison. As a juvenile, he had been through State School several times. As he told it, he had returned from Vietnam and then went on a spree robbing everything and everybody in sight. During his time in Raiford, he took in-prison courses, later transferring to Florida A & M University—and presto, here was our college graduate holding a social-work degree plus having plenty of hard time under his belt.

## Tuesday, May 22, 1984

"Do you still think it's a piece of cake?" I asked Foster. He offered a big smile in response but no comment. He had made that remark about Marco's entry into the program, but it applied equally to the others. Foster was no longer so certain. The honeymoon might not be over with this quartet, but for sure the dancing had stopped. They were fairly submissive for the first few weeks, enthralled with the idea of being taken off the bus. A lot of slippage occurred, however, as they struggled with the stern discipline imposed upon them. Two steps forward and one step backward was acceptable, but the possibility that the ratio might be reversed was disturbing.

Twelve-year-old Dwight Anderson (The Migrant) seemed to be doing best, perhaps due to his impressionable youth or his phlegmatic attitude of taking everything in stride. Other than one missed school date, he had followed Foster's regimen religiously. His large extended migrant family was not too involved, but didn't interfere either. My request for new housing was now in the HUD regional office waiting for a waiver, which wasn't likely. No basis existed for favoring my request because hundreds of other black families, similarly situated, were also waiting for decent housing, but a little political pressure never hurt a worthwhile cause.

Our newest recruit, fifteen-year-old Laurence Samuel, with us less than a week, was already back in the lockup. He's the big, black kid who is ready to fight at the slightest provocation, real or imagined. On the second day back in school, he punched another student in a dispute over who had the seating rights to a chair, his fifth assault charge among a batch of other crimes. In court, Foster asked that Laurence be detained while the state attorney determined whether or not to prosecute. All six feet, four inches of him bristling, Laurence made a run for it, only to be restrained by two child-care workers. Later in the day, he telephoned Foster to apologize for his behavior. He probably won't be prosecuted over this minor wrangle but, now suspended from school, he needs an alternative school placement. For the present, at least, he will be confined to a cell, sitting on a chair he can undisputedly call his own.

Marco Zargula, the fifteen-year-old Cuban, accompanied by his mother, came by to talk his way out of a penalty for violating curfew and missing school. Both Foster and I told him his stories were to no avail. If he continues to misbehave, back on the bus for him. His mother smiled in agreement, never before having had such support in controlling her son. Earlier in the day, his audiologist had advised me that Marco had only a mild hearing loss, confirming the JMH doctors' recommendation that high-pitched stereo be avoided. In view of the lacing he was receiving on his errant behavior along with the warning that he might yet need a hearing aid, Marco was a chastened boy as he left my chambers.

I was uncertain why Foster continued to describe sixteen-year-old Andy Sills as if he were a prime Phi Beta Kappa candidate. I saw this kid as a damaged little wimp and, unbeknownst to Foster, I was aware of the tongue-lashing he gave Andy the other day. It might be Foster's way of telling me that his white charge will receive as much attention as the black kids. Andy was going through all kinds of testing: at the vocational school, where it looks like air-conditioning may be his best bet; at a drug screening, to determine his need for alcohol and drug rehabilitation; at our School Support Program to determine his prospects for a General Education Development (GED) diploma. He was calling Foster daily for advice, confiding his problems to him and insisting he hadn't used drugs in six months and beer only socially. Despite my doubts, Foster continued to view Andy as a top prospect.

And of course there was Lester Burrows (The Runner), our first choice, who had never left the starting gate. He was gone but not forgotten. It was hard to believe that he had avoided a network of savvy, black street workers plus the police. He was like the "Scarlet Pimpernel," except he stole only for himself. Grandmother was victimized again, Lester cleaning out the house. Every time one of our people had a lead on him, he was out the back door as they entered the front, continuing to elude our best efforts. At this rate, he'll soon be a legend in Liberty City, and all his peers will wear "Lester Beat the System" T-shirts.

With about two months behind us, things are becoming clearer. No matter how much a program is designed to do *for* them, it still emerges as someone doing it *to* them. Being a big brother to downtrodden, deprived youths sounds impressive, but their response is far from brotherly. Why should they trust some stranger who is suddenly imposing all kinds of demands? It may be a lot easier adjusting to the routine and order of jail than the failure and frustration of competing in school. They dislike being locked up but recognize it is an acceptable risk. Conscience and remorse are not serious considerations on their part—survival for the moment is all they can contemplate. Depressing as is the thought, perhaps they have already crossed the borderline, no longer fearful or concerned with the consequences of crime. Thus far, none is a hard-core violent offender, brutalizing his victims, but day-to-day criminal behavior may already be a way of life.

When we started, I envisioned a golden opportunity to obtain behavioral insights as each of our charges chatted freely in my chambers: the avuncular judge and the remorseful teen in a soul-searching tête-à-tête, I the ace-in-the-hole masterfully filling vacuums in each of their lives, with Foster my agent. Instead, I'm the old curmudgeon—to be avoided at all costs—sitting in a black robe warning them that the bus is waiting. One needs to be reminded repeatedly that salvation comes only to those who want to be saved, and, at that, only after all parties agree on a definition of salvation.

The next few months will tell whether Foster can make inroads against all the years that have made each of our wards what he is. My absence for about six weeks won't make much difference.

# 2

---

## Running the Streets
## Is a Lot Easier
## than Walking to
## School

**Thursday, June 28, 1984**

People keep telling me about individuals they know who have had
hip replacements and play tennis as if nothing had happened. Meanwhile, over a month after surgery, I'm still on crutches, hobbling
from chair to chair, hardly ready to sit in court let alone jump over a
net. I'll be off the bench for at least another month, but meetings
with Foster and Manning will continue to keep me current. Their
reports suggest that none of these kids readily adapts to having his
life-style reconstructed. The summer ahead looks long and hard.

### DWIGHT ANDERSON *(The Migrant)*

It's not easy to reach a twelve-year-old who already has a mind-set
that burglary is an acceptable way to earn money. Foster thinks he is
reaching Dwight; I'm not so sure. During my absence these past six
weeks, the youth has been in the two-steps-forward, one-step-back
category. Despite several recommendations that he be placed in a
halfway house or the State School, our strategy has been to load him
with activity while he lives at home. Followers like Dwight easily
adjust to the demands of the institution but upon return home

quickly revert to old ways. He needs a lot of personal attention, and his mind needs to be opened to fresh experiences. His so-called progress at this stage may only be an ability to get along with whatever authority figure happens to be in his path.

Foster has inundated him with programs, in all of which he is doing well. Thus far, attendance and behavior have been excellent in his one-on-one learning situation at a special emotional behavior class. With the Explorers of the Homestead Police Department Crime Prevention Program, he has enjoyed Saturday picnics and sport outings. Lined up for the end of the summer is a two-week stint at the YMCA summer camp, payment for which will come from fines assessed to lawyers who arrive late for court.

The Anderson family is almost impossible to deal with. Migrant workers, constantly on the move, living from day to day, picking fruit or occasional jobs, they are an odd lot—the women mostly pregnant, the men drifting in and out. New faces appear often, somehow related, someone's cousin or nephew, each on his own, hardly aware of the abject poverty surrounding them in this makeshift apartment. Dwight moves among them, untouched, taking care of himself the best way he can. Personal conversation is at a minimum, and a twelve-year-old is completely excluded.

Social workers, specially assigned to the family, find it no easy task making contact with this band of wanderers, let alone establishing a dialogue. The Andersons simply smile at the onslaught of attention, neither accepting nor rejecting. All they want is their AFDC and food stamps and they'll manage. Despite all their handicaps and lack of any apparent structure in the household, somehow family life seems to survive. Despite heavy traffic and incessant quarreling, they willingly share what little they have.

Days before I left, word came down that the Housing Authority had granted special priority to the Andersons. They were finally going to move out of that urine-satured flat. Great! After all those nasty things I had been saying about the insensitive bureaucrats, they now conspired to embarrass me.

The Andersons haven't moved yet. For one thing, Mrs. Anderson kept the application in a drawer for weeks until Foster found out she had never returned it. She can't read or write and is probably scared to death of government forms. Foster completed the application and is now negotiating for an apartment. One will probably be available soon, but my best instinct tells me it's going to be a difficult task moving the Andersons to a strange, tall, project building among large numbers of unfamiliar people whose life-styles don't match their own. Manning agrees. Foster refuses to speculate: "One way or another I'll get them out."

Although Frank Manning, as Foster's supervisor, need only oversee his activities, he is so fascinated by these families that he volunteered to prepare social histories on each of them. The Andersons are particularly intriguing to him. Everyone is illiterate, many are retarded, and none has the slightest concept of acceptable social standards other than the most rudimentary. Dwight's eighteen-year-old, unmarried sister already has two children and a third is on the way. Manning is appalled at their casual attitude toward both the bearing of children and the identity of each father. Although ripe for some birth-control concepts, three generations have shown no such tendency. Good Catholic that he is, Manning surely is experiencing serious inner conflicts.

What kind of impression has Dwight made on Manning? His experience was like mine: one-syllable responses, one at a time, and then only with some effort. Foster, on the other hand, described Dwight as a running faucet: talking all the time; seeking him out; following two paces behind; and complying with curfew, school attendance, and any other requests. The good, white social worker and the good, white judge can't cut it with Dwight and probably not much with the family either. It looks like it is going to be Cornelius Foster, Master Counselor, and Dwight Anderson, lost twelve-year-old, all alone together.

Oh, yes. The one step backward. Dwight's grandmother sent him shopping to Jefferson's Department Store and he left without paying for a pair of sunglasses. When arrested, he claimed a friend tossed them at him and all he did was catch them. I cautioned Foster not to interfere with the court process, lest Dwight think he has some sort of immunity by being in the Master Counselor Program. I won't intervene either. Perhaps the experience earns him a few days in the lockup.

Despite his arrest and the absence of a stable family, Dwight still looks like a fair prospect for success. If he had a real family, his chances would be a lot better. Looking at the Andersons, one wonders about newspaper editorials demanding that parents be held responsible for the delinquent behavior of their children. What parents? Where are they? Life-styles and rules in the inner city are a lot different. How does one channel families like the Andersons into the mainstream?

## MARCO ZARGULA *(The Charmer)*

Everything went wrong with Marco. Had he gone to State School as Judge Gladstone originally intended, we'd probably be a lot better off today. Earlier, when taken off the bus, he impressed everybody: enrolling at Miami Edison Junior High, signing up for tough courses, achieving good grades, keeping curfew, staying in contact with Foster, and avoiding those older chums who had led him into trouble before. Slowly, the old ways began to worm their way back. First, he began missing school, saying his mother didn't wake him on time or that he was ill. Then, he broke his 9:00 P.M. curfew, hiding out and failing to come home for fear of being returned to detention. Back consorting with Jose and Osvaldo Calcon, with whom he had previously been arrested for car theft, he declared to his mother: "They're my friends. Nobody gonna keep us apart." Mark one for peer pressure over the system.

Home visits have deteriorated to a game of hide-and-seek, in which the family members provide Foster little support. On one occasion, while ringing the front doorbell, he observed Marco flying out the back, while the family members sat by as neutral observers. His mother has given up trying to influence Marco and says he comes home at night "so high he can't breathe."

At the beginning of Marco's slide, Foster was firm but conciliatory, offering to help him get back in line. Marco would telephone, mostly to offer excuses for his behavior. As his conduct worsened, the number of calls decreased and he avoided further meetings. In retrospect, Foster thinks one more face-to-face meeting might have made the difference. Had he been too inflexible in demanding conformity to curfew, school, and other requirements? I told Foster to quit the guilt scenario. A line has to be drawn demanding performance; otherwise, kids like Marco go through life relying on excuses.

The youth is now living on the street, running with the Calcon brothers and without doubt being involved in car thefts. Pickup orders have been issued and the police placed on special alert for him. Normally, I'd expect an arrest any moment but, if Lester Burrows is able to avoid it for several months, I'm not too confident Marco will be back so soon. Was Foster too optimistic, encouraging a heavy academic courseload that Marco was not ready to undertake, rather than a vocational program like culinary arts? Did Foster's two-week vacation right in the midst of Marco's decline leave a vacuum? Could it have been Marco's hearing loss?

Where did we go wrong with this youth? To some extent, it may have been our perception of his excellent academic potential, but, even more, it was probably our eagerness to succeed. We fell into the same trap as others before, believing that Marco was just one step away from a complete turnaround. His pleasing personality disarms everybody. I remember how excited his lawyer was when I told her he would receive another chance. "You'll never regret it," she said. "He's a wonderful boy." Sure. Our dream scenario had looked easy. First, a quantum leap by stabilizing him in school, followed by a college scholarship, and after that he will become a captain of industry. He'd have been the ideal cover story for the brochure describing the great Master Counselor Program. Back to the drawing board.

Foster, a bit dejected, didn't have too much to offer. Manning wanted a whole new approach to Marco, but wasn't sure how to begin. We all agreed that, once apprehended, he'd be placed on the bus to State School. That will be his summer camp. After he has a reasonable stay in pinstripes, we'll bring him back and start anew, a little wiser and a lot more careful. Of course, if he's more than a recreational drug user, State School may not be the right place. Meanwhile, you can bet that several automobiles, otherwise secure, will be missing or vandalized, thanks to the Master Counselor Program.

## ANDY SILLS *(The Drinker)*

Despite my reservations, Andy just keeps rolling along. No script writer could have created a more pronounced turnaround than that shown by our boy Andy. I've been waiting for the other shoe to drop, but thus far he's born again. Six months past his sixteenth birthday and a veteran of the court system, he's well tuned to playing some sort of game. With all of this, Foster has him wrapped up. It may be fear, religion, seeing the light, whatever, but Andy apparently is doing it all. Testing at the Miami Lakes Technical Institute placed him in auto-body repair. It didn't bother him that he never had the slightest interest in cars. He's participating as if this were the major goal of his life. Academic testing found him high in reading comprehension but weak in math. Without hesitation, he joined a math lab. Where every kind of school has always been the enemy, for the past month he has learned to take the classroom in stride.

Aware of my skepticism, Foster seems to relish telling me of Andy's progress. At our last conference, he rushed through the other reports, but dwelled on Andy. Foster had a little gleam in his eyes as he reported: "Andy is not only working for Morrison's Cafeteria, but also for his uncle's lawn service on weekends. He is absolutely sober at all times. Gets along great with his new daddy. He calls me several times a day, and is always doing the right thing when I drop in unannounced." This is a far cry from the past, when Andy regularly came home dead drunk and passed out. Both parents are totally cooperative, unhesitatingly coming up with money for Andy's tuition even though the family of five (two younger sisters) live solely on the meager income derived from the stepfather's salary as a security guard.

On Foster's most recent visit to check Andy's curfew, he observed the TV playing something like "Love Boat," Andy holding hands with his girlfriend and the older couple similarly situated. The counselor looked at the idyllic scene and tiptoed out.

## LAURENCE SAMUEL *(The Fighter)*

When last heard from in May, Laurence was safely ensconced in the lockup for assaulting a fellow student. That this arrest occurred only three days after the Master Counselor Program had reprieved him from yet another stay at State School came as no surprise. All the other kids in the program had behaved in the same manner: unconcerned about the likelihood of incarceration, unappreciative over sudden-found freedom, and indifferent to the special opportunities being made available. One would expect an immediate cessation of aggressive behavior as well as a cooling down of anger upon being taken off the bus—but apparently not. It is painfully clear that doing good for delinquents, when their own motivation is lacking, has virtually no impact.

Laurence is hardened to the streets, knows how to survive, and, at the slightest provocation, is ready to fight. Although his record for assaults and burglaries has him but one step from accepting criminal behavior as a permanent life-style, some soft spots still suggest otherwise. He's attending summer school regularly, encountering no problems there, doing household chores willingly, and enjoying a relaxed summer at home with the family. Foster finds him amenable to all requests and complying with the rules. Family counseling has been recommended in which all members are to participate. The more Foster describes the progress with approval, the more I worry. It is too easy. Marco had also sounded like a winner at the beginning, then simply disintegrated. We are moving slowly with Laurence, not

36

by design, but because we know so little about him. Coming out of what appears to be a calm family atmosphere, why is he always so ready for combat? His parents say little, accepting the involvement of the court as a necessity, keeping Foster at a distance, offering only as much cooperation as is required. Something is going on with that boy that we need to know.

Is Jan Mann Opportunity School the right place for him? This is a special school for students who are discipline problems. Although some may be salvaged there, its main function is accommodating disruptive kids so that the learning process in regular classrooms can go on unhindered by troublemakers. Can we discover some interest and develop it? A hobby or a sport? Foster said everyone tries to talk Laurence into basketball because of his size, but all he wants to do for recreation is sprawl out on the floor and watch TV. Manning, as tall as Laurence but a hundred pounds heavier, lamented that as a kid he had the same problem. His friends kept urging him to play football, while all he wanted to do was read books.

There's a sense of immediacy here, I pointed out. Unless we set a course for Laurence, he'll easily go back to his old patterns. Manning, the experienced hand, cautioned us: "Piling on programs may be equally disastrous. Laurence is what he is, and we only can move at his pace, not ours. Maybe Marco went off the track because we tried too much, rather than not enough." Manning may be right. Nonetheless, I requested that we accelerate activity with Laurence. There has to be a reason for bursts of unprovoked violence. He's not in a crisis situation yet, but for how long will that continue? We need to find out quickly. Sitting by, waiting for the flower to bloom, isn't my style.

## Monday, July 16, 1984

Halfway through the summer, results are mixed. Some kids are doing well, others not so well. As for me, I am down to one crutch. By the end of the month, I will be using a cane and back on the bench again. No telling which of our wards will be standing on his own two feet then.

### LESTER BURROWS (The Runner)

Lester Burrows is back in lockup. It's been a summer of bouncing around from the street to grandmother's or to rented apartments, depend_ng on his financial status of the moment. Although he continued to steal from grandmother, she always looked away and welcomed him back. His main operation apparently was to rent a room for homosexuals, then burglarize them, knowing that they avoid bringing the police into their problems. The first time Lester was caught, his theory worked because the victims refused to prosecute. However, after a series of successful scores, one of his homosexual landlords evicted him for nonpayment of rent. Lester, doing what he does best, broke into the apartment to recover his belongings. Caught in the act by police, this time involving victims apparently ready to prosecute, Lester's term of running the streets expired, at least for now.

In addition to homosexuals, Lester's modus operandi includes knocking down little old ladies and stealing their purses, though he claims he tries not to hurt them. According to Foster, Lester looks for these targets only when in dire need of money. Otherwise, he leaves others alone and wants to be left alone. Crime is not a vocation nor does it provide a thrill for him. His ability to survive under adverse conditions provides enough self-esteem so that he doesn't need to play the tough-guy role.

We both sensed that having Lester back was only a small victory, neither of us knowing quite what to do with him. Lester can be exasperating. Although likeable and sympathetic, he's a difficult person to help. Foster, thinking out loud, moaned: "All I want to do is hold him long enough to find a good foster home, this time a black one. Teach him to read and write, to hold a job. Once I get him thinking about a stable life-style, he'll forget about living in the streets." Foster didn't speak with much confidence; he was just talking. Our answer might be schooling or a stable family, but at this stage Lester's thinking was certainly on another wavelength.

Lester looked upon his present situation as regrettable but only of a temporary nature. He was quick to tell Foster that he offered no sex in exchange for his living arrangements with the homosexuals. Foster, of course, understands better. Lester recommended a foster home some friend had told him was a great place. We both laughed at that. Obviously, the foster home he had in mind was one that allowed kids to run loose, providing nothing more than a bed—and that to be used only rarely. Many of the foster parents are mainly interested in the few dollars they receive and pay scant attention to their charges. That would be perfect for Lester.

"Would he like to come back to the Master Counselor Program?" I asked Foster. He replied:

Sure he would. But it's only a question of time before he'd run from the program. He'd rather take his chances in the street than with what the state offers. In the streets he might get lucky and make a big score. He knows that with us it's only hard work, someone always looking over his shoulder, and no fun. He doesn't see anything at the end of our tunnel. The streets are exciting to him. It's an adventure. He can do something there. Running the streets has always been a lot easier for him than walking to school. Sometimes it's women, and drugs, and money, and sleeping in a nice hotel. Sometimes it's not. If he gets in on a drug deal or doing somebody, that's success. What we offer is just someone forcing him to do something he doesn't want to do. His attitude toward us is "Leave me alone. I don't need your help. I can make it by myself." That's Lester.

I'd never heard Foster speak so clearly or so forcefully. "Suppose," I asked, "we send him to State School for a few months and then put him back in our program. What are the prospects?" Foster just shook his head as if he had said more than enough. "Forget about what you would like to do, and tell me what we can do now," I insisted.

He thought for a few moments and then responded, almost reluctantly: "Lester is too wise, too slick, too everything for us to handle. He needs that wilderness program that keeps them for two years. After that, we might be able to do something for him."

Foster was referring to the new experimental Florida Environmental Institute (FEI), known as the Last Chance Ranch. Operational only for a short time, FEI is the juvenile system's response to the public clamor for punishment that fits the crime. Housing the toughest delinquents on a little spot in the wilds of the Everglades, the "ranch" concept is: build your own tent, cook your own food, and avoid the alligator as best you can. No fences, guards, or anything because escape means you end up deeper in the swamps of the Everglades. It's a kind of sophisticated Devil's Island, but structured in such a fashion that the undersocialized ghetto brute emerges two years later with a sensitized work ethic ready to be a contributing factor to society. That's the plan anyway. Critical observers are carefully watching the experiment. The Reagan administration loves it because it's tough, and the national media adore it because the whole concept is colorful and makes for good copy.

I told Foster, "Tossing Lester in with a hungry crocodile would make my day, but since he was only in our program for half an hour before escaping, we have some responsibility to give him one real chance."

My plan was to ship him immediately to State School, where for several months his daily regimen would be tight marching orders. On return, I envisioned a "new" Lester, much more receptive to what we offered. If we send him to adult court, he's sure to be placed on probation and be back at his old tricks. Foster saw him somewhat differently: "Lester isn't fazed by the prospect of State School and as a matter of fact could make it at Raiford State Prison. He's a survivor who will survive." We'll try State School.

Obviously, Lester is not a homeless, hungry waif sleeping in alleyways, waiting for the community to fill the vacuum in his life. He's already filled it. He's an entrepreneur on his own. We've been reading too much of Charles Dickens, where everything becomes a morality play. No moral issue, dwelling on the differences between right and wrong, is involved with Lester. That issue has never entered his mind.

It's difficult for me to accept the idea that a kid like Lester, whose major offense is that he has never had a real home life and whose crimes have been mostly nonassaultive, is beyond recall. To think that at age fifteen he's been completely weaned from a normal lifestyle is difficult to accept. Master Counselor Foster has mixed feelings. One day, he's all fired up about taking Lester on. The next time we talk about it, he is resigned to losing him.

## Friday, July 20, 1984

Observing these kids, not as a judge, but through the eyes of Foster and Manning, creates a different perspective. On the bench, it is simply a decision of fitting delinquents into an available program that somehow responds to their needs and the offense committed. Talking about them, meeting their families, seeing minor blemishes become deep scars, and watching them disintegrate at the slightest pressure make them real people. Not knowing any of them personally is clearly preferable. It makes the job of judging a lot easier.

### MARCO ZARGULA (The Charmer)

Although their personalities differ sharply, Marco and Lester show a lot of similar behavior patterns. Both are wise to the ways of the street and are totally alienated from conventional standards. Family, school, church, and government authority are all intruders and enemies, best avoided and ignored.

Marco has been running the streets, stealing cars, and being heavily involved with drugs. He too eluded our dragnet until he was finally arrested for a new offense. This time, it was armed robbery and car theft. Like Lester, he also contacted one of the counselors who was searching for him, offering to surrender if assured he would not be sent to State School. Occasionally he returned home, where mother served as a lookout for approaching strangers. Other times, he lived in a Biscayne Boulevard hotel, hanging out in Miami Beach.

Attending a radio station Splash-Down beach party along with thousands of other kids, he made the mistake of driving in the stolen vehicle. Stopped by a police officer for a traffic violation, he had no driver's license and the car checked out as stolen. His accomplice, probably one of the Calcons, fled. Fourteen hours earlier, the car had been taken at gunpoint in the Flamingo Park neighborhood on Miami Beach. According to Marco, it all began when he and a friend hitchhiked a ride on Biscayne Boulevard. He alleged that the driver stopped at his office and, once inside, locked the office door and made sexual advances. To protect himself, Marco grabbed a gun lying on the victim's desk, robbed him, and stole his car. The police were not impressed with his story nor was I by his explanation that he didn't surrender earlier for fear of being sent to State School.

Unlike Lester Burrows (The Runner), he appears terribly frightened by the prospect of incarceration, especially the fear of being sexually assaulted. He's slightly built, handsome, and not too adept at hand-to-hand combat. Foster agrees that the older boys in State School will "throw down" on him by nightfall. At one point, Marco burst into tears following Foster's dire prediction of what might happen in State School. Foster, untouched, warned, "I'm going to keep you there forever."

I reminded Foster again about his earlier comment, when one of Marco's counselors had warned that the youth would be impossible to handle. Foster, after interviewing Marco, had accepted him with a bit of braggadocio: "A piece of cake. A piece of cake." Foster no longer has that confident air about the boy. Like others taken in by Marco's guile, Foster now realizes that he is dealing with a tough, complex personality. Unlike Lester, who steals to survive, Marco wants to be recognized by others as a master criminal. He takes pride in knowing all the dealers, con men, and other criminal types. His air of bravado is notice for his peers to look up to him. Burglary and robbery are for the thrill, and he always travels with a group of like-minded youngsters. Whenever the system snares him, he suddenly becomes the tender, compliant youngster: "I'll go to school, stay away from the Calcons, quit drugs." He probably means it at the time he says it.

Marco is charged with armed robbery among other offenses, and the prosecutor's office may insist he be tried as an adult. Despite his macho air, he wept when Foster mentioned the possibility of being prosecuted as an adult. His experience with drugs worsened during his stay in the streets. He and his friends did it all: marijuana, speed, cocaine, and whatever. "Cocaine gave me the chills," he said, "but everything else went down well."

There's little sense in sending Marco to a local drug program, which is what he probably needs. He'd be fine for a while, and then one day the Calcon brothers would reclaim him. It will have to be State School and maybe then a drug program. He has the same problem he's always had. So long as he's under someone's tight control he behaves, but once on his own he goes bad. I hope he can protect himself at State School.

### DWIGHT ANDERSON *(The Migrant)*

My batting average has only been fair as to predictions, but I sure hit the nail squarely when I speculated that on moving day the Andersons would somehow manage to avoid the moving van. My concern was that the new apartment was too far removed from the extended family, but Mrs. Anderson's went far beyond that. Nothing about this proposed change satisfied her. She complained that the new, modern, three-bedroom apartment wasn't an improvement over their musty, one-bedroom walk-through. Even paying only $12 a month rather than the $238 they presently pay didn't impress her. The plastering job covering some holes in the wall wasn't to her satisfaction, nor did she like the way the walls had been painted. In addition, a truck was needed to move her belongings. Manning offered to paint the apartment and provide a truck. Foster said he was willing to help move, but he'd be damned if he'd paint her apartment.

"Is it leaving her friends and relatives behind that bothers her?" asked Foster.

"That's only a small part of it. Her real problem is that her boyfriend, the father of the baby she now carries, will not be permitted to live in the project since they are not married."

"You mean to tell me the project officials go door-to-door, checking closets and marriage certificates?"

"They know who belongs. He doesn't. And besides he sits around the living room all day in his underwear."

I just stared at Foster, wondering what I had ever done to deserve the Anderson family. "You just go out there and tell those Andersons to move. This is an order of the court! Tell them if they don't comply they are in serious trouble."

Foster wasn't quite sure whether I was serious, angry, or both. "What about the boyfriend? What do I tell her about him?"

I wasn't certain what to say. "Tell her that he can move in and, if the housing authorities object, I will talk to them in her behalf."

There I had said it. Imagine a circuit-court judge ready to throw his weight around against officials trying to keep a housing project in decent order! And no less to help a guy sitting around in his underwear, doing nothing. The hard-line Reaganites in Washington would have a ball watching this "liberal" approach to helping the underprivileged. "One more thing," I told Foster. "See if you can get that guy a job so that he gets his ass out of the living room. Refer him to Vocational Services or something."

I don't know whether Foster's smile meant he enjoyed my discomfort or that he knew chances were slim of ever getting our friend into the job market.

Dwight is all set to go to the YMCA camp. Court Administrator George LaMont has been gathering contributions from local civic groups to pay camp fees until I return to court and begin fining lawyers. He's provided Foster with money to purchase camp clothes for Dwight, but problems have arisen. Does he give the money to mother, who will probably use it for something else? Should he buy and deliver the clothes to the Andersons, who undoubtedly will divide them among all the children in the house? How bad will it look if he buys and then stores the clothes at the YMCA camp? I told Foster this was one problem he alone would handle.

## Monday, July 23, 1984

Recuperating at home with idle hours on hand, I decided to catch up on some of the youngsters I had earlier met, but who were not in our program.

### CLARK CARDEN

Only a casual interest had prompted my attendance several months ago at the Mental Health Clinic staff presentation of thirteen-year-old Clark Carden's cold-blooded murder of his father. He was indicted on a first-degree murder charge, awaiting trial in adult court. I didn't know at that time how effectively this case would demonstrate the problem of prosecuting juveniles in the adult system.

The psychiatrists, psychologists, and social workers present had agreed that a severely disturbed child was involved who needed long-term help. His abusive father has so warped the child's life that, as Clark stated, "execution is the only way out." Because the juvenile court has jurisdiction only until age nineteen, the adult court was the more likely place to address his long-term needs. At that time, my concern centered around two unacceptable possibilities: a sympathetic jury acquitting this thirteen-year-old, well-mannered, nice-looking, white child, victim of prolonged abuse by a brutish father; or the alternative, a conviction leading to confinement in the Florida prison system. However, it looked like the public defender and the prosecutor were in the process of working out a plea arrangement that would satisfy the concern expressed by the professionals attending the Mental Health Clinic presentation.

After almost thirty years in the criminal-justice system, I still haven't learned that criminal courts are a series of amusement-park mirrors that distort reality. Something always happens to change the script—usually for the worse. In this case, a young man in serious trouble, needing prompt and long-term remediation, was in the end treated like a boy who was suffering from growing-up pains that a simple change of scenery could easily correct. It wasn't planned that way; things just happened.

First, the publicity attracted a benefactor who provided funds to replace the public defender with private counsel for Clark; and, co-incidentally, the presiding judge resigned from the bench. Now new actors were to play out the scenario. Despite my fears, in due time the lawyers negotiated a plea acceptable to the court: the youth would be found guilty of the lesser charge of manslaughter, adjudication was to be withheld, a rehabilitation program would be approved by the judge, and Clark would be placed on probation for ten years. So far, so good. He'd receive some form of treatment, would have no criminal record, and the court would maintain jurisdiction for ten years in the event he violated the terms of probation.

As often occurs among psychiatrists and psychologists, they couldn't agree as to the extent of damage done to this young man and how dangerous he might be to himself or to others. It must be

**44**

noted that Clark had more than the usual share of examiners: three appointed by the criminal-court judge and others from the juvenile-court clinic. Some viewed his situation as dire, others were less gloomy, but all agreed that, coming out of a trauma of such proportion, he needed some stabilizing treatment.

At the clinic staff presentation, Dr. R. had flat out said that the boy was "plumb crazy," capable of repeating the act in another such stressful situation. His formal report stressed the need for immediate action: "Speed is of the utmost importance in this case as this boy is in a very serious state: he is volatile, vulnerable and quite treatable. I would strongly urge the Court to place this boy in a residential setting such as Grant Hospital, where he can be provided long-term effective treatment."

Another psychologist, Dr. N., agreed, recommending psychiatric intervention on a long-term basis: "Clark has an overwhelming rage and anger that has been building up in him. Serious emotional disturbances were apparent and schizophrenic patterns appeared repeatedly."

At the other end of the scale, Dr. O., a psychiatrist, noted, "He does not appear to be overtly dangerous to himself or others at present and does not meet the criteria for involuntary hospitalization." Dr. O. described the shooting event as a "reactive patricide," which if I understand the term correctly means that this is a one-shot incident (no pun intended) where the slaying of the father is a bizarre event in his life that could only be repeated under the exact same circumstances.

Dr. M., also a psychiatrist, stated, "Clark has a behavior disturbance of adolescence, but is not mentally ill, and does not need psychiatric hospitalization. Clark will benefit from psychotherapy in custody or as an outpatient. No medication is recommended nor isolation from other individuals."

A third psychiatrist, Dr. J., concluded that the defendant should be involved in an intensive treatment effort that would probably have to be residential. The wide diversity of treatment recommended by the psychologists and psychiatrists was echoed among the other disciplines involved in the sentencing process.

The probation officer recommended that Clark be incarcerated in the Youthful Offenders' Program for one to four years as part of a structured treatment plan to handle his emotional problems as well as being placed on probation for ten years. The state attorney proposed a two-year stint in the tough Florida Environmental Program followed by long-term probation. The HRS representative suggested the short-term, highly regarded, nonresidential Dade Marine Institute.

None of the above was accepted. As often happens in the criminal-justice system, every day begins life anew. The past is not prologue; it is nothing. The benefactor who had hired private counsel for the defendant now suddenly offered to finance Clark's stay for the next several years at a private military school. The judge described this as a "perfect solution." His only concern was that the anonymous benefactor a Polish count no less, would guarantee the money. The judge gave the defense lawyer ten days to work out the details and, because this was his last day on the bench, referred completion of the case to another judge.

The final hearing was a mere formality. The private military school recommended was moving out of Florida, and another military academy was substituted. This one had almost all Spanish-speaking students, a language unfamiliar to Clark. Ten years of probation was included in the sentence, but no treatment plan or follow-up examinations were provided. Oh, yes. The count not only guaranteed tuition for high school, but assured the young man's tuition payment for four years of college. Not bad.

The professionals at the juvenile-court Mental Health Clinic were guarded in their public reaction. Not one of them had been called to testify at the sentencing and they hadn't even been aware of the results. Knowing the vagaries of the court system, they shrugged and went on to the next case. Privately, they were aghast. Incredible! Unbelievable! Watching Clark deteriorate over the months in the detention center—and now this.

Dr. R., a clinic psychologist, said jokingly that the only program more inappropriate would have been an all-girls' school. Dr. O., a psychiatrist, questioned the choice of a military school because the object of Clark's hate had always been a military-type person who was constantly brandishing all kinds of weaponry. One of the clinic nurses who had worked with the youth pointed out that, when he became an upperclassman and had considerable authority over the younger students, he might well emerge as a "little Hitler," abusing them as he had been treated. Steve Levine, the public defender, who had been replaced in this case, expressed concern that putting Clark in such an untenable situation made probation violation highly probable. He was afraid the next judge assigned this case on such a basis, not knowing and not having time to find out, would as a matter of course simply lock him up for a long term of years.

**46**

For certain, this case highlights what's wrong with transferring juveniles to the criminal court. Dealing with hardened adults is difficult enough, but those judges simply lack the time and patience for youthful offenders. This is a classic example of the criminal-justice system meaning to do good but fumbling at every step.

The kicker to it all occurred when George LaMont, our court administrator, contacted the adult Probation Office to find out what provisions were made to monitor Clark's progress at the military academy. "None at all," said the chief probation officer. "His probation period doesn't start until he graduates. That's when we first get involved."

So not only have no provisions been made for any kind of treatment whatsoever, but also the state of Florida will have no official contact with Clark for the next four years. It's conceivable that the Polish count is right. And some of those psychiatrists, too. Clark may do great at the military academy, go on to college to study computer technology, as he says he wants to, and then fulfill his dream of living in southern California and becoming an avid surfer. We hope that things will go well for him. But I wouldn't bet on it.


## RUDY LANDER

Everyone is entitled to make a mistake, but, when judges make it, someone pays a heavy price. When I first saw Rudy Lander, back in April, I thought he would be ideal for the Master Counselor Program. At that time, he was before me for two robberies, both occurring within a seventy-five-minute time span, within twenty blocks of each other. In each case, a woman was thrown to the ground and her purse taken. Both victims and two witnesses picked Rudy out of a photo lineup and also unequivocally identified him in court. I recalled the cases because of the attitude of his mother: bristling with anger, insisting on his innocence, and complaining the proceedings were unfair, to the point of almost being in contempt of court. She viewed this in racist terms: her son, a fourteen-year-old black, couldn't receive a fair trial among a cast of witnesses, police officers, lawyers, and judge—all white.

Although he seemed like a good prospect at the time, I decided to waive him over to adult court and let him take his chances there. He would either get lost in that court, probably ending up on probation, or draw a tough judge and a long sentence.

His mother was proven right. She had claimed all along that he was home at a family barbecue during the period of time in question. It was an alibi often heard from mothers. Apparently, she gained a better audience in the adult court. Lawyers for both the prosecution and the defense agreed on a lie-detector test, which showed Rudy was telling the truth when he denied involvement in both robberies.

Case dismissed!

Rudy had spent three weeks in jail before he was released on bail. That is a long time for a guilty person, let alone one who is innocent. Yet four people had identified him as the culprit. No racial bias had been involved, but I can understand the mother's attitude. Notwithstanding her intemperate behavior in court, she was a spunky lady who would have been a great asset to her son in our program—assuming, of course, he had been guilty, as charged.

It is still hard for me to believe that all those witnesses were wrong. The lie detector is not infallible, but, as his mother surely would have said to me, "Neither are you." I will check on Rudy in six months to see if he has stayed clean.

## MARLON JAMESON

The reports from HRS in neighboring Broward County were glowing. Marlon Jameson, the legislator's son who suffered from a learning disability and demonstrated a propensity for getting into trouble, was showing "remarkable progress" according to his counselor. When I had heard the case on special assignment from the governor because the local judges didn't want to hear a legislator's case, my instinct told me this kid was just as bad as the Marcos and Lesters. They, however, unlike white, upper-class juveniles, don't come in well groomed and schooled to "yes, sir" the judge, along with a coterie of psychologists and hovering parents. The monthly reports on Marlon didn't support my speculation. He is gainfully employed, dutifully studying for his GED diploma, performing community service hours, and generally being a good citizen.

At least that is what his social worker says. I was still a little suspicious of these HRS reports. Too often, when families can provide a multitude of services on their own, social workers tend to back off and write "sweetheart" reports. Here, when a legislator was involved, that likelihood was even greater. To double check, I asked the prosecutor to request the police sergeant who handled the original case to conduct a private investigation for me. Both he and the prosecutor had entertained reservations at the trial about the presentation of Marlon as a misguided, misunderstood lad who only needed a bit of counseling to straighten out.

The police officer's report confirmed the observations of the social worker. The officer made a special point to contact the neighbors who earlier had expressed fear. They now found Marlon's behavior perfectly acceptable. Apparently the family has made an all-out effort to bring the youth around. They are either succeeding or have managed to perfect a cover-up beyond detection.

## Wednesday, August 1, 1984

All kinds of reports had accumulated during my hospitalization and recuperation. At an early stage, we had decided to test and retest each of our charges. Stacked before me were psychological exams, neurological and medical tests, school and program performance reports, as well as social histories of the families. Not only had our specialists at the juvenile-court Mental Health Clinic done their job, but the public-school psychologists and their staff had also replicated these tests. Much of the information had previously been reported, but some nuances were different.

I had asked Manning to digest all the reports, add some of his own investigation, and synthesize his findings. His social history of the families confirmed many of my conclusions, but added some new insights. First, he covered the Anderson family—a good example of how meaningless it is to "treat" the offender and ignore the family history. Reading a doctor's poor prognosis on Dwight's retarded older brother Derrick and realizing that the description was a mirror reflection of Dwight made one wonder how much progress really could be expected with Dwight.

### FRANK MANNING'S SOCIAL HISTORY OF THE ANDERSON FAMILY

The following is a brief social summary of Dwight Anderson's family. The information contained therein is brief due to the fact that family members are very uncommunicative.

Dwight's biological parents are Darrin and Latrecia Anderson. Although the couple never legally married, Dwight's mother uses the last name Anderson. She lived with him six or seven years producing four children (Erla Joy, Linda Bonnie, Derrick and Dwight). Mrs. Anderson gave birth to the first child at age fourteen. Subsequently she had four other children, Melenia, Talya, Carla and Harry from different fathers, eight children in total and presently expecting her ninth child in the fall.

Her physical health is good. She is currently about six month pregnant and receiving prenatal care through the Martin Luther King Clinic in Homestead.

*Comment:* Good news! The doctor says twins are expected, thus making ten.

Mrs. Anderson, thirty years of age, is the youngest of eighteen children, born in Robinsonville, Mississippi. Her mother and most of the family were migrant farm workers. Mrs. Anderson attended school only until the third grade when she began working in the fields with her mother. Talking with Mrs. Anderson it is obvious that she is intellectually quite remitted and possibly retarded. It is possible that her limitations are cultural as much as organic.

*Comment:* Good Lord! She is one of eighteen children and this will be her ninth (or tenth). What can be done?

Mrs. Anderson is extremely limited, depending on her mother and other relatives for much of her survival. In fact, when being interviewed, she prefers someone else to speak for her. She has very little insight into her own or any of her children's problems and while she thinks HRS efforts in behalf of Dwight are "good," she has made no other comment. Mrs. Anderson apparently has no comprehension of birth control or family planning and is not distressed in the least that she is having her ninth child.

*Comment:* All the psychologists suggest taking Dwight out of the home for placement in a residential setting. I don't agree. As dysfunctional as this family is—and I have seen few worse—a strong element of reliance on each other exists that is important to the boy. True and idealistic success would be for him to rise above the family and come out a new Dwight—a metamorphosis that would be miraculous. I'd like to go for the gold on this one.

Little information is available on Dwight's father Darrin Anderson, Jr. He reportedly has a history of criminal behavior, incarcerated in 1979 for Burglary and Grand Theft. However, his present whereabouts is unknown. He is not detained in Florida but possibly may be in Virginia. Inquiries will be made to that state.

The family living situation is quite poor. They live in a one-bedroom apartment without utilities on a monthly income limited to $243 AFDC and $213 Food Stamps. The only beneficial aspect of the present living situation is that it is close to Mrs. Anderson's mother and other relatives. Many of the children have been involved in HRS, two presently in custody, a third, Derrick, in a group treatment facility for the retarded.

Dwight Anderson is a nice looking twelve-year-old black male, extremely uncommunicative. He appears to be mildly retarded and as a result is in special classes at Cutler Ridge Junior High School. Dwight has responded quite well to the Master Counselor project, is open with his Counselor, relating to him as a father image.

Success in Dwight's case will consist of keeping him out of trouble, teaching him to relate more positively and allowing him to complete school to a point where he could obtain some vocational training.

Overall, Dwight's life has been unstructured and unstable. This is the first generation in his family that is attempting any sort of stability. For the first time Dwight and his siblings are attending school to a point beyond the third or fourth grade. It appears that Dwight and perhaps several of his siblings may be able to break the cycle of migrant worker/welfare recipient that has existed for several generations.

*Comment:* Diplomatically, I told Manning this was a fine report, well crafted for the bureaucracy of HRS. What I wanted was more feeling and less boiler plate. Manning, after six years, recently promoted to supervisor, is a rising young star in HRS and knows how to write reports that thoroughly cover a subject while avoiding controversy. He gave me a knowing little smile and promised a more revealing follow-up.

## FRANK MANNING'S FOLLOW-UP REPORT ON ANDERSON FAMILY

I continue to be horrified every time I see Mrs. Anderson. Here is a thirty year old lady who already has eight intellectually limited and problem children, expecting twins and is apparently completely unconcerned. Is she so limited and primitive that she cannot comprehend the unfortunate situation she is in, or is she insensitive and just wanting more children to increase her welfare check? I am not sure.

In addition to her lack of family planning, she is apparently unable either to think for herself or is unmotivated to make any changes in her life. When housing was arranged, and bills were paid, she failed to follow through. Her reasoning for failing to do so is unclear. It perhaps centers around her reluctance to leave the close proximity of her mother and other relatives or it may be because of pure stupidity.

With Cornelius Foster and HRS' assistance, Mrs. Anderson has become so dependent she can hardly do anything by herself. She calls Cornelius almost daily and he has taken her places, paid bills, etc. If it were possible, she would probably like him to move in.

I don't think by continuing on this course that we are helping Mrs. Anderson. We need to locate a program or individual that can help her to think and act independently. It is truly a shame that the family appears to have lost the housing that was so hard to set up.

With regard to Dwight, I think he is very happy. We are doing an excellent job of entertaining him. We took an impoverished boy, intellectually limited, and sent him on outings and to summer camp. We also bought him a lot of new clothes, so he feels nice and looks nice. We are rewarding him for being a "good boy" and keeping him busy. He has no need at this time to associate with older peers who used to get him into trouble. As long as we continue to entertain Dwight, he will not be a problem.

*Comment:* Manning's acid "truth" cuts to the bone, but doesn't help. A lot of groping around with Dwight will be required before a clear path emerges.

My concern is our long range goal. What will Dwight do after Master Counselor? How do we maintain his interest? Will he always need a "big brother?" Certainly we can't count on mother! Dwight is doomed to fail in school—he will need vocational training and would perhaps benefit from a job. I know he is only twelve, but I feel it important to plan well in advance for him. Maybe the answer in this case is for Cornelius to adopt Dwight as you jokingly suggested.

*Comment:* He gave me more than I asked for. Skilled bureaucrat that Manning is, the message was diplomatic but clear; we (meaning I) may have misread all the signals. Is Manning more realistic than I, or am I more patient than he?

## FRANK MANNING'S SOCIAL HISTORY OF THE SILLS FAMILY

Andy's biological parents are Ralph Sills and Mary (Sills) Waite. The couple was never legally married but lived together for over twenty years. Mr. Sills was employed as a waiter. He was also the father of Andy's younger sister. In July, 1983, he left the family taking the youngest child with him. His present whereabouts is unknown. Mrs. Waite relates that Mr. Sills was an alcoholic who was mentally and physically abusive to her and the children. As a child he was in foster care, and also had been involved in delinquent behavior.

*Comment:* Mr. Sills appeared in court at Andy's first hearing and offered to take him to a small upstate New York town to live with his grandparents. The court declined the offer because Mr. Sills was in the process of completing an alcohol rehabilitation program and Andy had no memory of his grandparents. Besides, the bonding between mother and son was too strong to sever it summarily.

Mrs. Waite has a similarly disturbing childhood with a history of running away from home. Rejected by her parents at a very young age, she was raised by her grandmother. At age thirteen, she met and moved in with Mr. Sills, having her first child at age seventeen. Mrs. Waite has an eighth grade education. She admits to abusing alcohol and marijuana but states she no longer does. She also admits to neglecting her children and attributes it to the many problems she has had. Mrs. Waite has an unstable work history working as a waitress and also as a cashier. She has also received AFDC for periods of time.

She recently married Mr. Ron Waite, a friend of Andy's who is quite a bit younger. He has been employed by Dade County as a school guard for the past two years, earning about $312 bi-weekly. Although there is an age difference, Mrs. Waite states that they get along well and that he has helped her and the children. She attributes giving up alcohol to his influence and states she is now together enough to the point where she is looking for employment.

She feels Andy's physical development was normal and he has had no serious illnesses or injuries. Mrs. Waite did state she felt Andy was influenced by the many problems that existed in the home (i.e. alcoholism, abuse, etc.), and that he was exposed to this a great deal.

*Comment:* Here's a troubled youth, growing up in the midst of family turmoil, who still has a chance. As a child, he had difficulty sleeping, woke up afraid, cried a lot, and had tantrums often. Yet, despite this background and excessive absences, he tested academically as a bright student making good grades.

His behavior at home is good and for the first time the entire family is interacting positively. Two events have greatly affected this family. The first, the Master Counselor Program, has provided Andy with the

**53**

guidance and attention he was desperately seeking. The second plus is Mr. Waite who has been for Andy's mother, what the Master Counselor has been for Andy. For the first time, Mrs. Waite has someone she can count on.

## FRANK MANNING'S FOLLOW-UP REPORT ON
## SILLS FAMILY

Are the parents maladjusted adults raising a maladjusted child? I'm not sure. Although I initially thought her new marriage might help stabilize things, I now feel that this is not the case. Marital problems are already beginning to surface. Many of Mrs. Waite's problems have accompanied her and flourished in adulthood. She continues to place her problems above those of her son, pressuring Andy to get a job to help with household expenses. Andy has been doing well but is torn by the job issue. I recommend that we force Andy to remain in vocational training. If he wants to work, he can do so part-time in the afternoons and evenings. If Mrs. Waite is not working, we should push her to do so. Family counseling is sorely needed to stress the importance of family stability for Andy.

*Comment:* Some time back, I had directed Foster to order her to obtain employment, relenting only when advised that she was fully occupied with the problems of the two younger daughters and that Mr. Waite's small salary was adequate for their needs. Apparently it isn't. Now bus fare for school can no longer be provided, and his mother prefers that Andy drop out of school to work full time as a dishwasher. This is all very confusing to him. In addition, his former friend, now his stepfather, has started to order him about. Andy's fragile psyche won't be able to handle too much of this.

Andy relates to Cornelius Foster as a father image, replacing the one that does not exist. His step-father is more of a sibling. There appears to be no racial conflict between the family and Foster. It never became the issue I thought it might be. Andy is very close to Foster, emotionally dependent on him, calling him when he is upset, and also sharing good news. He has suffered in the past from parents who just had too many problems of their own. If we continue to be firm and supportive with Andy, he will not decline. We must also work with his mother because her deterioration would greatly affect him. It might be helpful for us to get together with the client and his family to share feelings, concerns and ideas. Our "concerted" effort may not be as apparent to the family as we think.

*Comment:* Manning's follow-up report suggests the bloom may be beginning to wear off. We'll need to do more to keep this family going.

## FRANK MANNING'S SOCIAL HISTORY OF THE SAMUEL FAMILY

Laurence's mother, Mrs. Gloria (Barrett) Sumter, was born January 1, 1952, in Lena, Mississippi, the third oldest child of a family consisting of twelve children. At the age of eight, the Barrett family moved to Miami, Florida, and resided in the Brownsville area.

Laurence's father, Walter John Samuel, and Gloria Barrett were never married. Both attended Miami Central Senior High School. When Gloria Barrett was in the tenth grade she became pregnant with Laurence. Both dropped out of school, with the idea of working and marrying, but their families refused permission.

From her marriage in 1969 to Howard Leo Kirsten there was one girl, Tara, now twelve years old. Their marriage lasted approximately two years. Mrs. Sumter and her current husband, Jackson Sumter, lived together for approximately three years before marrying in 1973. They have no children but Mr. Sumter has three from a past marriage. His youngest son Arthur resides with them.

The Sumter household now consists of Mr. and Mrs. Sumter, Laurence, fifteen, Arthur, sixteen, and Tara, twelve. They live in a three bedroom, two bath house in the Brownsville area that is neatly kept and appears very comfortable for each family member. The area, once known for gang fighting and considered a high crime area, has in recent years improved its image. According to his mother, Laurence gets along well with each family member and has a close relationship with his stepfather.

Mrs. Sumter, employed at the Veteran's Administration Hospital as a Dietician, earns $12,000 per year. In the past she has been employed as a telephone operator and a Nurses Aide. Mr. Sumter, a native of Miami, Florida, graduated from Northwestern Senior High School in 1960, served in the U.S. Army, and now works with the Marriott Flight Catering Service, earning approximately $15,000 per year.

Mrs. Sumter states that Laurence started causing problems at the age of five during pre-school, disrupting school functions. This has been a continuous problem. Laurence has attended several schools and each time is transferred because of his disruptive behavior. At one point the public school psychologist recommended placing Laurence in a class for emotionally handicapped but his mother refused to sign the consent form. At age thirteen, Laurence began committing burglaries—four—before being sent to State School. When asked why he committed these burglaries, he stated he didn't know.

*Comment:* Physical examination shows that Laurence has a serious hearing problem: complete loss in one ear and impairment in the other. This could have been a major factor in his deterioration. The problem has been known for several years and apparently ignored. It may also be important to find out why Mrs. Sumter refused to permit Laurence to attend the class for emotionally handicapped. He's the newest of our charges, and we need to learn a lot more about him.

Since participating in the Master Couselor Program, his behavior at home has been satisfactory but not so at school. For some reason, Laurence has a very hard time communicating with school teachers, especially female. Laurence is a workable client who needs something to attract his interest in a vocational training field because he isn't going to last in a public school setting.

Laurence's parents take a passive role since Master Counselor has become involved. They appear to be more actively involved with their other children. Perhaps counseling might be beneficial. We must encourage Laurence's parents to spend a great deal more time with him if we are to be successful.

*Comment:* Manning's report doesn't add much. It only says that he's still a problem everywhere except at home, but that's probably where his troubles begin. The Sumters are well intentioned, but their level of involvement borders on indifference. It's a stable family that gets along by avoiding each other. This may be the result of several marriages on both sides and three children, all coming from different sets of parents. There must be awesome competition among the siblings, vying for parental attention.

## FRANK MANNING ON CLIENT MARCO ZARGULA

Marco is the Master Counselor client who concerns me most. I am fearful he is likely to be involved in serious crimes. His home situation is extremely unstable. The family consisting of Marco, his mother, two sisters and a married brother and his family, reside in one of the worst crime-ridden housing projects in Dade County. They have a history of problems which Marco tries to avoid by staying away from home. His performance in school is erratic, truancy dominating his school record. Although of average intelligence, his poor behavior and lack of impulse control prevent him from having any success.

Small for his age, everyone likes him. He's a follower who would like to be a leader. Marco abuses drugs which intensifies his out-of-control behavior. As for planning, we must consider an alternative living situation for Marco. Considering the multiple family problems and the negative influence of Marco's peers, a residential drug program might be appropriate.

Again I stress the fact that this boy concerns me greatly and I feel we must have very close control on him.

*Comment:* Manning's pessimism is warranted, but nobody promised a rose garden when this project started. Frankly, I expected some of our charges to be difficult, not dead ends like Marco and Lester. I also hoped we'd get lucky through some immediate turnarounds. That hasn't happened, either.

### FRANK MANNING ON CLIENT LESTER BURROWS

Lester presents a challenge frequently faced in foster care involving older adolescents. Where do we place clients like Lester after they have already been in and out of twenty-five foster homes? We must immediately initiate a search for a living situation for Lester. A conventional foster home is out. The only alternative is either a group home or perhaps a very unique single male who would be interested in helping someone like Lester. We have to begin talking with Lester to prepare him for his release from wherever he is placed. He needs to be "hooked" and "sold" with some type of interest, preferably vocational and motivated toward preparing for independent living which is not too far away. The living situation is crucial. We must hold him before we can work with him. He must buy into the idea or he will certainly run and return to his old ways.

*Comment:* Manning sounds like we need a team of professional negotiators to mediate.

Manning pulled no punches in response to my request for a critique of the Master Counselor Program. Like every other social worker, he felt uncomfortable about lacking a formal long-range treatment plan as opposed to my flexible, keep-all-options-open approach. Another concern of his referred to the likelihood of families becoming overdependent upon the many resources we now were making available. He cited instances where Cornelius Foster was filling the void in every family problem, bringing a "baby sitting" aspect to the job. "Eventually," he insisted, "both the family and the child should be weaned away from this constant support. We don't want them to be cripples, relying solely on Foster."

My repeated exhortation to Foster from the inception was that he view the delinquent in terms of the entire family, that he infiltrate, strengthen, and guide them. It never occurred to me that this might weaken the family.

Foster listened politely as I described Manning's assessment along with my reaction to it. "You're both right," he concluded and said:

Families always take advantage of whoever does things for them. They use me more than necessary, but they also trust me more. I can help when they trust me. About the programs—don't worry. It don't make much difference how they are planned. Truth is, bad dudes don't want no help. They want to be left alone. Sleep late, stay away from school, watch television, and run into a girl now and then. If they can get a little pot, maybe a snort, life's perfect. Go to the park in the afternoon to see what's doing. Maybe hit a parking lot downtown. Or if someone knows a house to break into, they do that. If one get arrested, it don't mean too much, cause someone's always getting arrested.

"Which kind of program works?" I persisted.
"Most don't," he answered and then continued:

They make a kid get up early in the morning, study, listen to his counselor, and do a lot of things he hates doing. After a while, he figures it's easier to go along with the program. At this point, the program sends a report to the judge saying how great the kid is doing. We're finally reaching him, we think. Meanwhile, the kids who didn't get caught make fun of him wherever they see him, calling him a "sissy" and "pussy." When he finishes the program, there's a graduation and he gets a certificate. Then he's glad to be home, can sleep late, and be with the fellows in the park again. Maybe tomorrow after he checks in with his counselor, they'll hit a parking lot downtown and he'll show them he's not a "pussy."

Foster's matter-of-fact recitation was not angry or judgmental. "What do we do?" I insisted.

His answer was simple. "We stay with them as long as we can, until they begin to hear us. Just what we are doing." It is becoming increasingly evident that one year of intense involvement will not be enough. Foster's hands-on approach may be needed for a lot longer.

## FRANK MANNING'S SOCIAL HISTORY OF
## CORNELIUS FOSTER

It is important to note that Mr. Foster was reluctant to discuss in depth much of his past as he felt it "opened up old scars."

*Comment:* When I asked Foster about this, he said that some things are better left unsaid and forgotten. His scars, he said, "had never healed."

Cornelius Foster was born June 2, 1946, in Miami's Liberty City, Florida, the eldest of eleven children. His mother was sixteen years old when she gave birth. When his mother left home to be married, Cornelius' maternal grandmother actually assumed full responsibility to raise Cornelius and his younger brother. His grandmother worked for Florida East Coast Railroad and his grandfather was a carpenter. Their income and living situation was adequate, the family never lacking anything. Cornelius considers his grandparents to have been his actual parents. His grandfather died of cancer when he was about ten. Grandmother raised him until maturity. She was the matriarch, always taking care of everyone in the family. She was good with money and bought several houses for her family. Cornelius was well provided for by his grandparents and does not attribute any of his difficulties later in life to his upbringing. As a teenager, he was greatly influenced by his peers and became involved in delinquent and ungovernable behavior. He was committed to HRS and spent time in the Kendall Facility and several other HRS placements.

Cornelius graduated high school in 1964 when he voluntarily joined the Air Force. He served in Vietnam in 1966 and 1967, working as a clerk and also a heavy equipment operator. He did not see intensive combat but was exposed to some action and honorably discharged in September, 1968. Upon return to civilian life, Cornelius found it difficult to find work and when he did, became easily frustrated and often quit his job.

He associated with a group of fellow veterans, who, due to mutual frustrations, became involved in robberies and burglaries, coming close to killing or seriously hurting their victims. He also admits to abusing alcohol and narcotics during that time. In January, 1969, Cornelius was convicted of Robbery and Assault and sentenced to ten years in the Raiford State Penitentiary. He spent time in several facilities until August, 1973, when he attained Educational and Vocational Status and was placed at Avon Park Correctional Institute.

He completed several vocational courses in prison, eventually moving or to Valencia Community College under a work release program. After release from prison, he completed his Bachelors Degree at Florida A & M with a major in Sociology and minor in Corrections, graduating in June, 1978.

While in prison, Cornelius participated in several drug and alcohol abuse programs frequently serving as a facilitator for the groups. Cornelius was then hired by HRS and has functioned as a Community Control Counselor since that time.

He feels his time in prison really turned his life around and that the experience set him straight. He hated confinement and avoiding return was a real motivator. He shares many of his past experiences with his clients in the hope that he might "scare" them into staying straight. He feels it has worked in a good many cases.

*Comment:* When prisons start promoting public-relations campaigns extolling their virtues (as colleges do), Foster will be an ideal endorsement. It was the tough prison incarceration that reformed him, not the juvenile-court rehabilitation or even service in the army. Score another for the hard-liners.

With regard to his family, Cornelius has been married three years but is in the process of divorce. He has two children, a stepson, Milton, age fifteen, and a daughter, Shanta, age two. His wife Mary Foster, also an HRS employee, works with the retarded as a supervisor at Sunland Center. When questioned with regard to his divorce, Cornelius responded that he and his wife still love each other but can not be together on a day-to-day basis. They have been separated for several months. Cornelius thinks some of the couple's problems stem from his job. His wife constantly tells him not to treat her like one of his kids. He is very close to his own children and unhappy that he is not able to be with them as much as before. He feels his personality may be very demanding and directive as a result of the relationship he must have with his clients. It is my opinion that he has always been that way. Cornelius has difficulties as far as his personal relations go.

*Comment:* Manning is a bit tough on Foster concerning this subject. Cornelius has been anguishing over his marital problems. He doesn't know how to respond. Sometimes he's depressed, mumbling nothings; other times, he becomes animated and playacts the man-about-town role. Once, when kidding him about how much attention he was attracting from Mrs. Anderson, he quickly turned into the ladies' man, telling me his kind of woman was a vivacious, sparkling dame, clothed in high-fashion attire, ready to make all the hot spots in town. This hardly was Mrs. Anderson and it wasn't Cornelius Foster, either. He has his problems and, like everyone else, a few shortcomings, but they don't get in the way of what he has to do.

Cornelius is very pleased to be the Master Counselor. He dislikes the high volume of travel and the over-dependency of a few of his clients' parents. He really likes his pseudo-father role to Dwight and Andy, and the Probation Officer role that requires clients to do what he says. However, underlying this he genuinely cares for the kids. Basically he does not want the kids to go through what he has experienced.

*Comment:* There's a lot in Cornelius Foster that each of our youngsters can relate to, both good and bad. He's gruff, doesn't stress philosophy, but underneath it all he conveys a total sense of honesty. He's an excellent model because he's not idealized. Most social workers are clean-cut, live in a different milieu, and model the proper life-style. Foster is real, someone his charges see on the streets everyday with whom they can identify. I asked him how he managed to get along so well with these families. "I don't smile," was his answer. "I just tell them what to do, straight-forward, no grinning, no scratching my head like black folks do. I just tell them what to do. They know I mean business and they do it."

He bristled at being identified as a "social worker." His explanation as always was terse and to the point: "When you knock on a door in Liberty City at midnight announcing you are a 'social worker,' someone puts a gun to your head, throws you down the stairs. You say 'probation officer'—you are the law—they open the door and invite you in."

# 3

## Throwing the Key
## Away Only Means
## Finding Another One

### Thursday, August 2, 1984

As the summer winds down and we gear up for the new school term, report cards would show an "F" for Marco, an "Incomplete" for Lester, and decent grades for the others. It is much too soon to give up on anybody or to check the applause meter.

We may not agree on a lot, but Manning and I do concur that the five kids encompass every known problem encountered by juvenile delinquents. It wasn't designed that way—it just happened. My recommendation to Foster was to select youngsters who had long, serious records, were heading for more criminal involvement, and were young enough to be influenced but were neither psychotic nor organically damaged. Because half the juvenile crime and three-quarters of the assaultive offenses in Dade County are committed by blacks, they occupied three of the reserved spots, an Anglo and a Latin occupying the other two. Participants also had to be on the way to State School so that removal from the bus might encourage a grateful attitude. Aimed at transforming them into amenable participants, this ploy had, in fact, little impact on their behavior; only for the moment were they glad to be saved.

### Friday, August 3, 1984

It was a big jolt when Court Administrator George LaMont reported that both Manning and Foster were in the market for new jobs. Both

had spoken to him about employment opportunities, each concerned at my reaction. LaMont had assured them I would be both
understanding and helpful.

I advised Manning to stay with HRS because he was being
groomed for bigger things. He was eyeing a position as program
analyst in the Court Administrator's Office. Although a substantial
salary increase loomed large now, in the long run HRS offered the
better opportunity. Foster sought a counselor's job in the state attorney's new program working with delinquents who were waived
over to the adult court. This meant about a $4,000 increase. He
needs the money. I promised to help. The legislature is so shortsighted on salary structure for social workers, it is surprising that
any stay.

Our program will be decimated if either leaves, but the reality is
that this is always a possibility, perhaps a likelihood. However, if the
concept is valid, no one person should be indispensable. At least,
that's what the theorists say. Manning is a bright, perceptive young
man whose departure would be a loss, but a new supervisor probably
could fill the gap in time. But how do we replace Foster? What
happens to all that credibility he has built up with Dwight and
Andy? The empathy generated from the hours spent together fishing, talking, and listening won't be transferable to the next Master
Counselor. Foster may not be the textbook version of the ideal counselor, but to these kids he's the best role model they've ever seen.
Unfortunately, counselors leaving is the rule, not the exception.

## Monday, August 6, 1984

A different Marco Zargula (The Charmer) appeared before me for the
waiver hearing. On an earlier occasion, he was a jaunty young man,
full of bounce, hair slicked down, happy to be taken off the bus to
State School. HRS Hearing Examiner Bill Shapiro had earlier ordered
him there for violating probation on the old case. Today, the prosecutor wanted him tried as an adult on the new case, and it was my
decision whether or not he remain in juvenile court. Sallow, glum,
hair disheveled, wearing a ragged T-shirt, he had evidently under-
gone an unpleasant stay in detention.

When arrested, Marco had told a lurid tale of being picked up by
the victim at 64th Street and Biscayne Boulevard, driven to Flamingo
Park in Miami Beach, and there solicited to perform a homosexual
act. His story of thwarting these advances by grabbing the victim's

gun turned out be typical Marco fiction. The victim, a baseball coach at Flamingo Park, described Marco placing a Baretta in his back while his accomplice directed Marco to "shoot him if he moves." Marco cocked the weapon, but, instead of the gun firing, the shell fell harmlessly out of the chamber to the ground. Facing a fifteen-year-old with an obviously malfunctioning gun petrified the victim. He didn't move as Marco recocked the gun. The youths took his car, wallet, .357 Magnum, and other property.

Two police officers testified that Marco led them to a shallow waterway where he claimed to have thrown both guns, but divers came up with nothing but sand. After interviewing the umpires, the policemen concluded that the short time interval between the end of the game and the robbery made it impossible for the victim to have driven the distance claimed by Marco. Nothing else in his story checked out; he had obviously lied. Both officers emphasized that they had never seen one so young, so committed to crime, and so habitual a liar. They asked that he be kept off the streets for the protection of the community.

The victim, in an emotional plea, declared he had worked with children for many years, and, though accused falsely as well as shocked to face a fifteen-year-old gunman, he nevertheless hoped the court would help this youngster. At this point, the waiver hearing was continued to a later date for recommendations from Cornelius Foster and others as to social considerations. It's the classic tight-rope act, trying to provide punishment and treatment at the same time. Marco obviously needs to be convinced a serious price must be paid. Then he needs a friend.

Shapiro's probation violation hearing had produced little to un-ravel Marco's behavior. Shapiro tried the paternalistic approach, tell-ing him he deserved more than a life behind bars: "You are a bright young man with the ability to succeed in school. Why don't you quit running with the Calcons and those other bad kids? What's wrong with going to school?"

Marco looked at him with those innocent, round, black eyes and responded matter-of-factly, "I just don't feel like going to school." For once, he was telling the truth. Shapiro, who had about twenty-five years of experience in dealing with these kids, hadn't come any closer to him than the rest of us. When I asked for some special insight on dealing with Larchmont Gardens, Shapiro sidestepped, saying, "Marco's Larchmont Gardens housing project is a cesspool filled with young criminals whose lives are devoted solely to crime.

They have no other interest and seek none. Once, several years ago we went after the ringleaders and sent them to State School. Things improved. Now, there are others. There always are others."

"I know that," I insisted. "But, since lockup is only a temporary step, what can we do to make a lasting impact?"

Shapiro shrugged and waved his hands in resignation. At that point, Foster joined the discussion, observing that, after viewing the movie *Scarface*, Marco sees himself as the slim Latin killer who terrorized Miami. " 'Scarface' is his hero and model. That's today. Tomorrow he may be somebody else. There's no telling about Marco. We think he's scared about what the big guys will do to him in jail. In fact, he may really want to go to jail to make himself a tough-guy reputation there. When I was doing my robberies, jail was just another place to make a name for myself. Once you get it fixed in your mind that you are a criminal, then you expect to go to Raiford and you really want to find out if you are tough enough to take it."

Shapiro listened and chuckled. "I've seen a lot worse than Marco. This kid's just a little schnook. Why are you making him out a killer?" I looked up, realizing that at one time or another, all of us had agreed with Shapiro's version of Marco, though we were not so certain now. How does one determine which individual turns out to be the killer?

## Thursday, August 9, 1984

Not much planning was required to send Lester Burrows (The Runner) to State School. His latest crime plus his runaway status were overt violations of probation. Hearing Examiner Bill Shapiro summarily placed him on the bus. The youth will be back in a few weeks for a waiver, and I will probably do the same as with Marco: transfer him to adult court, but make certain he stays at State School and eventually returns to the Master Counselor Program. He does not deserve another chance in the program, but we deserve another chance at him. Lester, unaware of these plans, sits quietly in his cell, prepared to wait it all out. Meanwhile, Shapiro has found no more clues on Lester than he had on Marco.

Lester was candid with Shapiro almost to the point of indifference. He admitted violating probation and couldn't explain why, except to say, "I don't like people telling me what to do. I never make plans for anything. Yes, the Master Counselor Program has tried to help me, but I don't want to be bothered." Hardly a receptive client. Shapiro describes himself professionally as a probation officer rather than as a social worker. He views the former as realistic, and the latter as idealistic. In Shapiro's realism, Lester's world is one without a future. Handling probation violations, he sees the failures after the system has made its best effort: "Only the immediate moment counts with them—it's hour-to-hour survival. Whatever happens is spontaneous. Lester's kind doesn't plan to violate the law. It just pops out. Programs don't make much difference to kids this far gone. All you can do is chip away and in time his head may open up." I waited for another hopeful word, but as at Shapiro's hearing with Marco, no new insights came to light. Shapiro's conclusions apparently represent the current state of the art.

### Friday, August 10, 1984

Although Dwight Anderson (The Migrant) was described as slow and unlikely to make it in the outside world, his two-week trip to the YMCA camp was a revelation of sorts. Located at scenic Lake Placid, in central Florida, the camp conducts two-week sessions devoted primarily to water sports and recreation: ten campers, two counselors to a cabin, mostly proper kids from hardworking families, 10 percent black. A few were on scholarships but not Dwight. His tuition was paid from lawyer fines, and his background was not revealed to camp authorities. Could he respond positively in a normal setting with other kids his age? According to his camp counselor, a young, white college student, he had no difficulty concerning social adjustment in his cabin. It took a while for the others to understand his shorthand speech pattern, but in the end, he fit right in with the others. Although it was only an adventure to him, more importantly we learned he could handle an unfamiliar setting outside his own environment.

Camp also provided the opportunity to pull Dwight out of the Homestead Police Department's Explorer Program. This had included Saturday picnics and other wholesome diversions until the format suddenly changed to washing police cars. Foster might have tolerated some forced labor, but, when the police started to question Dwight about recent burglaries, Foster decided they'd have to find another informer. Finally, one afternoon, they caught Dwight testing car door handles in an adjacent parking lot and charged him with loitering and prowling. That was the end of a not-so-great summer experience. We are now trying to place him in the Boys' Club after-school program, but Dwight's home may be outside the geographical area. Of course, considering the unsettled state of where the Andersons live, that situation can change any day.

The saga of the Anderson move to a housing project appears to be coming to a "they-lived-happily-ever-after" ending. Mrs. Anderson may look retarded to some, but, as Foster says, "Mrs. Anderson ain't retarded—she's country folk. They a little slow but they wide awake."

She didn't want the first place HUD offered, tossing every conceivable roadblock in the way. It was too far; the plaster was peeling; her boyfriend was barred; no money for utilities; and whatever. It didn't help that the people at HUD were unhappy with the political influence used to jump her to the top of the list, and they were hardly enthralled with this "uppity migrant worker" being selective about the choice. Foster kept at it and his persistence resulted in a new HUD offer: a handsome town house, in mint condition, closer to her family. Everyone is satisfied for now. We'll see how Mrs. Anderson handles this one.

## Tuesday, August 14, 1984

The second part of the waiver hearing for Marco Zargula (The Charmer) was cut and dried. This time, he looked less bedraggled, his hair was combed, and he was more composed. Foster wanted him to stay in the juvenile system and the public defender agreed, but the prosecutor was opposed, pointing to his long arrest record. Nobody argued with much fervor, all apparently knowing what was in store, including Marco. I ruled that adult court was the place for him. Watching him leave the courtroom in the custody of Foster, I couldn't help but be bemused by the words on the back of his T-shirt: "I AM A WINNER." Winner indeed! Someone with a wry sense of humor engineered that.

Foster hustled him downstairs to his waiting car, and they immediately departed for Okeechobee, Florida, the home of the Eckerd Youth Development Center, commonly known as State School. The trip was expedited for tactical reasons. Marco was now in the unusual situation of being in both the juvenile and adult systems. If he stays around more than twenty-four hours, he will quickly find himself transferred to the adult jail to be detained for weeks or months until his trial is completed. To avoid this, Foster volunteered to make the delivery immediately.

My plan to shift Marco back and forth is not exactly standard procedure and may even be dangerous, but the textbooks contain few prescriptions offering sure-fire methods for the Marcos of the world. I want him to see enough of the adult system to be frightened, yet not be in it long enough to suffer some of the horrible things that happen to delicate-looking young boys. Hard-liners may differ, contending that someone whose record is as bad as that of Marco assumes the risk, but using the fear of jailhouse rape as some sort of deterrent doesn't say much for either our jails or our rehabilitation philosophy.

Joining Foster in the get-away car was Herman Perry, one of Marco's earlier counselors. It was Perry who had warned Foster that Marco was impossible to deal with and would waste the time of the Master Counselor Program. After interviewing Marco, Foster had scoffed at his colleague's warning and uttered his now-famous declaration: "Piece of cake, piece of cake." It is a statement I do not allow him to forget. Marco sat in the back and Perry in the front as they began their 300-mile trip. Perry is out of the same school as Foster: tough, fair, taciturn, indigenous to the ghetto, and ready to treat clients in whatever manner necessary. Marco plied them with questions, to which they responded with horror stories. It was black humor, unappreciated by the fearful youth.

Entering the Eckerd Center grounds, Marco still had that scared look about him, until he spotted a familiar face, another Latin inmate from the Larchmont Gardens Housing Project. After a two-minute conversation with his friend, the old cocky Marco began to return, already comfortable in his new setting. Before departing, Foster visited with Lester Burrows (The Runner), who was starting his second week at State School. As with Marco, his big concern was his upcoming waiver hearing and what might happen in adult court. Foster predicts both boys will easily make the adjustment at State School.

## Thursday, August 23, 1984

This was the first of a series of summit conferences to begin the next stage of our operation. The start-up had not been defined too clearly.

Although we had met the cast of characters and grappled with their problems, a sense of uncertainty prevailed. It's time for the Manning approach of solid bureaucratic planning: schedules, specific goals, timetables, the works.

For today, it was Andy Sills (The Drinker). Manning was right at home as he enumerated all the roadblocks ahead for the boy. Foster, somewhat defensively, responded that the school-or-work dilemma had been resolved. He'd do both. His most recent spat with his stepfather ended amicably with a night out together, and mother is back working and happy with her employment.

These were not great milestones and probably temporary at that, but they showed some forward movement and earned a few kudos for Foster. Not from Manning. He had his list ready to go. How intensive was the course on auto-body repair? Job guarantee? Is he still drinking? Can he get a GED diploma? Although Foster had already provided some of these answers, he offered no comment; he just kept taking notes. Manning ordered intensive family counseling, predicting that all the signs for a major blowup were present: the guilt-ridden mother, the only crutch for a weak son; the weak son now competing for her affection with the young stepfather; and the young stepfather—Andy's own friend—becoming family disciplinarian and breadwinner. Throw in two confused younger sisters who were disturbed by the struggle for power and add Andy's attractive, rich girl friend, who daily takes him for a spin in her Mercedes-Benz to visit her fancy waterfront home. Manning predicts that when this family erupts, a platoon of psychologists will be needed to put them together again.

Next week will bring in the Sills family for a round-table discussion. No telling which way it will go. A lot of lines need untangling.

## Monday, August 27, 1984

The summit for Laurence Samuel (The Fighter) didn't move very far. He's still the enigma of the group. Teachers are an anathema to him. He challenges them all with: "You ain't gonna do nothing to me," then shifts to being class clown looking for laughs. Misplaced in a junior high school and oversized at six feet, four inches, he has both students and teachers frightened. Our options are for McArthur Senior High School, where his size won't be a factor, or the Culinary

Arts Program, to learn baking. Foster, somewhat peeved at Laurence's intractability, prefers McArthur High School: "McArthur is a mean, tough school with dudes that will beat on him. He'll be on the floor in no time. It will do him good."

No matter what effort Foster makes, Laurence shrugs it off, a response Foster finds hard to take: "I tell him if you fuck up, your ass is back in jail. For two weeks, he's passive and then he's threatening again. He's at the stage now where he wants fancy clothes and silver chains, but doesn't want to do anything about earning them. He asked me to find him a job. I told him to get his ass out of bed and get it over to Burger King."

Culinary arts may be the change he needs. His days in the public-school system certainly are numbered. The next time he pushes around another teacher, it will surely lead to permanent expulsion. These antics represent more than the typical teenage growing-up process. Besides, mixed in with these assaults is a record of several burglary arrests plus other crimes. The boy bears serious watching.

Manning thinks we won't make any real progress until we know what makes Laurence run. "Have you thought of chemical imbalance or improper diet as causes for violence?" asked a young public defender who was sitting in as an observer. Manning perked up, and Foster looked doubtful. The public defender continued, "Some scientific studies show that lack of cobalt or low-blood sugar is evident among those prone to violence. It is all in what you eat." Manning asked for literature on the subject. Foster said mischievously he didn't want to learn that blacks are violent because they eat hogshead and collard greens, his favorite dish.

The family reveals very little about Laurence. Is it that they don't care or are they intimidated? Mother says he's had temper tantrums since pre-school days and accepts no direction. She leaves him alone. Stepfather was close to him, but now he too gives Laurence plenty of room. His natural father, a tough, street hustler who has a long rap sheet may be his real model. Unfortunately, we don't know who or what influences Laurence.

A card is missing somewhere. Manning has ordered a new set of psychological and neurological examinations. Without question, Laurence is ornery. He also has had a hearing problem since the day his half-sister punctured his eardrum with a pencil. There's little else to go by. We may yet end up changing his diet or injecting a little cobalt into Laurence.

70

## Tuesday, August 28, 1984

Any impartial group assessing efforts on Dwight Anderson's (The Migrant) behalf must conclude that we are right on target. Notwithstanding his out-of-touch "Li'l Abner" family, he is slowly moving into the real world. The questions for summit consideration: Is there evidence of impact? Has his behavior been modified? We don't know. Not enough progress has been made yet to plant any markers.

Undoubtedly, Foster has won Dwight's confidence and fills a major need in his life. Equally important, the summer-camp experience proved that Dwight was capable of normal social relationships outside his family setting. The new town house, compliments of HUD, also assures a normal living situation, though spacewise no sooner did the boyfriend move out than two brothers moved in, and all the women appear to be pregnant. Next week, Dwight returns to public school to one-on-one teaching in a special education class, followed by the Boys' Club After Care Program, which provides closely supervised recreation, tutoring, and delivery home at 9:00 P.M.

If things are going so well, why does he keep getting arrested? Last week it was shoplifting again, the third arrest this summer. Impressed with Dwight's progress, Manning is not too alarmed over these minor transgressions. Foster, less accepting than Manning, has Dwight scheduled to spend a long weekend in a detention cell as preparation for the self-discipline required in public school and the Boys' Club. Manning may be the introspective, indulgent parent finding excuses, but not Foster.

## Wednesday, August 29, 1984

As a follow-up to our Andy Sills (The Drinker) discussion, we met with the family. Stepfather Ron couldn't make it, but Andy, his mother, and eleven-year-old sister Rhoda were there. Andy looked more grown up than last time. Instead of cowering, he responded with assurance when I challenged him to take a test to determine drug use. Without hesitation, he agreed. I smiled, telling him that by his willingness he had just passed the test.

Andy's big problem of the moment is arriving at school on time, which his mother attributes to his lacking bus fare, but in truth Andy keeps late hours with his girl friend, Abbie, who takes off with

**71**

him every day in her stylish new car. Foster's solution was easy: a student bus pass plus an 8:00 P.M. curfew. Andy took the bus pass gladly, but wanted no part of the curfew, pleading, "Please, please don't set a curfew and keep me away from Abbie."

He's free of drugs, maybe even alcohol, going to school, working, and even getting along with his stepfather. That's darn good. Manning asked what one factor had influenced him the most, assuming our program would get credit. Instead, Andy offered, "It's because of Abbie I don't go out looking for trouble. We are always together. Abbie's mother even told me that, if I'm nice to Abbie, some day I'll own her father's tile store."

Now that's even more encouraging than completing the auto-body repair course. I looked for little signs of stress or fear in little sister Rhoda during the discussion, but none were apparent. When asked about Andy, she smiled and, in a warm tone, confided that he bossed her around as all big brothers do.

Foster gave me an I-told-you-so grin as they filed out. Although impressed, I'm still a bit skeptical about his mother's sincerity and how long Andy can stay in line. What happens if the love glow dims and Abbie drops out of the picture? That might spell disaster. Concern for Andy's mundane problems affords pleasant relief from the grimness of some of those the others face.

## Thursday, August 30, 1984

Today's agenda called for a morning conference with the family of Laurence Samuel (The Fighter) and an afternoon court date with Dwight Anderson. Laurence and his mother arrived without his stepfather, who was at work. It's noticeable that the men in these families either don't exist or somehow manage not to be on hand.

Laurence walked through the doorway, taller than ever. At the long hearing table, he was on one side next to his mother, opposite Foster and Manning. All sat on short, plain, wooden chairs; mine was an overstuffed, high-backed juvenile chair. The august solemnity of a judicial chamber made no impact on Mrs. Laurence. She responded to each question with no more than three or four words, making it more an interrogation than a discussion. Neither frightened nor bored, she just refused to let herself become involved, perhaps still unsure of our motives.

**72**

# Throwing the Key Away

The session was informal, but to a fifteen-year-old it had to be a serious test. Although he kept looking up at the clock, Laurence fielded all questions, talked in sentences, and acted sure of himself. He successfully managed his hearing problems by facing his good ear to the talker, never faltering in responding to questions. He wants no part of culinary arts or any other special program. He prefers the public school, which offers his kind of action and his kind of folk. A little tumult, a little schooling, a little discipline, and a little roughhouse. It's the interaction, the give-and-take with his peers, that he craves.

I watched him carefully and listened intently for some telltale message, but he looked and sounded like any growing teenager who has new muscles and a hazy idea of what life is about. Perhaps my concerns have been overstated. He may be less a menace than I thought. Every minor transgression need not be treated as an omen of a major calamity. No new cases are pending, and, even if we aren't sure about his direction, what fifteen-year-old, in the best of circumstances, has a plan for life all mapped out?

Foster, somewhat impressed with Laurence's improved attitude, also sees him as less threatening and has plans for an administrative promotion to Jackson Senior High School, where the basketball coach will try to convert those long legs and arms to "dunks." When we had discussed this months ago, I thought little of it, and still do. This time, however, Laurence seems more amenable. A contributing factor may be that half-brother Arthur, a year older, has already earned a college football scholarship. No one admits to sibling rivalry, but, because of all those half relationships and parents who have little time for any of them, the rivalry is bound to be strong. Maybe basketball will be the ego-builder for Laurence. For sure he'll be able to expend his excess energy more appropriately, and the team regimen will instill some discipline. Jackson is the kind of school where he might even learn something.

Dwight Anderson's court hearing was only a formality because the case had already been plea bargained. As planned, he entered a plea to shoplifting and went straight to a detention cell for the weekend. He looked disoriented, didn't seem to understand the questions, mumbling and shrugging his shoulders. It was the same old Dwight. I had no reason to expect an urbane, sophisticated twelve-year-old to emerge after two weeks at summer camp, but I had hoped for some encouraging sign.

73

## Friday. August 31, 1984

Foster had been after me to select another youngster for him. Because three of his charges were fairly stabilized and routinized and two were safely ensconced at State School, he has time for another one. I have two prospects in mind: Rudy Lander and Jamie Forest.

Rudy continues to lead a fascinating life. He should be keeping a diary. He's always in the middle of the action, and his mother keeps coming to the rescue. Every appearance is a new saga. The robbery cases I had referred to adult court were dropped, then suddenly refiled. A short time later, Mrs. Lander and son were again before me, this time on new burglary charges. Unflinching, she entered a denial on the new charge and then reported matter-of-factly that a jury had acquitted her son on one of the robbery charges.

Out of curiosity, I telephoned the adult-court prosecutor to find out what had gone wrong in the robbery-case trial. Still angry at the result, he almost shouted his response: "Rudy may have convinced the polygraph examiner, but I never believed his story. His mother's behind it all. Not only was she obnoxious and abrasive, but she disregarded the judge's order, not to mention the polygraph examination, which was not admissible into evidence. The judge should have held her in contempt, but didn't. It wasn't the truth that got him off. It was his mother."

Yesterday, to my surprise, I looked up and there stood Rudy and his mother yet again; now the charge was assault and battery for pushing his teacher against the wall. Trial dates were set for both cases. She's an unusual woman. Never a hint that her son may need help. No remorse. Only a struggle against the system.

A part of me is sympathetic to her battle. As much as the juvenile system talks about rehabilitation, deep down we know that too many of these kids pass through untouched. Although overzealous, perhaps someone as strong as Mrs. Lander can successfully steer him through the next several years better than we can.

My description to Foster of the other prospect, Jamie Forest, was limited. He's a black fifteen-year-old whose rap sheet shows eleven burglary arrests, among others, over the past four years. His mother sounded like most of those we see in court: worn out, unable to account for what's happening, always blaming it on bad friends. She seemed a bit wearier than the others. "Why can't you spend more time with him?" I asked.

She groped for an answer, finally saying, "I work. There's no one else at home. I'm tired of going to police stations in the middle of the night to get him, and to school to explain to the principal and to court all the time."

We'll sit with these two for awhile. Both are prime prospects, but Rudy can't be saved until we get him on the bus to State School, which he, through the diligence of his mother, thus far has managed to avoid.

## Tuesday, September 4, 1984

This was one of those days when bureaucrats emerge, like an arthritis attack—painful, aggravating—but something we survive. As a result of Foster's bill for gasoline and other expenses, a high-level HRS official broached the high cost of the Master Counselor Program to me. I listened, arched my right eyebrow, thinned my lips, gave him a steely glint, and, in my best judicial manner, uttered: "Bullshit! What else?" Thwarted, but not enough to quit, he forged on, suggesting we select kids living closer together. Later in the day, Foster told me he had cut down on weekend fishing trips because he was having a hard time with expense vouchers. I directed him to renew these Saturday get-togethers and promised to eat alive any HRS bookkeeper standing in his way.

I actually felt good about the prospect of devouring some HRS penny pincher until a Boys' Club supervisor called to tell me that the admission of Dwight Anderson (The Migrant) to their program was being reconsidered. It seems that the fifty-mile distance to the Anderson residence is too far for the pickup driver to travel. Another gasoline problem. "How far does Dwight live from the driver's furthest stop?" I asked. There was a pause for calculation. "Ten miles" was the answer. "You are making an issue of ten lousy miles!" The rise of my voice prompted him to hang up quickly, saying, "You are the boss."

Another telephone call I could have done without awaited my coming off the bench. Manning was the first choice for the job with the Court Administrator's Office. He had only to be approved by the chief administrative officer at an interview scheduled for tomorrow. This was pro forma. They wanted him to start in two weeks. I literally screamed, "It's bad enough to raid a sister agency [HRS] but to cripple a program [mine] is disgraceful. I need Manning for two months more," I insisted. He said they couldn't hire him under those conditions. He had me. I wasn't going to stand in Manning's way. After twenty minutes of badgering each other, we reached no agreement.

Still stewing and too angry to eat lunch, I was apprehensive when Foster walked in to bring me up to date on the saga of Mrs. Anderson's new living quarters. I knew I wasn't going to like what I was about to hear. The good news was that she had given birth to a baby girl. She was disappointed at not having twins, as the doctor predicted, but it means one less child for AFDC welfare payments. The bad news is that, because of the additional child, she is no longer eligible for the town house because the HUD formula now puts her in another classification. Still a bit glassy-eyed from my earlier encounters, I was not quite ready to take on the federal bureaucracy.

"Besides," said Foster, "I'm mad because we finally paid the utility deposits. Do I get it back from her or the utility company?" I looked at him incredulously.

"I? We? You mean after all our conversations about not giving her money *you* paid the utility deposits? She foxed you into it. Was it a loan or a contribution?"

Foster shrugged off my outburst, saying that, when he arrived at her apartment, he found an incomplete application for utilities that had to be paid today. To save the situation, he had filled out the application and rushed down to pay the bill. "It's only a loan. It's only a loan," he kept repeating. "I'll get it back."

"Sure," I replied. "You'll get it back from the next lawyer fined for coming late to court." Will we ever get Mrs. Anderson and family a new apartment? I wonder.

As I was leaving for home, the phone rang. It was Foster again. The prosecutors in adult court had "lost" Marco Zargula (The Charmer) and were ready to put out an all points bulletin. Apparently their colleagues in juvenile court had failed to advise them that the boy was safely locked up in State School. I told Foster to relax. In due time, the bureaucracy will unravel itself and not only locate but even manage to transport Marco to his next court hearing.

## Wednesday, September 5, 1984

Foster's second trip to Okeechobee drew a lot more attention. This time the *Miami Herald* sent a reporter and a photographer along to do a feature story on the program. Foster's guests were a welcome sight to the Eckerd authorities, who have been struggling with lawsuits, legislative investigations, and other disappointments. They want to show a good face and obtain a good press. Lester and Marco, like two politicians, saying all the right things, handled the reporter with consummate skill. They admitted the errors of wayward youth, told of plans to rectify their lives, and lauded the efforts of the state in their behalf.

As expected, Marco Zargula (The Charmer) has made an ideal adjustment. If this were college, he'd be voted the student most likely to succeed or at least win the most popular student award. He mixes mostly with Latins, but is comfortable with everybody. All the staff know and greet him as he moves about the grounds. His prior vision of life at State School as one long series of battles, defending himself against rape, turned out to be only old-fashioned fighting between cottages, more akin to fraternity-house rivalry than to ugly prison brutality. He's in Honors' Cottage, has earned certificates in auto mechanics and auto-body painting and only failed to win a GED diploma by three points. What does he want most? He'd like underwear, cigarettes, shampoo, and deodorant.

Foster describes a new Marco: "He's put on some weight. Now he laughs at his 'Scarface' period and, other than his adult court trial, doesn't have a care in the world."

Manning, unimpressed, says, "Sociopaths always adapt to these conditions. They are bright, sociable, but amoral, chameleon-like people. It is a serious mistake to do anything but keep Marco under lock and key. Only time will provide the answer."

In all probability, the youth will survive State School, and my antennae tell me he'll also manage to make it through adult court. The answer to what happens when he returns to society probably lies with his family.

Foster stopped by Marco's home on the way back from Okeechobee. Things have gone from bad to worse there. Because of unpaid electricity bills, the lights have been cut off. Twin sister Rosita has taken up where Marco left off, running the streets with the Calcon brothers, using drugs, and becoming involved in an auto theft. Older brother Newton, who provided discipline and income for the family, has departed the household. Marco's mother, Mrs. Roman, is so depressed with her family situation that she is seeking psychiatric help at a local mental-health center. She is both pleased and fearful that her husband is due out of prison in six months— pleased that he has forgiven Marco for informing on him to the FBI, and fearful that he is a drug addict who beats everybody in the house when under stress, which apparently is always.

Even if Marco comes out of State School with a fresh new attitude, what happens in this crisis-ridden household? Manning plans to work on the family. He wants Foster to follow up on Rosita, find some financial help for the family, and assist Mrs. Roman in getting back to beautician school, to which she earlier aspired. Perhaps Foster and the psychiatrist together can enable her to function adequately, though in this family situation it looks like we need a magician, not a psychiatrist.

Lester Burrows (The Runner) did not become a recognized figure on campus; he stayed neutral, just getting along, keeping out of trouble. He, too, wanted cigarettes, underclothes, shampoo, and deodorant. On his next trip, Foster planned to provide these amenities, making certain the deodorant is the roll-on not the aerosol type, which can be sniffed. Sniffing and cigarette smoking are two of the major problems in juvenile lockups. Sniffing glue, gasoline, and other chemical properties is a deadly game. It's against the law, but worse it leaves permanent brain damage. Smoking, while lawful, is prohibited in most juvenile detention centers. The urge is so great, however, that some detainees prefer State School or adult jail only for the opportunity to smoke. Youthful inmates aren't deterred by the surgeon general's warning on cigarette packs or the devastating effect of sniffing. Like everything else in their lives, it's the instant gratification that counts.

According to the formal report on Lester from State School, titled the "Comprehensive Student Growth Plan," he was eligible for release no sooner than January 1985:

> Client Burrows, fifteen years of age, was very limited in his responses in the initial interview. Reports from the Orientation Cottage indicate no significant problems. He is a sociable, alert and cooperative person lacking guidance and supervision. Inwardly he is insecure and immature but tends to hide these feelings behind a mask of guardedness and bravado. He appears to be a non-aggressive person who may be vulnerable to peer influence. No evidence of thought disorder at present time. Intelligence appears to be low average. Lester will be exposed to a variety of career opportunities through the Career Awareness group which meets twice a week to discuss possible vocations.

The report was prepared by a Growth Plan Development Committee, which includes a counselor, a case manager, a psychologist, and a psychiatrist. It was an interesting document indeed. All his academic testing showed him at about the sixth-grade level, several years below his grade for age level, but, considering that he never stayed put in any school for any length of time, he still managed a lot of progress. Without being overcritical of the Eckerd effort, there's a smugness about it that almost guarantees failure. They seem to miss the essence of Lester. He is like an eel, amorphous and lacking anything tangible to grasp. It is almost naive to think that exposing him to biweekly sessions on Career Awareness will somehow energize him to accept a new life-style. A cursory run-through like that can, at best, only touch the surface.

To Foster's suggestion that we find a better foster home for Lester upon release, Manning reacted with a resounding NO! He said, "That's a waste. He's already been in twenty-five foster homes and a twenty-sixth won't mean a thing. All he ever gets is a bed among strangers. They don't care about him and he ignores them. This time we need a group home where there are professional counselors present and a structured existence can be maintained."

Good for Manning. In view of Lester's background, I am not sure anything will work, but repeating failure makes no sense.

A hopeful sign is the reemergence of his heretofore almost nonexistent family. Despite his constant mistreatment of his grandmother, she still wants him back. His mother, who literally tossed him into the street years ago, has been contacted in Winter Haven, Florida, where she is employed by the local Health Department. Although she hasn't seen him since early childhood, she offered to provide a home for him. It is unlikely that either one can handle him. It would be the same scenario again, but their presence may open the door to some family life.

As expected, the prosecutor couldn't locate the witnesses and dropped Lester's waiver case involving the homosexuals he had burglarized.

## Thursday, September 6, 1984

Some of what seemed important yesterday is no longer a problem. Frank Manning didn't get the job. In his final interview, it was decided he lacked experience in statistical analysis. Major problem solved. Great.

The Andersons signed a lease (rent free) and moved in yesterday. Wow! I never thought that crisis would end. The HUD formula we were concerned about was a bit of misinformation. Manning is so pleased he's arranging for a Catholic church to contribute furniture, even though the Andersons aren't of that faith. Foster was so pleased he said he'd convince them to turn Catholic. Oh yes. Mrs. Anderson returned the fifty dollars Foster had paid for utilities, then immediately borrowed thirty dollars.

According to Manning, order can be brought to the Anderson family life-style by teaching the mother some concepts of money value. She can't add or subtract, and, as soon as she receives her monthly welfare check, she doles it out to assorted relatives with no thought given to tomorrow's needs. Manning, ever the traditionalist, suggested that Foster find an adult education course that teaches the rudiments of arithmetic and the basics of family budgeting.

Foster, the street guy, struggling to keep her son, Dwight, in school can't envision Mrs. Anderson suddenly becoming concerned about her own lack of education. "She may not be too good at budgeting," he responded lightly, "but she's an expert at borrowing." Doubtful that she would attend or could adjust to any adult education course, Foster changed the subject, describing how grandmother delivered the new baby, called the paramedics to cut the umbilical cord, and then sent mother and infant over to Jackson Memorial Hospital for a post-delivery checkup. As in all her other deliveries for the extended Anderson family, the doctors approved her midwifery.

A sharp difference in values is represented here. Manning and I view people like the Andersons as failures who lower our middle-class standards, while Foster sees them as struggling survivors who have learned to cope the best they can in a world where they don't count for much.

The plan to transfer Laurence Samuel (The Fighter) to Jackson Senior High School to play basketball went awry when the coaches neglected to notify the registrar. Instead, it looks like he will attend McArthur Senior High, a place for behavior problems, primarily a school where only the tough survive. At one time, we thought a stint there might cure Laurence of his bullying tactics, but on reflection the more stable Jackson Senior High and an athletic emphasis seem the better opportunity. We'll have to start pushing some buttons to move him to Jackson.

## Monday, September 10, 1984

It's off to Washington, D.C., and New York City for a series of meetings this week, leaving Foster to his chores without my overseeing.

During the 1970s the American Bar Association (ABA) had put together twenty-three volumes of standards for the operation of juvenile courts. This was the era when standards were ground out with regularity by many national organizations, funded primarily by the federal government. Most eventually found shelves upon which to rest, but in the process all made some impact on upgrading their respective fields. As the crime situation worsened, interest in standards lessened and funds were diverted to action programs.

The president of the ABA, not satisfied to allow the ten-year effort to languish, established the Implementation of the Juvenile Justice Standards Project. I chair its Advisory Board. Abetted by a few small grants, the project staff has resurrected the standards and established the goal of familiarizing practitioners with them. Our advisory panel is a status group made up of several judges and national leaders. The meeting, held in Federal Appellate Judge Patricia Wald's chambers, needed only the ninety minutes allocated to take care of business.

I remember all the vying in the 1970s to be placed on national committees establishing standards. At that time, eligibility for federal funding required local and state government also to produce standards. The mails were full of copies of local, state, and national standards flying back and forth. The cost of that paper flow alone was probably a major contributor to the current national deficit.

## Tuesday, September 11, 1984

The SAG Conference was only a drop-in visit for me, in between other scheduled meetings, but probably the most dramatic. An air of tension was obvious to any chance observer. SAG, an acronym for State Juvenile Justice Advisory Groups, had 300 representatives from all the states and territories in attendance. These groups had originated in the late 1960s during the Johnson administration when fighting crime became a cottage industry for planners, data collectors, and funnelers of federal funds. In every state capital, a SAG-type unit received with one hand and dispensed with the other.

Today, because of a reluctant Congress and a parsimonious administration, SAGs have fallen on hard times. As a matter of fact, this was the first national meeting of this type not funded by the federal government. Participants came via local funding or at their own expense. They still had the name, but the game had changed. Now federal funds focused only on projects carefully chosen by the OJJDP staff. OJJDP (Office of Juvenile Justice Delinquency Prevention) is headed by Alfred Regnery, a man steeped in the Reagan philosophy of destroying the evil criminal empire in America but cutting all criminal-justice budgets in the process. The SAG people were cut from different cloth; OJJDP was not their kind of administration. And Regnery, whom they considered remote, uncommunicative, and inexperienced in the field, wasn't their kind of man.

This afternoon, Regnery and his lieutenants told of their accomplishments with a polished flourish. It was plain they weren't looking for grass-roots solutions. The words "innovative" and "experimental," heard so often in the past, were not part of their rhetoric. Their programs hit responsive, emotional chords: runaway children, restitution for victims, abused children, drug abuse. No long-term funding or never-ending research. The questions from SAG representatives were unfriendly but guarded. They didn't like the Regnery crowd, but enough funding was still coming out of Washington not to be outwardly antagonistic. It was a smooth OJJDP performance, particularly when Regnery complimented SAG for being able to conduct the conference without federal assistance. "It's a sign of your strength and growth," he said, with a straight face.

Regnery finished to a scattering of polite applause. The SAGs had been had, knew it, but couldn't do much about it. It took the last panelist, describing an administration project on pornography, to revive the audience. Involved was a $600,000 grant to study the relationship of *Penthouse, Playboy,* and *Hustler* magazines to juvenile crime. Distant before, the audience now warmed up, and the muttering was audible. "The nuts are running the country." "The researcher is Nancy's friend." "What can you expect from the Moral Majority mentality?" New life was crackling all around. A Regnery staffer standing alongside me whispered softly, "Don't you agree *Hustler* magazine is bad for kids?"

## Wednesday, September 12, 1984

The conference for the next two days was devoted to the skeleton in the juvenile-justice closet, namely, probation. Even before the advent of the Reagan administration, the concept of counseling young criminals, urging them to be nice, had gone out of style. The Reaganites, led by Regnery, merely performed the coup de grace. Dutifully assembled were the national heads of agencies involved with juvenile probation along with other activists in the field. I was invited because of my ABA association. The first day was to feature a think-tank discussion, identifying the problem; the second day, a formal presentation to Regnery and staff of a plan to uplift probation.

After a round of introductions, which showed a well-credentialed group, the fifteen participants began their dialogue. All the probation people present were articulate, hard working, and idealistic, but today they were supplicants, asking only that their efforts be given a chance. This hardly seemed the place and Regnery and his crowd, hardly the people. It was almost lunchtime before it became obvious that no agreement, even on the definition of probation, could be achieved.

Admittedly, the need was to repackage probation by marketing the positive aspects, so that both the practitioners and the public could see visible and effective results. Requiring the offender to make restitution and perform hours of community service work would be hard to sell to an already disillusioned public, but there wasn't much else to offer. The strategy for the next day's conference with Regnery was to emphasize the positive role of the private sector because this conformed to the doctrinaire Republican approach of less government.

## Thursday, September 13, 1984

Al Regnery sat in the middle taking notes, and spotted around the room were his aidès, doing the same. One thing about the seat of government: no matter who is in power, a shortage of note-takers is never evident. Circling Regnery were the think-tank participants. It was a very homey, relaxed setting. The first presenter started things on the right track by referring to an old Irish proverb describing the dilemma of the conferees: "If you don't know where you are going, every road will get you there."

It was all uphill after that. Regnery accepted the need to alter the negative image of probation and saw the private sector as providing genuine assistance. He cautioned against being cynical about the failures of the past, agreed to convene representatives of ten major cities to explore the expansion of probation services, and indicated he was favorably disposed to other requests we made.

Just before the meeting ended, he asked me to address the group, introducing me with flowery comments that were more appropriate for my eulogy. Not only had he finessed me by his surprise attitude toward probation, but he had thrown in an ego-massage for good measure.

## Friday, September 14, 1984

Ending my series of meetings in New York City at the ABA Juvenile Justice Committee meeting, I sat there listening to this group of brash young public defenders and academes discuss Regnery's efforts with disdain. "Untrustworthy, not too bright" were some of the milder comments. The critics were strong in criticism but light on action. It's easy to criticize Regnery, but at least he's willing to take a fresh look at old problems.

All the philosophical and political chatter of the past week left me with a sour taste. Things haven't changed over the years no matter what the rhetoric of the party in power. It all seemed far removed from the reality of coping with the problems of a Lester Burrows.

## Wednesday, September 19, 1984

I knew that Mrs. Lander could be difficult, and she didn't disappoint me. Rudy's waiver hearing to determine whether or not he should be prosecuted in adult court brought on the fireworks. The prosecutor produced fingerprints showing he had burglarized and vandalized the house in question, but was Rudy beyond help in the juvenile court?

Fed up with Rudy's long arrest record, the social worker recommended transfer to adult court. She put it aptly: "Either he finds trouble, or trouble finds him, but he isn't trying to shun it. I can't get to him His mother is overprotective, covering up for him, and he keeps getting arrested."

The public defender, urged on by Mrs. Lander, produced testimony that Rudy had changed significantly over the summer months. I ruled for the prosecution, sending him to adult court, noting that he had been rearrested as recently as last month for striking a schoolteacher. He may be a "new" Rudy, but how long should the juvenile-justice system continue to forgive and then gamble one more time?

Only when I ordered him into the lockup did the action begin. Until then, Mrs. Lander had sat quietly, tight-lipped, looking a bit drawn, occasionally whispering something to the public defender. Rudy also was more reserved than in the past, apparently realizing that one more time he faced a crisis that needed his mother. She asked to be heard. Then, in a quavering voice, she spoke out: "All you people do is abuse my child. You arrest him, lock him up. Then arrest him and lock him up again. He needs to be in school, not in jail. The whole system is a lie. The social worker doesn't care about my child. None of you do." All restraint was gone as she scornfully pointed to me. "A black person doesn't have a chance in your court. You let white kids go free and put black kids in jail." Embracing Rudy, she turned to me again, crying out, "What are you doing to my child?"

There was nothing for me to say. Stunned at being labeled a racist, I was only grateful that the social worker was also black. I learned later that, outside the courtroom, Mrs. Lander lost complete control, continuing her verbal abuse to the point that security guards had to restrain her. In chambers, LaMont envinced an "I-told-you-so" attitude, reminding me again of his unpleasant experience when she had cursed in response to his request that she be seated. Trying not to show it, I was nonetheless upset and offended by her allegations. I suppose that in her bitterness she strikes out heedlessly at everything in her way.

During the afternoon session, my mind kept wandering back to Mrs. Lander. Suddenly I was brought back to reality by a seventeen-year-old black girl in a dependency case who wanted to give up her five-month-old baby, saying she had no money to take care of it. The social worker filled in the picture of this unmarried, ghetto teenager, faced with her third baby, this one defective and needing hospitalization, perhaps for a long time. I asked the mother if she were receiving Aid to Families with Dependent Children (AFDC) and why this money wasn't enough. Still expressionless, she answered, "I ain't getting enough." To each of my questions, she gave the same monotone answer: "I ain't getting enough money." Exchanging glances with the social worker, I realized this teenager had no concept of mothering other children. Her way of coping with life was childbirth, then an AFDC income. If one baby were defective, she'd discard it and hope the next one was healthier. That's a terrible accusation, I told myself, but I entertained no doubt as to its accuracy. What would Mrs. Lander say if she were in the courtroom this time?

## Thursday, September 20, 1984

In the course of one week, Laurence Samuel (The Fighter) has been assigned to more schools than most kids see in a lifetime. Getting him into an appropriate school is as difficult as getting Mrs. Anderson into a housing project. To locate the right niche, Manning has built a paperwork trail from school to school. Fortunately, this entire tour was only on paper. Considering Laurence's short emotional fuse, imagine his reaction had he actually gone through this series of frustrations. Finally, Laurence will be admitted to Jackson Senior High in the emotionally handicapped class, and also in the basketball program. One small caveat: he needs to go back to McArthur Senior High for a complete psychological workup to determine his eligibility for the emotionally handicapped class.

## Monday, October 1, 1984

The small caveat turned out to be a large cave. Because the school system at one time had sought to place him in a class for the emotionally disturbed, testing to admit him now should be perfunctory. We didn't count on the school psychologist, Dr. N., to whom Laurence was a dream come true, a gold mine of neuroses and fears. In our telephone conversation, the doctor told me that, despite Laurence's laundry list of dysfunctions, none qualified him for the emotionally handicapped class. According to Dr. N., "Laurence is in a homosexual panic, preoccupied with his sex identification. Although Laurence appears quiet, intense anger surrounds him all the time, ready to erupt. Women are unsafe in his presence. He'll wait for the right moment, then strike. Although he clowns around in class, watch out. He is moody, lonely, denies responsibility and is impatient. He not only is violent towards others, but he is also suicide prone."

We have long been aware of Laurence's aggressiveness, but homosexual? Suicidal? According to Dr. N., Laurence remained unreadable until the Rorschach test. Then, those inkblots did the job. He insisted that, though Laurence's functioning is impaired by willfulness associated with psychosexual preoccupation, this is not an emotional thought disorder qualifying him for the emotionally handicapped class. I find psychologists helpful, but sometimes I have reservations about their conclusions. They do a lot of educated guessing under the imprimatur of a highly honed air of authority. What does Laurence need to do to obtain special help in the public schools?

Andy Sills (The Drinker) also had a surprise for us. His mother left for a trip to New York to reclaim her youngest daughter, and in her absence Andy went into a tailspin. He quit his job, left school, and couldn't be located for several days, probably staying at girl friend Abbie's house. It is evident that Andy needs every support available, especially his mother. She's back and he's back. Apparently Mr. Sills's alcoholic rehabilitation collapsed and, not able to handle the situation, he dumped the five-year-old child with some friends. Mrs. Waite, hardly a tower of strength, arrived to rescue the daughter, then flew back to Miami to revive Andy.

Now that a new sister was in the house receiving most of mother's attention, Andy faced some difficult days. Because of the additional mouth to feed and Andy being out of work, we needed to draw on the Children's Fund for a hundred dollars to pay for Andy's tuition and another school bus pass. Andy's situation of the moment is so fragile that Foster ignored the violation. Right now it's important he return to his studies and obtain some after-school employment.

The Dr. E. assessment of Andy made before this latest incident had given him mixed reviews. Where I expected a weakling, constantly in need of crutches, Dr. E. stated that Andy's self-esteem was relatively intact and that he was not apprehensive about the future or dependent on others. Dr. E. dwelled on Andy's lack of conscience, predicting that, whenever a crisis occurs, violating the law was a likely direction. The youth's positive motivation for change, according to Dr. E., arose chiefly from fear of incarceration. Translation: It may look like there's a new Andy, but, when the going gets rough, he likely will revert to his old self.

## Tuesday, October 2, 1984

Suddenly transported from State School, Marco Zargula (The Charmer) is back among us, beginning to understand more about the uncertainties of the criminal-justice bureaucracy. He'd been in the juvenile detention center a week entertaining some vague idea that he was waiting transfer back to the Master Counselor Program. After a day of phone calls, the prosecutor learned that Marco had been sent back to our detention center by criminal-court Judge Ed Cowart, who feared for his safety in the adult jail. Irritated, scared, but still showing that wholesome look, Marco appeared in juvenile court, never quite certain what he was doing there or what would happen to him. I explained the events of the last few days, emphasizing his upcoming trial date in adult court. He nodded vaguely, obviously befogged by the process. Foster put him on the bus and said he'd never seen a kid so happy to head for State School.

Dwight Anderson (The Migrant) continues to inch along. Foster plans to buy him a used lawnmower to cut neighborhood lawns. This will provide spending money and keep him busy on weekends. I approved the Children's Fund payment for the lawnmower, but cautioned against involving Mrs. Anderson in the transaction. Foster is no match for her financially. Somehow, she'd come out ahead.

We agreed to take Jamie Forest as another client, but first he'll do a tour of duty at State School. Both the victim and the prosecutor insisted he do some time, notwithstanding the good intentions of the Master Counselor Program. The victim, a police officer, still angry over his house being burglarized and vandalized, was not impressed with Jamie's two-month detention. The prosecutor agreed with him. So did I. The mistakes made earlier with others will not be repeated. Jamie will have to earn his way into the program by exemplary behavior at State School. Frankly, Rudy Lander would be more challenging, but that's not in the cards.

## Friday, October 5, 1984

A week gone by, still waiting for further testing on Laurence Samuel's admission to the emotionally disturbed class. It will be only a few more days, they say. School authorities tell me it will be difficult to admit him over the objection of Dr. N., the school psychologist. I'll try anyway. Laurence, once again, was involved in an incident shoving a teacher, but fortunately the teacher refused to prosecute. The youth explained the situation, saying sometimes he can't help himself. Apparently he's never met a teacher he didn't like to hit.

Again, I brought to Manning's attention the article describing the testing of hair samples to determine shortages in copper and excesses in sugar, which, according to the author, lead to aggressive behavior. As earlier, Manning was noncommittal, suggesting we first try more accepted medical approaches.

Andy Sills (The Drinker) made an impressive recovery upon his mother's return. He's back in school, making good progress, and things are normal again. Although neither will admit it, a strained relationship exists between him and his stepfather, but both are avoiding conflict situations. Mother, now holding a part-time job, still manages to keep an even keel in the household.

After all those extensive plans to move Marco Zargula (The Charmer) back and forth in his impending robbery trial, the scheme went for naught. I want that case as a club over his head to induce a fear of going to prison that would cause complete cooperation with the goals of the Master Counselor Program. When he left here to go back to State School, the plan seemed to be working. He was scared and confused. So what happened? After all my planning, the prosecutor suddenly dropped the case; the victim, annoyed with lawyers and depositions, wanted out.

Meanwhile, Marco's twin sister, Rosita, had been before me on an auto-theft charge along with Marco's buddies, the Calcon brothers. Threatening to lock her up if she misbehaved, I set the case for trial and released her. She had that dazed, glazed look seen on first-timers in court and showed no reaction other than promising to behave. One more victory for the Larchmont Gardens Housing Project. Manning, like others, describes Larchmont as a hellhole that eventually traps all its young people into criminal behavior. He wants to arrange a housing deal for Marco's family similar to that of the Andersons. Cornelius Foster will try the regular channels, and, if he is unsuccessful, I'll exert my charm on the housing authorities.

I tried to obtain the measure of our newest recruit, Jamie Forest, observing him in court, but he just sat there, as most do, expressionless. Later, I learned that he had turned to the police officer-victim, and threatened him with, "I'm gonna fuck you up when I get back." That's pretty heavy stuff for a fifteen-year-old, especially directed toward a police officer.

## Monday, October 8, 1984

Reports from the Boys' Club After Care Program on Dwight Anderson (The Migrant) are all positive. Now attending their after-school recreation and tutoring program for three weeks, he has been described by the staff as: "Perfect kid," "Never misses a day" and "Attentive in class." Three weeks, of course, hardly suggest a major shift. He was in court this morning and, unlike previous appearances, was composed, relaxed, and almost responsive. He's our youngest, just turned thirteen this month, and, despite a bad family situation and an already long record of arrests, is probably the most workable. In the past six months, every resource has been made available for his migrant family. Highly successful with youngsters like Dwight, the Boys' Club program may succeed in instilling some kind of study and work ethic. This will be difficult, but, if Dwight is reachable, the personnel there can do it.

## Tuesday, October 9, 1984

We've talked a lot about assessing the needs of the families of our clients, but efforts have been mostly on an ad hoc basis. To provide a holistic approach, the Dade County Department of Youth and Family Development (DYFD) has volunteered its services. Just as HRS represents the state of Florida's effort, so DYFD represents the role of Dade County, specializing in providing a full gamut of long-term services for neglected and dependent children as well as their families. Theirs is a smaller staff whose focus is limited, but most of the people hold masters degrees, receive higher pay, and experience less turnover. Generally, they rate a few notches above HRS. When asked, they promptly agreed to do an analysis, assigning counselors for each of our clients.

### MARCO ZARGULA (The Charmer)

"Good looking, friendly, charming manner" was the phrase used by the DYFD social worker in her Psycho/Social Assessment and Treatment Service Plan She, too, was good-looking as well as charming, and Marco, the ladies' man, obviously went all out to impress her.

She described Marco's mother, Mrs. Roman, as a forty-year-old attractive Cuban, the mother of five children. Her first marriage, pre-arranged by her parents to M. Zargula, lasted eighteen years and produced four children. After living in Detroit and New York, she moved to Miami and married Frederick Roman, Marco's stepfather. He is forty-two years of age, of Puerto Rican descent, and is presently serving a ten-year sentence for armed robbery. Mrs. Roman describes him as an "alcoholic and junkie," who for the past five years has been both a child- and wife-abuser. According to Marco, "his stepfather led him into stealing and then sold the stolen merchandise." An earlier statement that Mr. Roman would be out soon on an early release was not confirmed.

**90**

## Throwing the Key Away

DYFD Social Worker Mrs. A. deems Marco to be street-wise, but, considering his background and chronological age (sixteen), she feels he has not had the chance nor the climate to develop his emotional maturity. She recommends: "Marco needs to be provided with the structure and supervision of a benevolent authority which he has lacked all his life. I do not perceive this as being effected in anything other than a long-term residential treatment facility where the treatment is guided by professionals trained in working with hard-core delinquents."

"Benevolent authority?" That's exactly what we are trying to be. But what happens when he returns to Larchmont Gardens? Does Foster move in and baby-sit him? In looking at the total family, Mrs. A. says: "The family seems to have assimilated a certain feeling of hopelessness, as well as acquired a long-term history of anti-social behavior, some very serious. Their dysfunctional life style has now become chronic and therefore makes for a poor prognosis."

As for the mother, Mrs. A. was on target again:

> Intellectually Mrs. Roman may be able to acquire vocational skills such as going to beauticians' school. Emotionally, however, I do not feel she is able to follow through with these intense plans with any consistency, unless provided with intensive outreach support where she could establish a trusting relationship. She must be encouraged and "led by the hand" throughout the entire training process and thereafter, until she finds employment, acquires new patterns of behavior and increases her self-esteem.

Care of the mother would virtually require a full-time therapist. As intense as is our program, I cannot visualize Cornelius Foster devoting half of every day to her needs. Mrs. A. further suggested the family move out of Larchmont Gardens and recommended therapeutic treatment in terms of parenting skills for Mrs. Roman as well as group therapy for daughter Rosita.

We had already set the wheels in motion for obtaining better housing, but Mrs. Roman insisted that she's comfortable in Larchmont Gardens, knows the people, and prefers to remain there. Because I do not intend to endure an experience similar to that of Mrs. Anderson, I told Foster to try persuasion, and, if that doesn't work, we'd do our best amid the horrors of Larchmont Gardens. Several of the other family programs recommended are available through DYFD, and we will avail ourselves of these services. It's not likely we can shape up the family in time for Marco's return to Miami.

## Throwing the Key Away

## LAURENCE SAMUEL *(The Fighter)*

DYFD Social Worker Miss O. provided a word-picture of Laurence that was worthy of an accomplished portrait painter. In a few short paragraphs, she laid him bare:

> Laurence is a tall, approximately 6'4", medium built, young man who is very clean in appearance and neatly attired. He speaks in a slow, low pitched voice and responds only to what has been directed to him.
>
> He volunteers no additional information other than what has been asked. He appears to function at an average intellectual level for his age. However, he tends to leave you with the impressions that he feels he is way ahead of you in knowing a lot more than he chooses to share. Laurence's assessment is "he has no problems." It seems his egocentric attitude implies others should take on responsibility to insure all goes well with him.
>
> Laurence expressed little to no interest or concern about his contacts with the Juvenile Justice System. In recounting his many law violations, Laurence's response was one of nonchalance and disinterest. He showed no remorse or concern for anything he did. His attitude and visual responses were that of a sociopath enroute to being a full-fledged psychopathic personality. Laurence lives in a comfortable environment where his mother acknowledges he has little to no responsibilities.
>
> He has never worked nor has he ever sought employment. He doesn't know what he would like to do for a career in the future; nor has he ever given this matter any real thought. He is seemingly at ease and very "laid back" in his present setting where he apparently does as he chooses. Although Laurence expressed no real concerns about the future, he did indicate he would like to finish high school, after which he would probably join the army.

The treatment plan recommended for Laurence was a halfway house, additional examination by a psychologist, and some form of employment. A DYFD parenting treatment group was advocated for the parents.

Miss O.'s report confirmed one done earlier by Dr. E. that described Laurence as angry, hostile, impulsive, contemptuous, socially alienated, resistant, unhappy, sociopathic, and potentially quite violent. Treatment would require years of consistency, dedication, tight controls, and patience. Prognosis for adjustment to society, according to the doctor, must be regarded as extremely poor at this time. One of the most reliable psychologists around, he is not prone to be an alarmist, but confirmed all the worst fears others have expressed about the youth.

We are still not sure about what to do with Laurence, but a half-way house will only change the setting; it won't influence his motivation. As to seeing another psychologist, he says that, if he has to explain one more inkblot, someone will get punched out. Overexamining Laurence may breed rather than curtail hostility. He already has enough of his own. Meanwhile, he's added two more assaults in school to his record.

Discounting school psychologist Dr. N.'s ominous report, I've tried to read less into Laurence's situation, but these new reports and his continued assaultive behavior are disquieting. Medication to calm his outbursts may be in order. I am wary of this approach, having seen these mind-numbing medicines turn troublemakers into zombies. This easy way out is too often used in jails and mental institutions. Because Laurence is being groomed for basketball stardom, we can't very well eliminate all his aggressiveness.

## DWIGHT ANDERSON *(The Migrant)*

DYFD Social Worker Mrs. C.'s report on the Anderson family needed extra pages just to list the current status of the numerous children. Four are with the mother; three with HRS; one with grandmother; and the oldest, Erla Joy, now seventeen and pregnant with her third child, is living with her boyfriend.

This history of the Andersons as migrant workers and breeders of children is well known. Mrs. Anderson declined to identify the father of each of her children, perhaps because of uncertainty. In their early years, her children were raised by her mother and sister so she might work as a farm laborer. When several were taken by HRS from her sister, she began to raise the current crop at home. Her daughter, Erla Joy, has followed the same path by leaving her children with great-grandmother. Erla Joy, however, doesn't even bother to work.

Mrs. C.'s assessment of Mrs. Anderson was in line with others who had come in contact with her. The social worker offered a series of programs for the family, some of which are already in progress and others to be considered. Her prognosis was that "the family will require long term involvement and their progress will be slow."

From among the recommendations, Manning decided to initiate a homemaker service provided by DYFD that brings a helper into the home several times a week to assist in maintaining a clean, orderly household. This service usually is provided only for the elderly and the infirm. In addition, a home-management course is offered nearby in which Mrs. Anderson can learn the rudiments of budgeting for a family. Manning, beginning to see the light, suggested we send her to a clinic for an IUD fitting. She seems reluctant, but probably can be persuaded. I told him the right of the state to intervene in the lives of others is limited, and that it was improper to use the power of the court to force an IUD upon her. We let it go at that.

The effort to make Dwight a lawn-mowing entrepreneur cost sixty dollars, and the big test now is whether he will be the all-American boy mowing his neighbors' lawns on Sunday at five bucks each or will he sell the lawn mower, claiming it was stolen? After a long discussion, our strategy is to make him responsible for the security of the mower. He must earn and pay thirty dollars to the Children's Fund, at which time full title to the lawn mower will vest exclusively in him. His mother may outsmart Foster, but this little kid isn't going to "take" Manning and me for sixty dollars.

## ANDY SILLS *(The Drinker)*

The Sills story as recounted by DYFD Counselor Miss K. is a sad one, yet hopeful:

> At best, the background of this family can be described as tumultuous. Andy's mother, the oldest of five children, was born in Newport News, Virginia. The paternal grandparents were her primary caretakers. Her father, an alcoholic, who assumed no responsibility for his family, spent seven years in prison for robbery. The union of the natural parents ended in divorce and her mother remarried. Although the mother and step-father attempted to provide a home for her, she repeatedly ran away.
>
> When she was twelve years of age, her grandmother died and she began living in the streets. At the age of thirteen, she met Ralph Sills, then nineteen, and the two began living together. She knows little of Mr. Sills' background except that it was very chaotic. He once told her he had been put in a hospital for crazy people because the family could not control him. Although never married, they lived together twenty years having five children.
>
> Both used alcohol and marijuana to excess. In the beginning she

enjoyed her "wild" life style but her infatuation with Mr. Sills diminished as he became increasingly physically abusive toward her and the children. She was forced to do "horrible things" which could not be mentioned in front of the children. Her efforts to leave were in vain since she had nowhere else to go. On a number of occasions, charges of child neglect were filed, leading to temporary placement of the children. Once, at his direction, she forged checks, resulting in a jail sentence.

Since her marriage to Mr. Waite, a sense of stability has been added to the family. She describes him as "hard working with old fashioned values." Neither she nor Mr. Waite use alcohol. The whereabouts of the children are known at all times and regular bedtimes have been established. Although the family is burdened financially, Mrs. Waite has a positive outlook. Her husband has helped her see herself as a worthwhile individual. She has lost a considerable amount of weight and enjoys being a homemaker.

At this particular time, Rhoda, age 12, is the child for whom Mrs. Waite is most concerned. Rhoda was described by her mother as "very emotional" and "crying all the time." Rhoda is fearful of all men and is having more difficulty than the other children relating to her stepfather. Currently, Rhoda is in a math learning disability class. She also has difficulty in school socially because of her "shyness."

Audrey, age 5, has been back with the family for approximately two weeks. The mother is fearful that Mr. Sills will again try to take Audrey since he has legal custody. Audrey's baby teeth are decayed, and she and the rest of the family are in need of dental care.

Andy views his difficulties as a thing of the past. Warmth and caring were demonstrated in Andy's interactions with his mother and younger sisters, who excitedly ran out to greet him when he arrived home.

Miss K. concludes thusly: "Considering significant changes already by this family, the prognosis appears quite good." She recommends family counseling, particularly in enabling the children to adapt to making Mr. Waite part of the family, but on the whole is impressed with progress thus far made. Score one for Cornelius Foster.

I was particularly optimistic because that morning I had enjoyed meeting Abbie Iglesio, the treasure of Andy's life. And indeed she was. A cheerful, dark-haired girl, full of smiles, she obviously adored Andy. They sat as close together in their separate chairs as they could. Oblivious to all, this was puppy love at its best. She was in her senior high-school year, already accepted at UCLA, but choosing Miami-Dade Community College so she could be near her beloved.

She had been born in Italy, but after six years here she showed no traces of her foreign birth. Her father, a successful merchant, was in Italy on a buying mission. Both parents, she said, like Andy very much. She wanted him to finish his vocational training and then study for a GED diploma. If we can hold on to her for another year, we may yet have a new Andy.

Watching and listening to Andy talk with confidence about himself, it occurred to me that Dr. E.'s earlier assessment may have correctly described his rising self-esteem. Can all this have happened in six months amidst so chaotic and turbulent a family? That's hard to believe.

## LESTER BURROWS *(The Runner)*

Because Lester is at State School, DYFD Social Worker Miss O. was only able to interview Betty Hearns, his grandmother. These are excerpts from her report:

Lester Burrows is a fifteen year old, black male, who has been involved in numerous delinquent activities. Efforts to assist this young man have resulted in his being placed with various state agencies and countless foster homes.

His grandmother Betty Hearns seems to be the only person with whom Lester shared a close relationship. His natural mother gave Lester away to an Allie May Gray at about age three. Reportedly HRS took Lester from Mrs. Gray because of alleged sexual battery against him by her son. Next time grandmother saw Lester, he was eleven years old and HRS requested she take custody of him.

In his grandmother's care, he was always respectful and obedient in her presence. Away from her, he would lie, stay out late or overnight, take money from the church, was disobedient and created a lot of problems in school.

Grandmother's health began to suffer from worrying about the client. The last straw was Lester's attempt at age twelve to have sexual intercourse with his five year old cousin. At this point, grandmother refused to keep him. Placed in foster home or shelter, he would run away and return to the grandmother. Grandmother sees him as very street-wise and adept at making it on his own. He told her he hates his mother. Last contact with grandmother was over one month ago, when he came to visit, then left with his cousin's jewelry. Since then, however, he has called her from State School. She says his early life lacked any parental affection and he has become accustomed to being on his own too long, without any love.

*Comments:* She's a very insightful old woman. Maybe if Cornelius Foster had been available to her years ago, Lester wouldn't be so tough to reach today.

> Lester is an intellectually bright young man whose early life of neglect and forced independence has left him with a protective wall around his feeling and emotions. Although not hostile or aggressive, Lester is unable to openly display feelings of affection even with persons he seemingly cares about. A lack of nurturance and stability of parenting from an early age seems to have led to the development of a distrustful and fiercely independent adolescent. In addition, a multiplicity of short-term placements has only contributed to the inconsistent patterns in his life. Apparently, a highly developed sense of self-dependence coupled with the acquired skills of making it in the streets and a strong distrust of "others" would make it very difficult for client to accept or follow through on any plans or discussions designed by "others."

Lester's pattern of preying upon homosexuals and his attempt to have sexual intercourse with his five-year-old cousin may be attributable to the sexual abuse he suffered at an early age. Social Worker Miss O. insists that any future planning for his release from State School must include him in the decision-making process. Otherwise, he'll be long gone, no matter what penalties are imposed upon him. She recommends a combination of vocational training and independent living.

Manning agrees and recommends an ex-offender's group home for eighteen- to twenty-five-year-olds that accepts a few younger teenagers. Lester, at fifteen, will fit in. If he stays put there while studying for a trade, he may eventually be ready to live on his own. Of course, we'll first confer with him before firming up any plans.

The more we delve into the backgrounds of our charges, the darker it becomes. Each of these families has closets full of frightening apparitions: Lester, literally tossed from hand to hand, growing up in the streets; Andy's alcoholic mother, an abused child herself, now an inept parent; the Andersons, out of another civilization; Marco, surrounded by crime; and Laurence, being chased by all kinds of demons.

# 4

---

## Caring Goes a
## Long Way but
## a Little Lockup
## Doesn't Hurt, Either

**Monday, October 15, 1984**

State School authorities, though not knowing much about the Master Counselor Program, are impressed with Foster's periodic 300-mile visits. In their view, most local courts use State School as a dumping ground and demonstrate no interest in delinquents until they turn up again on a new charge.

For this trip, Foster carried packets of deodorant, cigarettes, and other goodies for each of the three boys, plus a special surprise for Marco his mother. Bringing her may have been a mistake. Instead of his usual role as The Charmer, he was "hyper," screaming, shouting obscenities, angry at the world, and frightening to his mother. As much as she wants him back home, she admitted to Foster on the return trip that he didn't seem ready.

Disappointing as was Marco's behavior—and it may have been only a bad day—Lester Burrows appeared promising and seemed to have been transformed into a concerned, reasonable young man. In Foster's own words, "Lester is sincere and appreciative, thinking about life, feeling that somebody is really trying to help him. Everything he never was before."

Manning cautioned that Foster might have to eat those words, but Foster, always the staunch supporter of his charges, firmly believes

# Caring Goes a Long Way

Lester (The Runner) is ready to come back to stay. We agreed to chance it, but need to be better prepared than in the past. As soon as a workable plan is prepared, the youth will again be foisted upon the community.

Our newest charge, Jamie Forest (The Nuisance), is also about ready to return. Two months in the detention lockup and a month in State School should have softened him enough for our program. The threat of incarceration over the heads of the others didn't make too much impact. Imagery failed with them; now we'll try reality. Will this taste of State School make Jamie truly appreciate the Master Counselor Program? Tune in tomorrow. The plan is to admit him to Dade Marine Institute, a highly structured, private-sector program that has been effective in putting boys like him on the right track.

Jamie Forest is a just-turned-sixteen-year-old black male, small for his age, one of nine children living in a single-parent (mother) household that is supported by AFDC and food stamps. His father lives in the city somewhere, but maintains no contact with the children. It seems as if I've been here before.

Like many of the kids we see, Jamie is in an emotionally handicapped class. Our clinic psychologist reported, "Jamie functions within borderline to mild retardation. He may have been born with a higher intellectual potential but an early bout with meningitis may be largely responsible for his cognitive impairment."

He is sickly, suffering from anemia and frequent colds, and doesn't like most people, particularly those in authority. He barely responded to questions, telling the psychologist, "I don't care," "I don't know," "If my mama ain't here, I ain't talking."

The maternal attachments are still strong. He is obedient and respectful to her and will often leave his bed to sleep on the floor in her bedroom. The psychologist concluded, "Jamie is a very immature child with poor judgment due to his limited intellect. There's an outward show of bravado to hide internal feelings of fear. His tolerance level of frustration appears low. He will show his hostility through sullen and obstructionist behavior."

First arrested at age twelve, the total is now fourteen, eleven for burglary. His early preference was for breaking into cars, but he has now moved toward private homes. These capers are always planned by someone else, and Jamie is usually the lookout. His choice of nonviolent crimes and his small stature have never raised any red flags in the juvenile-justice system. His is a typical juvenile-delinquent career, and the HRS response to him has also been typical.

After several arrests and unsuccessful counseling sessions, he was placed for a short term in the TRY Center, an all-day schooling and counseling program for crime neophytes. The first report was promising: "Jamie's difficulties can be handled. He is very polite, and his mother states that he abides by all the rules and stays home every night."

The report a month later raised some questions: "Jamie is self-centered with difficulty in expressing himself and has benefited very little from group participation." In the third month's report, Jamie was improving, and the following month he graduated. Five weeks later, he was arrested for burglary of a house, released while awaiting trial, and within ten days rearrested for burglary of another house. Enough said about the effectiveness of the TRY Center.

Jamie's travels through the juvenile system have produced little. The programs change, but he's the same. Foster's comment was revealing:

> Judge, the more we learn about these kids the harder it gets. When I first met Jamie, he seemed like a little pussycat, getting arrested, doing what the big boys do. Now I come to find out at State School that he goes around challenging everyone to fight. I suppose if there were something he was good at, he'd behave better. Right now he's small, a pest that can't hurt anyone. The bigger guys don't pay attention to his threats. He's only a nuisance now, hanging around, following the bigger guys, but in a year from now, when he can hurt someone, he won't be a nuisance anymore. He'll be big trouble.

If the three- to six-month programs don't lay a glove on Jamie, what makes me think that twelve months of intensive involvement with a Master Counselor is the magic number?

## Wednesday, October 17, 1984

Abbie didn't waste time getting Andy back on track. Both are working after school in a mall; he takes orders at a food stand and she at a nearby shop. Our young migrant, Dwight, not faring so well, is back in the lockup. It started with a harmless fistfight in class, followed by his refusal to work on a clean-up crew as punishment. This led to a three-day school suspension. Foster, upset by the boy's recalcitrant attitude, decided to let him serve the stint in detention.

It's amazing how these kids change from day to day. They are so volatile, up and down like a yo-yo. It's almost as if the shape of the moon or the flow of the tide determines their behavior. At any given moment, the mask slips off. Patience is the quality most needed in dealing with this explosive energy. This means forbearance and forgiveness, two attributes not always present. It's a kind of Catch-22. The rehab programs must enforce strict control in order to instill a sense of order. Miss curfew, smoke a joint—you are drummed out of the program. But delinquents exist only because they have grown up undisciplined, ignoring rules. Do we emphasize patience and forgiveness or strict enforcement? It can be a no-win situation either way.

## Monday, October 22, 1984

"Bad news, judge." Whenever Foster sidles up to me with that whispered comment as I walk the thirty yards between courtroom and chambers, I know deep trouble is ahead. Brushing off two lawyers who wanted continuances, I quickly closed the door to my chambers and turned to Foster. It was bad news. Big, tough Laurence was in jail, charged not with one, but two robberies, in both of which the victims were assaulted. Goodbye, Laurence! Details were skimpy, but apparently he and some friends strong-armed a car in Miami for a joyriding spin on the Florida Turnpike. When they spotted a car in distress, in Hollywood, Florida, about thirty miles from Miami, they jumped the woman driver and stole her purse.

Nothing like a good day's fun for active boys. Foster went off to the Broward County Jail to obtain more details while I sat and contemplated the vicissitudes of life. Certainly we had made an honest effort. Placing Laurence in a proper school setting had seemed the most sensible approach. We had tested him upside down, backward, and forward to gain some insights. Next on the agenda had been psychiatric and neurological probes to discover a medical technique to cut down his aggressive outbursts. But these weren't explosions triggered by some friction he couldn't handle. They were casual, don't-give-a-damn, malicious acts showing deep hostility toward anyone who happened to be around.

At that point, Manning came by to inform me that Jamie had been admitted to Dade Marine Institute, even though he was reading below the fourth-grade level. Yesterday that would have been glad news. Manning tried again, telling me that Andy and Abbie solved their little spat with her parents, who thought they were seeing too much of each other. No response. Not giving up, Manning observed that Dwight's mother is too lazy to arise early in the morning to wake him for school. Still immersed in Laurence, I told him to quit bothering me with trifles. End of meeting.

Hard times are ahead for the intractable Laurence. Clowning around in class, punching people he doesn't like, and intimidating his parents are now part of the past. Boyhood is over. The police reports showed a two-day crime spree that made little sense. Foster found Laurence's version mostly denial and totally inconsistent with the police version.

According to the affidavit of the sixty-eight-year-old, white, female victim, she was approached in her parking lot by two tall black males, choked, and thrown to the ground. They seized her purse, which contained thirty-five dollars, and fled in her 1979 Buick LeSabre. The following day, the second victim, a twenty-seven-year-old, white female, telephoning for assistance while stalled on the Florida Turnpike, also was attacked by two tall black males. They grabbed her purse, striking and dragging her as their car sped off. Two hours later, the car was found abandoned, the victim's purse still inside. Shortly thereafter, Laurence and his three accomplices were apprehended trying to leave in a taxicab. The second victim positively identified Laurence Samuel as one of her attackers. Upon being advised of his Miranda rights, he promptly confessed his part in the robbery. The policy affidavit further stated that he gave a sworn statement also admitting the assault on the first victim.

He is now in the Broward County Jail, where the state attorney will file for a waiver hearing before a juvenile-court judge to determine where to prosecute him. The same procedure will be followed in Dade County. Facing two serious felony cases, two confessions, at least one eye-witness identification, and a likelihood that one of his accomplices will gladly turn state's evidence against him, Laurence is a long way from deciding between playing basketball or joining the Culinary Arts Program. For sure, we'll never discover his potential as a basketball star, and I won't learn how cobalt and sugar affect aggressive tendencies.

His mother was calm, almost nonchalant, talking to Foster. "What can I say? He knows better," she said. My guess is that beneath the coolness, she has for years been anticipating and dreading that knock on the door telling her of some catastrophe involving her son. Maybe she never seemed to cooperate because she knew Laurence a lot better than we did.

## Wednesday, October 24, 1984

> Evian has a very active fantasy life. He tends to act out what other youngsters merely dream about. His paranoia makes him very aware of people who may be watching him. He is certain that teachers single him out and do not teach him on purpose, and that many of the students talk about him and make fun of him. When he was arrested he was dressed all in black, including gloves except for white shoes. He said he was wearing white shoes because if he wore his black combat boots he would have looked suspicious, especially at 4:00 A.M. in a public school building.

Most reports describing a young man acting out his fantasy never get beyond the fantasy. The patients usually begin treatment early enough to forestall violent acts. This psychologist's report had a different tone: "As Evian develops he may lose contact with reality and not distinguish fantasy from real life. When that occurs he will become exceedingly dangerous to himself and others."

I had seen a number of those predictions before, but the hurricane signals didn't flash until the next paragraph. It described why, when Evian chose to break into the school at 4:00 A.M., he possessed a forty-five caliber automatic, cocked, loaded, and ready to fire and was carrying an additional magazine clip inside his gloved hand as well as a 4½-inch double-edged dagger in his sock. His explanation said it all: "If I were to burglarize a house instead of a school at 4:00 A.M., someone was sure to be there and *I would have to kill him.*"

The psychologist had underlined the last phrase, and it came at me like a body hurtling through the screen in a horror movie. The psychologist concluded, "Left untreated, this youngster who has threatened suicide in the past will certainly do great harm to himself or to other innocent victims." And then, almost as an afterthought, the report added, "Evian is not psychotic at this time, does not need to be hospitalized and a competent psychiatrist can successfully treat him as an outpatient."

The psychiatrist examining Evian found it rare for an adolescent to be so depressed. He recommended intense outpatient psychotherapy and, like the psychologist, saw no need for hospitalization or incarceration.

This is Evian's first arrest. His stated purpose was only to vandalize classrooms, but he fled when he sighted the silent alarm system, which never went off. Police K-9 pursuit cornered him in deep brush, and he surrendered only after a police dog nipped parts of his body. What do we do with him? Is he another Hinckley in the making? Supposing he's not locked up, how do we explain any subsequent violent act? Should he be institutionalized in a mental-health facility even though the psychologist and psychiatrist say he's safe in the streets?

Evian Vilars is an intelligent sixteen-year-old Latin who scores in the highest group on standardized country-wide school examinations. He is an eleventh-grader by day, and in the evening takes courses in auto mechanics. His father, a truck driver for the U.S. Postal Service, formerly a regular army sergeant in Cuba, has lived in this country for fourteen years. The family supports Evian's penchant for hobbies—guns, motorcycles, automobiles, and the civil air patrol—and gladly foots all the costs, despite his failure to stay with any of these activities for long. Neither parent speaks English and both are uneasy about all the attention their son is attracting. His behavior started to change about two years ago when his best, and perhaps only, friend, a cousin, was killed in a motorcycle accident. After that, Evian kept saying, "I wish I had died instead."

The family social history revealed more pertinent information. The father, apparently a macho man who is disappointed with his son, constantly belittles him. Evian responds by wanting to do something important to feel better about the miserable way he sees himself. At night he sneaks out of the house, wandering the streets, thinking about his problems, and of course fantasizing. Perhaps most revealing was the fact that he had experienced difficulty entering puberty, suffering what was described as "penile infantilism." This required hormone injections and may have been the cause of his father's scorn, as well as an embarrassment in his relationship with other youngsters.

Evian and his family are in treatment, shocked at what is going on. The father and mother are totally confused, and their son keeps asking his counselor and himself: "Am I crazy?" For this case, a special HRS counselor is teamed with one of our Mental Health Clinic psychologists to maintain daily contact with Evian and his family as well as with the treating psychiatrist and his staff. The boy is receiving antidepressants and all the attention we can muster.

The doctors maintain he can be handled as an outpatient. How long will the antidepressants keep him turned off?

## Thursday, October 25, 1984

The fresh batch of reports in front of me plus a scheduled meeting with Jamie Foster (The Nuisance) and his mother would need to follow my annual rap session with inmates at the Juvenile Detention Center. Every year the local Mental Health Association and the Public School Volunteer Program cosponsor a workshop featuring a "Talk-to-the-Judge" session. It's one of those man-to-man, let-your-hair-down melees where the kids feel a little better by making the judge listen for a change. As the president of the Mental Health Association put it in his letter of invitation: "It is the cooperation of professionals like yourself that makes it possible for us to spread a little mental health among the youth of our community."

Notwithstanding the lofty goals of the mental-health advocates, my primary aim is to convey the message that responsibility for the inmates' incarceration is theirs alone. Their aim is to convince me the other dude did it, the police mistreated them, the system isn't fair. None expressed remorse or reflected upon how he or she might change. In response to their complaints, I admitted to shortcomings in the court system and conceded the police tendency to overreact, but I ended with a warning: "The public doesn't give a damn how you are treated here. All your problems are risks of the trade. If you can't do the time, don't do the crime. Until you quit beating on people, the system will continue beating on you."

They'd heard these little homilies before and just laughed. It sounded tough, but they, better than their elders, understand the roles we all play. They were friendly, all talking at once, and exhibited short attention spans—like any group of school kids except that these were charged with burglary, armed robbery, and two with murder. The seventeen-year-old charged with murder asked if he could receive a long sentence if convicted as a juvenile. He looked shocked when told he would probably be tried as an adult and face the electric chair. The kids obviously enjoyed the opportunity to pepper a judge with questions, but, other than the recreational value, the session hardly made an impression on them. Mental Health Association members may feel a sense of accomplishment sponsoring these sessions, and I'm glad to do them, but to the audience it's only another opportunity to sell their "story." They are in, want to be out and that's the sum total of their interest.

I left hurriedly amid the thanks of several sponsors who sat through the sessions and were enthralled with the lively and, I suppose, democratic give-and-take. Awaiting on my desk was the latest on Laurence Samuel. I wanted to get back to reality.

## Friday, October 26, 1984

Laurence (The Fighter) is a mess and is in a mess. At the same time we were so carefully testing him for admission to school, he was involved in hand-to-hand battle with the 22nd Avenue Players, a notorious gang of toughs who somehow concluded that he had transgressed upon their turf. There followed gunfights and struggles in the park that Laurence barely survived—all this while we were blithely testing him for proper school placement. Meanwhile, continuing to maintain his innocence, he told Foster his confession only admitted to being there, not participating. He added additional details that further contradicted his earlier version. His mother, accompanying Foster on the jail visit, later said her son was an absolute liar because he had told her a completely different story, and his grandmother yet another.

This kid's in bad shape. It will only get worse. He's angry now, complaining that "Everyone has turned his back on me. No one cares." That's not true, but he sure makes it hard to care. His family is torn apart: mother, depressed; stepfather, furious; siblings, confused. The Broward County prosecutor doesn't yet know of Laurence's extensive prior arrest record, and the Dade County prosecutor doesn't yet know his whereabouts. Shortly, they will get their act together and then really go after him. I keep thinking about his behavior. Actually, he spent only one day at Jackson Senior High School, never even bothering to show up for basketball practice. What makes a kid act like that?

## Monday, November 5, 1984

Foster's reports today were more pedestrian, a relief from Laurence's dilemma.

Marco's sister Rosita, back working at Burger King, seems to be calming down. It's important to stabilize her before Marco returns so that he has some positive role model other than the Calcon brothers. The Calcon family includes seven brothers, all of whom are in or have been through our jails and prisons. The two closest to Marco's age are presently with him in State School, but others are temporarily at liberty, ready and willing to commit crime. When I had sentenced Osvaldo Calcon, age fifteen, he seemed to be a carbon copy of Marco: slight, wiry, wavy dark hair, unemotional, silently challenging the judge to do his utmost. His handsome features were unmoved and unflinching as I sent him off to State School. As troublesome as Marco has been for the Master Counselor Program, suppose we had drawn Osvaldo and the Calcon family!

Lester Burrows (The Runner) looks like our next big project. He was our first failure, and maybe we can recoup some of our losses. Foster is eyeing a Dade Country Group Home for fifteen- to seventeen-year-olds along with a vocational assessment leading to culinary arts, auto mechanics, or any trade training that will keep Lester intact. On my trip to State School this week, I'll talk to both him and Marco about their return, but Foster wants to hold up on Marco for a while.

Still no progress with Dwight's lawn mower. He neatly trims his own yard, but does not earn a dime from the neighbors. School's still a problem, though he does well at the Boys' Club.

My meeting with Jamie Forest (The Nuisance) and his mother was canceled. Apparently his stellar performance at Dade Marine Institute (DMI) earned him enough points for a boat trip and he's out to sea. According to the staff, he is a bit mouthy but a good prospect.

Other than continued friction with his stepfather, our "star," Andy (The Drinker), is still doing his thing. He had a bad experience last week when he was attacked by three blacks as he exited a bus, stripped of gold chains as well as money, and given a black eye. He didn't appreciate the role of victim.

## Wednesday, November 7, 1984

My one-day visit to State School had a full appointment schedule. First was The Runner, Lester Burrows. His conference went a lot better than the one later with Marco. This was my first opportunity actually to meet Lester since his abrupt departure from the Master

Counselor Program seven months ago. Like all the others at State School, his first question was "When can I get out?" I approached him gingerly, mindful to include him in the decision-making process. He's an engaging fellow, smiling when chided about running away and laughing when I brushed off his explanations. Despite having run away from as many as twenty placements, he still feels compelled to justify each instance. Apparently, he had also made an escape effort at State School, but avoided punishment by convincing the Grievance Board of his innocence. He left full of smiles when told we were ready to accept him back. Convincing Foster of his sincerity was all that stood in the way of freedom. Lester could surely handle that.

From the moment of arrival, Marco was agitated, whining "When can I go home?" Whereas I was flexible with Lester, I was unyielding with Marco. When told he was scheduled for four more months, that his behavior didn't warrant an earlier release, he did what he does best. He cried and, amid sobs, reminded me, as do most of the others, that he was there unjustly. He was hardly The Charmer with me.

Perhaps I was too harsh with Marco. Watching him in the bake shop in his long white smock, I could see he was a favorite of both staff and students. Helping one student squeeze icing on a cake, cutting a meringue pie, and offering a tray of cookies to the guests, he was all over the place. When I asked about his performance, the baking teacher, a tall, husky black woman, grabbed and hugged him to her ample bosom, saying as she playfully pushed him away, "Marco's a good boy, he can do whatever he wants—if he wants to. He's spoiled sometimes."

State School, at Okeechobee, was still the same sprawling complex I remembered from my last visit several years ago, but, since the Jack Eckerd Foundation took over two years ago, significant changes have taken place. Then, HRS was in charge; now it's the no-nonsense businessman's approach. Today some big gains have been made at State School. Buddy Streit, the new superintendent, a short, sturdy, energetic, young lawyer, bounced among us, freely sprinkling good news:

The educational program now produces 100 GED diplomas a year rather than averaging twelve before Eckerd; all fourteen live-in cottages have been renovated; a new concept—Child Advocates—now speaks for the needs of students; and special education classes plus a wider choice of vocational courses are available. Most of all, there's a fresh new staff attitude and the quality of life has improved for the students. Even the ambience of the cafeteria is better: plates instead of institutional trays, overhead fans, and best of all, a daily salad bar just like Burger King.

Streit is right. A relaxed atmosphere and a sense of purpose do prevail, but, though obviously better run under Eckerd's reins, the institutional air of hopelessness and marking time still dominates.

Our presence created a bustle of activity. The inmates are throwaways at home, maybe, but here they were special enough to attract important visitors. A friendly reception committee awaited us at each cottage entrance. Juvenile Court Administrator George Lamont recognized many individuals, and every few steps a familiar face hailed one of us with a big "hello." I was their ticket out, each rushing up, reciting his name, and asking the identical question: "When can I get out of here?" All assumed I recalled full details of their cases while assuring me they had seen the error in their ways. Even those not seeking special consideration were pleased their judge had come to see them. At each stop, they called out, "Hey Judge Gilbert," mispronouncing my name, "remember me, I was in your court."

I chatted with as many of the boys as I could along the tour. Osvaldo Calcon, who had been sent up only a few weeks earlier, joined me in the cafeteria during lunch, asking the usual "When can I go home?" Because his wavy hair was shorn, those black luminous eyes looked larger and deeper. He hadn't flinched when sentenced, and now his eyes only looked colder as I told him he'd need to stay for a while longer. Marco had cried at that news, but his friend Osvaldo didn't even waste a shrug as he moved away. Among the others, I did discover two who deserved an earlier release date and made a follow-up note. Mostly it was a pat of encouragement and a few platitudes, which the inmates accepted good-heartedly.

State School didn't work before and isn't working now, but with one important difference: the staff no longer accepts the old attitudes. Buddy Streit is a good example. I asked him why he left big-city comfort for the boondocks of central Florida. His answer: "I went from on high to rock bottom because I'd rather be on the ground here with reality than in a boardroom up in some cloud." Sounds good but, despite his idealism, State School still accommodates a ragtag collection: hard-core delinquents mixed with minor offenders sent by rural judges who don't have enough local programs; a few disturbed youths who carve their names on their hands; and some sex offenders, heavy narcotic users, and many others who are equally inappropriate for the limited resources of the school. Motivation may be a great propulsion, but miracles need more than desire. Tomorrow morning, Streit joins our caravan on a visit to Florida Environmental Institute (FEI), fifty miles away.

## Thursday, November 8, 1984

Our destination is the FEI camp, nestled in the central Florida wilderness somewhere along Fish Eating Creek. This project is the most glamorous of the private-sector experiments, attracting the attention not only of the media but also of professionals in the field. Dubbed "Last Chance Ranch," "Survival City," "Alligator Feast," and other colorful designations, it's where the mostly bad, bad black dudes of Liberty City become countrified and learn basic moral values.

En route, the Florida flatlands were characterized by long stretches of grazing cows, a few citrus groves, an occasional church, and intermittent placards stuck in the ground calling for the selection of Joe Shepherd for sheriff and appealing to the occasional car or cow passing by. I later learned he won. After passing Old Venus Road over a couple of rickety wooden bridges, a pickup truck bearing FEI insignia led us on to a cut-off road, obviously dug by hand during Ponce de Leon's time. It was sand, rock, and palmetto stumps at five miles an hour for the rest of the way.

Through the brush, we came to an opening in which stood a corral holding one spavined horse, a couple of hitching posts, some makeshift tents and trailers, and a few other nondescript buildings. Out of the cab of the truck jumped Danny Grizzard, head of FEI. With a sweep of his hand, as if describing the grandeur of Niagara Falls, he exclaimed, "This is it; you should have seen it before we got here." This was the great experiment, extolled on TV, highlighted in newspaper features, and adored by Al Regnery as a model for his theories on fostering the work ethic. Grizzard invited us to stay for lunch, but, looking at the sparse surroundings, we collectively envisioned cold Spam and graciously declined, certain a Wendy's was somewhere up the line.

Grizzard, a husky, football type attired in cowboy boots, work

**110**

jeans, T-shirt, and baseball cap, provided a quick summary before turning us over to one of the detainees for a tour. "This wilderness," said Grizzard, "belongs to the Lykes Brothers, one of the wealthiest conglomerates in the nation. They leased FEI the seven hundred acres for one dollar. The first twenty kids sent here two years ago from Dade County came in with machetes, hammers, saws, nails, and carved out these five acres, setting up a tent, a kitchen, and whatever else."

As Grizzard went on describing the camp growth, my mind picture stayed with those twenty Liberty City kids who were struggling in the dark of the wilderness, amid weird noises and snakes, without utilities or utensils. Nothing like fright to build a wayward boy's character. Grizzard explained that surviving the six months of Phase I leads to Phase II, which takes the inmate out of a tent into a more civilized trailer for an additional six months. After a year of roughing it in the wilderness, it is Phase III for six more months at one of seven Marine Institutes associated with FEI, then a job in the community under supervision of an outreach counselor. "There are few idle moments in camp," said Grizzard. "It's all hard physical work, some classroom studies but mostly clearing palmettos, working in local sawmills and dairies, building outhouses and rec halls, tending horses, planting vegetable crops, and doing what has to be done."

Most of the thirty charges at FEI had been rearrested after release from State School. If State Schoolers are throwaways, these are untouchables. The first FEI inmate we met, Troy Sultan, had been sent to State School twice by me. All I remembered was his just sitting there in court, tight-lipped, surly, grunting some incoherent words. Today, he was Grizzard's emissary and our guide, prefacing every comment with a "yes, sir." He was composed, articulate, in control. "State School didn't do a thing for me," he said matter-of-factly. "In four months I'll be out of here to Phase III." Then, with a lilt in his voice, he added, "I know how to get along with people now. When I first came here I fought with everybody. Now I want to make it. I'm a different person today."

I had heard that song before, but nonetheless the little speech was impressive. Grizzard beamed as Troy pointed with pride to the living quarters he had built and the blue card he had earned that meant privileges such as hot showers and canteen. When asked how many times he'd been arrested, Troy answered, "thirteen," but then, as if truth were very important to him these days, added, "I actually committed forty-five burglaries in Dade County." Do these kids really keep score? One of Troy's fellow inmates chimed in that he was a three-time loser at State School, but he, too, was making the adjustment here. Fortunately, no one chose to ask him about his prior criminal activity. Dade County police could probably clear half their yearly burglaries just walking through this compound. Buddy Streit meanwhile stood quietly by, taking copious notes as he listened to some of his graduate students describe their past State School experiences.

In between holding on for survival, the boys attend educational classes leading to GED diplomas. As Grizzard described how city-bred boys were converted to country-style work, the success story became clearer. It was Grizzard and his top staffers who made things go. Each had made this his life's work. Grizzard spoke with pride, telling how his charges carved out this wilderness, how they rounded up wild cattle and hogs on neighboring property, how the Lake Worth Methodist Church contributed 150 hens for a hatchery that now produced eight dozen eggs a day, and how the camp hosted 120 people for Thanksgiving dinner with all but two turkeys coming from their own harvest. Here was a man who could transfer Liberty City to Fish Eating Creek and make Liberty City love it.

FEI and Danny Grizzard are part of a statewide network of programs that include the Dade Marine Institute and half a dozen other sites, all under the banner of the Associated Marine Institute (AMI). I remember attending an AMI statewide meeting, and the excitement reminded me of a fundamentalist revival meeting. All the staff members were pumped up to save the world. Their reward was satisfaction—not salary. A kid going bad was a personal loss to their onward and upward mission. Although AMI is a high-powered, private-sector operation today, the sense of individual commitment by the staff members is still the underpinning of the organization. Impacting on their wards requires almost a religious conversion that only the likes of a Danny Grizzard can perform.

Out of the twenty starters who graduated from FEI, about six are in trouble again; the remainder are employed, doing well or at least staying away from the court system. Three were so taken with rural life they have given up Liberty City and moved to Fish Eating Creek environs, one moving in with the Grizzard family until he can get established. I cautioned Grizzard to expect a lot more failure based on our experience with the Master Counselor Program. His response rejected that possibility. Pessimism was not in his vocabulary: "If all twenty are rearrested, FEI will still have been an experience for each that somewhere in their lives will be meaningful and helpful."

He was particularly proud that FEI doesn't terminate offenders for violating camp rules. They stay until the end, bitter or otherwise. He's right about that. Most programs turn violators out at the first sign of failure.

I came away from FEI remembering the movie *Cool Hand Luke,* a version of Florida chain-gang days. "Last Chance" differs by using modern sociological terms and has a more progressive focus, but many of the elements of forced labor, fear, and intimidation, though more subtle, are present. The big plus is that, unlike other programs seeking only amenable youngsters, it restricts the clientele to chronic violent offenders. FEI has accepted the challenge that others avoid.

These were two worthwhile visits. There's some hope for State School under Eckerd, and Last Chance Ranch provides a vehicle to meet even the toughest challenges in the juvenile system. Lofty as the goals of the Master Counselor Program may be, without the availability of these tough programs we'd be hard pressed to deal with Marco Zargula, Lester Burrows, and their ilk.

## Friday, November 16, 1984

The Laurence Samuel saga continues as this tough guy shuttles back and forth between detention centers while dates are set for his waiver hearings. Do we help him because he's in the Master Counselor Program or let him take his chances in the adult system? Laurence (The Fighter) is the archetype of a mean, indulged, truculent youngster whose selfishness overshadows other redeeming qualities. Why help him? I suppose because he's ours, and we have some sort of commitment to him. Foster agreed.

I had thought about Laurence during the tour of FEI. What better therapy to dilute his self-centered arrogance than a stay at Last Chance Ranch? In a week, they'd have him on a steady diet of "yes, sir" and some of those gargantuan inmates, toughened by the regimen of camp life, would surely take care of all his aggressions. After two years, he would emerge as an eighteen-year-old with a fresh look on life. I dispatched Foster to feel out the parties for a plea bargain that would satisfy the victim, police officers, lawyers, judges, and, of course, Laurence.

My feelings toward this boy are not too kindly. I almost hope he rejects the offer and goes to trial facing the long term he is certain to get in an adult penal institution.

## Monday, November 19, 1984

When I told Alberto Valdez, the specially assigned HRS counselor, that Evian Vilars could be the most important case in his career and mine, he almost jumped to attention ready for marching orders. "We don't want another Hinckley running loose," I emphasized. Valdez, a fifty-two-year-old former lawyer in pre-Castro Cuba, understands that his success is based on this client never becoming newsworthy. Valdez immediately began an intensive effort to stabilize Evian by making his family sensitive to the boy's personal and medical needs. He and court psychologist Dr. R. are also keeping in close contact with the hospital psychiatrist and the therapist.

The hospital therapist reported: "Evian is now able to express his feelings. He needs continued individual therapy as well as family counseling sessions. The future looks promising for him." Evian meanwhile maintains his heavy academic schedule, but is still somewhat depressed and insomniac, notwithstanding all this new attention.

Dealing with Evian brought me back to Clark Carden, the young man sentenced to a military academy stay for killing his father. The sentence was obviously inappropriate—it offered neither punishment nor rehabilitation. Worse yet, no provision was made for any agency to look in on him when attention was most needed. Four years from now, when the Probation Department takes jurisdiction, it won't matter. I dispatched Court Administrator George LaMont to the military academy for an unofficial visit.

When LaMont rang the doorbell at the Aerospace Military Academy, he was braced by a four-foot-ten-inch juvenile in full military regalia, wearing more braid than a head movie usher. Introducing himself as a captain, he referred LaMont to the appropriate officials. After passing several more pint-sized youths in full military dress, none of whom had ever heard of Cadet Clark Carden, LaMont finally met a secretary who knew what was going on. Clark was there under an assumed name. "He's doing well," said the secretary, "other than going back to the seventh grade academically." That was all the information provided. LaMont saluted his way out.

At the moment, it appears that both Clark and Evian are holding their own despite marked differences in their treatment. Certainly their problems can't be resolved in the Master Counselor Program or the Last Chance Ranch. With the Laurence Samuel types, community pressure is powerful to get them off the streets. With the Hinckley types, the community reaction is mostly uncertainty and indecision.

Caring Goes a Long Way

## Tuesday, November 20, 1984

"Your mother," I said to Rudy Lander, "has now seen you through ten arrests in the juvenile and adult courts. How long," I asked rhetorically, "will this go on? When does your mother get a rest?"

She looked me squarely in the eyes, answering in his behalf: "He's had a few problems. One time he was innocent. The police like to bother him, but he's a good boy and will be all right."

They were in court for sentencing on his latest case, involving a school trespass and assaulting a teacher. Neither was a serious wrongdoing. Rudy shouldn't have been on the school grounds; he then jostled a teacher when told to leave. I accepted the social worker's recommendation that he perform forty hours of community service and ordered family counseling. His mother's reaction was slow but certain: "If you order it, we will go. But it is not needed. I can take care of his problems. The police keep bothering him and going to court doesn't help. He's better off in my hands."

They left in friendly fashion, Rudy offering to do eighty rather than forty community service hours with the Tacolcy Rangers, a neighborhood program he apparently enjoyed. Mrs. Lander, beaming at her son's comment, paused in the doorway and very sweetly said, "Thank you, Judge. Thank you for your help." Had I not known her true feelings, I could have believed she thought I was on her side.

Before me was a request to terminate supervision of Marlon Jameson, the legislator's son, by HRS in Broward County. Six months later, he has earned a GED diploma and is enrolled as a full-time student at Broward Community College. No violations have been reported, sessions with the psychologist continue, and he voluntarily performed forty-five more community service hours than ordered by the court. His mother had called me several times during the summer to obtain permission for vacation trips, impressing me with the intensity she devoted to her son's welfare, even attending his street-law classes. Mrs. Jameson, the state legislator, and Mrs. Lander, the ghetto mother, both sense that only they, each in her own fashion, have the staying power to do what needs to be done.

## Wednesday, November 21, 1984

Head bowed, Laurence Samuel (The Fighter) walked through the detention door into the courtroom, sat down at the defense table, wondering no doubt how he had ever managed to get into this awful predicament. Close behind came his co-defendant, Dan Hollings, who wore a towel around his neck like a second following his fighter into the ring. Laurence had flat turned down the plea bargain worked out by Foster. He denied participating in the crime, admitting only to being present at the scene, adamantly stating he wouldn't do two years at FEI for that.

The victim, a slight elderly woman, haltingly described Laurence knocking her to the ground, putting his hand over her mouth to silence her screams, and last seeing him from the ground up driving away in her automobile. In tape-recorded statements taken on the day of the arrest, Laurence admitted being there, but claimed he only held the car door open for his friend and drove away with him. Co-defendant Hollings's confession admitted that they had both committed the robbery and vehicle theft. I found probable cause to believe Laurence had committed the act. His long prior arrest record plus a failure to cooperate in the Master Counselor Program made it easy to bind him over for prosecution as an adult.

Facing another equally serious charge in Broward County, Laurence is unlikely to avoid conviction. At the moment, he is playing Russian roulette with the adult criminal-justice system. Many slip through the net, but the few snagged can do hard time. Later on when full realization sets in, he may be anxious to plea bargain. Meanwhile, I canceled the phone call to Danny Grizzard at FEI to determine if Laurence were acceptable. No one is going to take him off the bus this time.

I still don't believe Laurence is all bad. Two years with Grizzard might salvage him while a long prison sentence would surely bring a potential killer back to the community. Laurence's mother sat through the hearing, but as in the past had nothing to say, just looking glum. Our eyes met once, but no message was transmitted. On the way to my chambers, Dan Hollings's distraught parents halted me with a barrage of questions: "Can my son be released? Is it too late to change lawyers? He's a first offender, why must he be tried as an adult?"

It suddenly struck me that young Hollings had only been extra baggage at the hearing—one of twenty cases set for trial today. I had never seen him before and likely never would again. Laurence was a person I cared about. Poor Hollings was only another case number. I started to explain the court process to these two unfortunate people, then stopped in the middle, telling them, "I no longer have jurisdiction over your son. It's out of my hands. Get a new lawyer. He'll help you understand what is going on." I was sorry later on about brushing them off, but it was the end of the day and I was tired.

Caring Goes a Long Way

## Monday, November 26, 1984

After a testing period challenging the staff at Dade Marine Institute, Jamie Forest (The Nuisance) is settling down, and to quote a staff report, "He has shown remarkable behavioral improvement." He also did well at State School, but performing appropriately in institutional settings is a long way from adjustment to the daily rigors of home and street life. How will he perform when all controls are removed? That's the supreme test. One good report does not a turnaround make.

The psychosocial evaluation of the Jamie Forest family by Counselor G. showed that this slow sixteen-year-old youth, who had an extensive record of delinquent activities, grew up in a household of twelve children, nine birthed by Mrs. Forest, plus two live-in nieces and one cousin. There were several absent fathers, but no male provider present. The family, living on AFDC and food stamps, paid thirty-nine dollars monthly rent for a HUD apartment. It was a profile seen before of ghetto families, breeding children and crime. To Mrs. Forest's credit, every child attended school except the oldest, age nineteen, no longer living at home, and the youngest, age one. In my interview with her, she seemed troubled but devoted to the large brood, hopeful they could survive.

Like the other psychosocial reports, this one was an incisive look at the personalities of the subjects. Mrs. Forest, born in a small town in Georgia, came to Dade County at age two, married Jamie's father at eighteen, from which union came the three oldest children. Pregnant with daughter Kara while her husband was serving seventeen months in prison, she divorced him, claiming physical abuse. According to her, he has little interest in the welfare of their son and makes an occasional child-support payment only for fear of jail. Like most mothers similarly situated, she has simple explanations for Jamie's antisocial behavior: he hangs out with the wrong crowd; is a follower who tends to buy friends; bigger boys tease him and force him into fights and crime. Counselor G. summed up Mrs. Forest's relationship with her family thusly: "She has the love and respect of her children, but appears to be overwhelmed with the problems of raising such a large family and has resigned herself to the fact that she can only dream of a better life for her family."

The interview with John Forest revealed a father justifying estrangement from his son, blaming it on his ex-wife: "She never stays put in one house. Moving all the time. When I find her she always has a new boy friend staying with her. I don't feel right visiting my son with strange men always around." Part of Jamie's problems, he admitted, results from lack of a healthy role model during his developmental years. He described his son: "A slick, fast talker who thinks he knows everything. He does crazy things to prove he is a man. The boy needs a lot of help."

Interviewed by Counselor G. at the Dade Marine Institute, Jamie was cooperative and relaxed:

**Q.** Describe your father.
**A.** He has an Afro with a patch up-front, a mustache, brown skin and walks like I walk . . . like a pimp.
**Q.** Describe your mother.
**A.** She has a curly perm, brown skin, gold in her mouth, jewelry around her neck and rings on her fingers.
**Q.** Why are you here?
**A.** To change my life around. To stop hanging around with the rogues and thieves in my neighborhood.
**Q.** What did you learn at State School?
**A.** I entered weighing ninety-eight pounds and left weighing 110 pounds. I now do 150 push ups a day. I learned how to fight better.
**Q.** Would you like to become a boxer?
**A.** No. I'm just tired of getting beat up and blamed for things I did not do.
**Q.** Are you afraid of getting beat up?
**A.** No. I m not afraid to fight. I've lost quite a few but now that I know how the pain feels, fighting doesn't bother me.
**Q.** Why do you get into fights?
**A.** I don't like anybody to boss me around. When they do, I get mad and lose my temper.

In his assessment, the counselor wrote: "Jamie is a personable youngster. He is extremely protective of his sister Kara, sensitive and guarded in his feelings. He desires a close and trusting relationship with a male figure, but doubts his ability to establish one. He has learned that aggression is the best way to handle conflict. He has a natural survival instinct and is undaunted in the belief that he can make it."

Counselor G. approved the approach we are taking, suggesting that Jamie's natural father assume a more active role in his son's life. The boy is classified as a slow learner, participating in special education classes reading at below fourth-grade level, yet from Counselor G.'s report I see flashes of humor and alertness suggesting a quick, bright youth who somehow got lost in the shuffle. Tomorrow morning, Manning will have my request for a battery of new tests to determine Jamie's real potential.

## Tuesday, November 27, 1984

Linda Berkowitz, the new HRS district administrator, replacing Jay Kassack, was paying a courtesy call. After we exchanged pleasantries about all the bad things we had heard about each other, I jumped into the Master Counselor Program. This was a great experiment, I assured her, designed to test the ability of the social-work system to deliver under idyllic conditions. She was absolutely entranced as I recited the efforts by Foster and Manning to remodel the likes of Dwight Anderson, Andy Sills, and company. Recognizing the appropriateness of emphasizing the positive, I bypassed Laurence's current predicament, Lester's uncertain future, Marco's unstable behavior, and the other negatives we face.

When I had sold Jay Kassack on this program, neither of us doubted that a year later we would be taking bows, amid the accolades of our colleagues and the general public. Now closing out our eighth month, what appeared to be a sure thing for the rehabilitation process is moving inexorably toward a punitive model. The likelihood of applause is diminishing considerably. For certain, the second year, which had been planned as merely a follow-up to chart the success of our clients, would need to be utilized for continued heavy involvement.

The new district administrator was pleased HRS was involved in so exciting an experiment and, just as Kassack had done months earlier, she offered whatever resources were available. I thanked her, avoiding any reference to the fact that I was now in the midst of negotiating a plea bargain to save one of these prospects from a long prison sentence at Raiford State Prison. Somehow that didn't quite fit into the picture of what had been anticipated when the program came off the drawing board.

## Wednesday, November 28, 1984

After calling his counterpart in Broward County and learning the government's case was even stronger than expected, Laurence's lawyer once again tried to convince him that the FEI two-year plea offer was a "good deal." Unmoved, Laurence insisted on his innocence, expecting to be released on bond in adult court and willing to take his chances on a jury trial.

Clearly, Laurence is receiving extra-legal advice from jailhouse lawyers. They know that too often continuances weaken the state's case, clogged calendars make for dismissals, witnesses tire of repeated depositions, time blurs facts, and for all these reasons many guilty people walk free. Not in this one. Unfortunately for him, Laurence is in the Master Counselor Program and everyone is watching. Witnesses will be carefully shepherded, prosecutors on the alert, judges concerned with the attention the case will draw.

Foster laid out Laurence's options, which showed he wouldn't be freed for a long time. Release from adult court is unlikely because his stepfather refuses to post bond and, even if he does, a new probation violation filed in juvenile court will keep him imprisoned for an indefinite period. In addition, Foster warned Laurence to expect his co-defendant Dan Hollings to testify against him on behalf of his own plea bargain. The walls are moving in on Laurence. We'll see how tough he is.

Since my inquiry earlier this week, Manning referred Jamie Forest (The Nuisance) to Dr. E. for a new series of tests and sent me a batch of reports by public-school psychologists back to 1979. They had found him to be a borderline mental deficient performing below his academic potential, and had placed him in a special class for the learning disabled. Their paperwork showed staffings, follow-ups, and placements aimed at providing specialized attention. Results? Within a short time, he had become involved in a series of burglaries leading to State School. Had the school system failed him? Can we in turn expect DMI to do a better fix-up job? Why not?

Thus far, the DMI reviews are mixed. On one occasion, Jamie's excellent attendance won him a boating trip, but punishment followed for failing to follow staff instructions. On another occasion, he refused to go on a canoe trip to central Florida because he wasn't allowed to take his radio along. Overall, his supervisors like Jamie. He complies with rules, attends classes, and, other than an occasional flash of anger challenging a fellow student or a staff member, he gets along well. A tendency to tell tall stories about his $200-a-week job and the two cars in his garage are accepted good-naturedly by listeners. Jamie seems to be settling in at DMI, but it's only the beginning.

**120**

## Thursday, November 29, 1984

Plans for the placement of The Runner, Lester Burrows, are going slowly. On his most recent visit to State School, Foster carefully outlined the game plan to him. A group home in north Dade County has been chosen, and he will be enrolled in the Culinary Arts Program, located nearby at Miami-Dade Community College. Lester was relaxed, expressing concern over his mother, sister, and grandmother. Because he has spent his life running away from them, this new attitude is impressive. Of course, this may only be a play-acting bid for early release, followed by another thirty-minute stay with his family. Foster thinks not. I'm once burned, twice careful—still hopeful.

Marco's mother came along with Foster. This time, Marco's behavior was acceptable. No shouting, no profanity, no tears—just a friendly mother-son visit. He was back to being The Charmer. According to his client advocate, he was "performing satisfactorily except when negatively influenced by his peers."

Twin sister Rosita has been another story. While we were deciding whether work or school was best for her, she unceremoniously quit school, abandoned her job, ran away from home, and, according to her mother, has taken up with a group of Puerto Rican drug dealers, serving as a drug courier from Miami to New York. Arrested on a pick-up order, she was back before me, no longer the uncertain little girl, but a disheveled, hard-looking, don't-give-a-damn tough. She'll stay in the lockup awaiting trial on her auto-theft case. Marco's mother told Foster that in view of all her other troubles, she may be evicted from the Larchmont Gardens project, which may be a blessing. We'll get to that problem next week. At four o'clock in the afternoon, I don't have the energy to take on one like that.

## Friday, November 30, 1984

On the priority list of the migrant Anderson family, education ranks at the bottom. Nonetheless, Dwight is making progress, albeit slowly, in his public-school special education class, as well as in the Boys' Club remedial tutoring sessions. According to his tutor, he reads at a pre-primer level and needs to recognize consonant sounds before moving on to advanced reading. Both teachers are hopeful. One area of marked improvement is the lawn mower. He has thus far earned twenty-six dollars, of which none has been returned to the Children's Fund, by virtue of a Cornelius Foster decree: the kid earned it, let him keep it.

Things have settled down with the Sills family. Both Andy and his mother seem to be putting their drinking problems behind them. She has a steady job, the relationship with the stepfather has improved, and all attend counseling provided by the Dade County Youth and Family Development. Andy is having minor difficulties with school attendance, and his auto-body repair instructor reports the quality of his work down from "Good" to "Fair." This may all be accounted for by his recent transaction, selling his motorcycle to buy an automobile. Owning a first car can do a lot to a teenager.

I was just about ready to leave for the weekend when Cornelius Foster poked his head inside the door and announced that Laurence (The Fighter) has surrendered. He's ready for FEI. Reaching Danny Grizzard on a late Friday afternoon wasn't easy. He finally came to the phone, cheerful as ever, saying he was out on the tractor tending the cows. None of the movies I had ever seen showed anyone using a tractor for that purpose, but I wasn't up to inquiring. He said he'd be glad to have Laurence; just send him with the next shipment going to State School, and he'd be dropped off at FEI. I told him Laurence was six feet, four inches tall, mean, tough, and lazy. "No problem," responded Grizzard. "No matter his size, we've got three bigger and meaner, and a few hours pulling stumps will take care of any laziness." Before the next question, he said he still had a long day ahead and hung up. I instructed Foster to contact all the parties on Monday to work out the plea bargain.

## Monday, December 3, 1984

Almost at the three-quarter mark of the first year of the experiment, it is time for us to look back to discover where we are heading. Because this is not one of those quantitative studies that includes a built-in evaluation component, we chose a round-table, self-assessment discussion:

> *Gelber:* "What does the Master Counselor Program have that the others lack?"
> *Foster:* "We are not in a hurry. We take our time. The other programs have to meet deadlines. They worry about budgets and writing reports."

# Caring Goes a Long Way

*Manning:* "Counselors working in the traditional programs, particularly those run by the government, have to concentrate on getting along with the system. Here there is only one focus: the child. These kids know someone is out there ready to go to bat for them. They know Cornelius works for the man, but they also know he's in their corner."

*Gelber:* "Is it possible that the Master Counselor does too much for his clients?"

*Foster:* "Sometimes I get scared thinking that these kids and their families can't function without me. I know that, when we started, I was to be the male image, but I never expected to be the father, the mother, big brother, and even husband. Whenever they have a problem, I get calls because there's no one else to talk to at home. The kids call me at all hours, Mrs. Anderson when she needs clothes, Mrs. Zargula worries me about Marco and Rosita, and Andy's mother when there's trouble in the house. They all need someone. Sometimes I think they are lazy and are taking advantage of me. But who else can help them?"

*Gelber:* "How can we get the message to them that we are on their side?"

*Foster:* "They don't trust us. We do our thing. They do their thing. If they knew what was good for them, they wouldn't be in our program. They haven't asked for any help. We force them to go to school. They hate school. We force them to do things they can't or don't want to do. It takes a long time to make a friend."

*Manning:* "These kids don't play according to our rules. They've never been part of a family structure where the father disciplines by raising his voice or even an eyebrow. Until these kids recognize that everything and everyone and every place is not a battle ground, we'll have to impose the sanctions that are necessary. That's all they know."

*Gelber:* "If Cornelius is the saviour, what happens when Cornelius leaves?"

*Manning:* "Capturing them is the most important thing and releasing them from capture is the next most important. We have to build a rapport system they can rely on when Cornelius is no longer around. Weaning them away is our next big goal, but I'm not sure any of them are strong enough yet to go on their own."

*Gelber:* "How long will it take?"

*Manning:* "For some, less than a year. For others, maybe three years and for many, never."

*Gelber:* "Do they get involved in crime because they are disadvantaged ghetto youth or is it peer pressure or what?"

*Foster:* "They always blame their friends but friends don't make you climb through someone else's window. You lift yourself over the sill. It's what happens in the family. That's where crime comes from.

These kids just grow. No telling what they come to. It makes no diference, poor or rich, black or white. Andy is white, but, when his mother came home every night from a bar with another man, it made him sick. And Dwight comes from a large, poor, black migrant family where no one takes time to talk to him. He was like a piece of furniture."

*Manning:* "They commit crimes because it's the thing they do best. Probably the only thing they ever did successfully and the only thing they can brag about. Convince them there's something they can do better and they might try."

*Gelber:* "Why aren't they grateful for being taken off the bus?"

*Foster:* "They figure if we do it, it's got to be bad."

*Manning:* "They expect the system will be as punitive as it has to be. If the system chooses to be less harsh, that's the system's problem, not theirs. When there's some trust established, as Cornelius is doing, only then will they begin to think that what is being done might be in their interest. How can a prisoner trust his jailer?"

*Gelber:* "If a prisoner can never establish trust with his jailer, why does this program lock them up so often?"

*Manning:* "You can't eliminate punishment for serious misbehavior. When we send a kid to State School, he's still in our program and we continue to work with him. We don't use jail to rid ourselves of trouble. We stay with it."

*Foster:* "That's right. I'm there for Laurence when he's in jail. He knows it. And Marco knows I'll bring his mother to visit him in State School. I give them chances to slide to the end of the rope. Then, when they are punished, I help them through the hard times. I am consistent. They can rely on me."

*Gelber:* "How can you continue to think so highly of this program when there have been so many rearrests?"

*Manning:* "Over the long haul, the Master Counselor Program will make a significant impact on their lives. We have routinized and stabilized their behavior. They see and understand that there may be another way. They may not be ready to make the leap yet, but the seed is planted in their minds."

*Foster:* "Punishment doesn't hurt anybody. It didn't hurt me. I spent five years in Raiford State Prison. It's how you treat punishment that matters. I stroke with one hand and then get tough with the other. I'm a good guy one day and a bad guy the next. Someone has to be an authority figure. I try to build relationships so that they don't have to lie to me. And then they can quit lying to themselves. I don't want them to be scared that I'll lock them up. I want them to know and expect there's a price to pay and at some point they pay. Whether I bring them in or somebody else does isn't important. What's important is that I'll be with them not only at the football games and fishing, but I'll be there when everybody else is gone."

*Gelber:* "Does change take place with them by rational decision or because of fear of consequences?"

*Manning:* "They are neither rational or fearful. They don't think ahead for more than a minute, and punishment is something everyone they know either delivers or gets. It's all a matter of timing. What we do is try to create an environment that will be conducive to change. When they are ready, the change will take place. I suppose the real answer is, I don't know. Nobody knows."

Foster's response was interrupted by an urgent phone message telling me that negotiations for the Laurence Samuel plea had broken down. Quickly calling the prosecutor and public defender to my office, I learned that both the Dade and Broward state attorney offices had cooled off to my earlier proposal. They want Laurence under adult jurisdiction so that, in the event he continues to cause trouble, adult court penalties could be imposed.

I told Foster to go to Plan Two. This bypasses the prosecutors by addressing the violation charges earlier filed. These were based on Laurence's missing a few classes and curfews, normally overlooked but technically adequate grounds for a transfer from the Master Counselor Program to FEI. "Put that on the court calendar for tomorrow morning," I directed Foster. "Waiting for the prosecutors to make up their minds will take forever. I want him out of here in FEI." My strategy is based on the theory that the adult system is so overburdened that, when they reach these cases, perhaps months later, they will accept the fait accompli and be satisfied with placement at FEI.

## Tuesday, December 4, 1984

What the hell am I doing? I thought about this last night. Perhaps I need more help than Laurence. Why am I climbing a tree looking for shortcuts to help this kid? Surely he should suffer the penalties of adult court. My violation hearing looks like an effort to sneak him out in the dead of night. I'd better obtain some advice about this before I end up explaining it to the Judicial Qualifications Commission.

I started to call my colleague and friend Judge Bill Gladstone, but,

**125**

before I could, the public defender walked into my office. He, too, had been thinking about the problem last night. Early this morning, he had worked out an agreement with the prosecutors. Laurence comes back to my court, the waiver is dropped, a plea is entered, and I send him to FEI. The Broward County case continues on to adult court, where Laurence enters a plea and relies on the good sense of the judge to continue him at FEI. This is a much more prudent plan than mine. The victims, the police, and the prosecutors will be reassured that Laurence still runs a risk that the system can strike back should he mess up at FEI. Tomorrow he enters the plea in my court, and the following morning Foster will transport him to FEI.

## Wednesday, December 5, 1984

The hearing lacked suspense. Laurence, legs shackled and wrists manacled, was accompanied by a corrections officer from the adult jail. Every time I see him he looks taller and his shoulders broader. What a build for a basketball player! He gave me a friendly smile as I explained what was happening. A psychologist testified he had examined the youth an hour earlier, finding him neither retarded nor psychotic and appropriate for FEI.

In a few days, he'll board the bus with Foster for Fish Eating Creek and Danny Grizzard. Good luck, Laurence. As he left the courtroom via the security area on the way to the detention center, ever the fighter, he had to play out his tough-guy role. No sooner was he relieved of shackles and manacles than he threatened to punch out a child-care worker, announcing dramatically, "I'm going away anyway. They can't do any more to me." He then lunged toward the worker, but fortunately someone intervened.

Among the many regrets I have about our efforts with Laurence is that, despite the countless psychological tests, his tendency to violence never was tested for chemical imbalance and diet insufficiency. Analyzing that hair sample may have unlocked the secrets to his aggressiveness.

## Friday, December 7, 1984

The nice-looking boy sitting in the back of the courtroom wearing the Walkman headset looked like Andy Sills (The Drinker) and was in fact he. "Visiting, I hope," I asked and he nodded. He and Foster were about to approach George LaMont for ninety-five dollars from the Children's Fund for Andy's tuition. Family finances are tight, Andy is out of a job, and they are in need again.

LaMont reported to me later that he had turned down the request: "This kid walks in wearing eighty-five-dollar alligator shoes, fancy leather pants, Dior shirt, thirty-five-dollar haircut, and tells me he can't afford to pay tuition. Is he kidding?"

We both turned to Foster, who explained: "All those fancy duds are gifts from Abbie's family. They've offered him a full-time job in their tile business, and are willing to do anything for him. They love him." LaMont suggested they should love him for ninety-five dollars more. Later in the day, Foster called to tell me he had contacted the school authorities, who had agreed to waive the tuition on account of "unusual circumstances."

Bringing Marco (The Charmer) back to a family in total deterioration will create a difficult situation. Plans were for a return from State School in January or February, but he's slated for failure unless the family situation improves markedly. Some families have ups and downs. This one never gets any better. Marco may be a great charmer, but personality alone can't carry him through this scenario. Rosita is in and out of jail, her mother spending nights riding around town looking for her. Eviction is in the offing because of failure to pay the electricity bill, and a rental increase will make staying prohibitive, even if the lease is renewed. Rental fees increase according to the number of tenants, and apparently all the family members and their friends now live in these quarters. Foster, moving between officials of HUD and Florida Power and Light, has thus far avoided eviction, but it seems inevitable. A team of Dade County social workers has joined Foster in working with the family, but is making little headway.

We can, of course, place Marco in a halfway house or in a group home, but those are losing situations when the family is not at the end of the line waiting to take over. Foster describes Marco's mother as a brave and proud woman fighting for her children. Unless we can prop up the family, prospects are dim.

## Monday, December 10, 1984

Laurence (The Fighter) was a bundle of nerves driving up with Foster. No matter how Foster responded to his questions about life at FEI, the boy was worried. Foster theorizes: "Laurence isn't quite the

**127**

tough he plays. He may be scared that those Troy Sultan-FEI dudes may be more than he can handle. I've seen his type before. Laurence is a school-yard fighter while the FEIs are street fighters. School-yard fighters throw sneak punches, then wait for the phys ed teacher to break up the fight. Street fighters use whatever weapons they can find to kill you. My money is on Troy Sultan to do a job on Laurence if they ever tangle." This was Foster thinking back to his own old street days.

## Wednesday, December 12, 1984

Celebrating his sixteenth birthday on a patch of swampland in Fish Eating Creek, cooking over a camp fire, and chopping palmettos, Laurence was discovering life. According to his counselor, he has a good attitude, is taking everything in stride, and is getting along. In response to my concern about his low boiling point, the counselor explained: "All our kids are ready to explode. We expect it and are ready for it. Living in these woods is shock treatment. We try to make it acceptable. As soon as they learn there are good things at the end of the line, most come around." This is a real test for Laurence. He'll be roughing it day-to-day with all those other tinderboxes while conforming to the rules. No telling how that will go.

Laurence's adventure was on my mind as the morning calendar started. I did a double take when Troy Sultan suddenly appeared before me. Not quite. It was his older brother Travis, now seventeen, on a burglary charge. Both Sultans have two-page rap sheets, and Travis, like his brother, a year ago, sat there sullen and cold while anger poured out of him. When I told him his brother was doing well at FEI, he didn't even bother to look up. As he was led back to detention, he growled, "They shitting me around here."

The Sultan boys, out of a harsh, poverty-stricken ghetto life, have a long way to go. From outward appearances, Troy at FEI is giving it a try; for Travis, going from one crime to another, nothing good is likely. Laurence, on the other hand, from a relatively stable family, should have less trouble making adjustments. There's no apparent reason for the deep-seated anger on his part.

## Thursday, December 13, 1984

Every parent readily concedes that thirteen-year-olds are an absolute pain. That in-between growing-up year defies all predictions. Dwight is no exception, except that his problems are magnified because he is part of that floundering, migrant-worker Anderson clan. They have only a primitive understanding of family relationships and, where most families boost a kid over rough spots, Dwight receives no support when he needs it most. He never has been able to make the school bus on time. First, his mother didn't wake him, then he misunderstood the bus schedule, then the driver didn't show up on schedule, and finally, when Foster worked out each of the problems, Dwight decided he didn't want to be seen on the same bus with children who were classified as emotionally disturbed. Foster personally delivered him a few times, but that isn't the answer.

He's become unruly, courting trouble at every stop. His special one-on-one public-school teacher, who has taken a personal interest in his progress, has been threatened with slashed tires, and he bullies the younger kids at the Boys' Club. The most serious escapade lately was an attack on a twenty-two-year-old retarded youngster. Dwight approached him at a bus stop, demanded money, then punched him in the jaw. The police investigation will determine whether it was robbery, assault, or, one might hope for Dwight, just playful misbehavior. Not even Foster's comforting hand can pacify his erratic behavior. He's going through a mean streak period that calls for family firmness and understanding, neither of which abounds around him.

Mrs. Anderson never had much control, and now apparently exercises none at all. She makes excuses for his behavior, he lies about it, and between them he's a loose cannon. Foster is considering placement in a foster home, but will wait. Patience may yet be the best approach. Moving the youth out of his home will mean the end of both the public-school special education class and the Boys' Club After Care Program. It's hard to believe that all the resources poured into him can't right his direction.

If we were publishing monthly ratings on our charges, Jamie Forest (The Nuisance) would be moving up a bit on the latest listing. Reports from Dade Marine Institute continue to show slow forward movement. He still challenges anyone in his way to a fight, but his targets have learned to ignore him. Although he becomes seasick easily and other than on calm days is a landlubber, he has become immersed in other programs. Educationally, he's classified low, and his counselor says prospects for a GED diploma are somewhere between "slim and none." However, his supervisors like his attitude and believe that "high maintenance" (English translation: constant care) will allow him to come out of DMI in good shape.

What the DMI staffers say jibes for the most part with Dr. E.'s recent report, though his clinical analysis is considerably less promising than their estimate. According to the doctor, "Jamie Forest has the potential to function in an unskilled or semi-skilled job situation which will involve concrete and relatively repetitive tasks. He requires a protected academic and social environment where he is not subjected to other individuals who could take advantage of him because of his borderline intellectual ability."

I had hoped that Dr. E. would find some sign supporting my theory that deep down in Jamie an alertness and brightness was struggling to emerge. After reading his report, I called Dr. E., who shrugged off my theory. "Dullness" was the word description he most often used. "The early bout with meningitis may have cooked his brain, leaving the dull affect, or environment may be the cause, but don't keep your expectations high," he cautioned.

Master Counselor Foster finds Jamie funny, but he too is not impressed with his potential. Jamie plays word games; he often uses a deejay patter and always has quick quips in response to Foster. Yesterday, when Foster extended his curfew an hour to visit a girl friend, the youth said an hour was fine but that he had eight girl friends. "If you think he's so smart," asked Foster, "why can't he learn anything in school?" I don't know. Apparently he's borderline retarded and his potential for development is limited, notwithstanding his outgoing personality. That "high maintenance" DMI refers to sounds like a forever program.

## Friday, December 14, 1984

Foster made the pre-holiday rounds of his clients and found little comfort to report on each of the households. Mrs. Waite, Andy Sills's mother, reports that the family is infested with head lice, requiring special treatment before readmission to school. Mrs. Roman, Marco Zargula's mother, took the $200 AFDC monthly check intended for an electric-bill payment and instead gave it to a friend whose husband needed it for bond on a drunk-driving arrest. The friend will have a happy holiday reunion while Marco's family will greet Christmas in the dark. Mrs. Forest, Jamie's mother, pleased with his progress at DMI, has requested they keep him there even after he completes the program. Mrs. Anderson, Dwight's mother, has given up on his school-transportation problem, leaving it to Foster to make the delivery. Mrs. Sumter, Laurence Samuel's mother, is relieved that he avoided the state prison system, but is not too optimistic about his future at FEI. There's no cause for universal joy among these families.

# 5

## Going Up Is Only
## a Trip—Coming Back
## Can Be a Fall

**Monday, December 17, 1984**

Lester Burrows (The Runner) is due back from State School today. His homecoming reminds me of the treatment reserved for visiting out-of-state dignitaries. Every move has been choreographed. Foster has driven three hundred miles to Okeechobee to escort him home personally. All the possible county and state placements have been canvassed. Upon arrival, he goes to the local detention center to be thoroughly briefed on the likely sites and be interviewed by house parents. In turn, he will examine the homes offered so that all parties are satisfied. Upon placement, he will go through a two-week indoctrination period, adjust to his new home environment, visit his grandmother, learn about the Culinary Arts Program, and have a session in my chambers. If he runs away again, for the twenty-first time, it won't be because we haven't tried.

Lester's joy was Marco's bitterness. Watching Lester leave, Marco cried all day. After earning certificates as the best baking student and other awards for progress, he was sullen and resentful. Although he is undoubtedly the better prospect for the Culinary Arts Program, his home situation must improve. And it is. What looked like a dark Christmas suddenly showed light. It all came about with a $300 gift from heaven, heaven being New Jersey State Prison, when Marco's stepfather sent home that sum for Christmas. This reinstated the in-arrears Florida Power and Light account. Along with a $50 contribution from the Children's Fund for a new deposit, the lights are on again. In addition, Mrs. Roman has found employment and Rosita is back in school—this time a trade school—and out of the clutches of the cocaine traffickers. Best of all, the Calcons are leaving Larchmont Gardens, heading back to Puerto Rico. Foster suggested half seriously that the Children's Fund buy their plane tickets.

Bringing Marco back may prove difficult because he's a lot more volatile and prone to foolish acts than Lester. For Lester, it was survival in the streets and now it's a matter of convincing him that another life-style is worth trying. Marco, though, has not outgrown the childish desire to be a heroic figure. Among his set, that means pointing a pistol at someone's head, as he did in Flamingo Park. Had the shell exploded, rather than fallen out, he would have achieved "star" status. Foster, understandably, is a lot more cautious about Marco's prospects.

Each of these kids requires a different formula. For example, the problems of Dwight (The Migrant) are miniscule compared to those of the others. Nonetheless, it looks like he's heading for trouble. It all seems to revolve around school, particularly getting there. Although Foster still delivers him, Dwight found occasion to shove the Boys' Club bus driver and again threaten a teacher. As a result, both the school and the club are on the verge of expelling him. It may be the rigorous time schedule he's on because he's accustomed to just wandering on his own. Or it can be the absence of his mother, now working at a fruit-packing plant. Foster explains that Dwight is simply "smelling his musk" an old black expression for youngsters reaching puberty, who for the first time can smell their own body odor. According to Foster's folklore, this apparently incites aggression. Now that school is out for Christmas vacation, he is hopeful that Dwight's musk will be less active.

The afternoon court calendar brought two unexpected visitors. Rudy Landers checked in this time on an aggravated battery charge rising from a break-dancing fracas at school. Although the evidence against him only supported a simple battery charge, the victim had received serious eye injuries. As I sent the case to adult court for prosecution on the lesser charge, there stood his mother, muttering again about the injustices of the system. No one can tell what makes Rudy tick. All ten of his arrests except one for burglary were spur-of-the-moment acts, usually assaults, provoked no doubt by his musk level. Neither his mother nor any of the juvenile-system programs have deterred him.

My other nonfavorite on the calendar was Travis Sultan, before me for disrupting the detention center by ripping out a water cooler, tearing up the plumbing and striking a child-care worker, among

other violent acts. He's an absolute terror around staff, fellow inmates, and property. The request to transfer him to the more secure
adult jail was granted. It will be interesting to track the Sultan boys.
Troy, at FEI, seems to be moving toward socialization, but Travis
needs a straitjacket. Will the new Troy move on to full adjustment
and how will Travis fare heading for state prison? Neither of these
boys is in our program. Would Foster have made a difference? Then
again, Laurence is in our program, and how much can we show for
that?

## Wednesday, December 19, 1984

In the several days he has been here, Lester Burrows (The Runner)
has produced a tour de force, impressing not only his grandmother,
Foster, and the house parents, but me as well. His grandmother,
offering a cake for his sixteenth birthday, couldn't quit hugging him,
forgetting the things stolen from her house and the heartaches. Foster delivered him to my chambers, absolutely convinced a new mature Lester has emerged who is ready to quit preying on homosexuals and settle down. Wearing beat-up khaki trousers, torn underwear top shirt, and tattered sneakers, he looked like he had spent the
last week sleeping in the back of a car. His clothes had been stolen or
misplaced at State School, but his easy manner and friendliness
overshadowed all else. Whatever was asked he'd gladly do.

Already warned by Foster that running away again meant back to
State School until age nineteen, he quickly assured me the warning
was unnecessary. He wants to do the right thing and can't wait to see
his mother and sister, whom he hasn't seen in years and doesn't
remember. The laid-back, engaging manner about him overcame my
recollection of all the counselors he had sweet-talked over the past
few years. I agreed with Foster: this kid will make it. Obviously,
State School cannot create this kind of metamorphosis. Certainly
Foster and I know his background. How then can this little thug
create this kind of an impression? Deep down we know Lester is the
ultimate test. We'll grasp any sign, portent, or straw in the wind.

## Friday, December 21, 1984

Not much happens in court during Christmas week. It's mostly
marking time: witness subpoenas come back unserved; prosecutors

and defense lawyers declare a truce; continuances become the order of the day. Hallways leading to the courtroom are adorned with Christmas cards depicting humorous lawyer-judge scenarios. At our annual breakfast, once again the lawyers did parodies on traditional holiday songs, substituting each of the judges as the target for irreverence. Mine was a ditty from *Fiddler on the Roof* to the tune of "If I Were A Rich Man":

"If I were a Si Gelber . . . Everyone coming to my court knows well in advance,
Of being found Not Guilty there is very little chance.
Defense lawyers work goes all to naught,
My mind is made up once the client is caught.
If I were a Si Gelber . . . la la la."

Some clean-up matters had to be handled in court before the four-day New Year's holiday weekend. In the back row sat Cornelius Foster, presumably ready to exchange holiday greetings. Instead, when he rose to ask for a pickup order, I knew instinctively it was Dwight Anderson (The Migrant). This kid's been a problem recently. Who? Lester Burrows! I couldn't believe it.

Back in chambers, Foster told the sad tale. Last Friday, Lester and his house parents worked out details for admission to what was considered to be the best group home available in Dade County. Because he still lacked suitable clothes, they bought him two pair of jeans, underwear, shoes, and their own gift of a radio for Christmas. Foster, ever the sentimental soft touch, added five dollars for spending money. When Lester left to visit his grandmother, good times seemed to be ahead. Overlooked in the holiday spirit was his midnight return, violating the 9:00 P.M. curfew. On Christmas Eve it was back to grandmother, then a visit to his girl friend and their one-year-old son. It's hard to imagine Lester, the street urchin, as a concerned teenage parent. Many slum kids, like him, are casual about the birthing-parenting process, and that's how the Lester types come to be what they are. This time, he returned at 2:00 A.M., but again the house parents took no action. Christmas day his grandmother also gave him a radio—he sold both—and that was the last seen of Lester Burrows. The next afternoon, he returned, broke through a window to steal his clothes, and left. The house mother said that, had he come through the front door, his clothes were there for the asking.

**134**

A downcast Foster said, "Everybody was out to help give him back the world and for no reason he threw in the towel." Foster offered to spend his vacation searching Lester's old hangouts. I told him to visit his own children, work out his own family problems, and forget the boy. Obviously neither reachable nor tameable, Lester needs to be incarcerated until the system grinds him into submission.

## Friday, January 4, 1985

Plans now are for Foster to pick up Marco Zargula (The Charmer) at State School and bring him back home for placement interviews for the Culinary Arts Program. En route they will stop at FEI to visit Laurence Samuel (The Fighter).

Once again we face the problem of what to do with Lester Burrows (The Runner), if and when he is caught. Last week, fifty lashes, castration, and fingernail extraction would have been too good, but today, when we are calmer and more reflective, uncertainty prevails. Fortunately, he's still at large and no immediate decisions need be made. Foster has no reservations about what to do. He is personally cruising the neighborhood, alerting his contacts to watch grandmother's residence. She says Lester has been back seeking food and money. Reports have him sighted, but he apparently moves quickly. It is hoped that somewhere along the way, he will be picked up before committing another crime. When that happens, Foster wants him shipped posthaste to an adult youthful-offender institution to be safely housed for the next three or four years. Foster sees no point spinning wheels anymore, only to face defeat again. He's probably right.

Manning takes an entirely different view. He feels strongly that we cannot give up on Lester. This has happened on every prior occasion, he reasons, and our failure to break the cycle does not negate further effort. His theory is that the youth runs away by instinct, programmed to reject any structured family existence. Thus far, none of the psychological reports or social histories has provided any helpful insights. Equally distressing is the fact that not one of the interviewers discovered Lester was a father, certainly an important factor in his life. Manning brushes aside all the negatives and opts for one more chance, and then one more chance after that, and on and on. I was impressed with his pep talk. He's probably right, too.

## Wednesday, January 9, 1985

The trip from State School to FEI was uneventful, and Foster explained to Marco Zargula (The Charmer) what was expected of him, once back in Miami. Fish Eating Creek's wilderness and wide-open endless space was a revelation to Marco, as were the size of Laurence Samuel (The Fighter), Troy Sultan, and the other inmates. As on my earlier visit, Troy was the tour guide through the camp.

Laurence was pulling palmettos, an assignment he had earlier rejected, telling FEI Director Danny Grizzard, "Hard work is not for me." After Grizzard ordered a few nights in isolation, sleeping atop a pine platform in the middle of nowhere, communing with eerie sights and sounds, Laurence declared himself ready to accept work details. Upon arrival at FEI, he had pointedly told the staff of his "temper" and his effort to control it. He described it as if it were an entity in itself, like a teenager talking about acne. The staff response was that "temper" was his problem, not theirs.

Here's a kid who never worked a day in his life. His family and everyone else always catered to his "temper" to an extent that he shouldered little responsibility for his assaultive behavior. Despite that, the current prognosis on him at Last Chance Ranch is optimistic, but guarded. His resistance to authority at the onset earned him an additional month's stay in Phase I, but right now he's just one of the boys who are getting along. His parting words to Foster were that he would hang in there, do his time, and get out as soon as possible. A tough stretch lies ahead. Phase I consists of straight punishment, no visitors for six months, and only one phone call in that period. For an egocentric who has manipulated all those about him, this sudden change is pure shock treatment. This may do a lot more for Laurence than my tests for excess cobalt and sugar deficiency.

The trip from FEI to Miami provided an opportunity for Foster to do some missionary work with Marco. Last Chance Ranch, with its Spartan accommodations in a virtual jungle outpost, made State School look like a pleasant summer-camp outing. Foster filled Marco in with the backgrounds of Laurence and Troy, pointing out that FEI could well be Marco's next stop. He had little to say in response, but it was apparent the message was not lost on him.

Back in chambers, he stood before me, a few inches taller, but otherwise there were the same cold, unsmiling eyes and the wary responses. He said the right things: he couldn't wait to start in culinary arts; he wanted to help his mother. No more drugs, no more Calcon brothers, no more "Scarface" Al Pacino. He sounded sincere, almost. It's not his charm that comes across so much, but rather the wonder why a kid with such raw talent can't turn himself around. Foster will tap Court Administrator George LaMont's Children's Fund for one hundred dollars to provide proper attire for the latest effort to remodel Marco Zargula.

## Thursday, January 10, 1985

The problems of Dwight Anderson (The Migrant) aren't going away. It may be more than his musk. He studiously avoids going to school. On the days Foster doesn't deliver him, he either threatens or assaults someone. The Boys' Club bus driver first used an older boy as an enforcer, but, when that failed, he took Dwight aside, quietly threatening to smash him if he continued causing trouble. Dwight responded by swinging at the burly driver. His teachers, finding him equally obnoxious, are grateful for his frequent absences. If this is a stage to outgrow, a lot of people are waiting patiently, some not so patiently, for his glands to stabilize.

Nursemaiding is not Foster's style, and the need to cart Dwight around has added an edge to his normally placid personality. He becomes even more upset talking to Dwight's mother. Arriving in the morning to check on the school departure, he usually finds both mother and son fast asleep. Enlisting her aid produces only a broad grin, a shrug, and some irrelevant comment. When Foster gestured that Dwight was only this much away from going to State School, she gave him a vacuous smile. Although their quarters are more livable than before, the Andersons are still the same collection of aimless wanderers, hardly touched by anything other than survival. Foster's effort as Pygmalion may be beyond reasonable expectations.

Reading Dwight's most recent psychological examination provided little comfort. The psychologist recommended placement in a residential treatment facility specifically designed for retarded delinquents. Dwight essentially remains illiterate, reading on the level of a first-grader, even though he is in special remedial one-on-one classes in both the public school and the privately run Boys' Club program. Of course, his numerous absences and lack of cooperation account for his lack of progress. Tomorrow, he gets top review billing.

## Friday, January 11, 1985

"Stump the experts" was the name of the game, and Dwight had us all guessing. It was one of our periodic reviews. Lock him up for a short spell? Place him permanently in a structured facility? Lecture from the judge? None of the above. We were in agreement on only one point: the situation had become serious, and he needed support more than punishment. Manning theorizes that, considering Dwight's minimal educational potential and lack of family support, our expectations have been totally unrealistic: "The fault lies in the zeal of the Master Counselor Program to succeed, rather than with Dwight, whose slow progress is all he is capable of giving."

We tossed Manning's theory about for a while. If the extensive, collective experience of a street-wise counselor, a highly trained social worker, and a know-it-all juvenile judge can't fathom a way out of what appears to be a simple problem, what can ordinary folk do? In truth, I asked myself what could be expected from someone in Mrs. Anderson's circumstances? I didn't wait for the answer. Foster will confer with supervisors at school and at the Boys' Club, while Dwight and his mother spend a few friendly sessions with one of our clinic psychologists. Maybe we'll hit on something.

Speculation and uncertainty may cloud Dwight's future, but it's a brighter story with Andy Sills (The Drinker). Foster has already declared him a winner and recommends honorable discharge from the program. Andy is doing well at school, his mother has a job, social workers are helping with the three young sisters, no problems exist with his stepfather, and Andy happily drives around town in his girl friend's new car. My hesitation surprised Foster. Because Dwight was going downhill, a victory would come in handy, but I still have reservations. At the first sign of a personal crisis, Andy may yet collapse and revert to last year's alcoholic burglar. It is essential he complete his auto-mechanics course and earn a GED diploma. When that romance peters out, as it surely will, little will be left to fall back on. Foster, having heard this line before, shrugged and left without comment. His faith in Andy hasn't wavered from the very beginning.

Another score for Foster is Jamie Forest (The Nuisance), now fully acclimated to DMI. He can't wait to arrive in the morning and participate in every activity. Other than for a few scuffles, he is well liked by the staff and his fellow students. He continues to tell tall tales, fantasizing about the rich life he leads, which amuses his

**138**

classmates. Manning wondered out loud if this continued fantasizing had some deeper meaning. I responded that poor kids playacting the rich didn't need to be decoded by a team of psychologists. When rich kids daydream about the great life of the poor, then a call for the analysts is needed.

Nothing new on Lester's whereabouts. The head of the group home program he so suddenly departed understands the problem and is willing to take him back. Because we don't yet have him, that decision is a bit premature.

## Monday, January 14, 1985

Mental-health problems certainly surround these two young men, but, though the approach to their treatment differs markedly, they continue to function without incident. Clark Carden, who, by his own admission, executed his father, is still at military school, apparently none the worse for being ignored by both the psychiatric and criminal-justice communities. Evian Vilars, a prospective Hinckley, seems to be thriving under the close monitoring of HRS Counselor Alberto Valdez and the regular therapy sessions at Children's Psychiatric Center.

Once more, George LaMont's mission to obtain information on Clark Carden's progress found him on a shuttle to nowhere. He only wanted a copy of the probation report describing the youth's current status. At my request, criminal-court Judge Ed Cowart had earlier clarified the situation so that reports were to be forthcoming from the adult Probation Department. LaMont spent an unproductive morning on the telephone with the department hierarchy. What information did he want? Why? Who needed it? Which court had jurisdiction? And on and on went the questions. Clark's probation officer never surfaced, if indeed one existed. Ultimately, the final word. No status report exists. No probation officer has seen or talked to him, and no treatment is provided. Periodically, they receive calls from the military academy advising that Clark is doing fine. "What's the difference?" the probation supervisor asked LaMont. "If he does anything wrong, we'll be told." Whenever despairing over the inadequacies of juvenile-court services, I reflect on the indifferent approach in adult court and my spirits are refurbished quickly. Equally distressed, Judge Cowart assured me he'd motivate the Probation Department.

Reports on Evian are optimistic. He's an ideal patient who is building an excellent therapeutic relationship with his therapist. Because he's bright, always on the go, and has a variety of interests, it's hard to understand why he has no friends and continues to be depressed. HRS Counselor Valdez hovers about him, clucking over every move, forming even closer ties.

No sooner had Evian given up evening classes than he found employment as a movie usher four nights a week. As expected, he scored high on preliminary exams for the military service. Enlistment apparently is his prime motivation for successfully completing treatment. Although outward appearances suggest he would be an ideal candidate for the U.S. Army, he would be a menace around weaponry. Unlike others, his fantasizing is serious business, for he has committed a break-in, armed with a cocked automatic, dressed in black, "to get into action." In a command position, to which he will surely rise in the military, who would trust his finger on a red button? What would happen when he faced a crisis? Would he follow military procedure or his fantasy? Predictably, both Clark and Evian, whose problems rise from authoritarian situations, are gravitating toward the military.

## Wednesday, January 16, 1985

Foster is not the type to become agitated. This time, his words came so fast I asked him to start over. It sounded like something about Marco (The Charmer) running away with one of the Calcon brothers. He had. He left Monday night and hasn't returned or called. His mother saw him driving away with one of the Calcon boys in a blue Chevrolet which a neighbor said was stolen. Today's scheduled interview with culinary arts was scratched. Instead of proudly presenting State School's finest baking student, Foster stood before me more embarrassed than angry.

It is hard to understand why Marco chose to run away. Unlike Lester, he has a family and certainly the Culinary Arts Program poses no threat to him. Facing as he did a long term back at State School, what could prompt this foolish act? Both he and Lester (The Runner) had adjusted fairly well to State School, but no sooner were they released than they immediately reverted to their old mode of behavior. Usually the criticism of institutional confinement is that, upon release, the follow-up supervision and support services are in-

adequate. Here, however, we have carefully crafted post-release programs where Foster is in constant attendance, and yet both could
hardly wait to put on their new clothes before disappearing.

Lester's loss was not so devastating because he never stayed long
enough to develop any relationships, but Marco had a lot of Master
Counselor Program nurturing. Some of it should have created
enough trust to hold him, at least for a while. Can it be that once the
line of serious criminality is crossed, nothing works? I'd hate to
believe that. We keep waving the banner of a full charge ahead while
all around the troops are falling. First, large doses of individualized
treatment didn't work. Short-term lockup was added, which didn't
work either. Then came the get-tough approach, incarceration at
State School; that also failed.

I suppose the message is that this is only a game of inches, not
miles. Given enough time, a Cornelius Foster can reach a Marco
Zargula. But how long will a community wait? Meanwhile, dis-
heartened but determined, Foster will be gone the next few days,
searching, running up his gasoline-expense tab, and hoping he lo-
cates the two fugitives before HRS auditors complain anew about
his travel expenses.

## Thursday, January 17, 1985

Not having anything to report on his two fugitives, Foster came by
to pass the time and commiserate about life in general. I had a touch
of the flu, and, along with his chatter, Foster brought a bag contain-
ing a pint of gin, four limes, and a jar of honey. "Heat the honey,
squeeze the limes, pour gin freely, and the flu goes away—a guaranteed cure my grandma gave me," assured Foster. My bailiff, Barry
Young, echoed the guarantee, saying that every black in Liberty City
subscribes to this prescription.

Obviously thinking about Lester and Marco, Foster reminisced
about his own youth:

> I grew up in the street like these kids, but I had my grandmother. I
> think I was her favorite. She whipped me when I wouldn't listen. I was
> bad. Stealing money. Liquor. Drugs. Jail. She got me out of jail every
> time. I always had a place to stay with her. She'd say "Be a man. Be a
> man. Stay out of trouble." She was a proud lady, never allowing any
> stolen goods in her house like other folks did. When I sold news-

papers she opened an account for me in postal savings. She was sure proud of me when I joined the U.S. Air Force. You know, she saved enough money to buy each of us a house. She never went to school, but she was smart. She sure was good to me.

I told him we needed to bottle people like his grandmother and franchise them all over Liberty City. That would solve the crime problem. Foster liked talking to me about his grandmother. Suddenly, he changed direction: "How about me taking a job with Metro Rail. They pay clean-up men three thousand dollars more than I get. Then I just pick up trash and don't have to worry about Lester and Marco." I shook him off with the observation that we had a lot of cleaning up to do before he went anywhere else.

## Friday, January 18, 1985

Here we go again. Another story on the rapacious, predatory, kill-for-the-sport-of-it juvenile delinquent. The journalist, this time from the *Ladies Home Journal*, flew in this morning, knowing absolutely nothing about Miami crime except lurid tales of Mariel refugee mayhem, international drug traffickers shooting up the streets, and gangs terrorizing the city. I told him that, unlike the juvenile crime in Los Angeles and New York, ours has been declining for several years.

He had other fish to fry: "How often do juveniles commit gratuitous murders? Do they kill for amusement? Do you see defendants who by their very presence are frightening? Why is the modern youngster more inclined to savage criminal acts?"

This was going to be red meat for the gentlewomen reading the *Ladies Home Journal*. I told him no more than a handful of juvenile homicides were committed yearly in Dade County, most arising incidental to another act, such as a fight or fleeing a burglary. Brutality is occasionally displayed, but mostly by psychotics, in genuine need of treatment. I then went on to describe various approaches in some of our better programs. He listened patiently, always returning to the theme: What has happened in America to turn friendly Boy Scouts helping little old ladies cross the street into teenage barbarians pillaging the neighborhood? The interview ended a draw: I, unable to convince him we had a better class of juvenile delinquents in Miami; he, unable to persuade me that his article was one I'd want for my scrapbook.

# Going Up Is Only a Trip

## Monday, January 21, 1985

There he was, trailing behind Foster, a little abashed, holding the baking certificate he had earned at State School. The afternoon court session was to begin momentarily, and I was hooking up my robe when Foster and Marco Zargula (The Charmer) came into chambers. Last night, he had voluntarily returned home after staying several days at a girl friend's house. He denied being with any of the Calcons or knowing their car was stolen, claiming that it belonged to a friend named Junior and that his absence had involved no drugs or crime. To each of his statements, Foster kept shaking his head negatively. Not having time or patience, I threatened an immediate trip on the State School bus unless he told the truth. "Yes, José Calcon and I stole a car. We drove around town just for the hell of it. Smoking joints, visiting girl friends, having a helluva time. We didn't commit no crimes. Just having fun." He hesitated a few seconds before adding, "He's my friend." Again, so much for the contest between official sanctions and peer influence.

What next? Foster and I examined the options, knowing we'd try again. Probably culinary arts. Things at home are about the same for Marco. Sister Rosita has shed her boy friend, who, it turns out, has been the very same José Calcon. Apparently a beating by José's current girl friend convinced her to stay away. The impending departure of the Calcons to Puerto Rico is only a conversation piece because no definite plans are confirmed as yet. Mrs. Roman straightened out her electric bill, but, when she fell behind in her rent, the Children's Fund again came to the rescue with $74.00. Culinary arts? Looking at Marco, listening to his guarded admissions, knowing where he comes from, and worse yet, where he wants to go, I'm not so sure.

Departing, Foster turned to say that things aren't going well with Dwight Anderson (The Migrant) either: "He's absent from school a lot and, when he's there, the teachers wish he was absent." This may yet be more difficult a problem than Marco's transgressions.

According to clinic psychologist Dr. C. and others who come in contact with Dwight, his situation is hopeless unless he is removed from home and placed in a residential facility. Everyone seems to recommend that, but it's too easy a solution. Take him away from home at age thirteen and he'll start running and be another Lester Burrows. Dr. C. has offered to see Dwight on a regular basis, which may be worth trying because he seems to have a knack of getting through to such suspicious youngsters. Besides, he's black—and that may open a door.

## Tuesday, January 22, 1985

Visiting the Dade County Juvenile Justice Center was Al Regnery, head of the federal Office of Juvenile Justice Development (OJJDP), who was in town officially to look at a State Attorney's Office program that was funded by his agency. The program was progressing slowly, and, though he made no direct comment, his expectations apparently had not been met. At the first opportune moment, I made a pitch for the Master Counselor Program, telling him all the twists and turns Marco and the others had taken in our testing of the theory that even bad kids are salvageable if they receive enough attention. Where most people are fascinated and respond with a bushelful of questions, he listened without comment. He finally asked, "How did it come out? What are your conclusions?" I said it was too early to tell, but probably a mixed bag. He seemed a bit disappointed, but, like his reaction to the State Attorney's Office program, I wasn't certain how he felt. I tried to hold him with an analysis of Lester Burrows's motivations, but my audience was lost. "What documentation do you have?" He wanted supporting data; without them, these were just "war stories" he hears every place he goes.

Regnery left some serious questions to mull over. How important would the results of our experiment prove to be? Suppose all six individuals had been transformed into paragons? Without empirical data and a control group, would professionals in the field be impressed?

## Wednesday, January 23, 1985

No matter how much the behavior of Dwight Anderson (The Migrant) is minimized as a passing phase, everything about him suggests a long struggle ahead. Despite Foster banging on the windows to waken the household, the boy cannot or will not get out of bed in the morning for school. Bus rides are a struggle and school an ugly experience for all involved. It seems older brother Derrick offended a housing-project gang, who are taking it out on Dwight. Mrs. Anderson keeps Dwight indoors until it's safe to leave. He then spends his day smoking joints and making himself scarce. Foster says that, though the gang threat to Dwight is real, it is only an excuse to skip school. Dr. C. found him depressed, dejected, totally beaten down

**144**

and alienated. Whether the gang threat is real or not, Dr. C. says it's another signal to Dwight that life is stacked up against him.

Andy Sills (The Drinker) is now on his second motorcycle, this one, like the others, obtained through trade-ins, courtesy of Abbie and her parents. Foster keeps close tabs to make certain Andy attends classes, which he sometimes tries to avoid. He is helping the mother obtain Medicaid for one of her daughters, but she is fearful of applying because of an earlier involvement in Medicaid fraud. Poor Foster never envisoned, when becoming Master Counselor, all the directions he'd be going.

## Thursday, January 24, 1985

HRS Counselor Valdez was outside chambers waiting for me. I recognized the look, having seen it before on Foster. He was going to break it to me gently, as if I had a vested interest in only good news. Quality HRS field counselors not only are out there when clients need them, but suffer with them as well. Valdez, formerly a successful lawyer in Havana, a Castro émigré, now totally immersed in his new career, was suffering. His tale indeed was sad.

Each time he has met with Evian Vilars and his parents, another guard has come down. As a result, the youth is more open with both Valdez and his therapist, and the parents look upon Valdez as a confidant. The final veil was brushed aside yesterday. It wasn't a pleasant revelation. The parents are frightened for their lives and for the sanity of their son. Unburdening themselves was difficult. For months they had viewed their roles as protective and supported Evian's line that things have changed for the better. Yesterday morning, the father telephoned Valdez, urging an emergency meeting: "You are the only person I can talk to." Over a cup of coffee, Mr. Vilars, on the verge of tears, admitted he had deceived Valdez. "Evian has two personalities," he said. "Here at home my wife, the two children, and I are frightened to death of him. He threatens us all the time. In the outside world, with you and the therapist, he's a fine young man. None of the medicine or therapy have helped him, but as loyal parents, we covered up for him. Lately, it has been getting worse."

Last time his vision of breaking into a school as a military maneuver brought out his illness. This time, he was at war with Trans-Ams, Porsches, and Camaros. Among his other fixations, he apparently dreams of owning expensive cars and has been demanding the family buy him one, an impossibility on his father's postal-employee wages. Upon their refusal, he flies into a rage, threatening to rush into the street, kill all drivers of those vehicles, then return to the house to put a bullet through his head so that they may see and know how strongly he feels. The mother confirmed these actions. He wakens her at 2:00 A.M. to continue the discussion on his obsession with fancy cars. She says they are so fearful for the safety of the two younger children that they dare not go to sleep.

I listened transfixed. This unfortunate family was protecting a menace in their household, while the "system" is unaware and smugly goes through its rituals, pretending expertise when in fact it's pure guesswork. We might as well be using incantations. "He needs to be in a hospital," pleaded Valdez. In the past, the experts had always testified in court that the problem could be handled on an outpatient basis. Besides, how do I know they'll do anything more for him in a hospital?

Trying to keep calm, I directed Valdez on a course of action: "Have the police pick him up immediately. Make certain they know he is dangerous. Once he's in the lockup, call Dr. R. and arrange a conference. Maybe the doctors will listen now."

Reflecting on what has happened in this case, I was first grateful that no one had been hurt while we were exploring the avenues of treatment for Evian. Not until the realization struck me that he was receiving special attention only because of my chance involvement did the real truth sink in. Under normal everyday conditions of a crowded court calendar, this case likely would have passed through in the rush of others, unnoticed and unattended.

I had some questions for Dr. R. that needed answering. He works in our clinic and has been monitoring Evian's treatment by the Jackson Memorial Hospital doctors:

"Why had the outpatient treatment rather than hospitalization been recommended at the first sign of illness?"
Dr. R.: "It is important to first determine if the patient can adjust in a normal setting with medication and therapy since the ultimate goal is to stabilize the patient in his regular surroundings."
"Why didn't the therapist want to meet with the parents?"
Dr. R.: "He first wanted to establish a relationship with Evian."
"Is confinement better for him medically or is this only for security purposes?"

*Dr. R.:* "Confinement will bring him to grips with the reality of his problem and he'll get closer observation by the staff."
"What can be done immediately?"
*Dr. R.:* "I will set up a battery of tests to determine if he's schizophrenic. He'll need hospitalization or treatment in some security facility."

I told Dr. R. that neither U.S. Supreme Court Chief Justice Warren E. Burger, the College of Cardinals, nor Freud's return to earth will get Evian released. He nodded in agreement, scheduling tests for next Tuesday.

Evian was no problem, going quietly with the police. Counselor Valdez was there waiting at the detention center. "Why am I here?" Evian asked. When told, he said he had only been teasing his parents about a car, as other kids did. That afternoon in court, confirming what had gone on, I formally ordered him held for psychiatric examination and asked the public defender's social-work staff to look into this case. We are going to need all the help available.

## Friday, January 25, 1985

Foster's glowing reports on Jamie Forest (The Nuisance) are so broadbrushed that I decided to visit the Dade Marine Institute (DMI) and view him firsthand. It was visitors' day, and Jamie was assigned as my tour guide. He took me from classroom to classroom describing the use of air canisters and masks for underwater diving as well as navigation charts for the boats to enter and leave Biscayne Bay. He only had a rudimentary understanding of the process, but made a serious effort to sound informed.

DMI, located on Rickenbacker Causeway, nestling alongside the Seaquarium, consists of a compound of portable classrooms placed in a circle around a thatched chickee that serves as an outdoor gathering place between classes. DMI has a dollar-a-year lease with the Seaquarium, for which the institute occasionally performs chores involving dolphins, whales, and other performing mammals. Because of the glistening seascape amid the sand and palms, it is an idyllic location. The youngsters, most of them black, spend the day there, while living at home, and seem to have made the adjustment from hot Liberty City pavement to cool open waters.

Jamie readily admitted not knowing much about seagoing experiences, explaining that he had asthma and besides he didn't like the water. He pointed to the plant nursery, saying that's where he spent most of his time. His earlier conversation had been jumbled, uncertain, mixed with nervous laughter. Now he spoke slowly, telling me about each of the plants. Maybe they've found something Jamie can latch onto.

In one of the classrooms, three older boys were sitting at a table poring over charts relating to budgets, bank-deposit interest, and other monetary matters. These were graduates of FEI, now in the last stage of their sentence: living at home, going for job interviews, preparing for release to society. They were businesslike, telling me their plans and describing how their "attitudes" had changed. Each spoke clearly and directly to me, showing confidence in their ability. How long, I wondered, will it take before those neighborhood gangs win them over? Would all the civilities drummed into them by Danny Grizzard at Last Chance Ranch outlast the realities of their old neighborhood? How many job turndowns would be required to make them forget the new and go back to the old ways? Where was Troy Sultan, I asked? As far as they knew, he was still at FEI.

On the way out, I stopped to chat with Nick Millar, director of DMI. He was the all-American type you'd like your daughter to bring home. A lot like Danny Grizzard, he could do it all: boating, hunting, athletics. Whatever the manly art, Millar, a six-foot-five-inch bearded Viking, looked and acted the part. He was cautious about Jamie's prospects, being particularly concerned about his reputation for selling stolen property. When I had asked Jamie about that earlier, he gushed with laughter, denying the charge. "It's just talk," he said. Millar likes Jamie, even though he alternates between being the camp cutup and the camp troublemaker. But Millar fears the youth will return to his old ways once no overseer is around. He sees Jamie as the hustler and survivor who believes a black street kid can only make it through fighting and shortcuts. I told Millar my theory about the boy's undeveloped intelligence. "Do you see a glimmer of quickness and alertness in him?" I asked.

"Jamie isn't retarded," he answered. "But he isn't bright either. He may make it out there, but it won't be on hard work, intellect, or morality." That's a tough sentence.

Millar wasn't more helpful with Troy Sultan. Apparently his family still can't be located and, because housing is not available for him in Miami, he'll stay at FEI until some relative or friend comes forward. That's too bad. Troy's progress at FEI earned a transfer to DMI, but no one is on hand to aid in transition to the community. George LaMont's staff will check old court files in the hope of finding some relative to look after Troy.

## Monday, January 28, 1985

Laurence Samuel                                        January 21, 1985
FEI, Venus, Florida
To: Mr. Seymour Gelber
    Well I'm glade you gave a nother chance, but i wish that i would
have learned but i'm learning from my mistake. i'm up hear learning how to work and make a living, cause they teach you a lot
about your self, and you learn alot of things you never knew, i
wish it would have stop at state school, but it went a little longer i
no it's going to stop at this, it's taking a lot of time out of my life
up hear, but i've got to deal with it until the time i go home and
that going to be a little while form [from] know, so i'ma doing
good, and mr. foster came up hear to see me and talk for a good
while. well i'm running out of words to say but i think this is
going to teach me, and we went to a prison today and i don't think
i wan't to go there so i'm going to stop going the wrong way know.
                                                    from: Laurence

Laurence's command of the English language is primitive at best. It's a sad commentary that, despite such dismal communication skills, our best option for him is a "social" promotion out of junior high to pursue a high-school basketball career. He hasn't the slightest idea how to construct a sentence, and spelling is pure happenstance. This is the first letter I have received from an FEI inmate, so I assume it was not a class assignment, as often is the case in other programs. Usually, the mail from imprisoned youngsters lauds the program, describes the great change effected, then asks for help on an early release. Laurence's letter is a bit more reflective, and I suppose, if he is thinking about who and what he is, his stay there may be worthwhile.

## Tuesday, January 29, 1985

It looks like culinary arts will never receive one of our students. Every time I point one of Foster's kids in that direction, something

**149**

goes awry. This time it was Marco Zargula (The Charmer). Repentance after his last escapade was short-lived. He arrived promptly for his first class and proceeded to wow the instructor with his skill. I knew that would happen. Friday, the second day, Marco was a no-show. On Monday he didn't appear again, and Tuesday morning he once more straggled into my chambers behind Foster. I had a hunch that would happen. He was barely upright, only able to utter the weak excuse that he didn't have bus fare for school, and then collapsed in the chair, out of breath, obviously disoriented.

Foster's explanation that Marco had been on a drug binge this past weekend was hardly necessary. Never looking up from the morning newspaper, using a slow deliberate tone, I told Foster to take him out of my chambers and put him on the first bus to State School. Marco was numb to my displeasure, the effects of the weekend still with him.

Marco always had a drug problem, but it seemed something he could handle. He managed to have survived without drugs at State School, but since his return he's hardly been off them. Foster describes it thusly: "This time he's into cocaine—free basing to get a quicker, higher sensation. It will burn up your brains. Larchmont Gardens is an open drug market. Everyone has it, uses it. There's no way for a kid like Marco to escape."

We had a quick conference with Manning, concluding that this kid is an absolute loser. No matter what we do, he will play out his own scenario. Manning, the last remaining optimist in the world, predicted, "One of these days, on a drug spree, Marco will kill someone, or be killed."

Foster, in disgust, said, "This kid is so fucked up, he'll never be able to stand up."

I agreed with their worst estimates. "Now that each of us has that out of his system, what do we do?" I asked.

We decided to remove him from Larchmont Gardens by placing him in a local residential drug program, ultimately readmitting him to culinary arts. At least for now I want him near home. Foster favored an out-of-town drug program: "Some of these local drug programs have more drugs inside than outside. Besides, if he stays locally, he's sure to run back to Larchmont Gardens."

Back in court, I found Frankie Calcon, the youngest of the clan, before me on his first arrest. His mother sat there, rigid, knowing too well what was in store. A lot could be learned from a mother of seven—all regulars in the jail system—but she did not understand much or could not describe it. I asked the obvious question: "Why are your children always in trouble?" She looked for help from the Spanish interpreter and talking directly to him said, "I know the others are bad. I can do nothing. But Frankie my baby. I pray every day he gonna be the one. I cry when he arrested."

After that, what does one say to a mother, even the mother of those dreadful Calcons? "Is it true the Calcon family is returning to Puerto Rico?" I waited for the interpreter, but I had already seen the negative shake of her head. "Puerto Rico's gain and our loss," I muttered under my breath.

The afternoon calendar had another surprise. Getting Troy Sultan down here from FEI has not been a top priority, but the idea of studying him to test the effectiveness of FEI has intrigued me, as well as comparing him with brother Travis, who is going through the adult system. Everyone is lending a hand to locate the Sultan family, if one exists. The only contact seems to be brother Travis, who never has a parent present for his court date and only grunts when asked about his family. This afternoon, luck brought Travis's mother to court for the first time.

"Troy's coming home," I assured her.

"Troy's not my son. He and Travis are not even related. Travis is bad enough," she laughed, "I don't need Troy."

However, she did know the Troy Sultan family and would provide their new address. That's good news for Troy, bad news for my grand research experiment. Mrs. Sultan, not quite sure what this was all about, asked how long she would have to keep coming to court because she can't afford to take off from work. I told her that, as long as Travis continues to behave like Travis, she has a lot of visiting ahead.

## Wednesday, January 30, 1985

The lunchtime case staff presentation at the Mental Health Clinic for Evian Vilars was similar to the one I had attended some months back for Clark Carden. That one I had wandered into out of curiosity. This one involved a decision I would soon have to make that might affect someone's life. In attendance were psychologists, psychiatrists, clinical social workers, field counselors, and Evian's public-defender lawyer. Most of it was repeat information, but each new bit fleshed out the hapless Vilars family. What incident made Evian cross the line? Where did his life go so wrong that he felt it necessary to dress in dark garb that night with pistol cocked waiting in an empty school for an enemy that existed only in his mind? How did family relationships impact upon him?

Each staff report made it clearer that his father was the focal point. From a long line of military men, he dominated the household, ignoring his wife and daughter, and favoring Evian's younger and more aggressive brother. Although better educated, the mother accepted her subservient role, catering to the men in the family. Poor judgment seems to be their common bond. On one occasion, the parents set out to buy a modest $5,000 automobile, but a salesman talked them into a $14,000 Thunderbird, which some weeks later they traded in for an even more expensive car. Monthly payments for this car have so strapped the family that money is lacking for household expenses. Seeing the car only made Evian hate his father more. He asks why an old man should own a beautiful car while he has nothing He hates his mother for giving birth to him, and hates himself for being bald, ugly, and unpopular; actually, he's a well-proportioned, nice-looking young man who has a full head of black, curly hair. Both parents are frightened, knowing he has $200 he earned as an usher, with which he threatens to buy a gun.

Everything seems to be bound up in concerns about his sexuality. He is convinced girls laugh at him and people are always watching him. This probably all began with his "penis infantilism," for which he took hormone shots. In his early years, he confided these concerns to his father and in return would hear tales in detail how his father was a great lover. Instead of providing reassurance, Mr. Vilars cruelly referred to Evian's virginity, offering to take him to a prostitute. The boy vividly remembers his first day in school, upon arrival from Cuba, when he was beaten because he didn't fight back. Today, he sees driving a sleek automobile, playing military hero, and joining the Civil Air Patrol as tickets to transform himself from an unappealing drudge to a sophisticated man about town. In his case, however, these normal teenage visions become bizarre. The sight of young couples enjoying a drive in a car brings on an urge to kill. Identifying with serial murderers, he uses as models Christopher Wilder who went on a cross-country rape spree; Carl Brown, a local schoolteacher who became unhinged and machine-gunned eleven people to death; and Son of Sam, New York's wanton murderer of several years back. Evian was certain that some woman had misled or mistreated all of them.

**152**

As each new bit of information was presented, he loomed more menacing to me. The doctors, agreeing he was a serious problem, were uncertain about immediate action. What bothered me was their clinical attitude. To me he was a monster ready to break loose. To them he was a patient needing assistance like any other patient. They kept insisting he wasn't psychotic; therefore, mental hospitals would only provide short-term attention before returning him to outpatient treatment. True, he knows what's going on and is aware of his problem, but if that armed foray into the school in the middle of the night wasn't a departure from reality, what is?

Dr. R. said, "He's a danger to his family, but not a Hinckley yet. He will be a problem the rest of his life. Now he's only a menace to his family. Later he may be a threat to anyone around him." I asked Dr. R. how he could determine professionally the line of demarcation between being a life threat only to his family and not to anyone else who happens to be around at the wrong time. He said he meant that, at this time, the likelihood of action against those in closer proximity, namely his family, was greater. Dr. R. suggested a psychiatric hospital for adolescents.

Dr. B. was no more optimistic: "His prognosis is poor. Extremely volatile. He has only a tenuous touch with reality. He is not appropriate for long term institutionalization. Unless contained, he will kill himself or others." When asked the alternative to hospitalization, Dr. B. said Evian needed to move in with a relative and be placed under the care of a psychiatrist to both treat and medicate him. I wondered out loud what relative or friend would bring a ticking time-bomb like Evian into their home. Dr. B. said he didn't know.

Dr. O. commented: "He needs long term hospitalization and treatment. The Grant Hospital has an ideal program for him, but they are very expensive."

"Why can't he be placed in Florida State Hospital?" I asked. "Don't they have beds for people like Evian?"

His answer was to the point: "They will medicate him and, as soon as he quits hallucinating, they'll pronounce him cured and discharge him. He'll be out in thirty days. That's the goal of a state hospital. They don't want long-term serious problems. There are loads of people like Evian walking the streets, recently discharged from a state hospital."

Dr. B. joined Dr. O., saying that Evian was better off staying in the detention center lockup than in South Florida State Hospital. Someone else said that perhaps Evian should continue with the present therapist, who, drawing on the added knowledge now available, may begin to make progress.

So where are we? Dr. R.'s battery of tests plus this conference told me Evian was a schizophrenic psychopath, but not psychotic; his prognosis was poor; he needed intensive psychiatric help; his parents are likely to face death; and any others around him have cause to fear for their safety. The family health-insurance policy can't begin to meet the high cost of private hospitalization; the South Florida State Hospital will unload him; and HRS Purchase of Service is already way over budget for cases like this.

It was 2:00 P.M. and time for court. Ed Tutty, administrator of the Mental Health Clinic, who had chaired the staffing, closed the meeting with a question posed to me. "Have we been of any help?" "Not one damn bit," I answered. I could have been more polite, but I had hoped somehow to push this case out of the court arena into the medical domain, where it belonged. I walked out with Steve Levine, the young public defender, who told me we needed to find out a lot more about Evian's state of mind before taking action. Curtly I told him what I thought: "We know Evian's state of mind. Any number of additional psychiatric exams will only reaffirm that he's going to kill someone. My main concern is for the people out there, not Evian. Sure I want him to get better, but more importantly I don't want anyone killed while he's in the treatment process. And I don't want to get blamed for it."

I was upset, but there was no reason for me to be upset with the clinic people. They are doing their best with what they have. Everyone is edgy because we sense little can be done other than to hope medication can tranquilize Evian for the next thirty to forty years, assuming he takes his medication.

## Thursday, January 31, 1985

"Would you be available for a CRB meeting?" inquired the caller. It was scheduled for 2:00 P.M. tomorrow and I had a full calendar. "What's the problem?" I asked Willie Sims, director of the Community Relations Board. He said:

> There's this new place called Disco 183 up in the Carol City Shopping Center. It's the only activity for black kids on the weekend. On Friday night, there are 2,000 kids inside the disco, and 2,000 more in the

parking lot. There's at least one shooting every weekend. Last week, four were shot, one died. Police confiscate an arsenal of guns and knives, but mostly the police officers assigned there are intimidated by the crowds. The youth gangs have a ball causing disruptions. Most of the action takes place in the parking lot, and therefore management doesn't feel responsible. They hired five off-duty police officers and that's all they are willing to do. It's an explosive situation waiting to become a disaster. We want the state attorney to file an injunction in circuit court closing down Disco 183 as a public nuisance.

The injunction suit was assigned to a court other than mine. He only wanted a bit of encouragement. I told him most judges are reluctant to close down a business unless evidence is strong that every effort has been exhausted, but it was certainly worth the effort. For months I've been trying in vain to involve Dade County officials in proposals to set up an outreach program to channel gangs into more productive directions. A violent outburst at Disco 183 will probably be required to shake the powers into action. Regrettably, only a riot brings the Chamber of Commerce and other leaders to life . . . the day after.

## Friday, February 1, 1985

Dr. C. believes his counseling sessions with Dwight Anderson (The Migrant) may be bringing him out. After one of those visits, I chatted with the boy and found him as noncommittal as ever. To my probing questions, he responded with a few garbled words, turned his head away, or just glared. "Why do you beat up those little kids on the bus?" I asked. "Some of them are bigger," was all he said in reply. Going nowhere in our conversation, I ended with my shape-up or ship-out speech. "I'll do good," he mumbled in response, then glared again as he walked out of my chambers.

Dr. C. and I agree on one thing. He now supports my position that Dwight is better off at home under the guidance of Foster and the Master Counselor Program. That troubles me too because I'm no longer so sure home is the best place.

## Monday, February 4, 1985

Lester Burrows (The Runner) is as elusive as ever. If some of that adroitness could be channeled in other directions, he'd be a captain

**155**

of industry. His weakness is getting into trouble; his strength is managing to avoid paying the price. A few days ago, while looting someone's living room, he was confronted by the returning home-owner. As the victim rushed by him to phone the police, Lester ran out the front door. A half hour later, accompanied by a police officer, the victim identified Lester several blocks away, quietly playing a pinball machine in a game room at the Omni Hotel. This is a high-priced hotel that provides not only expensive suites for visiting South Americans, but also two floors of wide arcades featuring handsome boutiques, as well as play and food areas aimed at attract-ing the young city crowd. Although not the intended market, large numbers of black and Latin kids, living nearby, who don't have much money to spend, come to enjoy the excitement of fancy surroundings.

Unlike Lester's modus operandi in the past, on this day homosex-uals were not his prey. This victim's house happened to be near the Omni Hotel at a time when he ran out of pinball money. Lester broke a jalousie in the kitchen door, gained entry by pushing in the screen, and was collecting valuables when interrupted. Like most teenage burlaries, this caper was neither planned nor executed with any foresight. He hadn't the slightest idea when the occupant might return, and, instead of hurriedly leaving the area, he sauntered back to the arcade, where police usually look for suspects.

When identified, Lester calmly pinged the last pinball, gave a bogus name, and accompanied the Miami police officer to the police station, where he was placed in a holding cell while the officer filled out the arrest form. Lester had been this route many times before. Leaving for a moment to get his sergeant to sign the form, the officer returned to find the cell door open and its occupant gone. He had just walked out of the holding cell, down the stairs, and out the building.

Foster asked why I was laughing. The last time I had been at the security-conscious Miami Police Department building, I had to pro-duce an I.D., was given a badge, and provided an escort to make certain I wouldn't wander off course. Here was little Lester casually strolling through the security checkpoints, untouched by human hands.

Perhaps the embarrassed Miami Police Department will now make an all-out effort to locate Lester. We learned from the incident that he is flitting around town, scrounging for funds, patronizing pinball machines at the Omni Hotel, and using the alias of Keith

Mervin, which name we'll check out in the computer. We also learned that his luck at avoiding the system is still holding. Foster is certain that real soon, somewhere along the way, he'll be caught again. Sure he will.

## Tuesday, February 5, 1985

After his brief stay at culinary arts, terminated by a weekend drug binge, Marco Zargula (The Charmer) spent a week in the cooler. He now looks like his old self. Hair slicked back, wearing a borrowed U.S. Olympics sports jacket, he is a lot more relaxed and seems amenable to the drug program chosen for him. The Here's Help program prescribes a strict thirty-day orientation period. No visitors, no leaving the campus, and someone with the client at all times. If he makes it through this regimen, then perhaps we'll follow with culinary arts.

In order for these kinds of drug programs to work, 110 percent cooperation from the clients is essential. It's hard to believe Marco is so inclined. He'll go along only so far as necessary. As a residential facility, Here's Help is not secure. The program has a fairly good reputation, but it will take magicians to hold Marco, let alone cure him. A sliding-scale fee arrangement is in effect. We may have to fall back on lawyer fines from the Children's Fund.

## Wednesday, February 6, 1985

Today, in court, I signed the order sending Evian to the Jackson Memorial Hospital Crisis Center for a three-day examination. He sat there, dejected and confused at what was going on. Small signs of beard growth were showing on his face as he glanced up at me from the defense bench. He looked wan and worn, obviously deteriorating in lockup. Two weeks have gone by since I warned the top HRS brass that this case will become a public scandal if adequate services are not provided.

After my public statements that Evian would receive the best attention the state could provide, I am beginning to have some doubts. Everyone is cooperating, but not much progress is evident. The JMH recommendation will be crucial as to follow-up treatment, but I fear they will find him a bright, amiable young man, whose occasional fantasizing needs no more than proper medication on an outpatient basis. If they do, they'll hear some screaming, and it won't be coming from one of the wardrooms.

## Thursday, February 7, 1985

Progress with Dwight Anderson (The Migrant) can be measured in inches, but we are grateful for any signs of forward movement. Today, I signed a check for ten dollars to buy an alarm clock, compliments of the Children's Fund. The bus is still the problem. He hates traveling on the special school bus for retarded kids, who he says slobber over him. He won't arise at 7:00 A.M. for the public transit bus that would deliver him to school on time, and he has to fight the gang to make the next bus that arrives late. We are hopeful that he can learn to set the alarm clock in time to make the early bus before the neighborhood toughs begin harassing him.

Dwight's attitude seems to have improved. He acts as if he wants to attend school. If the bus problem can be resolved before he is suspended for excessive absences, he may yet get on track. Reports from the Boys' Club are also more favorable, and the best sign yet is that Dwight is trying to repair his lawn mower, which apparently collapsed about the same time he started downhill. Small signs, indeed

## Monday, February 11, 1985

This morning has been all Dwight Anderson (The Migrant). First, his classroom teacher, Ms. Edison, telephoned to commiserate with me about the frustration of getting him to school. "It's now 10:05 A.M.," she said, "and he's still not here." Hers is the Very Exceptional class for kids who are mental retardees or suffer from learning disorders or learning disabilities. Dwight has a little bit of each. She has a special interest in him, but every effort has been rebuffed. At the onset, she contacted the school transportation department to make certain the bus arrives on schedule. It does, but Dwight doesn't. On one occasion, physically threatened by him, she refused to press charges, thus avoiding his expulsion. When he looked downcast at not receiving Christmas gifts, she organized a party, specially for him, including an extra large tree and all the trimmings. She has provided incentive rewards to maintain his interest in class work.

He has responded with indifference. "What more can I do?" she asked. In the middle of my pep talk, urging her to continue being patient, I could hear Dr. Pat Mooney, supervisor of the Boys' Club, telling my secretary he too wanted to talk to me about Dwight. Ms. Edison concluded on the sad note that Dwight only admires and pays attention to brother Derrick, who is still on runaway status from a residential program for the retarded.

Apparently Dwight is an all-American irritant. It was now Dr. Mooney's turn to be unhappy with him. "The Boys' Club can't stand Dwight's odor," complained the doctor. "He's going fine with school work, but they can't get too close to him. His clothes are never washed at home."

First it was musk, now it's his clothes. The problem seemed unimportant, but, aware of the general frustration, I listened sympathetically to Dr. Mooney. We were interrupted by Cornelius Foster's entry announcing that Marco had run from the Here's Help drug program. Ignoring that fact, for the moment, I asked him about Dwight. He reported that the alarm clock had been provided but had not yet been put to use. Mooney, now talking directly to Foster, continued complaining about Dwight's odor, until finally Foster asked, "Am I supposed to bathe him? Wash his clothes? Wake him in the morning? You know I didn't take him to raise."

Dr. Mooney, not wanting to offend Foster, said the Boys' Club wouldn't give up on Dwight. They would do whatever had to be done, even toss him in a shower. Foster smiled, so did I, and then Mooney joined in with a big grin. All together for our boy Dwight. His situation borders on the pathetic. Ms. Edison, Dr. Mooney, Dr. C., Cornelius Foster, and others are vying to befriend him—all rejected—while Dwight prefers his retarded brother as a model.

Marco's sudden departure from the Here's Help drug program came as no surprise. He claimed to be homesick and after two days was gone. The program is willing to take him back because many youngsters run away in the first few days, only to return to become receptive students. Foster is off to Larchmont Gardens to locate and return Marco.

## Tuesday, February 12, 1985

Thus far, the effort to find effective treatment for Evian Vilars is still at a standstill. He's been sitting in lockup for almost three weeks, untouched by medical attention. Last week, he was to be screened at

Jackson Memorial Hospital (JMH) for long-term admittance as a mentally disturbed patient to South Florida Hospital. When he arrived, no one knew who he was, why he was there, or what to do with him. One JMH psychologist declared he was not a crisis patient, a nurse made another appointment for next week, and someone else mistakenly sent him to Ward D for adult felons. He was finally unceremoniously shipped back to our detention center carrying a message that he didn't need emergency attention and would we be kind enough to learn appropriate admission procedures. The foul-up occurred because our people were so busy talking to each other about the boy that no one had contacted JMH to make clear the purpose of the examination. Three wasted weeks.

Still stewing over this bureaucratic ineptness, I faced a sad Mrs. Vilars, in court, wailing over what was happening to her son: "He has lost his school, lost his job, lost his mother, lost his medicine. Please let me take him. I will find a hospital for him." Several weeks earlier, she had feared for her own life, but now her maternal side wanted help for her son at any personal risk. Agonizing and unhappy, all her feelings welled over. The poor woman, unaware of the long, troubled road ahead, believes that once her son is hospitalized, recovery is sure to follow. I avoided responding, knowing things are not likely to improve.

Back in chambers, a hurry-up plan was put in gear to recover the wasted weeks. Should we shift gears, avoiding JMH and instead shooting for a private hospital? Call the newspapers and make Evian a cause célèbre? I sat there wondering what to do.

In the midst of my ponderings, Nancy Traad walked in, telling me she was agitated, angry, and frustrated, needing to talk to someone or she'd explode. She is an activist volunteer, currently trying to raise half a million dollars for a shelter home for abused children and then convince the state Legislature to provide another half-million dollars for the project. Her group has thus far raised only about $50,000, but she is undaunted. A woman of boundless energy, wife of a prominent surgeon, she is a new-style Junior Leaguer, no longer interested in teas for debs. Whenever a cause for children appears, Nancy hears the call. She complains about the horrible conditions in foster care: children packed in back rooms; hospitals ignoring them legislators and social workers, callous. She wanted to file a lawsuit closing down one of the worst foster homes, where she said a baby is dying from lack of nurturing. "Failure to thrive" is the official designation when the child has lost its desire to live. Both the hospital and the foster home mother have ignored the baby, who she said looks like one of the starving children in Ethiopia. Listening patiently, telling her I was sorry about the situation, I in fact envied her. The chance to express anger and be righteous over good causes is a wonderful luxury. "You have an advantage over us. As a volunteer, you can afford to explode. We don't have the time. Maybe that's why social workers seem callous to you. They have a whole slew of reports on their desks topping your horror stories and they can't get to any of them."

Mrs. Traad departed, barely hearing me, brimming with determination to file the lawsuit. I sat there, still uncertain about the direction to take for Evian.

## Wednesday, February 13, 1985

Gaining admittance for Evian to any hospital becomes more and more complicated. Talking to our clinic staff, I keep hearing the same line about public hospitals: "There are so many crazies out there a lot worse than Evian that the state rejects almost everybody." It was a flat turndown for him at the private hospital. It wants $8,500 up-front money. No ifs or buts. At best, his insurance covers only a few weeks, and the hospital is not about to be stuck with some long-term psychotic carrying short-term insurance.

Back to JMH and South Florida Hospital. This time, Clinic Director Tutty will make certain no snafu occurs in processing Evian for admission. Tutty was not too optimistic as to the likelihood of acceptance: "The JMH doctors will not refer him to South Florida Hospital unless he's actively psychotic, that is, he is out of touch with reality when they interview him. Little attention will be paid to past behavior. Then there's a court hearing before a special master who must approve commitment. He finally may be admitted, but that doesn't mean they'll keep him." Bucking the system isn't easy, even from the top.

## Thursday, February 14, 1985

The voice recited, "There was a little boy who had a curl right in the middle of his forehead. When he was good, he was very very good. But, when he was bad, he was horrid." It was Nick Millar, head of

**161**

Dade Marine Institute, describing Jamie Forest (The Nuisance). He is impossible to control. Yesterday, he fashioned a stick with nails, attacking one of his fellows. The day before, he used a hatchet to attack someone else. He has a quick fuse as well as a short attention span and alternates between telling farfetched tales and reacting violently when called "retard." Millar says one moment he's a lovable card, and the next second he explodes. He's frightened of water, sleeps through classes, and, other than showing an interest at the plant nursery, is a complete hindrance to the DMI program.

His presence is suffered only because of my involvement. I asked Millar to hold on with Jamie while I sought additional help. The youth has been examined in every possible way by psychologists, and that route is no longer feasible. Some time back, Judge Gladstone suggested a neurological workup at the Mailman Center for Retarded Children. Perhaps they can medicate him, at least to control his outbursts. He and Dwight Anderson (The Migrant) display the same erratic behavior patterns, though Jamie is a lot more outgoing, probably because of a very caring, concerned mother. Dwight, withdrawn, Jamie, open—the results with these two have been the same.

It was one of the few cold days in Miami, and Foster knew Marco Zargula (The Charmer) would be enjoying the warmth of his bed that morning. He covered the front of the house while Deputy Court Administrator Larry Hanes guarded the back door. They were ready. Several days ago, when Foster came looking, Marco rushed out the back before Foster could ring the front bell. This time, both were inside the house, surrounding Marco's bed before he was awake. He came quietly. What to do with him? Manning and Foster nixed trying a local program, agreeing on other sites available in Fort Lauderdale, Orlando, and Tallahassee. "Choose whichever you like, but send him far away from Larchmont Gardens," I instructed.


## Monday, February 18, 1985

Pressure needs to be exerted on the examining doctors at JMH to make certain Evian receives the attention he needs. They don't want bad publicity, malpractice suits, or judges leaning on them. My message to them was clear: reject Evian and be held publicly responsible for any further criminal act he commits. This form of pressure may raise a few medical tempers, but hardball is more relevant in this case than professional gentility.

Going Up Is Only a Trip

## Wednesday, February 20, 1985

Getting Marco admitted into a residential drug program may not be as difficult as obtaining bed space for Evian, but it's still no easy matter. Because the drug problem is flourishing, ample programs are available, but most are voluntary, all are expensive, and none are short on applicants. For Marco, out-of-town was preferable and security essential. The Disc Village program administrator in Tallahassee accepted him, but the board of directors insisted on first priority for local residents, putting Marco's admission about two months down the road. What to do in the meantime? The Orlando and Fort Lauderdale programs were rejected for other reasons. Fortunately, Foster found that the Humana Hospital was willing to take him at a cost of $7,000 for a forty-five-day treatment program. I blanched at the fee, but Foster assured me that was the going rate. This hospital, located in nearby Hollywood, Florida, is part of a national chain, famous for introducing mechanical heart procedures. It is a lockup institution, able to hold Marco, and reputedly an effective drug program is operated. Marco reacted to all of this by saying he was now ready to return to Here's Help, in Miami, to which Foster responded, "Oh no! We aren't going through that scene again."

Before the day was out, Foster had worked out the mechanics for admission to Humana Hospital. If, upon completion, Marco needs more help, Disc Village will be available, and, if drug-free, back to culinary arts. The turn of events brought a spark back to Foster. He needs an occasional upper after these daily struggles.

"When does he start?" I asked. Looking at his watch and walking briskly out the door, Foster replied, "In forty-five minutes; that's how long it will take me to drive him to Humana."

Good ol' Foster. Every time I begin to wonder why we are doing all this, he evinces a new spurt of enthusiasm and a little bit brushes off on me.

## Thursday, February 21, 1985

Apparently heat applied in the right places has a salutary effect. HRS Counselor Valdez and the public defender's social worker, Judith Lieber, accompanied Evian to Jackson Memorial Hospital, where a red carpet awaited them. An immediate examination by the head of the JMH Crisis Center found "some evidence of psychopathology

**163**

warranting further intensive study." Good. In addition, administrators at the state's South Florida Hospital indicated a willingness to accept him—if he were "appropriate." "What does all this mean?" I asked our clinic director, Ed Tutty. "Will Evian now get the attention he needs?" Tutty measured his answer, making certain I received the information due me, but equally certain the medical fraternity he dealt with daily was not placed in too bad a light: "You have attracted their attention. They don't want to take you on. Evian will get what he needs for now. As to long range, they may not have the answer. It could well be back to outpatient therapy."

Translation: "Don't be overimpressed with your influence. In the end, JMH and South Florida will do what they want."

We'll wait and play it one day at a time. Right now Evian is in the hospital under the care of high-quality clinicians. Should it appear that their conclusions represent the state of the art, I'll have to accept them, despite my own intuitive feelings. If, on the other hand, it looks like they are hastening Evian out of their medical care because of lack of space or budgetary limitations, then I'll use the court and the media to force other actions.

At least Evian has a chance for treatment, but what happens to those other disturbed kids whose case histories Tutty's group presents weekly?

## Friday, February 22, 1985

Whenever Foster reports on Dwight Anderson (The Migrant), I feel like a captive, hands tied, lacking ability to influence what is happening. Other than taking him out of his home permanently, what more can be done? His biweekly visits with Dr. C. offer some hope, but psychologists don't possess magic powers, even though a black psychologist probably cuts down some of the barriers.

This was a positive report, but there's always tomorrow. Believe it or not, Dwight has been setting the alarm, arising at 5:30 A.M. to make the early public bus, thus avoiding both the gang waiting to waylay him as well as the company of his retarded classmates.

"What about the smell problem?" Foster beamed in response: "His mother is finally cooperating. She bought a bottle of cologne, but didn't know whether it belongs on his body or his clothes. She put it on both. He still smells a little."

"Why not suggest a bath?" I asked. "So long as we can keep the alarm clock going, we'll somehow manage to keep the cologne going," he assured me.

## Monday, February 25, 1985

The computer didn't tell us anything about the Lester Burrows (The Runner) alias, Keith Mervin, except that he also uses the name Gary Pittman. Without much ado, Foster has been quietly scouring Lester's old Liberty City haunts, and George LaMont has had police units on prowl for him. No one has had any success. Lester is somewhere, but obviously always a few steps ahead of law enforcement.

## Tuesday, February 26, 1985

Foster was wrong about the cost of treatment for Marco at the Humana Hospital drug program. It wasn't $7,000 for forty-five days, as I had been told. How about $9,000 for thirty days? Three hundred bucks a day on Marco. Payment is mostly through Medicaid. It is ironic that early intervention programs get short shrift from legislators, yet these kinds of astronomical costs, when it is almost too late, go relatively unnoticed.

# 6

---

## Watching the Dark
## Side Get Darker
## Makes It Harder to
## See the Light

**Tuesday, February 26, 1985**

Foster delivered Andy Sills (The Drinker) like a father escorting the
bride down the aisle to the waiting groom. Among all his charges,
Andy is the one big plum, particularly because my early predictions
had been all negative. Here was Andy, in the Judge's chambers, still
unsure of himself but now able to carry on an extended conversation,
something neither he nor most other delinquents would usually care
to engage in with a judge.

In the past, he had always been accompanied by his mother; it
seemed appropriate for the "new" Andy to be here on his own. He's a
part-time counterman in a mall, carving sandwiches, and Abbie
works in the same mall at an Italian restaurant. I asked if he had his
lunch in the big paper bag he carried, and rather proudly he opened
it, showing me his counterman's uniform.

Although pleased with his progress, Foster and I had wondered
about his source of money to purchase cars and motorcycles, continuously trading them. All the used-car dealers we know always demand cash on trade-ins. Gifts from Abbie and her parents were possible, but a burglary here and there is also a possibility. Andy
laughed at the suggestion: "Abbie and I saved some money. Her
mother gave us the rest for the first car. It broke down. I fixed it and

traded for a motorcycle, which ended up a tree. I fixed it. Traded for a car which never got started. Traded again for a motorbike. That also broke down. Ended with nothing. I'm now down to my old bicycle."

Somehow he sounded more like a kid seeking to find his way than a burglar: "I want to get a better job now so I can make some money. Why do I have to go to school six months more? I can get twenty-eight dollars an hour fixing dents and welding parts. I'm good at that right now."

This was a powerful statement from someone who, only a year ago, favored all-night beer-drinking and some housebreaking on the side. He didn't need much prompting to talk about his family, telling me with pride in his voice that no serious problems existed in the household.

I couldn't resist asking the question every social worker saves for the end of an interview: "How do you feel about yourself now?" He gave the answer every social worker wants to hear and believe: "I don't drink beer anymore and I feel better about it. I stay away from my old friends because I don't want to go to jail. You and Mr. Foster have helped me become better. I think I have grown out of all my bad things."

Wow! Not only did my perennial beamer, Foster, beam, but so did I. Most interesting was Andy's apparent lack of dependence on Abbie. He talked about her, but he sounded independent, with some new fiber in him that he alone controlled. Could it be that the collapse I expect when Abbie is no longer in the picture may never materialize? I offered a compromise by suggesting he find a job as an auto-body repairman and work out an agreement for work-study credit, in lieu of attending class.

Andy may be a shrewd number who knows the right chords to play, but I think, even if it's only pretense, the good guys are slowly co-opting him.

## Wednesday, February 27, 1985

The several-hundred-mile mission to Fish Eating Creek was worth it. Foster returned buoyed at the experience and was certain Laurence Samuel (The Fighter) appreciated seeing his familiar face. Laurence is still in Phase I, considered the punishment stage, entitled to neither visitors nor telephone calls. It's all cold water and pulling palmettos. On yesterday's work assignment he was planting vegetables, and before that he was riding horses, rounding up cattle, and stacking sod on trailers. He doesn't like any of it one bit. In May, Phase II will bring a less taxing living situation.

Foster describes him as suddenly sprouting in all directions, with bony shoulders turning to hard muscle, a few inches taller, and about fifty pounds heavier. He's working on his GED, controlling his temper, and the staff consider him to be a model student. It's all "yes, sir" and spit-and-polish attention. Laurence still has a long way to go, but, because Foster is alongside, his chances will be a lot better.

## Thursday, February 28, 1985

It took a while but Foster finally convinced the Mailman Center doctors that he wanted a neurological rather than a pediatric examination for Jamie (The Nuisance). In all probability, the neurological will only confirm what we know. Meanwhile, Jamie drifts along at DMI, sometimes the friendly little sprite but at other times an absolute disaster. Last week, he was a menace; today, he's everybody's favorite. Over a cup of coffee at this morning's DMI board of trustees breakfast meeting, DMI Director Nick Millar extolled Jamie's behavior, at least for today. He's been working diligently aboard a fishing boat helping wire the electrical system. So long as others don't provoke him, he gets along fine.

Waiting in chambers for my return was Jamie. He had to be back at the Mailman Center in an hour and was on hand for one of those quick, friendly little chats with the judge. Unlike the others, Jamie enjoys these dialogues. As usual, he was relaxed, smiling, full of talk, obviously performing for me. I said, "Would you like to learn how to cook so that you can earn a good salary?" (Somehow I'll get one of these kids into culinary arts yet.)

"I'd rather work in a service station or Burger King. If I become a cook, I'll see a nice young lady come into the restaurant and while I be looking at her, the food will burn."

"The DMI bus driver says you gave your mother a hard time this morning. How come?"

"She gave me the hard time, shaking and pushing me. It was all about garbage. Who takes it out. It was my brother's week. Last week it was my cousin's. My mama doesn't know much about the garbage and beat on me for not taking it out. Next week, I'm putting a list on the wall. Let her beat on somebody else."

When I told him his mother deserved a medal for putting up with him, he roared in appreciation. Foster doesn't enjoy Jamie's little quips, as I do. He thinks they are a cover-up for a refusal to deal with reality. Nick Millar sees an equally bleak future, citing Jamie's failure to function in a group setting. The slightest provocation creates a tinderbox. It will be interesting to see how their assessments match those of the experts at the Mailman Center.

## Friday, March 1, 1985

Here we go with Dwight Anderson (The Migrant) again. He missed school all week. Monday it was a toothache; Tuesday, no clothes; Wednesday, the alarm didn't go off; and on and on. Foster is totally frustrated. The youth is indifferent to his threats, lacking both motivation and fear. Either he doesn't believe Foster will lock him up or doesn't care if he does. This is where we started. What to do? "Why not place him in a halfway house for a month to see how he performs away from that family?" asked Foster.

This was the action I have been avoiding for months, but the evidence is clear that Dwight is in a no-win situation. Considering his limited potential and his horrendous family situation, not even Foster moving in permanently, taking command of the household, could make a difference. True, Dwight has made progress avoiding law violations, but, without a rudimentary education and someone to look after him, this thirteen-year-old is doomed. I directed, "See if Dr. C. can perform some small miracle to get him back on track. If not, and if Dr. C. approves, let's find a halfway house." I made it sound like an ordinary order, but it was a big step for me. Making the kid whole again in his home situation had been a prime factor in the original concept.

## Monday, March 4, 1985

It was a gory Sunday. Dwight sported twenty-seven stitches in his head, and Jamie displayed a broken hand. Just children at play over the weekend. Dwight, visiting his grandmother, tried to halt a fight between two girl cousins. Instead, he caught a rock over the right temple, bursting his face wide open. Sewn up and swathed in a turban of bandages, he's back home, head still throbbing, but secure in the knowledge he's excused from school for another week. His appointment with Dr. C. has been rescheduled.

Jamie's story of his fisticuffs leaves a lot to be believed, but the evidence clearly shows a broken hand. On the way to the store, a gang of boys attacked him, and, according to his account, in the ensuing struggle he punched a wall hard enough to fracture a knuckle. He, too, received emergency hospital treatment and had a big bandage to show for the incident.

The weekend experience of Marco Zargula (The Charmer) didn't draw any blood, but it drew a lot of attention. As on past occasions in other programs, he passed through the Humana Hospital five-day orientation with flying colors. So impressed were the staff members that he received a four-hour pass to visit his family. That was a mistake. His mother picked him up, and, according to her version, he enjoyed a wonderful Sunday visit, happy to see the family, playing with the dog and watching television. In truth, he was hardly home before he was out the door in the company of one of the Calcon brothers smoking a joint. Then, in order to keep a supply available during his stay at Humana, they spent the afternoon concealing marijuana in a seam of Marco's shoe. Once back, he made arrangements for someone else to take his drug urine analysis exam. Sneaky as he is, the Humana screeners spotted his little ploy immediately. Marco cried, broke down, and confessed the entire scenario. Impressed with his honesty and their sympathy won over, they more than ever want to work with this potentially "fine young man."

Several conclusions can be reached from this incident. First and foremost, Marco is as manipulative and untrustworthy as ever. Secondly, orientation obviously made no impression upon him. In a matter of minutes, he was back to his old life-style. But, perhaps most significant, he did not run. He returned to Humana when he could have taken off with the Calcons. Maybe he really wants help this time.

## Thursday, March 7, 1985

Laurence Samuel (The Fighter) and I almost became pen pals, but it wasn't to be. Pleased at my response to his letter, he had assured

Foster I would be receiving return mail soon. Today, the message from FEI arrived, not in the form of a letter, but a frantic phone call from Gerald Johnson, the director of operations: "Laurence Samuel has gone off the deep end." Like all the FEI staff, Johnson is a cool character, and, though his voice lacked a frantic quality, the message was urgent: "For the past two weeks, starting the day after Foster's last visit, Laurence's bizarre behavior has the camp in an uproar. He seemed to be adjusting to FEI, but suddenly cracked up, or is pretending. First he set about burning the forest down."

Several thousand acres of combustible pine are located in this area, and, because Florida has recently had several mammoth forest fires because of lack of rain, this effort is a sure attention attracter. Johnson continued, and each statement indicated a worse situation: "We stopped him in time. Next he began sitting in the tractor, pretending to shift gears, driving the vehicle, when in fact he never turned on the ignition."

Every effort by staff to engage him in conversation was rebuffed with: "I'm James, not Laurence. Who's Laurence?" Johnson proceeded to explain that, no matter what Laurence does, he denies it a moment later. Names of staff and inmates change in the middle of a conversation. He will only talk to black counselors, threatening and throwing things at white ones. "Tonight," he challenges, "I'm going out to get some pussy-assed crackers." He is willing to talk to Johnson, who is black, but his conversation is no more lucid with him.

Both Johnson and Foster believe he's playacting, hoping for transfer to a mental hospital. Anything to avoid pulling palmettos. Conceivably, Laurence is clever enough to maintain this kind of charade, but it is also possible for a high-strung volatile personality to crack under the rigorous demands of Phase I. I told Johnson none of the psychologists had predicted this kind of behavior. He assured me FEI would continue to work with the youth and not overreact to his behavior. Should he, however, commit any crime, he will be prosecuted in their local courts, where they will throw the book at him.

Laurence clearly is traveling under a dark cloud. If he is "the budding psychopathic personality" described in an earlier examination, then he is destined for hospitalization and a lifetime of tranquilizing medications. If he's playacting, he's sure to mess up the game and pay a heavy price. No matter what happens, it will turn out badly.

## Friday, March 8, 1985

There was Marco Zargula (The Charmer) in a burgundy jump suit telling us he had just completed his daily two-mile run and a turn in the weight room. He's only been at Humana Hospital's Adolescent Drug Program a week and already has gained four pounds. The dietitian has him on supplements of vitamins and protein juice. One positive thing about him: he knows how to make an adjustment. No matter where he goes, before long he fits in. The life-style becomes his.

At three hundred bucks a day, Humana's claim to fame is to accept prospects other drug programs reject: the unmotivated ones, not wanting help. The goal is, with a thirty-day crash course, to instill a desire in the patient to want to help himself. Once that is established, the long-term treatment programs can take over.

Marco's counselor, a former drug-addict felon, looked and sounded like a man who had been there before. He spoke with authority as he described the youth: "He's a kid who'll get cocaine and marijuana however he can, and wherever he is. He's not an addict. It's just the excitement. He's a garbage collector, willing to take anything and try anything."

Marco sidled up to him, listening intently to each word, nodding agreement: "Now that I know the damage drugs can cause, I'll be different. The Calcons won't see me again."

There he goes again, acting The Charmer. Smiling in response, his counselor patted him on the head, saying, "Marco has the right attitude. Before long he'll be back in Larchmont Gardens free of drugs." Saying this mostly for the boy's benefit, he knew this would be no easy conversion. The counselor's statement raised an eyebrow of George LaMont, who was standing nearby. Foster shrugged in disbelief and walked over to the water cooler for a respite. No one was convinced.

Marco's therapist strongly believes she can make him feel responsible for his actions. That's unlikely in thirty days. It will take more than several weeks of common-sense talk to alter someone so complicated and confused. Drug programs, particularly expensive short-term ones, need to show fast progress. Despite the confidence displayed, it's hard to believe they can quick-fix the Marcos.

Sitting with me alone, Marco told me about his roommate, a young boy from a wealthy family who was scheduled for release

**172**

today, but wanted to stay rather than go to boarding school: "Last week this kid's mother and father came—both high, eyes pinpointed, holding on to each other. They don't want him home. The boy wants to get off drugs. He's afraid there are more drugs at boarding school. This is the only safe place for him." Marco's story may have been pure fiction, but, if true, it mirrors the kind of complexities that are associated with drug abusers.

Listening to Marco talk about his sister's problems, his brother's recent arrest, and his mother borrowing to raise bond for him made the whole effort seem futile. Why spend three hundred dollars a day to send Marco back home to this family of losers? As we left the Humana Hospital, the program director repeated the emphasis it places on motivation, and the therapist made arrangements to have Marco's mother in for a counseling session, while the counselor and Marco, side by side in their jump suits, jauntily walked through the security door back to the weight room.

On the way back to Miami, Court Administrator George LaMont, who hadn't said much during the series of interviews at the hospital and was apparently not too impressed, turned to Foster, telling him to call the Disc drug program in Tallahassee: "Maybe Humana will change Marco and maybe not. But it's going to be a long trip. We might as well start lining up all the residential programs we can find."

## Monday, March 11, 1985

The situation with Laurence Samuel took an even more confusing turn this afternoon as a result of Foster's two telephone calls to Fish Eating Creek. Denying any of the behavior attributed to him by the FEI staff, Laurence complained that he had offered to return to work, but instead has been confined to quarters. He sounded rational to Foster. The second call to Laurence's counselor reported that he was still playacting, creating turmoil in the camp. Foster's reaction to the two phone calls made sense: "It sounds like two different people. If he's really nuts, he would act that way with everybody. Why does he talk normal to me?" Monday morning, Foster will drive to Fish Eating Creek to see what he can uncover.

Before the day was out, Foster came by with still another page-one announcement. Jamie Forest (The Nuisance) has been arrested on

**173**

two burglary charges. Details are skimpy, but they apparently are old cases. Held in the Miami jail, he has been bombarding Foster with pleas for help, claiming he was "framed."

## Thursday, March 14, 1985

Last week's dramas continue to unfold at a rapid pace, but the puzzles are no nearer being pieced together. Foster, set to leave on Monday for Fish Eating Creek, had to cancel when advised that FEI had suddenly moved Laurence to a Ft. Myers jail. Saturday night, the youth punched a staff worker, brandished a stick threatening others, and, when the night-shift staffers were unable to handcuff him, the local police were called for assistance. Trundled off to Ft. Myers jail, he quieted down, claiming no recollection of what had happened. For the next forty-eight hours, a series of telephone conversations, Miami to Ft. Myers to Fish Eating Creek and back again, only confused the situation. Had FEI seized this opportunity to charge him with a crime as a pretext for ridding themselves of trouble? Last week, Laurence's strange behavior was taken in stride; now suddenly spirited out in the middle of the night, he was no longer welcome at FEI. A statement by an HRS intake worker in Ft. Myers confirmed my suspicions: "FEI has never done this before. This assault was of a minor nature. The local prosecutor doesn't want to prosecute. There was no need to have him arrested."

Further raising doubt was a call from FEI Operations Officer Gerald Johnson stating that Laurence was in Ft. Myers for a psychiatric exam but saying nothing about the criminal charges. I started to ask about Danny Grizzard's proud statement to me, months back, that FEI never gives up on their clients, but refrained for the moment. It was more important to get through to Laurence than debate FEI's motives.

Foster cranked up for another trip to Ft. Myers, but it wasn't to be. This time, the telephone called him back to drive his daughter to the hospital due to a bronchial attack: "It's in the family. We all have asthma." Since when do counselors have families with their own illnesses and problems?

Back to the three-city telephone dialogue. According to the latest word on Tuesday, the magistrate in Ft. Myers was declining to pros-

**174**

ecute, instead giving Laurence a stern warning to behave or else. That will hardly impress him. What about the psychiatric examination? Is he schizoid, a threat to himself or others? "It will take at least a month before we can see him," advised the Ft. Myers Mental Health Clinic. We can't wait that long. For Laurence, it's back in the van to Fish Eating Creek; another telephone call for me from FEI: "Can you arrange for an examination at the Dade County Clinic?"

"The minute he gets here," I responded.

It was Thursday before Foster finally arrived at Fish Eating Creek. They strolled the grounds together, Foster listening to Laurence complain about his treatment: "I don't know what I done wrong. All I want to do is do my time and go home. I ain't mad at no whitey. Why they treat me like this?"

It was a changed Laurence. He sounded normal but looked strange to Foster: "Eyes set in the back of his head. He don't remember anything. His hair is cut off and he keeps rubbing his head. He only wants to see his mother. I don't know if he's acting. He told an FEI counselor, 'I'm gonna beat this program. I'll be out in three months.' "

Foster came away uncertain as to the events. Operations Officer Johnson clarified the situation, quieting my earlier fears that FEI was giving up on Laurence. The FEI counselor in charge of the night shift had mistakenly involved the local police. According to Johnson, it was an error in judgment: "Until a medical examination finds him unfit, or he commits a serious crime, Laurence is our problem." I felt a lot better about FEI and Danny Grizzard after that statement.

The FEI staff was divided on Laurence's true condition. Some believe it indicates he needs hospitalization; others see it as a ploy. The believers were reinforced by the hard bump on the head Laurence had incurred several days before the forest-burning attempt. Because he denies knowledge of the attempted arson, in the best reconstruction of the event Laurence apparently is sleepwalking in the middle of the night, going to his cache of matches and then rushing to the woods. Sleepwalking or not, fortunately he was intercepted by a counselor.

Although the deep cut and scar on his head may be significant to the examining physician, the role of the matches may be equally telling. Because they are contraband at FEI, they are unlikely to be readily available. It is highly doubtful that they suddenly materialize to one allegedly in a catatonic state. Careful planning is more

**175**

likely. Another intriguing incident is the second letter I received from Laurence, postmarked Tuesday and likely written immediately prior to these events, or perhaps during a lull in his strange behavior. Other than butchering my name, the letter was as lucid as his first, perhaps even a bit more thoughtful:

> Dear judge geblert
> well mr. foster came up here and seen me and we talk about the programs and what i'm doing in here, and i'm doing fine better then what i was doing when i first came. i just had to get adjusted to what was taking place, and that i was going to have to work to make, and change my ways. and deal with life has it comes. well i have this letter and thanking you for answering my letter.
> from, Laurence

Next week, Dr. R. and his associates will have their hands full unraveling this one.

This week's drama for Jamie Forest followed Laurence's pattern: unforeseen turns and no ending in sight. Suddenly arrested by Miami police officers on what appeared to be two old burglary charges he is now accused of fifteen additional burglaries. He claimed both shock and surprise, as did we. Foster was no more successful in learning his status than he had been with Laurence. The arresting officers carefully avoided providing details of the arrest or his whereabouts. When it fits their needs, the police are unsurpassed in the ability to be unavailable, or to keep a suspect incommunicado. Foster encountered a trail of telephone messages that always ended in a blank wall. Three days into the week, despite neither Jamie nor the facts being visible, a few details were emerging.

Although Jamie had pleaded guilty before me to about a dozen burglaries committed last summer, apparently several had not been cleared and the Miami Police Department burglary detail needed his admission to balance their books. In these situations, the accused usually pleads guilty, walking out with time served as a sentence. This is the accepted police practice, but these officers wanted more. Jamie was to set up a scam to snare a neighborhood dealer in stolen merchandise. In fear, he readily agreed to cooperate. Held overnight in the Miami jail, he was a frightened little boy.

Jamie played his part, taking a stolen stereo down the street to the dealer, an elderly lady whom he had known for a long time. She offered thirty-five dollars, no questions asked. At this point, the police burst through the door arresting the surprised woman and her son. Not much of a score and, lacking consummation of the sale, not much of a case. Jamie, released after performing his role, went home a free man. It wasn't to be that easy.

Later in the week, a cryptic message to Foster from the police announced they were filing two cases: an old one and a new charge allegedly occurring about the time Jamie returned from State School. His troubles were only beginning. More than becoming a pawn of the police, he had violated the neighborhood code. Both his sister and mother have been threatened with bodily harm and told there was a "small contract" out on him.

Sitting in chambers describing his experience, Jamie waved his hand, still in a plaster cast, mustering up all the bravado he could, saying, "I'm not afraid of them. I can take care of myself. They better leave my mama and sister alone."

His usual affable, joking manner was absent. For now he's out of the neighborhood, living at an aunt's house, miles from Liberty City, attending DMI. When the neighborhood concern over his betrayal dies down, he'll return home. Meanwhile, he faces new criminal charges. The report from the Mailman Center, due in a few days, surely will assist in determining what to do with him. He will keep Foster busy for awhile.

The others survived the week without eventful moments. Dwight Anderson (The Migrant), still sporting his twenty-seven stitches, managed to make it to school three days, but excused himself early because of the continuing "pain." Reluctantly, we admit that it appears that a halfway house is next, though it means taking him away from Ms. Edison, his very caring teacher in the special public-school class.

Marco Zargula (The Charmer) is holding his own at Humana despite a slight fallback for violating a rule against pierced ears. The hospital code deems earrings as inappropriate dress for young men, a view Marco treats with scorn: "They don't really care how we look. They are afraid rich people won't send their kids here because only pimps and homos wear earrings." Marco's thirty-day treatment session runs out soon, and negotiations with the Disc program in Tallahassee have not been fruitful. Space is not available, and Marco will not be moved to the top of the list.

As we approach the end of this phase of the Master Counselor Program, all the participants appear to be at a critical-decision time for their future. A year ago when we started, each was also in crisis, but then we were optimistic and confident. Today, we are only certain that tomorrow some new concern will surface, requiring another four-alarm response.

## Friday, March 15, 1985

The question was not, what had we done for Marco, Lester, et al., but what had the Master Counselor Program done for Foster, Manning, and me?

> *Foster* "I had some hard times. It really hurt inside when Marco and Laurence were arrested. It was like family. If I had caught Lester when he ran away, he would have been sorry. I became more patient with problems. They always had problems. They needed me, but I was glad when they be pulling my pants leg, calling 'Mr. Foster, Mr. Foster.'"
> *Manning:* "The extent of our ability became crystal clear. Even coordinated effort doing everything is not enough. The inability of family to participate insures failure, no matter what we do. We learned more about what we couldn't do than what we could do."
> *Gelber:* "Working on a day-to-day basis with the likes of an untouchable Lester and an unreachable Dwight brought a sense of reality to our jobs—a reality that woke us up to what really happens out in the streets."

This was the assessment session to determine the impact of the Master Counselor Program and what we had learned. We agreed that success or failure could not be determined in any way. The year spent in this program was but one interval that followed many years of stunted growth and preceded many more years of probable frustration and failure. How much Cornelius Foster has fortified our charges to face the almost insurmountable problems ahead is still questionable.

What has been the impact on the lives of these kids?

ANDY SILLS (*The Drinker*)
*Foster:* "That's my boy! He's a star! A star. I knew it all the time."
*Gelber:* "His turnaround continues to amaze me. Both he and his mother seem to have licked their drinking problem. It's hard to believe he's the same person. Andy gives hope that something works."

**178**

*Manning:* "It was all caring. The family allowed Foster to become part of them. His girl friend helped, but everybody joined in supporting Andy."

### LESTER BURROWS (*The Runner*)

*Gelber:* "Losing Lester didn't bother me as much as the others. We never had him. He never gave us a chance. The system had so many other opportunities with him. Why couldn't someone have reached him early?"

*Foster:* "I really felt this one. Every time I thought I had reached him, he was gone. I tried so hard."

*Manning:* "He has seen one too many counselors and been under too many plans."

### MARCO ZARGULA (*The Charmer*)

*Manning:* "Marco is a dreamer who only realizes his dreams when high on drugs. He is on a course of self-destruction, and he will either kill himself or be killed."

*Foster:* "You can't survive in Larchmont Gardens without being hard-core."

*Gelber:* "Marco is bright and cunning enough to have a chance. Foster opened enough doors for him to see there's a better way. One positive influence in his life might turn him around. What that might be, I don't know."

### DWIGHT ANDERSON (*The Migrant*)

*Foster:* "If only his mother would do something, then Dwight might stay out of trouble. She wanted me to be his father so she could sleep all day. All these people want to do is sleep."

*Manning:* "They sleep all day because it's an escape. For the same reason the kids fantasize. Deep down they hate their lives. Dwight also has limited intellectual ability. There is nothing in his future except crime and incarceration."

*Gelber:* "Dwight is thirteen and unless there's a radical change by age fourteen, he'll be beyond recall. In one year the Master Counselor Program has done everything possible. He's young enough to be pliable. Dwight is the acid test. If he changes, a miracle indeed has been performed."

### LAURENCE SAMUEL (*The Fighter*)

*Manning:* "Laurence has a very low tolerance level and by isolating himself, help was not available. The true seriousness of his problem is only now being revealed. He faces a dismal future."

*Gelber:* "Absent this program, Laurence would have been forever a stick of dynamite with the fuse ready to go off. Things may continue

**179**

to get worse for him, but in the long run he may settle down now that his problems have surfaced."

*Foster:* "He was playing us all the time and still is. FEI is forcing him to discipline himself, which he doesn't like. If we let him off the hook again, then it will be the same old story."

JAMIE FOREST (*The Nuisance*)

*Foster:* "He does nothing but lie and fantasize. He needs our help but will do nothing to help himself. As long as I'm around he'll behave. How long can I be there?"

*Manning:* "Jamie will drift from program to program, obeying the rules, getting into fights, then do what he wants to do. Getting him a job earning some money might settle him down, but it will only be temporary. He will always be in trouble."

*Gelber:* "He has had some success at DMI and made a friend with Foster. Those are the things he needs. Some vocational training along with his mother's influence might stabilize him enough to avoid trouble. But unfortunately his inclination is toward 'easy money' and I'm afraid that's the course he'll follow."

It was noteworthy that Manning, the company man, always ready to look on the bright side of bureaucracy, was least hopeful; and that I, the perennial cynic, still saw hope for these kids. Foster, less sure about himself than at the beginning, was selective, seeing good prospects for some but recognizing the futility among others.

What did we learn?

*Gelber:* "Several significant things. Time is an essential factor. Most of our programs run three to six months. That is barely enough to scratch the surface. Long-term programs with less clients and follow-ups are necessary. For sure we are going to extend this program another year."

*Manning:* "We need to have a Master Counselor Program for first offenders, not the hard-core. That way we have a chance. It's too late with the hard-core. If we had devoted all this energy with first offenders, then they wouldn't grow into Marcos and Lesters."

*Gelber:* "The public has no patience for long-time investments in kids who are not an immediate threat to their safety."

*Foster:* "You need patience with the kid, too. Most of it is waiting. Nothing will happen until he's ready to make it happen."

*Gelber:* "Punishment and treatment are both necessary, but both can be equally ineffective unless something inside tells the kids there's a better way. The trick is to get inside."

*Foster:* "Fear wears away. After a while lockup doesn't mean anything."

## Watching the Dark Side Get Darker

*Manning:* "I'm more convinced than ever the parents are the problem. We can't help kids unless we first influence the parents. No matter how much is done, unless the parents can back us up, it's all wasted."
*Foster:* "How can you influence someone like Mrs. Anderson?"
*Gelber:* "I didn't believe this before, but now I think many hard-cores like Dwight and Marco need to be taken out of the home environment early, real early."
*Foster:* "I agree, but only for short periods, and then returned home."
*Gelber:* "For certain, dealing with problems of the entire family is correct. But for how long can the government baby-sit a family?"
*Manning:* "With our budget, not for too long."
*Gelber:* "Another thing we learned: that the usual counselor caseload of forty to fifty is a complete misuse of taxpayer money."
*Foster:* "With my regular caseload of forty, I was able to pay attention to only five. In this program, I am running a taxi service but at least they know me and I know them."
*Gelber:* "The next time I read about how jobs will cut down delinquency, I'll throw up. They need to learn basic skills to hold a job. What employer in his right mind will hire Dwight or Jamie or Marco?"
*Manning:* "You can force them to jail, but you can't force them to learn. They have concern only for what they want to do. Little else matters."
*Foster:* "Whether these kids go bad or not, I know that if you establish a relationship, get the kid to relax and trust you, pay attention to them, that somewhere along the way, they'll be better for it."

It had been a useful discussion clarifying our own views and providing a more rounded perspective. A year ago, I had anticipated that from these efforts would flow a list of concrete, crisp proposals, not necessarily a sure-fire formula, but surely moving in that direction. Now it came out a mixture of philosophy and conjecture. "What's your solution?" asked Manning. Everything that had happened this last year made me a little insecure in my response:

Incarceration doesn't do it and treatment programs fall way short. There's little to show for whatever is done. Everything we try is impersonal. Nothing reaches inside. Hard-core kids need someone at their side all the time: a conscience, a guide, a probation officer, a patron saint, a coach, a confessor, someone who can say "no" and at the same time point the way. Mine is a radical approach. A one-on-one Cornelius Foster type sitting with one family, maybe two, working with them for two years. It costs about $20,000 a year to keep a Jamie Forest locked up; why not have a Master Counselor take over that kid's life at home, minute by minute, day by day? Jamie would have a chance that way.

Manning sat silent for a few moments before responding: "That is rather drastic. Are you saying that 'state schools' over the country should be closed down and the hard-core kids sent home?"

"No. We'll always need a lockup. But, if every local community had a dozen Master Counselors, we could skim off those kids who had a chance and really work with them."

Manning didn't seem quite satisfied with my response, but offered no rebuttal. I wasn't too sure, either. We'd have to wait another year, when the experiment is over.

## Friday, March 22, 1985

Foster had anticipated a tough time bringing Laurence Samuel (The Fighter) back from FEI for his interview with Dr. R., but the two-and-a-half-hour trip from FEI was uneventful. Laurence, stretched out in the back of the car, insisted he wanted to get along with everybody. Most of all, he wanted to see his mother, who had not been allowed to visit him at FEI. He was calm, repeating his loss of memory claim. Foster found his appearance and behavior to be normal. Earlier, Operations Director Johnson had reported that Laurence was back on work detail, creating no problems and participating in all activities.

Bright and early, Foster had the youth in Dr. R.'s office. An hour later, the doctor walked into my chambers, Laurence behind him, grinning over the attention he was getting. Without any preliminaries, Dr. R. delivered the verdict in a few clipped sentences: "If you and I are crazy, then so is Laurence. His loss of memory is pretense and changing his name is playacting." Somewhat annoyed at the waste of his time, he minced no words adding, "If he doesn't alter his behavior, he'll end up in the penitentiary."

Dr. R.'s report was good enough for me, but I wanted eye-to-eye confirmation. Laurence's head had barely made it through the door of my chambers as he entered, arm in a sling. He was all smiles and affability. No signs of sunken eyes or unusual mannerisms. "Yes, sirs" punctuated his sentences, but most impressive was his willingness to converse. Where was the withdrawn Laurence, never saying more than necessary? The sling was for treatment of a muscle that had been pulled playing basketball. He denied the forest-burning

**182**

incident, treating it as if it were some rumor around camp rather than a witnessed event. He wanted only to talk about the future and was brimming with optimism about it: "I'm gonna make it this time. I'm getting my head together. There's only one counselor I don't like and it's not because he's white. He keeps hassling me to do things. I get along real well with Mr. Johnson and everybody else. I want to go back and convince them I'm going good. In two months I'll be out of Phase I. I'm going to be all right."

When asked about remaining in the detention center for the weekend, where his mother might visit, he declined, preferring to leave in the morning with Foster: "I want to show them I can make it. I want to show them I can make it." It was hard to believe that what had been described as a basket case was now this cooperative, resolute young man. If this is the third act of his play, he sure has me fooled. We shook hands as I wished him well. My parting words carried the warning, "Even if you burn three forests down, you are finishing your term at FEI."

Laurence turned on that big smile again and assured me things would be different from now on. I almost had the sense that he understood my uncertainty about his behavior and was enjoying it. Not too long ago, he was fighting and scheming to get out of camp, but now the folks at FEI are family and he wants to return to the warmth of their affection. If true, they earned it, staying with him. In any event, I owe Danny Grizzard an apology for suspecting FEI's motives. Who knows? Maybe Laurence can yet be helped.

## Monday, March 25, 1985

As expected, Marco Zargula (The Charmer) has quickly moved to the head of the class at Humana Hospital. He's the floor representative, allocating points to those displaying exemplary behavior. In every program, he follows the same pattern of success. No sooner discharged, it's back to the Larchmont Gardens life-style. Since my visit last week, he has been strutting around, bragging about the relationship he has with "his judge," confiding to some people that he would be out and home very shortly. This morning, Foster brought his mother to Humana, along with the news that the Disc Village Program, in Tallahassee, has reordered its admission list and was able to accept him. On April 15 Foster will fly him up, and he'll stay in this residential program for possibly a year. It was good news to us, but not to him. As soon as he heard it, he screamed, "Shit no. I'm not going!" and ran out of the therapist's office heading for the exit. A nurse collared him. Back to his room he went to cool his anger. Obviously, he doesn't yet have the serious motivation to overcome his drug habit. Perhaps Disc Village can work with his less than cooperative attitude. It won't be easy, but we simply cannot compete with Larchmont Gardens.

The situation of Dwight Anderson (The Migrant) has also changed—maybe even for the better. Dr. C.'s session produced a recommendation that he be allowed one more chance at home—again. The doctor sees a glimmer of hope, a willingness to comply. Foster says all he sees is a taller boy who gives his mother more sass and smells his musk. In chambers, he was still the same glum, taciturn youth except for one new factor. He has decided to be a star football player and wants to participate in spring practice for the under-125 pound league. To do this, he is willing to go to school and attend the Boys' Club, promising to set the alarm and make the bus on time. "Where have you ever played?" I asked. "Around my mama's house," he answered proudly. He said he was a running back and, when told the Boys' Club League was big time, including uniforms as well as coaches and drills, he said he'd take care of himself, don't worry. It's hard for me to believe that football will move him up the ladder.

The relationship between Jamie Forest (The Nuisance) and the Miami Police Department is still unclear, though a new burglary case has been filed. This one occurred six weeks after his release from State School and during his stay at DMI. It was a neighborhood break-in: Jamie was identified by a neighbor, and, as in all the others, readily confessed when confronted by the police. Coming shortly after release from State School, it tells how long the fear of incarceration lasts. And happening six weeks into DMI, one of our best rehabilitation programs, this also carries a message for us. Jamie barely recalled the event and merely shrugged his shoulders in response to Foster's inquiries. That burglary is just part of another day in Jamie's life, quickly forgotten.

The State Attorney's Office, fed up with him, wants him sent to FEI's Last Chance Ranch. Manning says Jamie, at 101 pounds, coupled with his childishness plus his temper, will never survive among the likes of Laurence Samuel and Troy Sultan. No matter, he cannot enjoy the luxury of crime without penalty. He probably needs my proposed Master Counselor, who has a caseload of only Jamie. Here's a kid who is absolutely amoral, lacking any conscience about his misdeeds, totally unconcerned, casually committing crimes. What's the next step?

The long-awaited report from the Mailman Clinic finally arrived. It was a long-shot hope that a complete neurological workup might reveal some of Jamie's secrets. The clinic threw in a pediatric examination, but both added up to zero. The pediatrician's report revealed "a somewhat withdrawn sixteen-year-old black male, cooperative, with bacterial meningitis at an early age with apparently no medical problems other than asthma for which he does not take his medication." That's old news. The neurologist concluded: "There are no neurological stigmata which point to a specific organic basis for behavior problems or below normal mental development. Clinically his mental deficiency is mild and while he requires special schooling, I would question and doubt that his intelligence rating (Verbal I.Q.-77, Performance I.Q.-73, full scale I.Q.-70) indicates an incapability of understanding right from wrong."

Nothing new there either. Whatever else the testing shows, Jamie is capable of distinguishing criminal from normal behavior. His early bout with meningitis cannot be blamed for his string of burglaries. What he learned must be unlearned. But how?

One-upsmanship seems to be the specialty of Andy Sills (The Drinker) these days. Whenever I set a standard he can't reach, he immediately sets out to prove me wrong. At our last conference, I suggested that in lieu of classroom studies he obtain a job in an autobody shop and convince the school to give him class credit. Yesterday, I received word that he had a job and was negotiating for school credit. He wants to be discharged from court supervision and has Foster's endorsement. "Show me the documentation," I requested of Foster. "If in fact he has succeeded, I'll have no choice." A year ago, I never would have believed that this little sniveler could have grown so fast in so short a period of time.

Lester Burrows (The Runner) is still among the unaccounted for. Too bad we never had a real opportunity with him. He's probably out of reach anyway.

## Tuesday, March 26, 1985

Evian Vilars' mother was angry, distraught, and confused: angry because the "shame" of Evian's behavior had been plastered over several pages of the *Miami Herald*; distraught because of her guilt feeling about being responsible for his hospitalization; confused because all the medical and legal voices she heard at today's court hearing seemed to be aimed at taking her son away from her. "When I ask to read the reports, what the doctors say about my son," she cried out, "they say no, it is confidential. Now my neighbors read it in the *Miami Herald*." (To conceal his identity, Evian had been given the cover name of "J" in the news story.)

Mr. and Mrs. Vilars sat stiffly through the proceedings as all the doctors, social workers, and lawyers paraded their views. Evian had been excused, staying outside in the company of Judith Lieber, social worker with the Public Defender's Right to Treatment Unit. Jackson Memorial Hospital (JMH) psychiatrist Dr. P. in his report described Evian's condition as chronic depression with paranoid features. He concluded that long-term hospitalization was unnecessary, despite the portion of his report stating that "under emotionally-laden or stressful situations, Evian has the potential to act out his repressed anger." However, no psychotic episodes had occurred in the hospital showing him to be out of touch with reality, and therefore outpatient treatment was recommended along with immediate counseling for the parents.

I was somewhat shaken by Mrs. Vilars' emotion, particularly when she said she didn't believe I had made the statement attributed to me in the newspaper: "Someone may die unless Evian gets help." When I had encouraged a *Miami Herald* reporter to write the story, some negative feedback had been anticipated, but it seemed more important to me to make the public and the legislature aware of our inadequate resources. As a result, Evian received a thorough evaluation at JMH, and he will undoubtedly continue to receive better treatment because of the press attention.

It had been a difficult court session. Dr. P., young, alert, sincere, made it clear JMH was not shrugging Evian off as another untreatable it wanted removed from the rolls. Nonetheless, we were virtually in the same posture as a month ago when Evian came under hospital care. He may not be another Hinckley, but certainly he's a threat. Can the medical profession really do anything in these situations even under the best of conditions?

Evian's father sat, fists clenched, jaws tight, in repressed anger, barely able to say he would cooperate with the doctors, then in the same breath challenging me: "I have my ways as a father like you and any man. Why do I have to go through all of this?" I chose not to reply. Watching the irate father and troubled mother, I wondered how we could ever presume to change their attitudes. Some eyebrows had been raised when, at the onset, our juvenile-court clinic psychologist Dr. R. stated matter-of-factly that psychological techniques properly administered could make adjustments capable of changing relationships within this family. I doubt it.

Dr. P., the JMH psychiatrist, recommended residential placement. Prosecutor Karen Kallman cautioned that our main concern must be protection of the community. I chose to delay ruling to reflect overnight on the problem. Despite Dr. R.'s confidence in his ability to change family attitudes, I seriously questioned that this father could ever be sensitized to appreciate Evian's problems. At best, any progress is years in the making. What happens while this process is taking place? Isn't it too late to realistically expect serious change?

Because Mr. and Mrs. Vilars and Dr. P. were absent, today's follow-up hearing allowed for a freer exchange. Everyone recognized that it was the father more than Evian who needed treatment. At one point, I offered to lock up the father and send Evian home, but no one laughed, though heads nodded in agreement. It was pointed out that a report by JMH psychologist Dr. E. described Evian as a serious present danger, more so than had his associate Dr. P., the JMH psychiatrist in yesterday's testimony. According to Dr. R., "In light of the fact that his reality testing can significantly become impaired under emotionally-laden situations, together with an abundance of data suggesting marked underlying hostility and paranoid traits, the potential for his acting out his anger in an overt manner is highly probable."

When yesterday I had asked Dr. P. to estimate the likelihood of Evian acting out one of his murderous fantasies, he said he couldn't predict. Yet, his colleague, Dr. E., whose findings were similar, predicted "highly probable."

After carefully observing the father in court, Dr. R. reversed yesterday's stand, now stating that little prospect existed of ever altering the father's attitude. Evian's resentment and fear of his father are so imbedded that only total separation may save him. The public defender, in a strong defense of the father, demanded: "What right does the court have, legal or moral, to break up this family and deprive Evian of his freedom because some few fear he may do something wrong? How can you expect his father, an uneducated man, not to be upset with court proceedings which he doesn't understand: where all the authority figures condemn his upbringing of his son, a son whom they are calmly taking away from him?"

Social Worker Judith Lieber reported that JMH has moved prompt-ly. Sessions with the parents as well as a treatment schedule for Evian have been set. He will stay at JMH for perhaps several weeks until enough progress is made warranting a return home. Prosecutor Karen Kallman shook her head, again reminding the court that more was at stake than Evian and his family.

The dilemma of Evian will continue for a long time. We'll respond to it on a day-to-day basis. He will enter JMH for treatment, and at the same time HRS will make applications for long-term placement in a residential facility. It is not likely that he will be admitted to the State Hospital, nor is the HRS Purchase of Service Committee able to fund emergency private placement. As a matter of fact, the mes-sage had already been sent to me that the committee will not buckle under to any outside pressure. Evian goes to the bottom of its list. Apparently, many individuals a lot worse than Evian need help.

That's all right with me. It had not been my intention to pressure the HRS Purchase of Service Committee. It consists of a group of volunteer citizens who deserve to be able to make decisions unin-fluenced by the pressure of a judge declaring an emergency.

I left the courtroom unsure but hopeful, determined to keep as many options viable as possible. The public defender's words stayed with me. Do any of us—doctors, lawyers, social workers—really have any answers for what is happening here? Walking through the waiting area, I looked for Evian, wanting to place my hand reas-suringly on his shoulder. He wasn't there. What made me want to do that? Certainly nothing had occurred in the courtroom to raise his hopes for better days ahead.

## Wednesday, March 27, 1985

The prospects for Evian may be questionable, but at least a strong effort is being made. Clark Carden, an equally serious concern, is hardly noticed. Today, after many months of badgering the adult Probation Office and enlisting the aid of criminal-court Judge Ed Cowart, a psychological examination finally emerged.

Dr. H.'s thorough examination confirmed the earlier description of a brutal, sadistic father and a mother, not only continuously beaten but also a victim of her first husband, who had departed with their six children and was never seen or heard from again. Clark appar-ently has made a reasonable adjustment at the military school, though he prefers living at home with his mother. She is the only stable entity in his life, and his main concern is her health and welfare. Dr. H. reported that the aftereffects of the traumatic murder still linger in Clark's mind: "I sleep only a few hours and have nightmares. I don't remember too many things about my father's death. All my childhood memories are gone."

According to Dr. H., the themes of loneliness and death appear frequently. Despite the enormity of his problem, Clark has the desire to achieve academically and overcome his present difficulties. Overall, the report did not raise any serious alarm for his present situation. Dr. H. concluded: "The boy's emotional refrigeration is intense and long standing. If it is not possible to arrange an ongoing therapeutic relationship, it is recommended that at least he be in touch on a monthly or quarterly basis with someone who can monitor his adjustments and current thinking and feeling."

Not directly addressed was the wisdom of his attendance at a military school. Why a military school for a child traumatized by growing up in a veritable prison-camp setting? Dr. H.'s response to my query surprised me: "The military school is good for him. He needs structure. They have rules and if he follows them he knows things will go well. They may be disciplinarians, but they are not unreasonable. His father, on the other hand, was an irrational tyrant who beat him for no reason."

Clark was described thusly: "A powder keg, cold as ice. I wouldn't say 'no' to him and feel safe going to bed. There is little likelihood of effecting serious change. So long as he is in warm surroundings and not unduly provoked, he may lead a normal life."

Some irony exists there. Clark, a convicted juvenile murderer, virtually ignored, apparently is faring as well as one might have hoped under the best treatment plan. In contrast, Evian, viewed only as a potential perpetrator of violence, has been the focus of all the resources the state can muster. Yet, in the end, he may be the worse for it.

# 7

---

# Helping Bad Kids
# Is Just Being There
# for the Bad Times

## Friday, March 29, 1985

Our kids differ from most in that they are perpetually in crisis, always under the gun, waiting for "the man" to do something for them or to them. Marco Zargula (The Charmer), for example, is on the way to Disc Village for a year; Dwight Anderson (The Migrant) appears headed for removal from home; and Jamie Forest (The Nuisance) is likely to try yet another program. None has ever lived in a normal family setting, and in our zeal to correct their lives, we bounce them from program to program—in social work jargon "to stabilize them."

Marco sat in court, listening as Foster and I ironed out details for his transfer to Disc Village, in Tallahassee. He was relaxed, amused as I expressed shock at Foster's announcement that Disc Village cost $900 a day. I assured Foster he was in error and asked Marco what he thought about the state spending that amount of money on him. He chuckled, "Why not?" Signing the order completing the transfer and reading the Humana Hospital therapist's final report, I had the feeling I had been here before:

> At his initial interview, Marco presented the image of a street-hardened youngster resisting treatment and denying any problems with substance abuse. During the interview he repeatedly averted the interviewer's questions by staring into space and refusing to consider the

consequences of his behavior. He also denied any need for therapy and threatened to run away if there were mention of further placement.

Marco's first two weeks in the unit were punctuated with periods of compliance followed by covert rebellion. It seemed as if the internal struggle to accept help was often at conflict with the need to maintain an "image" of the street junkie. This image seems to become his defense when he is asked to reveal any portion of his family history. He tends to fantasize and idealize the "glamour" attached to the dealer and street hustler. Marco has an idea that the only way to become successful (i.e., rich) is to deal in drugs, a fact which is readily reinforced by his previous peer associations.


The hospital therapist clearly identified Marco, as have other examiners in the past, but none has been able to break through his defenses. She claims some success: "It was very rewarding when Marco's covert behaviors began to mirror his overt acceptance of help. Marco began to become a positive member of the program, seeking out staff members in order to gain insight into his negative behaviors." That has also happened before, but never for any lasting period.

Dwight Anderson is still Dwight. His resolution last Friday to attend school and the Boys' Club in furtherance of a desire to become a football star withered almost immediately. He missed school Monday and Tuesday, claiming illness, lack of bus money as well as clothes, and an inoperative alarm clock. Choose any of the above. An exasperated Foster promptly deposited him in detention and made plans for a halfway house. After daily sessions with Dwight in his detention cell, Foster was back this morning suggesting "one more chance." Foster attributes the boy's behavior to the presence of brother Derrick in the household. Sleeping most of the day, wandering at night, he is Dwight's model. Foster's new strategy is to create a stable environment by removing Derrick from the household. I smiled in agreement, saying, "Master Counselor means glutton for punishment. Try. Try. Try. Release him for school on Monday and find a place for Derrick."

Jamie Forest is betwixt and between. DMI is terminating him without graduation because he has not made enough academic progress to warrant a diploma. He will not be one of the institute's success stories, though he received the Electrician of the Month award for February. DMI recommended placement in a learning-disability class and in the HRS Special Intensive Group for daily counseling. These are not likely because the prosecutor wants stronger action on the newly filed burglary charges. Jamie may deserve long incarceration, but where will he be when he gets out? We need a program tough enough to appease the prosecutors, yet still able to inject some worthwhile values into him.

## Friday, April 5, 1985

All week, Fish Eating Creek looked like any other wilderness outpost, quiet and industrious, until Laurence Samuel once again took over center stage. It all started innocently when he slammed the kitchen door. Admonished by a female employee, he responded with a torrent of foul language that the lady's husband, standing nearby, found objectionable. It could have ended there—not with Laurence. Flashing anger, he grabbed a pickax and swung it at the surprised husband. No one was hurt, but Laurence climbed the garage roof, threatening anyone who came after him. Finally descending, he calmed down. Quiet until midnight, he was suddenly jumping up and down in bed, standing on his head, shouting, "I'm going to kill myself and anyone who comes near me. That psychologist in Miami didn't do anything for me. He didn't even give me any medicine."

FEI Operations Officer Johnson was on the phone the next morning, asking for a psychiatric examination. I assured him clinic psychiatrist Dr. O. would be available as soon as Foster delivered Laurence. Johnson is convinced that, whenever something displeases Laurence, an eruption occurs. A few days earlier, in a similar situation, Laurence tore apart the supply shack. "We can handle him, if he's a malingerer," assured Johnson, "but we need a psychiatrist to tell us for certain."

If only it were that simple. No matter what Dr. O. finds, it will be no more than a clue to Laurence. The old saw that psychiatrists and psychologists can unravel the mind of a patient is a well-nourished myth. What better example can be found than their indecision and uncertainty in treating Evian and Clark? Anyone trying to understand Laurence would readily conclude that he's crying out for help. But what does that mean? Suppose his violent temper is indeed uncontrollable? The slightest stress will likely trigger violence. Conversely, if his performance is an "act," that too may suggest a disturbed youngster. Hospitalization? Medication? A padded cell? Where do we go from there?

Thinking back, I recalled that it was Dr. N., the school psychologist, who had warned that Laurence was potentially violent, particularly toward women, subject to extreme mood changes, and even suicidal. In his report, Dr. N. had noted that, at one point, the youth had asked to see a psychologist because "he felt strange." Several students had also stated that he acted "crazy" and needed help. Dr. N.'s dire warnings may have been accurate. The Laurence I had been seeing was a selfish, short-fused, clowning bully in need of tough discipline. He may, in fact, be a sick deviant in need of maintenance for a long time. Maybe his mother and stepfather kept a hands-off attitude because they sensed he was "different" and were in constant fear of upsetting him.

The drive down from FEI was unlike previous trips. Sulking, Laurence rejected any effort at conversation. Concerned about his own safety, Foster had him handcuffed in the back seat. Arriving at the detention center, Laurence refused to cooperate, calling everybody "Cracker," claiming his name was "James." As I described all this to Dr. O., he scribbled a few notes, asking no questions. "Here's one that will keep you up all night," I told him. "They all do," was his response.

Accompanying Foster to FEI was Jamie Forest (The Nuisance), scheduled for an interview for admission to the program. Earlier, plans for him had been uncertain, but insistence by the prosecutor's office helped make up my mind. They want Jamie to do some "real time," particularly for the burglary committed while in attendance at DMI. Because the prosecutor has the authority to bypass the juvenile court, by filing directly in the adult court, prudence suggested his views be given serious consideration. Foster, on the side of the prosecutor, summed it up: "Jamie is likeable, but if there's a choice between burglary and school, there's no doubt which way he'll go. If FEI can't impress him, nothing will."

Upon my return from court, Jamie was in my chambers, curled up in a big chair like a puppy dog waiting for his master. Fresh from his trip to FEI, he was completely unaware of the Laurence crisis. He knew a problem existed, but his concern was focused on his own little world. Addressing me as "mister" rather than "judge," he asked in his little-boy voice: "What you gonna do with me Mister Gilber?" I told him it was FEI or state prison. He answered, a touch of concern in his voice: "Can I set up a deejay program there? I got great records I can play." Then, as an afterthought, he added, "FEI is okay, horseback riding will be fun."

I explained this would be hard work, not a pleasant, camping experience, knowing full well the only horses he knew were those seen on TV westerns. Immediately, he took on his tough-guy stance. "I can do as much work as anyone," he declared. As soon as details are worked out, he will be on his way to Fish Eating Creek, perhaps as Laurence's replacement.

## Monday, April 8, 1985

Three months have elapsed since Evian's removal from his home, and we are now ready for a decision. Where once there had been spirited discussion, now Dr. P.'s recommendation was a foregone conclusion. Once more, he testified that outpatient treatment was the most appropriate medical approach. South Florida Hospital was out. The HRS Purchase of Service Committee had denied funds for private placement, recommending instead that Evian be placed in the least restrictive setting, namely, his home. No other options were available. Mr. Vilars, this time cool and contained, now satisfied to have his son home, thanked me politely, offering to cooperate.

It was all very civilized, more like a rehearsal for a play where everyone knows what comes next. I wondered whether the sense of relief that pervaded the courtroom was as uncertain as mine. My immediate goal had been accomplished. Evian's release came via a consensus of the best medical advice available. It had been a thoughtful, professional process. What disturbed me was that not for one moment did I believe that prospects for the boy had improved markedly after these three months. I wonder if others in the courtroom shared my doubts.

## Tuesday, April 9, 1985

Despite my concern that Marco Zargula (The Charmer) might run for it at the airport, no problems arose. He seemed to relish the importance of flying to Tallahassee, escorted by Mr. Foster, for this new adventure at Disc Village. Foster has this sublime confidence that his kids won't run from him, and, notwithstanding my suggestion, allowed him to roam free at the airport, without handcuffs.

On the plane, Marco was expansive, confiding to Foster a conversation he had with Laurence Samuel in detention. Foster was all ears, as was I in the retelling. Marco quoted Laurence: "I'm beating the system. I'm not going back to FEI. I got away with it. They are sending me to a hospital." Marco described Laurence's manner as "bragging." On his return to Miami, Foster interviewed several other cell mates in Laurence's detention unit, who confirmed the statement.

I'm not sure how this information will influence Dr. O. "Beating the system" is the major goal of jailed delinquents, and their success or lack of it is always uppermost in their minds and certainly in their conversation. Bragging or not, Laurence may be succeeding. Preliminary reports from the clinic doctors indicated he will need hospitalization. How much of his errant behavior is feigned, how much is real, and where is the line between the two?

Disc Village, on the outskirts of Tallahassee, is an idyllic version of FEI. Although sparse and institutional, the cabins are tastefully furnished, functional, and comfortable. Thirty-five kids are housed, six to a cabin, and a large staff provides intensive drug and alcohol programs lasting nine months. Special teachers from the public-school system and a variety of vocational apprenticeship programs are available. In addition to therapy sessions, students are able to participate in mountain climbing and camping—ten currently being gone on a trip to Nebraska.

The immediate reaction of the Disc staff was positive. The clinical psychologist stated with assurance: "I can work with Marco." It will be a strict regimen: no smoking, daily urinalysis, AA, Drugs Anonymous, and other controls designed to turn the mind against alcohol and drugs. The personnel take to Marco, and he likes them. Before long, he'll be a leader there. Will they manipulate him or will he come through untouched, as he has emerged from all the other programs?

## Wednesday, April 10, 1985

Far away from the rigors of Fish Eating Creek, Laurence Samuel (The Fighter) is once again a slow-talking, relaxed, casual young man. He's been here a week and not a child-care worker or a detainee has been assaulted or threatened. It's been all testing for Laurence, who is cooperative and compliant. His reputation, however, has preceded him and his mere presence brings out a show of force. Yesterday he was scheduled in court for a routine matter and, suddenly before he emerged through the detention door, the courtroom filled with security officers. As he approached the defense table, each of the six guards positioned themselves between his seat and mine, providing a protective cordon. Sliding into his chair, he spotted me, and, seeing a familiar face, a big smile broke out. I tried to put him at ease.

"Have a seat Laurence. How are you feeling?"

"Fine, judge. How am I doing? Will I be here much longer?"

"We will probably have you out in a few days, Laurence. Stay cool."

He smiled broadly as he left. It has never occurred to me to be fearful of him. My personal safety does concern me in court, but somehow with Laurence and the other Master Counselor kids it's different.

In addition to a psychiatrist, I asked our clinic psychologist Dr. C. to examine Laurence. Because the youth repeatedly expressed feelings about white authority figures, I enlisted Dr. C., who is black. To obtain some background, Dr. C. first interviewed an FEI supervisor, who told him: "Laurence would often be found in a trance-like state at night, daydreaming. He had to be physically shaken to wake him. He would often get into fights 'playing sex games.' Laurence would feel the other young men on their buttocks, which elicited an angry reaction. He would then flee, hiding on the roof. Later, Laurence would claim amnesia. At times, Laurence appeared to be very genuine in his lack of memory. At other times, his amnesia seemed phoney."

It's Dr. N., the school psychologist, again. He had made references to latent homosexual feelings, at which I had scoffed. Can this be an underlying factor in Laurence's behavior patterns? We've come a long way since I wanted to test his hair for abnormal levels of copper. The doubt raised as to Laurence's amnesia may be even more significant in view of his statements to Marco about "beating the system."

Reading Dr. C.'s reaction to his interview session with Laurence, one can sense an ominous situation:

> Laurence indicated very strongly that he did not feel that the program was "helping" him to resolve his problems. He would attempt to run away if ever returned to the facility. In addition, he expressed fears that he would hurt someone or himself during one of his violent outbursts. He could not recall many of these episodes, but the staff told him about the behaviors that he had exhibited. He was afraid that

he was experiencing serious illness and was fearful of losing control and hurting someone. Laurence reported visual hallucinatory experiences in which he felt that he was actually observing himself strangling with his hands a particular staff person with whom he had had a conflict.

The deeper the involvement with Laurence, the more complex the problem. None of his prior clinical evaluations suggested "hallucinatory experiences . . . observing himself strangling with his hands a particular staff person." He has either become much worse or has fabricated a more threatening scenario to avoid return to FEI.

Dr. C.'s testing confirmed the seriousness of the problem:

> His responses to the Rorschach were generally within normal limits; however, there were a few responses which could be categorized as strange or peculiar. His performance, however, on additional projective testing suggests episodic breaks with reality have been occurring. Laurence's current feelings and thoughts should be taken seriously as he expresses a strong desire to receive help and assistance. He appeared to experience considerable anxiety and confusion regarding his intense feelings of anger and loss of control.

Although only two weeks ago Dr. R.'s psychological examination had concluded otherwise, Dr. C. now stressed the need for hospitalization: "It is recommended that Laurence be placed in an inpatient psychiatric facility in which he can be observed closely for a period of several weeks in order to further add to the diagnostic and clinical picture."

Clinic psychiatrist Dr. O. concurred. He recognized the possibility that Laurence may be masquerading, but in his view, the symptomology requires hospitalization: "He is very convincing in describing his hallucinations. They are real to him. Laurence may be exaggerating consciously or unconsciously, but prudence dictates the benefit of the doubt be given to the possibility that he is seriously dangerous to himself and that there may be some diagnosable organic basis to some of his abnormal behaviors."

"What does this mean medically?" I asked Dr. O.

> *Dr. O:* "At med school the books describe it as the Ganser Syndrome. My professor said it was a 'crazy man trying to act crazy.' It happens a lot in prisons. There's a compulsion to act out as a means of self-protection. Other prisoners stay away from you if you appear strange

**197**

and violent. Sometimes it's an unconscious act which the party doesn't remember. You have to be a little deranged to behave in this fashion."

*Gelber:* "Psychiatrists can sure confuse a situation. You are stating that there's little difference between being crazy or only acting that way. It's plain to me that Laurence realizes that acting tough at FEI will not impress anybody because the others there are as tough as he is. Therefore, he now acts weird, so he can get the attention he wants."

*Dr. O.:* "If you think about it, your theory isn't much different than my professor's explanation, except Laurence may not have control over his actions and in truth may not remember."

Dr. O.'s explanation still had me confused, but I chose not to pursue it. Laurence's family has adequate insurance coverage for a forty-five-day full hospital examination. Foster will make the necessary arrangements. I'll let the psychiatrists sort this one out.

## Thursday, April 11, 1985

I had been delayed getting to court while listening in chambers to Jamie Forest ramble on about a $16,000 "gig" he and two older musicians had scheduled in Alabama for June. "Would I be able to do that before going to FEI?" he asked. Then, he went on to tell me about his $4,000 bank account and a girl friend he claimed he had impregnated, and on and on. Fantasizing may be healthy, but for this kid it surely is his antidote for fear of the unknown. I tried to assure him FEI was a tolerable place. He reminded me that he had earlier asked about setting up there as a disc jockey. I doubted that Fish Eating Creek in the desolate swamplands, was the ideal site for a deejay, but told him the staff might go along with it. A lengthy calendar faced me, and another judge's illness would double my normal caseload, but I stayed a few minutes longer with Jamie. He needed me more at that moment.

Rushing through the calendar, I made short shrift of the legal arguments tendered by the lawyers, still thinking about Jamie. "He's entitled to be released. He's entitled to be released," repeated the public defender, jarring me back to reality. The file in front of me was an automobile theft case, and the young man had been held an extra day in detention because no parent appeared to accept custody after I ordered his release yesterday. The prosecutor objected, wanting more information because the defendant had not provided the police with an address or date of birth; he also was using an alias when first arrested. He was charged with stealing a 1985 Cadillac and had originally given the name of Gary Pittman, later admitting his true name to be Keith Mervin. I was about to release him again when the jarring voice of the public defender repeating the request for his release suddenly righted the little wheels in my head. Mervin! Pittman! This has got to be my boy Lester (The Runner). Back home again!

"Are you Lester Burrows?" I asked.

"No. Never heard of him," was the answer.

"Bailiff, bring Cornelius Foster to the courtroom," I ordered. As Foster walked toward the bench, he passed by our subject without noticing him. I said, "Mr. Foster, will you examine that young man and identify him?" The courtroom was crowded, and I played it to the hilt. All the lawyers knew of Lester's escape-artist reputation, none had seen him before, and here he was being dramatically unveiled in court. Foster gently lifted Lester's head, now fallen between his legs, and eyeball to eyeball they both burst into laughter.

"That's him all right," said Foster while Lester grinned sheepishly, unhappy but impressed with all the attention, and finally admitted that he was Lester Burrows. Home at last.

Back in chambers with Master Counselor Foster, Court Administrator George LaMont, Prosecutor Karen Kallman, and Bailiff Barry Young, an air of victory prevailed. LaMont offered to strike a medallion for my investigative prowess, and the prosecutor reported that, when all the aliases were entered in the computer, it began to sputter, unable to handle the overflow business generated by our young friend.

## Friday, April 12, 1985

He didn't have many bargaining chips, but Lester was not about to give up. Yesterday's capture, plus facing three new felony charges, didn't faze him. He wanted to talk to his judge. Bailiff Young delivered him to chambers, and without any preliminaries he made his pitch: "I've been living with my father's friend, near my grandmother's house, going to welding school. I'm doing fine. Not bothering anyone. Why can't I be in an Independent Living Program?"

I tried to explain to him that life wasn't one series of program placements after another: "You are a hot number. The prosecutor wants you badly. With all those escapes and aliases, prison is what they have in mind for you."

He ignored my statement, continuing with his plea: "I was learning in welding. I can get a job." He's probably right. It is doubtful we will ever convert him, no matter how structured the program. At age sixteen and skilled in survival, minimal supervision may be the sensible route.

I tried again to help him understand his predicament: "Don't you understand you committed a burglary, stole a motor vehicle, and escaped from the Miami Police Department? There's a price you have to pay for those crimes. You can't walk away as if you are entitled to do those things."

He just looked at me empty-faced, understanding the words, yet not quite fathoming the full import of what I was saying. He is a nice kid, who with some schooling might be classified as bright, but he has no underpinning of values that ordinarily come from home or school or church. None has been part of his life. He knows that consequences arise from antisocial behavior, but no set of warning signals operate inside him telling him to stop when he's going in the wrong direction.

When it became apparent he could strike no bargain, Lester relaxed a bit, filling me in on what had been happening to him. His father, whom he hadn't seen for the past three years and only twice in the five years before that, made one of his rare appearances and arranged for Lester to live with a male nurse, who Lester quickly denied was a homosexual. For several months, the youth has been attending Northwestern High School in the evening, studying welding and expected a job soon. He said his escape was simple: "The police officer left three doors open, didn't pay any attention to me, so I just walked out."

As to the most recent arrest, he was leaving a skating rink when a friend, stealing a Cadillac parked outside, asked for assistance in starting the car: "I was behind the wheel, hot-wiring it—I learned that at State School from the other kids in the 'Small Engine' class— when this police car drove by. I didn't think he saw me and I was pumping the gas pedal. But damn it! There was no gas in the car. When he arrested me, I didn't know which name to give him. I guess I gave him the wrong one."

It's hard not to like Lester, but it's dangerous to like him too much. He deserves a lot of sympathy. At some point in his life, someone or something could have intervened in his behalf. Lacking any conscience, he may be close to turning violent. How can I justify giving him one more chance, then another and another? Next week I'll talk to the prosecutors about what to do with him.

During our conversation, my bailiff, Barry Young, hovered about in momentary expectation of Lester bursting out in a run for freedom. That's not Lester's style. Young is 250 pounds of solid muscle, also bred and grown in the streets of Liberty City. Lester would want no part of tangling with him. When he returned from delivering him to detention, Young, who in addition to looking like a fierce sumo wrestler is a gentle Baptist minister on weekends, smiled, repeating Lester's words on the walk back: "Damn. I believe I fucked up. I shouldn't have done those crimes, but I still think the judge will let me go."

Young chuckled, almost in admiration, and said, "That's some boy there. I wonder what would have happened to him if the car had gas?"

## Wednesday, April 17, 1985

Meeting with Laurence Samuel's mother to discuss hospital insurance has somehow opened her up to Foster. Uncommunicative in the past, she now was revealing family history—and what a history! Laurence's father has divided his adult life between crime and mental institutions. In addition, the youth's aunt, uncle, and grandmother on his father's side have all been in and out of mental institutions. At the age of four, she recalled Laurence calmly lighting matches, setting fire to a clothes closet, and just standing there laughing at the flame. Why not burn a forest? What reason could she have had for never revealing this in the past?

The rap sheet of Walter Samuel, the father of Laurence, identified a thirty-five-year-old black male, built like his son, six feet, three inches tall, weighing 180 pounds, presently completing the last month of a one-year sentence in county jail for possession of drugs. The offenses could have been Laurence's. Most involved violence: several armed robberies, half a dozen aggravated assaults, burglaries, probation violation, and other assorted forms of mayhem. On the surface, Laurence was part of what appeared to be a stable, middle-class family—the stepfather earning a respectable living and a stepbrother who was the recipient of a college football scholarship—but his closet was full of frightening skeletons.

Has Laurence spent his life fearful he too would end up in a mental institution? Or was acting crazy a pretext, learned from others in his family? How can we account for the similarity of assaultive criminal behavior, considering that he barely saw his father over the years, instead growing up with a traditional, law-abiding family? To think we were going to solve his aggression by making a basketball player out of him!

## Thursday, April 18, 1985

Undoubtedly, more will be heard from Jamie Forest (The Nuisance), now having successfully completed orientation at FEI, and Marco Zargua, adjusting to Disc Village, in Tallahassee, but for the moment both are content and amenable to their surroundings. Because Andy was moving closer to discharge and his other three wards were lined up for new placements, Foster should be relaxed and rested. It never quite works that way with this crowd.

An agreement with the prosecutor's office on Lester Burrows (The Runner) seemed imminent on several occasions, but somehow bottlenecks always emerged. Neither charmed by his personality nor impressed with his potential to survive in the street, the prosecutor prefers that he be tried in adult court, where he faces the prospect of a long prison sentence. In my view, he needs structure in his life, but not necessarily the kind prison bars offer. No sooner had an agreement on FEI been reached than someone discovered old records that showed Lester was not a tender youth who had recently turned sixteen, but instead was a hardened nineteen-year-old, no longer within the jurisdiction of the juvenile court. An inspection of HRS records confirmed his age as nineteen. Foster and state attorney investigators are trying to locate family members and checking the state registry for a birth certificate.

Smooth sailing for Laurence isn't in the cards either. His ticket out of FEI to a hospital has been derailed, temporarily at least. The family health insurance will apparently cover only a thirty-day hospital stay, but like most health-insurance plans, full coverage is lacking. Meanwhile, he sits in the detention center, a place much more restrictive than FEI. So far no incidents have occurred.

For Dwight Anderson (The Migrant), a new tactic is being tried: no threats, no gentle pursuasion, no Foster driving him to school. This "last chance" is based on what he does on his own. Will he, on a regular basis, attend school and participate in the Boys' Club program? Foster, staying in the shadows, is keeping score. After several more days, a final decision will be made. During this past year, have we shaken the old lethargic Dwight sufficiently for him to be aroused enough to see the value in attending school? Is he now strong enough to survive his family environment, or will a halfway house be necessary? None of us expects a small miracle, but nonetheless we are all rooting hard for him to turn on the "go" button.

## Friday, April 19, 1985

As expected, the Lester mystery darkens. The Dade County Bureau of Vital Statistics has no birth certificate for him, but it does for his alias Keith Mervin, February 22, 1966, the same date as shown on Lester's early HRS records. When faced with the hard evidence, Lester looked up, that little smile spreading over his face, and in a slow drawl said, "That's easy to explain. I met this kid at a shelter home and when he was sent to an out-of-town program, I took over his name and birthdate. He ain't me and I ain't him."

Of course, he lies so effortlessly and artfully that this perfectly logical explanation may be pure fiction. Living so many different lives must make it hard for him to distinguish fact from fancy. His story about helping a friend hot-wire and steal the 1985 Cadillac is also falling apart. It seems that he "borrowed" the car from two newly met acquaintances, failed to return it, and the owners, probably homosexuals, reported it as stolen. Now, they are declining to prosecute. The search for other family members and his birth certificate will continue.

The Laurence problem was solved quickly. Foster persuaded HRS to handle the amount not covered by insurance. On Monday, Highland Park Hospital will begin a thirty-day examination aimed at determining his mental capacity. Here we go again. Will they find he needs long-term hospitalization? And, if so, who will pay for it? How about outpatient treatment? Do we send him home while he laughs about beating the system? Is he suicidal and laden with serious sexual problems as Dr. N. suggests?

Getting him into Highland Park has been the easy part. What we do with him upon release is a tough decision. Departing the detention center, he attacked a white inmate, kicking him in the face because he was throwing food at a black inmate. When told he would be sent to the adult jail, Laurence sneered. "I ain't afraid of nothing or nobody. Send me to jail or prison. It don't make no difference to me. I'll fight anybody."

Foster, reporting on Laurence's behavior to me, commented: "I've seen this behavior when I was in Raiford Prison. These young kids suddenly realize the muscle they have in their body and they want to take their anger out on the world. Like Laurence, they really believe everyone is afraid of them. Most people are, but along the way someone gets killed."

We didn't create this monster, but we sure were present at the christening. We can only hope that Highland Park Hospital will help. FEI is no longer the place for him, and our detention center is in a state of siege when he is there.

## Wednesday, April 24, 1985

There we were, sitting around the table: Foster, the play-the-cards-as-they-lie pragmatist; Gelber, the cynic whose faint idealism still flutters; and Manning, the young realist, always hoping the world is really better than it appears, but knowing otherwise. Each of us had suffered disappointments, some unexpected, others likely, but all hard to take. Somehow, I felt that Manning's personal loss was greatest. Never saying it, always the good bureaucrat, avoiding emotion, he so badly wanted a "they lived happily ever after" ending. I sensed this in the sharpness of his criticism, which bordered on anger at what had not been accomplished.

Foster, on the other hand, was still ready to go—pushed around a bit, but undaunted. I sensed a disappointment in him that we hadn't scored a resounding victory.

> *Gelber:* "Let's play predictions on where you expect to find these kids five years from now."
> *Question:* Who among them will be most involved in criminal behavior?
> *Foster:* "It's close between Laurence (The Fighter) and Lester (The Runner). Probably Laurence with more serious crimes, and Lester greater numbers. They both think they can beat the system. Get away with anything. Laurence's body has outgrown his mind. When he started lifting iron, he thought he could take on the world. People will use equalizers. He won't learn until he gets to Raiford. Nothing we do will stop him until he kills someone. . . . Lester will play the streets.

# Being There for the Bad Times

That's his life. He's slick, highly sophisticated. Can work his way out of anything. Doesn't need to work. When he gets to thirty years of age, he'll burn out. Then he'll be nothing."

*Manning:* "It's too late for Marco (The Charmer) to get out of the system. His whole environment of crime and drugs are too much to overcome. The Disc program is too late. He should have gone there at age thirteen, not sixteen. He'll go through it, be 'rehabilitated,' and back again to the Larchmont Garden ways. Crime will be a natural for him. But Jamie (The Nuisance) may be even worse. He may be a child for a long time before reality hits him. He's a follower. When someone says 'let's go'—he'll go."

*Gelber:* "Five years from now it will be Dwight (The Migrant) or Jamie (The Nuisance) you are likely to see in the adult criminal court. As bad as the others are, they have enough internal resources to step away from crime and choose other alternatives. The positive things instilled by Cornelius Foster may take hold years later. They, at least, may have a choice. Jamie and Dwight, however, are slow, not likely to develop any skills and will probably fall back on petty crime and burglary to survive. They are locked in to what they are."

*Question:* Five years from now, who will have made the least progress straightening himself out—not based on criminal arrests?

*Foster:* "A man has to have some ego. Dwight doesn't. There's no desire. Nobody is pushing him. Last week, he was out picking beans in the field with his mother. He has no ambition to better himself. He'll soon be a migrant worker like the rest of the family. Perhaps no crimes, but nothing much else."

*Manning:* "Marco is smart but always returning to Larchmont Gardens will keep him from developing. Laurence has strong emotional problems, which will cripple him. Whether they get arrested or not, I can't see how they will ever overcome these handicaps."

*Gelber:* "I agree with Cornelius. Dwight has too many strikes against him. Jamie at least fantasizes about a better life. Dwight can't rise above anything."

*Question:* Five years from now, which of these six will be most "successful," whether in criminal or noncriminal activities?

*Foster:* "Probably Andy in the long run, but over the next five years it may be Lester. Right now, he has the experience of a thirty- to forty-year-old man—a smart street hustler making money. But after a while it will be all downhill."

*Manning:* "Andy will get married, settle down, own a business, and raise a family."

*Gelber:* "Manning would like to see the all-American ending, but I'm still not sure about Andy. Or Lester either. He doesn't have a fire in his gut to be a crime boss. Marco does. He could be the 'Scarface' who dreams about running a drug combine. Of course, he could also straighten out and open a fancy bakery. With all the surprises we've had, it is conceivable that some good will enter their lives."

*Question:* Speaking of surprises, what one thing in this program surprised you?

*Foster:* "I'm not a man for surprises. I look for the best and expect anything. Frankly, I thought I would be a lot more successful. What did surprise me was the families wanting to work with me. At the end, even Laurence's mother was looking for me. These families want help. They don't know how to ask."

*Gelber:* "The casual manner in which they accept violating the law. It's kind of reflex to them, at times a form of recreation. For Dwight or Jamie to commit a burglary requires little or no reflection. It just happens, like smoking a cigarette or drinking a glass of water."

## Friday, April 26, 1985

Highland Park Hospital was a debacle for Laurence Samuel. The proposed thirty-day treatment lasted only two days. He was surly, threatening, and resistant from the moment he arrived. Although the staff were accustomed to difficult patients, they weren't equipped for the physical fear induced by this boy. They were willing to try, but not he. Somehow, he managed to smuggle narcotics into the hospital, distributing doses to other patients in the ward. Foster believes he had secreted packets of marijuana in his old FEI clothes. The ward was in an uproar, and Highland Park sent out an SOS: get Laurence out of here. It was Friday afternoon and no one was eager to be involved with him. "Take him directly to the adult jail," I ordered Foster, "and pick up two sheriff's deputies on the way over." Foster, plus reinforcements, arrived at Highland Park, prepared for some rough moments, but Laurence was docile, claiming, as always, that he had done no wrong. He wanted no trouble. If the judge directed him to the adult jail, so be it.

Highland Park Hospital psychiatrist Dr. D. told a somewhat different story. First, it was physical fear, intimidation, then the drug situation, and finally Laurence's refusal to be examined. He was alternately "beating up on staff and banging his head on the wall." An injection of Haldol quieted him down while restraints were used to tie him to the bed. Dr. D. wanted a full examination—EEG, the works—to find a possible organic basis for his behavior. Laurence wouldn't permit it. What was Dr. D.'s opinion based on his observa-

**206**

tions? "Laurence wants his way and is determined to get it, but does not have obvious psychotic problems. There is no suggestion of trauma associated with deep-seated problems. He's a sociopath who wants to fight society. There's nothing wrong with him that giving him his own way won't solve." Apparently there are several Laurences, none of whom would anyone want to be marooned with on a desert island.

## Monday, April 29, 1985

The situation with Dwight Anderson (The Migrant) moves slowly and inexorably, but we are not certain where. When one problem area seems to be clearing, a leak springs somewhere else. Dwight passed the test, deciding on his own to go to school—not every day, but enough to show a strong interest. He's managed transportation to school, followed by afternoons at the Boys' Club and insists that he enjoys both. Wonderful! He has made enough progress to begin moving forward without Foster pushing him. What's the problem? A small gang war is going on in the housing project that threatens to escalate into a large bloodbath. Dwight's gang, led by his thirteen-year-old cousin Kenneth, and a much larger group guided by someone named Pedro have already had several armed face-offs. Rocks have been thrown through windows, autos turned over, screens slashed, doors broken—all by out-of-control thirteen-year-olds who are terrorizing the project. The gangs hold marijuana-filled councils of war; then, while on a "high," they go into action, making the housing project a veritable no-man's-land for the tenants. The housing manager stays indoors all day, avoiding complaints. Dwight's mother wants to return to the safety of her old place.

We've traveled the full cycle. Obtaining this apartment from HUD enabled the family to exchange a hovel for decent living quarters. The roomy town house was symbolic of the new opportunity to be provided to Dwight. Back then, it had seemed important, but now, listening to Mrs. Anderson explain life in the housing project, the move no longer meant anything. Relaxed, sprawling over my conference table, wearing an old-looking hat and sporting a big empty grin, she spoke, resigned to whatever came her way: "Pedro one bad kid. He and his gang shooting windows with a BB gun and waving a big knife at everybody. I talk to his mother. She speaks a different language. The police be driving by, but never get out the car. When we complain, the rent manager, he want to chase us out, not them. I get a gun, take care of Pedro, but I afraid to go to jail. Maybe I do it anyway."

Dwight listened to his mother, nodding agreement. This time he was the aggrieved, not the aggressor. His gang, far outnumbered, would gladly sue for peace. "I want to go to school. I like the Boys' Club. They jump me. Beat me. Won't let me go near the bus. They have guns. We need to get them." This was a somewhat different Dwight: more open and accepting. Looking for help against the bad guys, he was now part of the mainstream.

"Supposing we find a group home for you near your school? You would be able to visit home, but live away. Would you like that?"

Without hesitation, Dwight indicated agreement, expressing concern only about being available for the Boys' Club football season. We talked a bit more. He left, paused at the door, nodding to me as if we had a verbal understanding that I was on his side. Any kind of signal from him is impressive, so I should be grateful for these few words and the nod. Now all we have to do is hope that the group home, public school, and the Boys' Club keep him in line, while somehow the gang problem and that damaged family don't stand in the way. Dwight might make it yet.

## Tuesday, April 30, 1985

It has taken a year, but each tidbit brings Lester Burrows (The Runner) more into focus. An old report, unearthed in his dependency file, dating back to 1980, described his early years. He was born in Bartow, a central Florida citrus community. At age eleven, he came to Miami with his divorced parents. He lived intermittently with each of them as well as with his paternal grandmother. Both parents found Miami big-city life distasteful, his father soon returning to Bartow to pick fruit and his mother departing for parts unknown. Grandma did little more than tolerate Lester's presence, her house becoming only a way station for him. Father visited town every few years, and mother's occasional postcards from different Florida cities kept the dim memory alive. He knew he had an older sister who was living with his mother, but could not remember her.

This report was a psychological assessment performed by the Peace River Center, in Bartow. It was obvious from the report that Lester had been a problem child for many years, even before coming to Dade County. Interviewed in the Bartow report were his mother, Mrs. Alean Jackson, Lester, and a Mrs. Juniper, in whose home he was staying at that time. At age three, his mother had sent Lester to live with assorted relatives and friends. In each one of these placements, Lester was acused of stealing things in the household, eventually running away, often returning to his mother, who then farmed him out to yet someone else.

The report stated that, in the early years of his life, while staying in these different homes, he had often been deprived of food, causing him to eat from garbage cans. At one of these homes, he was sexually molested over a long period of time. His mother resented him at birth, didn't want him, and had terrible guilt feelings about her attitude. Mrs. Juniper, the woman housing him at the time, said that, when his mother came to visit, he would hide or run away.

According to the Peace River report, Lester stated that he started to run away because he felt like an outsider wherever he stayed. He talked about his father to the psychologist, as if a real relationship existed. He vividly described games they played together and the room set aside for him when he reached sixteen. In truth, his father, an alcoholic, hadn't seen him since infancy. The report concluded that he needed a structured group-home setting and mental-health treatment to overcome his feelings of rejection and depression. Almost as an afterthought, the counselor suggested that, if he were to continue in his current behavior mode, he could become suicidal.

Five years later, Lester's mold continues unbroken. Although permanently damaged, he seems to have absorbed all the negatives without cracking. Disaster? Yes. Suicide? Unlikely. Lester's birthday, according to records of the State Bureau of Vital Statistics, was December 30, 1968, making him sixteen years of age. The birth certificate showed two other children born of the marriage. He knew of his sister, but, when I apprised him of the existence of a second sibling, he shrugged his shoulders, expressing no further interest. We were in court for the formal entry of guilty pleas to the several charges recently filed against him. The lawyers had worked out a plea bargain; in exchange for not prosecuting him as an adult, he will go to FEI.

Afterward, I thought about his disinterest in the news of his unknown brother. Any normal sixteen-year-old would be excited over discovering a long-lost brother. It didn't mean a thing to Lester.

For the past several days, Foster and Lester have had cell conferences, as they have had on each occasion in the past when the boy has been incarcerated. This time, Foster is laying the groundwork, trying to convince him that cooperation, rather than an escape effort, is in his own best interest at FEI. As always, Lester is soft and buttery going along with the system. No sooner will he hit Fish Eating Creek than he'll be off. Foster has explained in language the youth understands that getting lost in the swamplands is a lot different than scrambling around Liberty City alleys. Lester, in return, gives him that round, innocent, moonbeam smile, which says exactly nothing. Danny Grizzard and his crew will all be mounted high in their saddles, waiting for Lester to make his move.

There was one special mission I wanted Foster to perform. This related to Lester's son. Where was he? Was he living with his mother? What was his name? Was any help needed? Was it possible to reach Lester through his child? Lester was mum, not wanting to divulge anything about his offspring. He would only tell Foster the mother's name, Swanee Smith, and the child's name. It was Lester Burrows IV or Lester Burrows V, he wasn't sure which. When informed in court that the birth certificate showed he was Lester Burrows IV and therefore his son was Lester Burrows V, he showed renewed interest. One could sense he was proud of the name, particularly the fact that each Burrows bore a numerical designation, showing continuity from generation to generation.

Despite an almost nonexistent family, poor Lester clings to the hope that things might be different for his son, a child who in all likelihood will not know Lester Burrows IV any better than the preceding Burrows generations knew their fathers. Foster will now start a search through school records, welfare files, public-housing records, and other sources to locate Lester Burrows V. His father keeps getting one more last chance; maybe we can give the newest Lester Burrows a better first chance.

## Wednesday, May 1, 1985

People don't expect judges to answer their own telephones, but during lunch hour, when my secretary, Janet Rosselle, is not on hand, I do the honors. The gag around the office is that, if I don't like the caller, I quickly identify myself as the "clean-up man" and the caller just as quickly hangs up. This time, it was Laurence (The Fighter), calling from the county jail and wanting to talk to his judge. I was glad to hear his voice.

## Being There for the Bad Times

"What went wrong at Highland Park Hospital, Laurence?"

"They gave me a hard time. I didn't do anything to anybody. Can't I get out of here and go to school to learn a trade?"

"We have tried to get you in school for a year and you have resisted every day. Those robberies are something for which you have to be punished. Don't you understand that?"

"I want to be near my mama. I love my mama."

"Try to make the best of it, Laurence. Mr. Foster is trying to get you admitted to Jackson Memorial Hospital in the next few days."

"I want to go there to find out what's wrong with me. I don't want to go back to FEI. Too much stress and strain. I had to put up with a lot of racial stuff."

"Stay out of trouble in the adult jail, Laurence. They are tough there."

"I haven't had trouble yet. But some of those dudes keep looking at me. I might have trouble."

It was a friendly chat. Nothing of real substance, but, as with the others, after a year, he, too, felt secure enough to carry on a conversation with a judge, even a white one. Laurence can still focus on only one subject in a conversation: himself. Listening carefully for signs of distorted reality as he spoke, all I could hear was an unsophisticated youth whose concerns were very primitive. He was to the point, never showing the slightest sign of someone with a dysfunctional thought process. This has been a rough year for him. The next year may be rougher.

In only fifteen minutes studying public-school attendance records, Foster had located Swanee Smith. Interviewing her was easy, too. Yes, she was a friend of Lester Burrows, had a nine-month-old child, and was not married. Is Lester the father? A scornful laugh was the response: "I haven't seen Lester in years. Never had sex with him. My baby's name is Talbert Toran. I wish I knew where to find the real father. He left town a long time ago."

Foster demurred at my request that he repeat Swanee's denial to Lester: "Judge, let him have it. If he wants to go around acting like he's the father of a child, let him. He doesn't have much of anything else."

I suppose. For all we know, Lester may have deliberately led us astray with Swanee, and in fact a Lester Burrows V may exist in some other ghetto tenement. Maybe we should leave him alone. We won't, but it probably will not make much difference.

# 8

---

## Inching Along
## with Six Bad Dudes
## Covers a Lot of Miles

**Six Months Later**
**Thursday, October 24, 1985**

### LAURENCE SAMUEL *(The Fighter)*

The lady on the other end of the phone identified herself as Maureen Appel, director of health services for Eckerd State School, at Okeechobee. She was responding to an earlier inquiry as to the status of Laurence Samuel: "Laurence is a very agreeable young man, working as an aide in our infirmary. He performs responsibly in his job and also holds the position of group leader in his cottage. I am happy to confirm that Laurence's behavior has been a pleasant surprise. He gets along well with others and performs all his responsibilities."

"You have the wrong file there," I interrupted. "That's not my Laurence Samuel." It was *indeed* my Laurence. Not the same personality who had created physical fear among Highland Park Hospital staffers, disrupted the Dade Juvenile Detention Center, and caused havoc at FEI, but some new being who had taken over the old Laurence.

Several months ago, he had been hustled out of Highland Park in the middle of the night, sent to the Dade county jail, and placed in the secure confines of Ward D awaiting psychiatric examination. Upon completion of the examination, he would be shipped immediately to State School unless doctors at Jackson Memorial Hospital determined that other treatment was appropriate.

After several days of testing, the doctors confirmed what we already knew. He had poor impulse control and was angry, unremorseful, and indifferent to any pain he inflicted. None of the examiners had been impressed with his loss of memory or change of identity. From interviews with his family, it was learned that, as a three-year-old, he had played with matches and that while growing up he was considered to be "the baddest kid in the neighborhood." The matches and his reputation may account for his acting out those roles as a teenager, but this information was of little value at this late date. He was a menace and needed to be locked up to protect innocent people who crossed his path.

I had called Buddy Streit, the head of State School, to prepare him for Laurence's arrival. Streit has always envied the favorable press afforded FEI as an innovative progressive experiment while his State School is often described as merely a warehouse for children. I teased Buddy: "Here's your golden opportunity to succeed where FEI failed. If you can do anything with Laurence, you deserve a medal."

During the first five weeks at State School, he was the same old Laurence: inciting a riot, verbal abuse of the staff, AWOL from class, extorting money from inmates, physical attack on peers. It would only be a matter of time before a Laurence Samuel explosion rocked the school. Streit was patient, placing him in the special Alpha Cottage for severely disturbed, physically aggressive youth. It's a no-nonsense, shape-up-or-double-your-stay program. Getting tougher hadn't worked before, but Streit assured me this program was different.

By August, the situation had worsened. Streit called with a message that Laurence apparently had a frontal-lobe seizure and was taken off the premises for psychiatric evaluation. Here it comes, I thought. This is the same script he used at FEI. When he returns, he'll probably try to burn the forest at Okeechobee. The examination showed no signs of illness, and he was returned to Alpha Cottage.

Meanwhile, during this period of Laurence's disturbing behavior, I had been receiving mail regularly from him. All of it, even during the period of his so-called seizure, was very rational, self-understanding, and controlled: "Thank you for helping me in life and not giving up on me." (June 4); "I'm proud of my attitude in life and my mind is made up to do what I have to do to make it in the outside

**213**

world." [July 29); "I received your letter and I'm ready to come home. The people up here say I have changed. I guess I can go home to my love ones." (August 8); "I have completed the Alpha Program and can deal with my problems for better. Give me a try and see how I do. I have showed you that I can make it up hear, so let me prove myself at home." (September 6)

Despite the fact that he continues to misspell my name in each of his letters, his requests are touching. There obviously are two Laurences. Maybe three. When does the good one take over?

The State School progress report, dated October 4, 1985, told it all:

> Laurence has been a client for approximately four and a half months. He was in the Alpha Program, which he successfully completed. Since his return to Kennedy Cottage, Laurence has exhibited acceptable and appropriate behavior.
>
> Since the last reporting period, there has been a significant degree of consistency in Laurence's behavior. Presently, Laurence maintains good behavior in the cottage and school areas. He is currently a positive group leader at his assigned cottage and his leadership is highly respected by his peers. Laurence has been consistent in exhibiting respect for his peers and authority figures while being very cooperative.
>
> Academically, Laurence has upgraded his standings. He qualifies for enrollment in our GED program and is expected to start studies in the near future. It has been observed by our staff that presently, Laurence exhibits no major behavioral problems. This reporting period he hasn't been involved in any major incident nor has he exhibited aggressive or violent behaviors.

Foster, returning from a visit with Laurence, is equally impressed with the new image: "He's clear-eyed, cooled-down, and relaxed. Maybe he forgot who he was supposed to be. He's excited about going home and says he wants to go to school."

"What do you attribute the change to?"

"I don't know." Further speculation is useless. Foster will bring him home for Christmas, make plans with him, and then hope for the best. This one has to be a miracle.

### LESTER BURROWS *(The Runner)*

Stubborn is the word for Lester Burrows. He won't give in easily to society. Six months at FEI and they haven't corralled or even slowed him down. He's done all the things expected of him: two escape efforts, an arrest for burglary, sexual misbehavior, and deliberately ignoring camp rules. He won't be socialized. I suppose that wandering the streets all your life makes it hard to conform to someone else's idea of how to live.

One of the escape efforts involved stealing an employee's rifle, then wading through the swamps for eight hours, using a log to cross a river to avoid moccasin snakes and alligators. He and his two accomplices were spotted by the police hiding in high grass just off the main highway. Real "Cool Hand Luke" stuff. Contrite upon his capture, he waited several weeks before breaking into the operations director's file cabinet and stealing money and cigarettes. Criminal charges were deferred.

Danny Grizzard, the FEI chief, preferred to ride out the storm with Lester, shipping him back to me for a judicial sermon. If anyone is not amenable to reasonable persuasion, he has proven to be that one. To satisfy FEI, I went the lecture route. Lester had a few new muscles and showed some pleasure when I mentioned it. He had that perpetual half-moon smile ready for me. I tried sternness: "I didn't take you to raise. Foster and I have tried to help, but every time you turn us down. This is the end of the line. I will not rescue you any longer. If they prosecute you, you are on your own. I am tired of sending Foster looking for you all over the state. If you want to end up in Raiford Prison, that's O.K. with me."

"I'm not going to run again. I want to study electronics. I'm going to do the right thing."

And so it went. Later in the month, back in Miami, representing FEI in a basketball game, he disappeared for several hours, and then reappeared claiming he had visited his grandmother and his son. In August, he was caught having oral sex with another inmate. Foster shrugged it off, saying, "Street people do that to survive, especially when confined. It's not a new life-style. The other kid is a straight-out faggot. He's the problem, not Lester."

The September FEI report on Lester had a few positives. He's made some improvement in responding to authority and his negative attitude has lessened. Best of all, no serious setbacks this month. A few small steps forward and none backward. Operations Director Johnson saw a faint light ahead: "Lester is a stone wall: he steals without concern, lies about everything, denies wrongdoing even when caught red-handed. He's not too friendly with other kids, fears they may take something from him. He's never had anybody care for him and he's afraid to let anybody fill the gap. He's improved a little. Escape hasn't crossed his mind since you talked to him. I'm the only one at FEI he trusts. We have a special relationship. I think there's some hope for him." Foster once thought he too had developed a special relationship with Lester.

"Are the prospects for Jamie Forest any better?" I asked Foster.

"There's no comparison," he replied. "Jamie is just a seventeen-year-old who refuses to grow up. There's still a chance with him."

## JAMIE FOREST *(The Nuisance)*

Unlike Laurence or Marco, Jamie is the kind of delinquent who quietly amasses a long record of offenses, but never attracts much attention. No one has ever impressed upon him the difference between right and wrong, so that violating the law has no meaning to him. At this stage, he is considered "mouthy," but no real threat to anybody. None of his crimes has involved serious violence, and he's small enough to be ignored. A year or two from now, when his anger and his failure begin to take further toll on his personality, he may not be so harmless.

After his failure at DMI and an arrest for yet another burglary, he was placed under the long-term, demanding regimen of FEI. They will either reach him or he'll be gone forever, certain to always be a small-time thief grooming himself for bigger moves.

Thus far, progress is slow. Jamie reluctantly accepts the requirements of Last Chance Ranch. During the summer work program, he earned money shoveling corn for farmers and was proud to send $150 of his earnings home to his mother. Staff reports show continued problems with his temper because he threatens other campers. Most are out of his range physically and they merely brush him off as a little fly, which upsets him even more. He works hard at not making friends, repeatedly uttering racial slurs at the white staff members. They, too, ignore him.

On his visits, Foster finds him talkative, in good spirits, and involved in the things he is doing. Working in the camp plant nursery is something he likes. He often goes there on his own, just as he did at Dade Marine Institute. "If only he'd quit being at war with everyone, maybe we could do something with him," mused Foster.

Jamie is going to require a long-drawn-out vigil. Readjusting his attitudes and standards is hard to do at age seventeen. He has a long stay ahead in the FEI program. They'll need to do a lot more than teach him to say "yes, sir." FEI Operations Director Gerald Johnson put it thusly: "He wants to be pampered twenty-four hours a day. If he can't have it his own way, he goes off the deep end. He's small and has to protect himself with his mouth. Last week, for the first time he came to me and promised to get his act together."

At one time, I thought that Jamie's mild retardation classification covered up a bright youngster. Apparently, I was wrong. His latest letter, written so childishly, confirms that what I had hoped for was not hiding in that shell. We'll have to settle for less—a lot less. If he can grasp sufficient survival skills and rudimentary knowledge of life about him, along with a slight tolerance of others, he may yet survive in the world outside.

## MARCO ZARGULA *(The Charmer)*

As my car slowed along the gravel parking area at the entrance to the Southeast Florida Juvenile Detention Center, I wondered how many more times Marco would be sitting in some distant Florida jail waiting for a visit from Foster or me. This time, the lockup was in Ft. Myers, on the lower west coast. In April he had been sent to Disc Village, in Tallahassee, where he did fairly well for two months. At that time, he glowingly told Foster how impressed he was with life in Tallahassee: "I want to move to this city and live here with my mother. That way I won't be near my bad friends in Miami. I can get a job in construction here. All my problems will be over." It was a short-lived euphoria.

Foster and I barely had time to speculate on how long it would take for the real Marco to emerge. The phone call came in the midst of one of our progress review sessions, at the very moment Foster was reciting the latest positive report from Disc Village. I listened to the caller and handed the phone to Foster to let him hear it first-hand from the supervisor.

Marco had run away. The honeymoon was over. It was the first of several escapes. Each time, a chastened boy returned to a forgiving Disc Village. Finally, the inevitable report: "On July 4, 1985, Marco again absconded from Disc Village, taking two other clients and was apprehended by the Tallahassee Police Department and detained at

**217**

the Leon County Juvenile Detention Center. Marco's behavior has gone completely out of control. Our program can no longer tolerate his behavior."

Foster was there the next day, listening to Marco's tale of woe: "They made me do dirty jobs. Scrub floors with a toothbrush. Sit in a chair facing the wall all day. I can't smoke a cigarette. I don't want to sit in a circle telling everybody why I'm a fuck-up." Of course, most of these tasks were punishment for rule violations. His last runaway involved walking twenty miles through the woods and hitching a ride to downtown Tallahassee.

At his exit interview, the Disc director concluded: "We recommend that Marco continue his long-term residential treatment in a highly structured and secure setting where he is not allowed the option to run away and put himself in a life-threatening predicament." Then, after embracing Marco warmly, the Disc director turned to Foster, saying, "Marco's a nice sensitive kid. We like him. If there are changes in him, we'll gladly take him back."

Good ol' Marco. Always The Charmer. They recommended FEI. Danny Grizzard, on the lookout for a few nonblacks, was receptive. Marco seemed unconcerned about going there. "Do they need a good cook?" was all he asked.

I suppose we should have known that, if he couldn't make it at Disc Village, he surely wouldn't survive the rigors of FEI. But we were running out of options. He lasted three months at Disc and two months at FEI. As in every other program, he made the adjustment at FEI. The staff saw him as a bright prospect. Even Foster, knowing him as he did, was showing some cautious optimism. Last Chance Ranch was living up to its name. Not for long. One of the other kids managed to steal a set of car keys, invited Marco along, and they were on the way to Miami and freedom. They were spotted before leaving the compound and never had a chance. The hundred-mile-an-hour chase lasted half an hour over a wet, dangerous highway and included sheriff's roadblocks and bumping the pursuit car off the road. Only good fortune avoided a fatal injury.

Now awaiting prosecution as an adult, Marco was temporarily housed in the detention center, located in Ft. Myers. It was a clean-looking facility and provided all the amenities: locked doors and bars but also shelves of books, ping-pong tables, and a nice mess hall. Relaxed kids moved about freely. Looking through the rec room window, I saw Marco immersed in a card game. One of the players, noting my presence, alerted him, and he wheeled around in his chair

**218**

flashing a dazzling smile—his judge was here. Word of my visit had preceded me, and, when I entered to claim him for my visitation, there was almost a cheer—"Marco! Marco!"—from the others in the room. Obviously, he was a popular member of the group. That's how it has always been. Why can't that engaging personality be turned into some constructive purpose? We sure have tried.

An office was made available for us, and Marco lounged at ease in one of the chairs. He needed a haircut, and a close inspection of his face showed the-sixteen-year-old was about ready for a razor blade. As we talked, it became obvious that FEI had made some impact. All his responses were prefaced with the compulsory "yes, sir," required there. He shrugged when I commented on that, replying almost sardonically that he was taught good manners.

This wasn't the time or place for the authority figure to demand answers. Mine was the role of an elder listening without being judgmental. He deserves whatever punishment is meted out, but there's something pathetic about a bright, popular boy, still too young to shave, whose options are all nearing the end. What makes him run? I let him ramble on, barely interrupting:

> I don't know why I screw things up. I'm a fool. The thought of being locked up makes me run. I want to be with my mother and sister. I only want it my way. I don't know why. The more they lock me up, the more I'll run away. I think coming to Miami did it. In New York all I ever did was skip school. All my friends in Larchmont Gardens are into stealing and dope. I'm part of it and hate to be left out. If I didn't steal or do drugs, I wouldn't have any friends. Everytime I meet someone who's into stealing, I want to do it.

No crying, no whimpering, or begging for another chance. As gently as possible, I told him this case was out of my hands and I couldn't intervene in his behalf. He would soon be placed in an adult jail awaiting trial. As if reading my mind, he said he was no longer fearful of being sexually assaulted. One of his fellow escapees, a homosexual, had twice been sodomized at FEI, but Marco, shrugging it off, declared him fair game. He seemed to be making the mental adjustment to hard time. It's apparently a lot easier to gear yourself for life in prison than life in the streets.

Departing with the promise that we were not giving up on him, I knew that Marco would be a career case. As long as Foster and I stay in the criminal-justice system, Marco will be there to keep us busy.

His Ft. Myers HRS counselor, Troy Brunley, waited for me outside. He was a country boy with a thick southern twang who had grown up on the banks of the Calusa River. Before his present job, he had been a counselor at FEI. He only knew Marco a short time but was the HRS counselor on duty when Marco had been arrested:

> That night Marco came into the police station as if he had been out for a stroll. He thought the escape was a neat idea, not taking his problem too seriously. He didn't say anything, but his body language said he didn't give a shit. He'd like to go back to FEI, but if he doesn't he'll make do wherever he goes. Most of these kids acting-out at FEI figure that the worse that can happen is transfer to another program that might be easier. I have no idea what will turn Marco on. He'll say what he has to and do what needs doing to get along. He's in big trouble here, but it hasn't set in yet. It may never.

So that's Marco's situation. Accompanied by Marco's mother, Foster visited him several weeks later. His trial is not scheduled until some months hence. Waiting, he works on his GED diploma and his suddenly found interest in religion. He goes to church every day, something he avoided while growing up. GED and GOD are two good things for Marco, but true conversion to anything won't be that easy for him.

## ANDY SILLS *(The Drinker)*

It had to happen to Andy. And it finally did. For a year, he's been doing the right things and avoiding serious trouble. Problems were plentiful, but he somehow managed. Labeled a "star" early by Foster, he never let him down—at least until this summer. These past few months were hard times for Andy, but to his credit in the end he was back again.

It was one of those hot, uncomfortable May afternoons. The air conditioning was inadequate for the crowded courtroom. It was a day when one hopes that nothing serious will need to be addressed. Outside, waiting for their cases to be called, lawyers were plea bargaining; social workers were interviewing their clients; and others were just milling about. Not quite a flea-market atmosphere, but not the hallowed halls of justice either.

There was Cornelius Foster against the back wall in my courtroom. Andy's mother stood next to him, a worried look on her face.

## Inching Along

The calendar didn't have Andy's name, which meant an emergency situation. I asked, "What can I do for you, Mr. Foster?"

A weak little smile crept over his face as if to send me a private message. I sensed it immediately. Andy was in deep trouble. The other shoe had finally dropped. "This is a detention hearing for Andy Sills," announced Foster. "He was arrested for burglary this morning. He and a friend broke into a trailer." Poor Foster! How hard it must have been to say that. His one pure success, and now it's back to the drawing board again.

It had happened because Mrs. Waite (Sills) chose to help a friend evicted from a trailer, providing her and her son space in the Waite apartment. The son, Andy's age, whose police record was even longer than Andy's, engineered the break-in that brought them some costume jewelry, a bag of pennies, and two witnesses who spotted them at the scene.

Andy's fall was more than peer influence. Everything else around him has been going downhill. He just didn't have enough inner resources to resist. Financially, the family is in trouble. The only breadwinner is the stepfather; mother and Andy are now both unemployed. Mrs. Waite has taken in three boarders plus her crippled father, making a total of nine occupying a house built for no more than four. In addition, Andy partitioned one of the rooms so that his girl friend, Abbie, could move in. Before the summer was many weeks old, she was pregnant. Mr. Waite screamed, "I don't want that whore around here," and the curtain dividing the room came down and girl friend Abbie was out. An abortion followed and, needless to say, Abbie's old-fashioned Catholic parents have lost their appetite for Andy.

The house has gone to pot because an assortment of cats, birds, and other animals are invited guests. Lice are also back. The three little girls have infested their school, Andy doing the same to our detention center. Everyplace they go, lice follow. Andy is being deloused at the center, and the social workers assigned to the family rescued the three girls, sending them to summer camp. Foster, observing the family scene, says, "I talk to them from the outside, standing on the porch, while the social workers scrub, spray, and shampoo them."

I suppose an abortion, lice, sisters playing with all the animals, no job, and people squeezed in around you can make life hard, but why suddenly go along on a petty caper to steal pennies and liquor miniatures. Foster had no answer: "He didn't go into the trailer. Nothing of value taken. Maybe they drank some of the miniatures. There was no reason for it, and he can't explain it." Andy's explanation wasn't any better.

It got worse. Andy's father came to town, presumably to assist him during the crisis. Released until his trial, Andy promptly left town with his father for parts unknown. Mother said they were in Boston, New York, or anyplace. I told Foster to check the neighborhood bars, and place an all points pickup for Andy. We had invested too much time in him to allow this ending. Meanwhile, unbeknownst to him, his burglary case was dropped, the victim declining to prosecute. So a nationwide search was being made for someone no one wanted—except Cornelius and me.

Two weeks later, that phone call came. It was Andy—a pleading Andy: "Please take me back. But don't put me in jail. I've been drinking a lot, but joined Alcoholics Anonymous. Will I have to go to jail? Abbie and I may get back together again. Will I go to jail? Her mother still likes me. But not her father. I'll turn myself in if I don't have to go to jail."

I told him to surrender, but no deals. Jail depends on Foster, and I said, "He'll make the decision." I hung up quickly. Half an hour later, he was back in detention. Foster chose the Dade Marine Institute, and without further ado Andy was enrolled. This meant dropping out of the auto-repair course before graduation, but a GED diploma was available at DMI. The youth needed structure and an opportunity to be productive. His family situation was chaotic, school was boring, employment opportunities had disappeared, and his love life was on the rocks. Something new was needed.

Thirty days later, Foster brought me a sack of award citations earned by Andy. Every ribbon that month had his name on it. I told Foster that DMI distributes ribbons like the Waite (Sills) family distributes lice. Nonetheless, I was impressed. Andy was coming back.

Another thirty days and Andy and Abbie are together again. Then, from out of nowhere, Foster walks in one morning and casually states that Andy may be leaving us. The story is a fairy tale. As he recites it, I realize Andy has a chance to live every child's dream.

Foster explained the situation: "There's this big millionaire from California who owns this big yacht. Every year, he interviews DMI students and picks three to serve on his crew. They get $750 monthly, all expenses paid. First they go to California to work on the boat for a month. They then come back to Miami, pick up passengers, and go on a Caribbean cruise. From there, they go to the ports of Europe, coming back a year later."

"Holy mackerel!" was all I could say. What more could a Master Counselor Program provide?


## DWIGHT ANDERSON *(The Migrant)*

Lasting for about a year, Dwight's musk period may be coming to an end. It has been a rough time. At the very beginning, he looked like an easy prospect. Starting as an undersized twelve-year-old, he was rescued from a dismal future and provided fresh new living quarters, a private summer camp, everyday attention by a caring counselor, and social workers to minister to all the needs of the Anderson family. At the end of the first year, he was taller, tougher, totally intransigent. Nothing offered met his needs. His fall continued unchecked: a gang war in his housing project, truancy, new law violations, and anger at the world.

Foster had opted for removal to a Dade County Group Treatment Home, something I had resisted for a long time. "These group homes have professional staffs who work with these kids," Foster assured me. "Besides, some of those kids are bigger than Dwight, and he may quit being a bully." Shades of Laurence. I had heard that song before.

Thirty days was as long as the group home cared to deal with Dwight. The June 5 transfer request was clear and to the point: "In spite of an all-out effort by the staff at Dade Group Treatment Home, Dwight refuses to stop his physical approach as an answer to all situations. On three occasions he has physically assaulted smaller fellow residents. He attempted to intimidate staff, . . . has broken numerous rules, . . . refuses to participate in group meetings, . . . will not follow simple directions. The Dade Group Treatment Home has no individual programs to fit this child's needs."

In addition to his other problems at the group home, Dwight contracted gonorrhea. He said, "I had sex with a little girl in the neighborhood." Foster, the man for all seasons, quickly took him to a doctor for penicillin shots.

We made a quick decision to ship Dwight to another program: the Nassau Start Center, located at Fernandina Beach, in north-central Florida. They provided the same kind of services as that of the group home in Miami, but what a difference was apparent three months later! Dwight's behavior warranted this laudatory report:

> Dwight continues to show improvement in developing relationships with the staff and his peers. He has shown that he can be consistent in accepting criticism and getting along with others. He has earned three (3) eighth grade credits and explored pre-vocational interests and training opportunities. The academic staff notes that Dwight has made considerable improvements in most of his skills. He has shown a sincere interest in working towards completing the long range goals set for him. Dwight was even elected to hold a house position by his peers.

"What happened between June and September?" I asked Foster, who had been visiting him regularly at both places.

"I don't know. It must have been his time."

Dwight has been home a month, and Foster is carefully shepherding him. The youth claims to be serious about school, even encouraging his cousin Kenneth to attend. Until the school bus schedule is worked out, Foster delivers him, checks with his teachers, and virtually tucks him in at night.

The family situation is the same. His older sister's two children have been taken by the state on account of neglect. Grandmother is in the hospital, and the disarray normal for the household continues. Foster finally convinced HRS authorities to remove brother Derrick from the home and place him back in the center for retarded children from which he had escaped.

Can it be that Dwight's other interests may overcome the overwhelming negative influence emanating from the family? Nevertheless, both programs made note of the attachment between Dwight and his mother. They are strongly bonded and need each other. His heart is at home.

The gang problem in the housing project has receded—at least for the moment. Pedro, the tough Puerto Rican kid, was killed in a car accident, and the housing authorities began tightening security rules. No more beatings at the bus stop from Pedro's gang, and those mini gun wars and window-shattering episodes are at a halt.

At my next meeting with Dwight, I found the same unsmiling, glum personality. He was almost a head taller and his arms were long and sinewy. I could see another Laurence emerging. Only when I said, "Smile, you are going home" did a little grin break out.

**224**

## Inching Along

"I want to play football. Go to school. Stay straight." That was all he said. The sum total of our conversation. The smile broke off. It was almost rote, as if he had been saving it for me. No matter. If Foster can keep him on track for six more months, Dwight may still go all the way.

The most revealing thing in this Master Counselor relationship is not the reaction of our charges to us, but ours to them. We are always looking for big gainers. Every day the message comes across emphatically that nothing worthwhile will happen in a hurry. It's only an inch forward—and, if we are lucky, maybe another inch.

# 9

---

## Putting Humpty Dumpty Together Again Needs More than the King's Men

**Friday, May 2, 1986**

It's over. The experiment ends today. Two years of twists and turns, unfilled expectations, some pleasant surprises, a lot of big disappointments. Mostly it's learning that there's no telling what a kid in trouble will do. The last six months have been more of the same.

### DWIGHT ANDERSON *(The Migrant)*

It's like a broken record. At any given moment, Dwight's in trouble, either becoming involved in it or emerging from it. During the five months since last October, when he returned from the Nassau Start Center, he alternately gets along at school or is challenging teachers. The housing-project gang members no longer bother him, but the school bus is a problem. The other kids on it still call him "retard." One can never tell when it will be a good day. Called to task, he bristles and says, "When I'm in a bad mood, I don't like school." That's the sum total of his statement. He refuses to burden his mind with explanations for his behavior. Problems vary little, and his responses are the same. It may be too much to expect a kid who has so few resources to react with any degree of understanding.

## Putting Humpty Dumpty Together

For Foster, running back and forth between the family and school authorities, the last six months was a losing struggle. Mother failed to wake Dwight in the morning, refused to make cuffs for the jeans purchased by Foster ("I can't find the needle and thread"), and brother Derrick was back in the house (HRS ran out of funds for retarded kids). The school people, optimistic for a time, now see little hope.

Each of these final six months has been a replay of the past. We tried harder at the end: Foster, grasping to find that little niche where Dwight might fit in; I, finally breaking through his stone wall of silence. He listened and at times responded, but somehow it didn't make too much difference. Whoever and whatever had molded him got there first. That collection of migrants wandering through his life did their job. Sometimes I saw a glimmer, but the next time it was the old Dwight again. In February for the first time, he spoke in full sentences, sounding realistic and receptive. His voice had a ring that replaced his usual rote manner of speech.

> *Dwight:* "I might make it at South Dade High School. They got football and basketball. I can get along with the teacher. I want a good job."
> *Gelber:* "What kind of work do you want to do?"
> *Dwight:* "Washing dishes, stocking canned goods, mopping floors. I don't want to be in the sun all day picking hampers of beans like Derrick does."
> *Gelber:* "You can do better than that. What's going to happen to you when you get older?"
> *Dwight:* "I'll buy me a house."

Primitive responses, but at least in February he was thinking ahead. In March, when I faced him across the table, listening to a report by an angry Foster, he once again retreated to silence. Arms crossed against his chest, glaring, he said nothing.

> *Foster:* "He fights with the teacher and threatens everyone else. He's smoking marijuana and, while he's not a junkie yet, he's on his way. On the street, I heard he stole a TV. He denies it, but street talk is pretty accurate."
> *Gelber:* "What about that, Dwight?"
> *Dwight:* "That was Derrick stole the TV, not me. They always blaming me for somebody else."

Foster, still angry, rising from the table, cuts off the conversation: "C'mon. Next time I'm not bringing you to the judge. You go straight to State School." One more chance. We have been nursing Dwight for almost two years now. How much longer to go? Is this the time to pull him out of school? Get him any kind of job—washing dishes? That's hardly progress.

In March, the decision was to keep going, at least for the next few months until the experiment ends. Who will be there after that to contend with a fractious youngster and a family oblivious to his presence?

Only two more weeks now remain in April and the experiment ends. Dwight's adjustment to me is evident. He sits across the table relaxed, responding, waiting for the next question; I am no longer the enemy. Not only has he grown about eight inches since we started, but he possesses a little more self-confidence. Or am I imagining what I'd like to believe?

His school-attendance record is atrocious. Eight absences in February, twelve in March, and five for the first two weeks in April. He's had fights with teacher aides, sulks when called on in class, and has been suspended for horseplay. He's an eighth-grader, but in performance is several grades below. No matter what efforts are made, the school system cannot break through to motivate him. The Master Counselor Program has opened doors for him, but none has resulted in a turnaround.

Foster listened as Dwight and I once again tossed around the options. They were few and time was running out. Finally, Foster observed, "You know, judge, we should be grateful. Dwight has kept out of trouble for over a year. For him, that's great."

Dwight's usual glum features lit up as he accepted the compliment. "I don't be doing no wrong now. I start using my head."

If keeping out of jail is our goal, then Dwight has made a lot of headway. He's learned how to do that, if nothing else. I made one last effort to impress him: "Don't you understand, Dwight? You need to learn to read and write before anyone will give you a job. What is it you want out of life?"

He stared at me for awhile, trying to understand the import of my question. Starting to answer, then reconsidering, he waited a few moments before replying: "I don't want to pick tomatoes anymore. I did it for a week. Can't make any money. My mom ain't picking tomatoes anymore, She have a job in a hotel washing windows. I can do that."

It's clear that vocational training is all we have left. He doesn't turn sixteen for four months, when he'll be eligible for those special trade classes. We can probably obtain a waiver until then. Anything to remove him from his mother's influence. Because only two weeks are left in the program, we need to line him up for the next few years. I questioned him: "How about it, Dwight? You ran a lawn mower. Would you like to learn to be an auto mechanic? Air conditioning? Plumber? Construction work? How about a cook?" (I'm not giving up on getting someone into culinary arts.)

Foster suggested a series of tests to determine his vocational skills. I looked toward Dwight for any hints, rattling off further possibilities, and said, "What would you like to learn to earn some money?" He replied, "I don't like those. I gotta make enough money to help my mama. I wanna learn computers." Why not computers? He certainly is entitled to the same American dream every kid aspires to. If only that were a possibility! Poor Dwight! He is not yet sixteen, and his last opportunity is probably gone. The regular public-school classroom isn't for him anymore. At this point, it's probably just as important to get him out of school as it was to keep him in during the past two years. This is another crucial moment in his life. We will settle for a lot less than learning computers. If we act promptly and set him up with some vocational opportunity, he may yet survive. Two weeks is such a short time.

## MARCO ZARGULA *(The Charmer)*

In November, Glades County circuit-court Judge James Adams put Marco on adult probation for two years, warning him he would be sent to Raiford Prison if he didn't pay the thirty-dollar monthly fee required of adult probationers. He was admonished to stay off drugs, to contact his probation officer weekly, and not to get arrested. This was the adult system's typical reaction to juvenile criminals: bypass any effort to work with a kid and then throw the book at him when he fails to pay the monthly fee to cover the cost of probation supervision—only a fiction anyway.

Marco was free at last. Not quite. Foster held a Pick-up Order from our court to take custody. He departed quickly with Marco in tow, en route to the Dade County Juvenile Detention Center. We had him once more. What do we do with him? He had started as a "piece of cake," bright, a good prospect. Before our eyes, drugs, the gang, and some twisted compulsion inside him made him resist everything. Humana, Disc, culinary arts, State School, FEI, Foster's handholding—nothing made an impact. Sure, the blame isn't entirely ours. His problems existed before we acquired him, but it's different when you are standing by watching it all unfold.

Home is still as disruptive as ever and leaving him on the streets is a sure bet for an arrest and a probation violation. Foster suggested shipment to the Marianna State School for a few months, and then try again in Miami. Marianna, in north Florida, is similar to Eckerd's Okeechobee State School except that it is considered to be tougher. Bill Shapiro, the HRS transfer hearing officer, agreed to handle the paperwork expediting the transfer.

It's not likely that Marianna can do for Marco what Okeechobee did for Laurence. Laurence is a relatively simple boy (though his problems are complex), concerned with creature comforts, and, when denied these, he strikes back. Marco is cold and cunning: his little mind works all the time, scheming, angling, and dreaming out his "Scarface" scenario.

His stay in Marianna is more for our benefit. We need the time to prepare. How will he do in Marianna? Foster laughed: "That will really be a piece of cake for him. The one thing he's learned the past two years is that he can handle jail. He doesn't like it, would rather be out but knows it will be over in a short time."

Three months later, Marco was back in Miami. As expected, he impressed the Marianna staff, earning a B+ in GED Preparation and a B in Vocational Training—Upholstery. As in most juvenile reformatories, he and the staff signed a performance contract that outlined their respective responsibilities. It's all very legal and proper. The earlier the goals are reached, the sooner the kid is released. Marco's responsibilities included: "Cooperate with Counselor. Keep an open mind on alternative programs. Display behavior in classroom and not be disruptive."

It's all a little too pat. The Marcos of the world absorb this with ease. Foster on one of his visits reported the youth was finding life relatively comfortable and safe in confinement. He's learned how to do "easy" time: core courses in the morning—reading, spelling, and math; furniture upholstery in the afternoon. His big problem continues to be the adult probation people in Glades County, angry because he hadn't sent his thirty-dollar supervision fee. When told Marco was incarcerated in Marianna, they still insisted on the fee. I told Foster to work it out, but certainly not to pay it out of our Children's Fund.

Marco came back by Greyhound bus, announcing he was sick and tired of running. Glad to be home, he wanted to be settled, but had no plans. Whatever we offered he rejected, no reasons given. He just didn't like the public schools, culinary arts, or furniture upholstery. It was a typical Marco response. Foster, determined to go all out, found something for him in Larchmont Gardens. This was a work-learn experience that filled his needs for the moment. The sixteen-week program included four hours of class in the morning, learning how to cope in the world of work: filling out applications, practicing interviews, and reading want ads. In the afternoon, clean-up chores at Larchmont Gardens paid $125 biweekly. At the end of sixteen weeks, regular employment was guaranteed. What are the chances of binding Marco to this?

Things at home are the same: two sisters are pregnant, brother is out of work, stepfather is still in jail, and mother is distraught over her inability to make ends meet. According to Foster, Marco is heading for trouble: "He's staying out until two in the morning. Mother can't control him. He says, 'I'm seventeen. I can take care of myself.' At the beginning, he attended all the classes. Now he's missing more than he makes. I think he's shooting cocaine. I told him his adult probation officer can tell him to drop his pants any time, fill the bottle, and you are gone to Raiford."

"What's happening with his adult court probation?" I asked. "They are transferring probation to Dade County, but the paperwork takes several months. They still want the thirty dollars for each month he was locked up in Marianna." I urged Foster to work out the financial problems with adult probation. It's time for another conference with Marco.

He is no longer handsome. As he approaches eighteen years of age, adolescence has taken over. His straight nose has hooked, and those innocent features are now gaunt. That careful smile is still there, emerging at the right times, but controlled. He claimed, "I won't get into trouble. I won't do no drugs. Don't associate with the Calcons. I'll finish this program and get a job." His big concern is the thirty-dollar payment, coming out of his earnings. As soon as a local probation officer is assigned, he intends to complain about paying for the months at Marianna.

I told him Judge Adams is looking forward to a violation: "He'll enjoy sending you to Raiford." Marco shrugged. Once more, we reviewed all the possible jobs that might interest him. He rejected each, again with a shrug. Finally, a bit exasperated, I asked, "What is it you want to do? Do you want to be a drug smuggler?"

He sat there for awhile, biting his nails, ignoring my question. "Maybe I'll take the GED," he responded. He is a tough kid. He's almost afraid of going straight, wary of being captured by anything even sounding like conformity. He's learned to like the adventure of drugs and crime. Unfortunately, we also taught him that the system isn't as menacing as he once thought.

Something is different about him. I didn't realize what it was until he left. He's lost his charm. Not only his looks, but also that winsomeness and the little sparkle that occasionally lit his eyes. He looked and sounded like all the others I see every day: drab and glum.

Two weeks have elapsed and Foster is about ready to give up hope. His description of Marco was depressing: "He's going down the drain. Very high on drugs. He's back with the Calcons. Doing cocaine, free-basing. He's lost weight. Looks like a skeleton. You can see his rib cage clearly. When I talk to him he just looks at me. Keeps repeating, 'I ain't done nothing.' That's all he says. Refuses to get up in the morning. Sleeps late. Doesn't go to classes. When they send him to a work site, he just sits. The lady in charge says he's always spaced out."

I suggested Marco be placed in the lockup for a few days to dry out; then we start all over again. Foster listened patiently, and, like a father explaining the facts of life, he said, "Judge, what do we do then? Put him in another drug program? You know what happened before. Besides, if he's locked up, he's in violation of adult probation and he'll be back before Judge Adams on the way to the chain gang."

Foster has a knack for puncturing my reality. He's right, though. I moved on to another area: "What about his adult probation officer? Is he interested in anything other than the thirty bucks? Has Marco been assigned one locally?"

The probation officer's concern for the monthly supervision fee is irritating me. Foster has learned his name, and perhaps bringing him into the process will make something happen. "Let's have one of those summits," I directed Foster. "This time bring in Marco and his probation officer. Maybe if we put all the cards on the table, Marco will be impressed."

The adult probation officer was Gregory Bridges, a well-dressed, well-spoken black man. He was all business, but reasonable. I thought he would begin harping on the monthly payments, but instead he showed a genuine interest in Marco, apparently not anxious to press his violation of probation. Firm and clear, he had no intention of cajoling or persuading Marco: "I left my card with Marco once. Told him to contact me. He didn't. I went back. Left my card again. Marco didn't show. If he's not in my office tomorrow morning, he's gone. I'm willing to take a chance with him, but not forever." Then, turning toward Marco, he looked at him a moment and speaking slowly, added, "I definitely am not playing games. You are under adult probation. You better act like an adult. If you don't abide by the rules, you go back to Judge Adams in Glades County and then to state prison."

It's good to have someone else playing the heavy. Foster added, angrily: "You don't deserve another chance. I keep giving them to you and, before you go two blocks, you are high on drugs, looking for the Calcons to do a job. You'll get no more help from me."

Marco sat there under the onslaught, a pathetic-looking figure: hair overgrown, features darker than ever, furrows under his eyes, thin, almost emaciated, barely responding and not too coherently. Only drugs can take someone down like that in a few weeks. "Give me another chance," he said, lacking conviction, almost as if the situation required it. Bridges and Foster ignored his plea. I too, sat silently.

Three weeks later and another summit. This time, Bill Shapiro, the HRS transfer hearing officer who had shipped Marco to several programs, was there, mostly out of curiosity. Adult Probation Officer Bridges reported that Marco was performing beyond expectation. He was totally immersed in a work-in-the-morning, study-in-the-afternoon program, and was up-to-date in his monthly probation-fee payment. Bridges, smiling somewhat smugly, recounted his success: "Marco's attitude has changed dramatically. He shows up every day. Does his work. Studies for the GED. He's doing fine. When he finishes the program, he's guaranteed a job."

Bridges obviously was pleased with the progress of his charge. I was too. Foster made no comment. He'd been here before. Marco sat there quietly as though other important things were on his mind. There were, but at that moment I didn't know. Shapiro, sensing something awry, jumped in: "What's wrong, Marco? You're not the same kid I sent away a couple of times. Where's that big smile? That's the longest face I've seen in a long time."

He was right. Marco looked bad. He had needed a haircut at our last meeting. Now his hair tumbled down to his shirt. Some natural color had returned to his face plus a few pounds to his body, but something was wrong with him. He just shrugged when I asked what was bothering him. Foster finally told us: "Marco got arrested last week. He was a passenger in a stolen car. The cops charged him with possession of marijuana. He was doing so well, I didn't have the heart to tell you."

Bridges looked up slowly from his note pad, disappointment in his voice: "That's too bad, Marco. You were doing so good, I hate to report this to Judge Adams."

Now it was time for Foster to spring into action with a direct plea to Bridges: "It was only a cigarette he had behind his ear. The policeman arrested everyone. I'm going to ask the state attorney to dismiss the case. He's finally doing o.k. Now is the time to give him another chance. I've got another job waiting for him if this one doesn't work out."

Bridges, impressed with Foster's plea, said he would wait until the case finishes in court before reporting back to Judge Adams. Turning to Marco, he said, "You are skating on thin ice. From now on you will be required to take weekly urinalysis tests to prove you are free of drugs."

That's were we left it. Foster will try to extricate Marco one more time while Marco no doubt will find a way to court trouble. Shapiro, the onlooker, shook his head in disbelief and queried, "How can a kid in trouble with adult probation walk around with a marijuana cigarette tucked behind his ear?"

None of us bothered to answer this rhetorical question. Shapiro continued: "He's in a box and it looks like he doesn't care if he gets out of it or not."

I think Marco cares. Foster does, too. And probably Bridges does, also. Maybe even Judge Adams. We all care. But, how long can we keep him out of the box?

## ANDY SILLS *(The Drinker)*

I suppose that Andy is the living example of the uncertainty involved in dealing with unstable youngsters. Still, what happened to him was more our fault than his.

After his setback last summer and subsequent placement in Dade Marine Institute (DMI), things began to brighten. Apparently that assignment was perfect for him. He was truly a "star" again, winning awards on the ballfield and in the classroom. On DMI Visitors'

Day, he was there to greet me at the gate, flaxen hair, sunburned face, the picture of health and confidence. Mother and stepfather looked on in admiration, basking in his recognition. He was scheduled to complete his GED in October and graduate from DMI by Christmas. Cornelius had been on the mark from the beginning. It could have been that way except that we wanted a miracle. No miracles happen with these kids.

Disaster came in the form of Captain Bill. He was the millionaire from California who owned the big yacht and was to take Andy on an around-the-world tour. We bought it all, brushing aside any doubts about the captain. They were scheduled to fly to San Diego in ten days. Andy and Captain Bill had been working together on plans for their trip, and all seemed idyllic. In the interim, the youth received permission to attend a relative's funeral in Richmond, Virginia. Upon his return, they would leave amid an airport farewell party we had planned for Andy. His mother returned from Richmond, but Andy didn't. He was absent for three days, and we had no leads as to his whereabouts. Still unconcerned, I knew he'd walk in any moment with that tear in his voice and some weak excuse.

Departure day came and went, Captain Bill saying he'd wait a few more days for Andy. I should have been suspicious then. Why delay for a kid so unreliable? A pickup order was issued; the police in Richmond were notified. Maybe foul play? Andy in a drunken stupor somewhere? Captain Bill says he must leave this weekend. Foster goes into high gear in his search. Finally, a message arrived from Captain Bill. Andy is back in town, frightened, in hiding, afraid he will be locked up. Telephone calls are made back and forth between Foster and Captain Bill, negotiating. Andy and his girl friend are staying at the captain's hotel. What's going on? The captain has airplane tickets for departure on Sunday. Furious, Foster accuses him of hiding a fugitive and threatens him with arrest. My message to Captain Bill: be in my chambers in one hour with Andy or both of you are in deep trouble.

It was now Friday afternoon and seated around my conference table are Captain Bill, Andy, Foster, and Tom Williams, a representative from DMI. The captain sat next to me. He is in his mid-fifties, well over two hundred pounds, his overflowing stomach causing his sport shirt to flap up and down every time he spoke. His hair was barely combed and double-lens glasses hid his eyes—not quite the hardy sea captain I had envisioned. He told me a story of his wife's death several years ago in a horrible accident, leaving him a severely maimed son. It was a ghastly story and I felt sorry for him. I got right down to business:

*Gelber:* "I don't know whether you are a boat captain, a child molester or what, but apparently you have helped conceal Andy from the authority of the court, for which you may be held in contempt of court. If you were a child molester, you wouldn't be stupid enough to come here. So what's your game?"

*Captain Bill:* "I am not a child molester. I have airplane tickets for Sunday. I'm ready to take Andy along. I owned this 180-foot ship valued at three and a half million dollars and had a deal to sell to a Detroit millionaire. The deal fell through and, instead, it was sold to TV Channel 9 in Australia. It's being fitted for use by Channel 9 for the American Racing Cup in 1986. Australia now holds the cup, and its defense will be prime news. From there, we go on to New York for the unveiling of the Statue of Liberty and then on to Australia for several months."

*Andy:* "I ran away because I didn't have bus fare back to DMI and was afraid of getting locked up."

*Comment:* There has to be more to it than Andy's weak explanation and Captain Bill's fanciful story. Something was obviously going down. I should have been more suspicious. Damn it! I should have been more suspicious.

*Gelber:* "How many young boys in the crew and how long do you keep them?"

*Captain Bill:* "There are a total of fifteen in the crew, including some wives of the crew men. There are four the age of Andy. They are hired to be stewards and stay as long as they want to."

*Gelber:* "Why did you select Andy?"

*Captain Bill:* "I spent a few days in the hospital for sun poisoning, and he was the only one of the DMI kids who came over to see me. Besides, I felt sorry for him. I was shocked at conditions in his house. All those people living in a room the size of a closet. Kids barefoot. No one taking care of them. Very little food in the house. I spent $400 buying Andy clothes. He'll never have a chance there."

*Comment:* That hospital story was a little too much, and the $400 for clothes seemed more than a normal outlay for an employee. But I wanted to believe him. I really did.

**236**

# Putting Humpty Dumpty Together

*Gelber:* "What does DMI know about Captain Bill?"
*Tom Williams, DMI representative:* "As far as I know, he's legitimate."

*Comment:* Tom Williams was in his early twenties, absolutely captivated by Captain Bill. To think I allowed myself to be swayed by the assurances of this awe-struck youth!

I directed the captain and Andy to step outside in the company of my bailiff, Barry Young.

*Gelber:* "This is the moment of truth for Andy. We are now at risk-taking time. What do we do? Is Captain Bill for real?"
*Tom Williams:* "Captain Bill is all right. He's offered me a job on the ship and my wife and I might join Andy."

*Comment:* If a DMI instructor and his wife are accompanying them, how unsafe can it be?

*Foster:* "I'm not too happy with Captain Bill, but the important thing is what's best for Andy."
*Gelber:* "I was ready to lock both of them up until Captain Bill said, 'Andy will never have a chance here.' That got to me."

*Comment:* Captain Bill's story is hard to believe, but it's so far-fetched, it must be true.

*Foster:* "Let's give Andy a shot at it."
*Gelber:* "All right. Now hear this. First, I want Captain Bill and his ship operation investigated thoroughly by DMI to make certain he's not in the slave-trade business and that this world cruise is legit. Meanwhile, I want Andy in lockup for the weekend for going AWOL. If all goes well, he'll be on the Sunday plane to San Diego."

I shook hands with Captain Bill, wishing him well. I wanted badly for him to be what he said he was. In the back of the room, bailiff Barry kept shaking his head back and forth. When they left, he said. "Judge, I never went to college, but my street sense tells me you all are crazy if you think this guy is o.k. He's a fake. He ain't no more a ship captain than I'm a judge."

That Sunday morning, Foster called to tell me that Andy had been released from detention to the custody of Captain Bill for the flight to San Diego. I envisioned the airport scene right out of a movie scenario: a rainy Sunday morning, Foster delivering Andy from the detention center to this fat, unkempt, double-lensed, unsavory character. What was in store for Andy? Was it the chance of a lifetime or an uncertain fate? They never boarded the plane. Captain Bill explained: "We will leave as soon as a large draft of money arrives from Australia. In the meantime, I will find a job for Andy at a local dockyard."

Still confused about the status of the captain and still buying his story, neither we nor anyone at DMI had learned anything new about him. Was he a legitimate boat captain? A child molester? An imposter? We still didn't know. Foster described the captain succinctly: "He's a mess." Luckily, the plane trip was delayed. Time was still available to find out about the captain. Maybe he's what he says he is. If we deny Andy this opportunity, we'll feel both foolish and disappointed.

Contact was difficult to maintain the next few days. Captain Bill stayed at a hotel, Andy and Abbie apparently with him. But we weren t certain. Appointments were made and broken. Telephone calls were for the most part ignored. Andy made himself scarce, only his mother seeing him occasionally. There was no sign of him. There was no sign of the draft from Australia either.

When the dawn came, it didn't break—it erupted! Captain Bill was a fake. But what a fake! Arrested by the Dade County Sheriff's Office for grand larceny, it all came out. The crime was a relatively crude one. He and some accomplices (not Andy) had stolen a boat engine, boldly lifting it from a docked boat and transporting it in a van. He was caught in the act. But, there was more. Found in his possession was a directory of names and addresses—all male. Suspicious? Yes, indeed. The Sheriff's Task Force on Exploited Children moved into action. Pornographic child exploitation films were found in his room. He associated with known pedophiles in the community, who were identified as running child-prostitution rings. Was he part of an international network, shipping children around the world to customers at every port? The police weren't sure, but some of their information pointed in that direction. For certain, they could tell a pedophile when they saw one. This was a bad one.

His arrest record told some of the story: three larceny arrests involving swindles, worthless checks, and resisting arrest. What was Andy's involvement? The police interviewed them both, the boy denying any criminal role. He heatedly rejected the suggestion that

**238**

he had sex with Captain Bill, saying, "Abbie was with me all the time."

Captain Bill stated otherwise. In any event, there could be no prosecution because Andy was over sixteen years of age. Satisfied that Andy had committed no crime, the police released him, asking him to "stick around" to help investigate Captain Bill.

That was the last the police saw of Andy Sills. With the police certain to be constantly on his tail, with Foster badgering him, and his whole world turned upside down, he disappeared. Daily visits to his home, contacts with Abbie, stakeouts at his old haunts—all to no avail. No Andy. He did what he does every time he faces a pressure situation: he ran. It's true it wasn't his fault, but, if he had trusted Cornelius Foster a little bit longer, we could have overcome this mishap.

How could I have missed all those signals? Why hadn't I questioned Andy more about his relationship with Captain Bill? Surely, DMI wouldn't vouch for an imposter. Wasn't it strange that Andy disappeared and then reappeared in the company of the captain? In view of all my experience, how could I have been deceived by this consummate liar?

What happened to Captain Bill? He's a survivor. He became an informer for the FBI, CIA, Dade County Sheriff's Organized Crime Unit, and who knows whom else. I'm told he's supplying information to the FBI on bank-fraud cases. Good luck! Coping with such a creative mind, the FBI, too, will be dealing with bank drafts from Australia before long.

Bill's new position as an informer earned him a release from jail. In gratitude, he promptly wrote a $1,000 worthless check for Neiman-Marcus and was placed back in jail. He talked his way out again and is now living in the plush, exclusive Cricket Club, compliments of the federal government. If its cases are based on evidence supplied by the likes of Captain Bill, justice isn't blindfolded; the lady's just winking.

Christmas has come and gone and still no Andy. Had we not become involved with the captain, Andy would now be graduating from DMI, still the "star" of the Master Counselor Program. The search has intensified. One night, Foster and Assistant Court Administrator Larry Hanes sat waiting in a car for nine hours outside the Sills home. The police also visit occasionally, and all Mrs. Sills says is that she thinks Andy is working in Orlando. Nothing else. Foster believes she and Abbie know more than they admit.

# Putting Humpty Dumpty Together

It's time for a conference with the women in Andy's life. Maybe an in-chambers session will bring out the truth. It works sometimes with lawyers. Before I could impress Mrs. Sills with the consequences of misleading the court, her words tumbled out: "The police just dumped him on my doorstep. I never even saw him. He didn't bother to say hello or goodbye or come inside for his clothes. He just ran. He has never called me since then, and he hasn't been back. I don't know where he is. I wish I did. I don't know why he ran away."

She paused for a moment, as if to gain full control of herself:

*Mrs. Sills:* "He liked Captain Bill. He trusted Captain Bill. He wanted to go badly. I thought going with Captain Bill would help him a lot. Why did it have to turn out so bad? What did Andy do that he had to run away? It wasn't his fault that Captain Bill is a sex pervert. Andy didn't know."

*Gelber:* "It wasn't Andy who made the mistake. We weren't suspicious enough. All we want now is to get Andy back and put him on the right track."

*Mrs Sills:* "That boy has a lot of problems. His drinking is terrible. He stops. Then he starts again. I thought going with Captain Bill would help him stop drinking. Whenever he has a problem, he drinks a lot and runs away from home. You know, I don't drink anymore. Haven't had one for two years."

*Abbie:* "Captain Bill was a creep. He was weird. I didn't like him from the first minute, but I went along with it because Andy wanted so much to go on this trip. Captain Bill was nice to Andy. He bought him clothes and other things. But, there was something about him I didn't trust. I think Andy ran away because he's ashamed of what happened. He wants to start his life over again, forgetting Captain Bill and his past. I don't know where he is. He called me once saying he was living in the streets and wouldn't come back. I think he's afraid he'll be locked up again. He hates that. Why should he be locked up? He didn't do anything wrong."

*Gelber:* "I don't want to lock him up, but, if he doesn't return soon, I may have to do that. When he calls again, tell him the judge, Mr. Foster, and DMI only want to help him. We made the mistake with Captain Bill. Andy was only the victim. Tell him to call me."

The conference brought us no closer to Andy. This whole scenario is hard to believe. It's a kind of allegory conceived by a fiendish scriptwriter. Captain Bill is the vision coming out of the clouds to save a weak, alcoholic youngster, instead turning out to be an evil

**240**

child molester. We, the innocent good people, sensing something wrong, ignore it, hoping for some miracle to save the child. It represents all the dreams we have dealing with these badly damaged kids. A real, pure Captain Bill must exist somehere!

Cornelius Foster sat there quietly during the conversation. Not a word out of him. Probably more than any of us, he wanted Andy to have his big chance. Whereas I always had doubts about the boy, Cornelius had never wavered. He knew Andy would make it. "What do we do now, Cornelius? What do you think?"

"I think I'm going to go out and find him, bring him back, and start all over again with him. What happened with Captain Bill was yesterday."

"That's fine, but how many chances do we get?"

Cornelius rose to leave, looked at me for a moment, then said in a cracked voice, "You know, judge, Andy didn't have to be in the Master Counselor Program for this to happen. Guys like Captain Bill are all over the streets looking for kids like Andy."

Finding the youth should be easy, but it hasn't been. His mother and girl friend insist he has a job in Orlando, but no one believes them. Captain Bill may be the key to finding him, assuming one can find the captain. I checked with the Dade County Sheriff's Organized Crime Unit and was told my message would be relayed to the FBI. A week later at 8:15 in the morning, a sharp, crisp voice interrupted my coffee and newspaper reading: "This is Captain Bill. You wanted me."

He was friendly, open, wanting to please. To my simple question "How are you?" he volunteered all I wanted to know and more. He was a paid informer for the FBI and the Sheriff's Office. "I have this wonderful apartment at the Palm Bay Club [even fancier than the Cricket Club], got a new car, plenty of money. Life couldn't be better. I work fifty hours a week and love it. Morning, noon, and night. They even give me time to work on my own. I'm a dockmaster."

Good listener that I am, I allowed him to go on as he extolled the work he and the FBI were doing. Finally, I mentioned my concern for Andy. Did he know of his whereabouts? He hadn't seen him since December, the day of his own arrest. Now, almost three months later, his only contact had been one phone call from Andy, angry over Captain Bill disclosing Abbie's address to the police. The captain's best guess is that the youth probably works and lives near Abbie. He suggested we comb the restaurants in the area of 163d Street and Collins Avenue on Miami Beach. It wasn't much of a lead,

**241**

but Foster will start trekking from drive-in to drive-in looking for a blond seventeen-year-old kid on the lam.

The captain gave me his private phone number, inviting me to call for any further help, and then volunteered, "I am working on a big one now. This morning we are busting up one of the biggest kiddie-porn rings in the country. You'll read about it in the paper." He paused for a moment, then, referring to Andy, added with some emphasis: "It's all right to have one of these kids for yourself, but to exploit them—that's bad."

That's our man, Captain Bill—a true-blue American, saving our children. For the next few days, I scanned the papers closely for the story on the breaking of the kiddie-porn ring. Not a line.

A few days later, we almost found Andy just as Captain Bill had surmised. Foster, on one of his periodic visits to the Sills home, spotted a delivery truck outside the house. "Joe's Pizza" was painted on its body and it bore an address on 163d Street and Collins Avenue. Mrs. Sills hurriedly claimed she was the driver, not her son. Not too likely a story. Foster quickly took the twenty-minute ride to Joe's Pizza, where he was told that "Andy is working the six o'clock shift tonight."

That evening, Foster and three sheriff's deputies surrounded Joe's Pizza on all sides. The FBI tracking down John Dillinger wasn't better prepared. Andy walked in and the deputies sprang, poised with handcuffs. Foster shouted, "No! No!" before any damage could be done. It was a fellow named Andy all right, but not our Andy. The innocent party will wonder the rest of his life what that was all about. Mrs. Sills does deliver pizzas for Joe. She sure has made a lot of progress.

We did gain one more opportunity with Andy. It was in the final days of the program. Foster was driving downtown to HRS headquarters to report on the Master Counselor Program to the district administrator when he sighted Andy on a bike carrying a messenger's pouch for the Ace Delivery Service. First he cried, then he was angry, and then rather aggressively he informed Foster that he was eighteen years old and no longer under control of the juvenile court. Foster calmed him down, told him we had jurisdiction until age nineteen, and assured him he was in no trouble. Andy sat dejectedly as Foster called me for further instructions. Talking first to Foster and then to Andy, I scheduled a meeting the next morning in my chambers. Reassuring Andy that he faced no punishment, I urged him to stay on his job and told Foster to release him. He was back and we wanted his trust.

Foster accompanied Andy to his lodgings and checked out his work site, all the time emphasizing our desire to help him. Later in the day, Foster reported to me. He was not too optimistic: "Andy lives in a run-down seedy hotel in the drug and wino section of town. His room has a padlock on it and smells somewhere between a toilet and a bar. He's been living in the street the past few months. He's not mad at anybody. Just doesn't want to be bothered. He delivers messages. They call him by beeper whenever they have a delivery. He doesn't want to talk about Captain Bill. Says he doesn't see Abbie any more or keep in touch with his mother. He never smiled once. His only concern was about being locked up. I told him, 'If the judge wanted you locked up, I'd be taking you in.' I think he believed me. I hope so."

The next morning, Andy was not at my chambers. Nor the next day. Foster went to the hotel looking for him. The door was padlocked. The man at the desk said Andy had moved out. It was the same story at Ace Delivery Service. Andy had called to say he quit and asked, "When can I pick up my check?" He never showed up for the check. He's out there somewhere, surviving.

## JAMIE FOREST *(The Nuisance)*

Nine months of hard labor at FEI's Last Chance Ranch didn't dampen Jamie's spirit on his return. Back at DMI in January, he quickly was the Jamie of old: refusing to attend class and challenging counselors, telling all in earshot, "My judge brought me back and he the only one I listen to." Familiar with his antics, the DMI staff didn't take him too seriously. Their mission is to finish the job started at FEI, to produce an individual who can survive. Making him marketable will require a lot of doing. Once stabilized, he needs to be released from "programs" and make it on his own.

Wearing his blue Windbreaker jacket, on which his name was hemstitched, a gift from Cornelius Foster, courtesy of the Children's Fund, Jamie was aglow. Sitting in my chambers, he had his judge, Cornelius Foster, and the FEI After Care Counselor Rose Regins, all there to make plans for him. He immediately began to perform: "Heck, I was such a good cook at FEI they don't want me to leave.

243

Do you know I made more money at FEI than any other kid? The other day in court I stop a kid from running away. I tell him you want to go where I just came from? Everyone liked me at FEI. Ask Rose. She like me."

Rose did indeed like him. She liked all the kids—maybe Jamie a bit more. They seemed to hit it off well. Rose, a large black woman, obviously pregnant, reached over, touching the boy gently on the shoulder. He placed his hand on hers, lightly. The electricity was there. Around Rose, Jamie was sure to be at his best. She confirmed this: "When I'm there to mother him, he's good. When I leave, he's back to giving people a hard time. I can get him a job at Winn-Dixie, but I'm afraid to send him over there because of his attitude. If he won't take his sunglasses off in class when the instructor asks him, why will he listen to the boss man on the job?"

Jamie listened intently to all the comments, occasionally interjecting a murmured "no," sometimes nodding in agreement. Mostly it was ' I'll try to do good." He enjoyed every word and every minute. We agreed that he stay at DMI for January and February to prepare for job-hunting, and that adult education classes in reading and auto mechanics were in order. Now seventeen years of age, he needs some preparation for life in the big city. His interest beginning to lag, he commented, "I look for that little garden when I come back to DMI. But, nothing there. It all grass."

Foster answered my question before I could ask: "We tried to get him a job in a plant nursery, but there are no nurseries where he lives and he has no transportation to get where they are."

Nothing much happened in January or February. Jamie can't find a job. All the usual places—fast-food, bag boy, errands—turned him down. He can't fill out an application form and acts so childish in his interviews that employers reject him.

The DMI people say he's calming down, trying to learn. One incident particularly impressed them. Leaving DMI for home on a local bus, Jamie encountered three kids standing around a pregnant woman, laughing as they puffed marijuana smoke rings in her face. Annoyed but too frightened to object, she sat there rigidly. Jamie rose to her defense, asking them to quit bothering her (maybe thinking of Rose). They refused, surrounding him instead, threatening him. According to the passengers, he talked his adversaries off the bus, thus avoiding any conflict to further endanger the pregnant woman. Several passengers called DMI lauding his behavior. Perhaps he's finally learning to control his temper.

Finding employment for him will be a large task. A menial job may be all he is capable of doing. Despite his shortcomings, he managed to earn about $2,500 at FEI, much more than any of our other charges were able to amass. Even though doctors declare his capabilities limited, I still see flashes of a productive, normal human being. He certainly handled that bus situation in adult fashion. When I told him that a large share of the $2,000 balance of his FEI earnings would go for restitution, he understood. "You owe those people whose homes you broke into. The money you earned building irrigation ditches in orange groves will pay them. Then you'll get a job earning for yourself."

"All right. I pay them everything I owe." That's not likely. The damage for destruction and loss to his victims is well over $10,000. They'll gladly take ten cents on the dollar.

In March, Foster finally placed Jamie. It was a work-school program that might discipline him to the routine demands of life in the job market. This morning, a month of work under his belt, he walked in unannounced, saying he took time off from work to talk to me. Sporting sunglasses, gold around his neck and on each of his fingers, wearing a baseball cap, a big comb in his hand, and a beeper attached to his belt, he looked like a caricature of the black street kid. The psychiatrists always said that Jamie was slow and somewhat retarded. Don't expect too much from him, they had cautioned. I don't, but he continues to surprise me.

"What's your problem?" I asked.

"Ain't got none. Just wanna talk to you. Tell you about my work."

I tried keeping up with his story line, but Jamie talks so fast, flits from thought to thought, never finishing a sentence, that I needed my bailiff, Barry Young, to interpret. After all these years, I still need help with the ghetto patois. It's a shorthand that somehow eludes me. I sat back as Jamie rambled, Young interrupting and clarifying for me. "That job Mr. Foster got me o.k., but they don't pay enough money. Two dollars an hour. Do clean-up work in park. Need more money. Want to get job at Burger King. Maybe I work at two jobs—in daytime and at night. Need to help my mama pay rent. Want to buy my sister bicycle. I'm the man in the family now. We got thirteen moving in and out. They move around so fast I can't count 'em. My older sister has three babies. Can't stay with boyfriend any more. She on welfare. Wants to come back. Mr. Foster took me to bank to get some money [$200] out so I can pay light bill for my mama."

Jamie obviously enjoyed telling of his virtues, real or imagined. "What are your plans?" I asked, still not certain why he was visiting.

Off he went again: "I'm gonna keep working like this. Maybe two or three jobs at a time. Save money for my mama, and then when I'm nineteen or twenty I go in the army for four years. After that, I come home and buy a big house with a pool in the back for my mama."

I tried to shift from his grandiose plans to more mundane matters. How to keep him out of trouble with the law? Can he stay at a job? I was about to ask a question when he began a new ramble, this time about his disc-jockey experience: "See this beeper. Some man has all my DJ equipment. He gonna call me to move it. He hold it for me while I was at FEI. I make a lot of money playing at a park last week."

Bailiff Barry Young interrupted with a question about the beeper: "All the kids I know carrying beepers are selling drugs. You selling drugs on the job?"

Jamie didn't even break stride at the accusation in Young's voice: "No. Don't sell drugs. I follow the rules. FEI taught me everything. They my parents. I respect them. When I come home, I learn to respect my mama like that. Don't let anyone in the house show disrespect for her. I'm gonna start going to church. Be on the good side. Listen to the preacher. Earn money the right way." He had touched every base: motherhood, family, church, and community, representing all the good things in life.

An hour later, talking to Foster about Jamie's visit, I heard a different reaction: "He probably was looking for an excuse to skip work this morning. Told them he had to see the judge. His supervisor at the job site says he still gives them too much lip and sometimes he's lazy and doesn't show up. That disc-jockey business is only a story he likes to tell. He's right about his mother though. I took $200 out of his bank account to pay a light bill. He has $400 left and wants to help his mother. He's a family boy."

When I repeated Jamie's parting words about "earning money the right way," Foster scoffed: "That sounds like a commercial he heard on TV. To tell you the truth, I'm worried about that beeper of his. Barry may be right. Why is he carrying a beeper?"

I don't know about the beeper, and the DJ chatter may all be fantasy. With all of that, what he says about his own behavior and

**246**

his attitude toward mother and family may be more a reality than even he realizes. Foster will be out in the streets tonight to learn if Jamie has any drug connection.

## LAURENCE SAMUEL *(The Fighter)*

Laurence couldn't wait for Christmas. His two phone calls from State School persuaded me to accept an earlier return home for a Thanksgiving family reunion. Fresh from the Okeechobee bus, he walked into my office wearing one of those flowery Miami shirts and a big smile. Whatever we wanted, he was ready. Vocational? Basketball? Counseling? Whatever. He was a pussycat, listening as Foster and I batted around the options. At each suggestion, Laurence's smile grew bigger, and he, more willing. "That's all right with me" was his response to each proposal.

Foster enrolled him in the tenth grade at Jackson Senior High School, making certain that he received school credit for progress at State School. His mother is happy to have him back, but things at home are strained since she and her husband have separated. Many of their problems arose from Laurence's behavior and his return is not likely to bring an early reconciliation. His half-brother is at the University of Texas on a football scholarship, and his father is out of jail, living around the corner with Laurence's grandmother. I had considered sending him for a series of psychological and neurological testings (maybe even for chemical imbalance) in January or February, but his adjustment over the first six weeks was so favorable that I chose to delay any testing.

Two months later, on January 16, he was arrested. Here we go again. It was a loitering and prowling charge. Normally serious but not the end of the world. For Laurence any brush with the law is serious. The police officer's arrest form said it simply: "7:50 P.M. Three black males seen crouching alongside a parked vehicle, possibly attempting to gain entry."

The officer told Foster that this parking lot in Coconut Grove has had many car break-ins lately. One of Laurence's friends had a screwdriver, and, when the youths were approached, Laurence refused to cooperate. He couldn't understand all the fuss: "Me and some dudes, standing on the corner, talking about girls, like we always do. This police officer comes by, decides to search us and finds a screw-

driver on one of the guys. I ask him why he bothering us and suddenly I am in a police car going downtown. What did I do wrong?"
It was time for another conference:

*Gelber:* "Did you learn anything from that arrest?"
*Laurence:* "I growed up at State School but not enough. I have to learn not to ask policemen questions."
*Gelber:* "How are you doing at school?"
*Laurence:* "I passed all my grades except physical education. I got an 'F' because I forgot to bring my gym shorts."
*Gelber:* "How are you getting along with your teachers?"
*Laurence:* "I get along with all except my science teacher. He's grouchy and short. He doesn't like me because I'm tall and always laughing at what goes on."
*Gelber:* "Is he white?"
*Laurence:* "No. He's a black grouch."
*Gelber:* "How's your athletic career coming along?"
*Laurence:* "I didn't play basketball because I hurt my toe at FEI. Right now, I'm in weight training for the football season. I weigh 200, want to weigh 230 to play defensive end. I'm gonna be good."
*Gelber:* "What went wrong at FEI?"
*Laurence:* "I just didn't like the people. And I didn't like sleeping in a tent. It was freezing cold. And then sometimes during the day, working, you'd burn up from the heat."
*Gelber:* "Was there anything you liked about FEI?"
*Laurence:* "The food was o.k. and I didn't mind riding a horse bareback, but whenever they put a saddle on the horse he'd go his own way and throw me. I didn't like that."

I chose not to question him about the forest-burning, his hallucinations, and other wild behavior. Maybe these were things of the past, best forgotten.

*Gelber:* "What brought about the big change in you at State School?"
*Laurence:* "At first I had trouble there. But then there were people I knew who I could get along with. Besides they didn't work us so hard."
*Gelber:* "Was there anything there that made a difference?"
*Laurence:* "Mrs. Appel. She gave me a job in the camp hospital. She became my friend. She was like my mama. I had something to look forward to, talking to her. She brightened my day. She's white, but she's my best friend."
*Gelber:* "Have you talked to her since your return?"
*Laurence:* "Talk to her? I visited her twice, and I am going up there again to stay with her and her daughter."

## Putting Humpty Dumpty Together

*Gelber:* "You took a bus 300 miles to Okeechobee for a visit? Why?"
*Laurence:* "She my friend."

Laurence had found a friend who made the difference. That's the secret of life. Whatever chemistry brings this about is the formula we need to discover.

*Gelber:* "What are we going to do with you now?"
*Laurence:* "I want to go to school, play football, and work part time. I don't want a job in a fast-food place hustling hamburgers. I can work on a construction site or in a warehouse stacking supplies. Man, I want to earn some money and get a lot of girl friends."

There was Laurence chatting about teenage needs like all the kids at school and on the corner. He was at ease, all six feet, four and a half inches. Raring to go, ready to meet the world. As he walked out of the front office, exchanging greetings with my secretary, Janet, she put her head in my doorway, saying, "I like him. He's a nice boy."

Turning good is a lot harder than going bad. Good requires a lot of planning; bad just happens. That's how it was with Laurence. He couldn't resist what the boys were doing—one more time. More than a month had passed since the loitering and prowling incident. We hoped that we could work out one more chance for him. It wasn't to be. Foster described the events of that fateful day: "I ran into Laurence walking in the street. It was by accident. He had been doing all right in school and his mother was happy with him. He said he had overslept and was late for school."

"When I offered him a ride, he said, 'I'm gonna catch me a ride with a friend.'"

A long pause ensued. "I wish I had given him that ride."

The police report, written ten hours later, told the full story: "The victim, a woman, observed three black males in a white Cadillac parked across the street when she exited her car. As she was taking packages out of the back seat, she felt a tugging at her purse. She turned and the accused [Laurence] pulled her along the ground, causing pain and lacerations to her shoulders and legs. Fearing for her life she let the purse go."

Within minutes of her call to the police, a white Cadillac speeding at seventy miles per hour was apprehended. The victim identified Laurence and his accomplices. One was Dan Hollings, the boy I had cautioned him to avoid only two weeks earlier. The third, an adult,

**249**

had a long record. Laurence denied involvement, gave a false name to the police, and devoted the next twenty-four hours to threatening child-care workers at the detention center and fighting with other inmates It was the old Laurence in full bloom, bristling with anger, claiming innocence, challenging the world.

His prospects are grim. A rash of recent front-yard attacks on women unloading groceries has angered and frightened the community. The judge sentencing Laurence will show little compassion for his age. Transferred to the county jail to be tried as an adult, he was upset that his mother cannot post $10,000 bail. She lacks the $1,000 cash required, and her estranged husband refuses to place title to their house as guarantee for a bondsman. Medicated to calm him down, Laurence refuses to discuss his plight with anyone. He wants out. That's all. Visiting him in his cell, Foster had a short stay. Laurence didn't want to be consoled. Why couldn't his mother get him out? Why? Why?

Telling Mrs. Appel wouldn't be easy. I telephoned the clinic at State School. She was with a patient. Later, she returned my call. I couldn't bring myself to deliver the bad news. We chatted about Laurence. She must have been wondering why a judge had called for chitchat. Mostly, I listened as she described the Laurence she knew:

> He visited me at my home. I returned the visit in Miami. He and his mother came to my hotel. She was a very nice lady. He insisted that we come to his house so that I could see where he lives. He told me about his job with a construction company—how he planned to buy things for his mother. He explained his arrest several weeks ago for loitering and prowling, saying, "I was only talking to a girl on a street corner." I told him I understood. He seemed relieved that I accepted his explanation.

I thought this was the moment to tell her about the strong-arm robbery but she went on: "After visiting at his home, he suggested we walk through the arcades at the Omni Hotel Mall. As his mother and I walked ahead, she said rather dejectedly, 'He talks about working, but in truth doesn't have a job, and never has had one. He really doesn't want to work. I am worried about him.' He rejoined us and we talked about school. Despite what his mother had said, I had a good feeling about him."

This wasn't the time to tell her. I let her go on: "His mother says he's lazy, but at that age you can't ask for much sensible decision-making. He's going through tough times. He fantasizes the good life and does the same for the bad life. All this business about being 'James' and losing his memory is only a ploy. It's a game he plays to avoid punishment. When I tell him there's no room for 'James' here, he just smiles."

I interrupted her: "Laurence was arrested yesterday charged with strong-arm robbery."

There was a moment of silence. No comment. I continued on, filling in the details. Finally, she said, "He had been asking to see me, but I've been very busy lately. Putting it off. Maybe I should have seen him."

I assured her Laurence hadn't been alone during that period. He was just being Laurence, doing things no one could fathom. Again, a long pause as if allowing herself to digest the news. "How could he do that? I would trust Laurence with my life. He was always protective with my safety. When we were walking in the Omni Mall, he looked out for me as if he were guarding me. He was always concerned for my safety. In the car, he told me to put my purse under the seat, saying 'They can't steal what they can't see.' It's hard to believe."

It was clear she didn't want to talk anymore. Almost as an afterthought, she asked me to keep her informed as to the status of the case.

The prosecutor's office has been interviewing witnesses for the past two weeks. What seemed like an open-and-shut case is now doubtful. The victim only recalls a tall, black male. One of the two passersby who witnessed the robbery cannot identify Laurence. Meanwhile, he sits in county jail, waiting, unaware that the state's case depends on the testimony of the other witness later in the week. Although disappointed in not being able to make bond, he has made a favorable adjustment to jail life. No violent behavior. No pretending to be "James."

Foster expects that, when the novelty and excitement of being with the "big guys" wears off, he'll return to his old ways. On each of his visits, Laurence is all over him with speculation as to what may happen: "Can't I get probation? This is my first offense as an adult. Is the judge gonna help me?" No remorse. No second thoughts. No admissions. Only feeling sorry for himself.

Although Foster has offered him little hope of release, back in the confines of my chambers, the story was different. Foster posed the difficult question: "I know he's guilty because he admitted it to his mother and she told me. Suppose they can't prosecute and they release him? What do we do then?"

I didn't hesitate in answering: "That's no problem. Get him back in school. Find him a tutor and you baby-sit him twenty-four hours a day. Then we'll bring down Mrs. Appel—put her up in a hotel if we have to. We'll start all over again." Foster nodded agreement in response, but not with any enthusiasm. It's easy for me, sitting in chambers, to get all charged up. It's a lot harder for Foster, however, struggling in the field.

The prosecutor's decision whether to prosecute was taking longer than expected. A few days later, I called the medical clinic at Okeechobee to talk to Maureen Appel. She and I were becoming old friends on the telephone. As always, Laurence was the subject of our conversation. I wanted to know what kind of person took this much interest in Laurence. She had an interesting background. Holding college degrees in nursing and in behavioral science, she had worked for many years as a nurse with a large pharmaceutical laboratory in Pennsylvania. Tiring of the corporate world and because a daughter was attending college in Florida, she accepted the challenge of working with delinquent kids at Eckerd's State School in out-of-the-way Okeechobee, Florida. She had been there two years, but still found it to be an exciting experience.

She met Laurence when he was in Alpha Cottage, under restriction, and medication had to be delivered. At first, only casual daily greetings and pleasantries occurred. Then he began asking questions about the clinic. After that, he always sought her out, until one morning he showed up at the clinic.

"Can I work here?"

"Why do you want to work at the clinic?"

"Because you trust me. Don't you?"

She told me she never forgot that simple exchange. Then it all came out. Her rewards were plain to see:

When you are nice to them, suddenly they are on your doorstep. We take them in. When Laurence first came to the clinic, I would ask him to do something. He'd say "I don't have to do that." Then a few minutes later, I'd come back. He'd be there cleaning the windows or mopping the floor, a big smile on his face. I once asked him why he liked the clinic. He said, "This place is comfortable for me." You know he didn't see black or white in me. He only saw someone who liked him. He was a terrific kid.

I almost wanted Laurence to get another chance for her sake. She continued: "We can't throw somebody like Laurence aside. I'd like to believe he didn't commit anything violent. His mother knows about all the help he has been getting. She doesn't know what to do. He and I talked about his future a lot. Does he have a future?"

I told her the prosecutor's decision was only a few days away. I'd call her. We might still salvage Laurence.

When my secretary, Janet, told me the prosecutor was on the line, I excused myself from the visitor in my chambers. I had been waiting for several days for this one. Whatever the decision, I was prepared to accept it. Something deep inside was rooting for the presence of a huge pine tree that obscured the vision of the witness. Still uncertain as to the reason for a judge's unusual interest in this case, the prosecutor was matter-of-fact in her description: "The witness identified Laurence without question. He's a sergeant in the Marine Patrol and will be great on the stand. The police chased Laurence's car and found the victim's purse, a gold charm bracelet, and $229 in cash on the floor, next to Laurence. The other two were not charged, but we've got Laurence cold."

I thought it appropriate to congratulate the prosecutor, and when I did she responded, "We'll go all the way with this one." I've got one more phone call to make. That one will be hard.


### LESTER BURROWS *(The Runner)*

FEI didn't want to release him. The new director, Rusty Russell, held all kinds of reservations: "He's not ready yet. He barely gets out of Phase I before he's in trouble again. When we caught him cold with a ten-pound ham in his bunk, he denied it right to my face. He stole a videotape out of my locker, even though he had no machine to show it. He steals just for the practice. He's been here ten months and hasn't learned enough to go back."

Not so. Lester may be intransigent, but he's not dumb. He's got the message. Pulling palmettos is not for him. Now is the time to take another chance. No point waiting until he turns bitter. He'll never follow all the rules, but maybe he's ready to listen to some.

One more time, Foster prepared a return-home agenda, carefully consulting with Lester. On the drive back from FEI, they discussed each step in the planned scenario. Temporary housing would be in a group home, awaiting independent living quarters. Foster found a program in which Lester would be paid a stipend while learning house painting. Visits with grandma would be arranged, and contact reopened with his mother. We had been here before.

Foster deposited Lester at the Zigler group home, telling him to be ready for a visit to the judge in the morning. The first night home was crucial. In the past, Lester never stayed too long. Bright and early, Foster was at the home to accompany Lester on a visit to the judge. Foster's doubts were dispelled: "I was the most surprised guy in the world to find him there ready to go, all smiles. One thing, I made sure not to give him four dollars to buy a soda."

There it was, that moonbeam smile, as he came through the door.

"Hiya, Moonbeam!"

"Hello, judge."

"How long do you plan to stay this time?"

"Judge, I ain't gonna run again. Not going through that anymore."

"What do you want to do?"

"I want to take the GED."

"C'mon, Lester. Who are you kidding? Someone told you the best thing to tell a judge is that you want to take the GED. Right?"

Unlike Marco's charm, Lester's was still intact. In his own quiet way, ol' Moonbeam could pour it on.

"Why were you so difficult at FEI?"

"It was mostly me. I wanted to do what I wanted to do. I found out I couldn't. I didn't want to work. Sometimes I woke up on the wrong side of the bed."

"How do we know things will be different now?"

"I really want to take the GED. I'm not gonna get arrested again. That's all past tense."

"What are you interested in doing?"

"I told you. I want to pass the GED. And I am curious about electronics."

"Electronics? That's interesting. Because that's what you told every social worker and psychologist who interviewed you over the last six years. How come? Do you know you need a background in science and math for electronics?"

"Listen judge. I'm curious. I once started to fix a radio and it fell and broke. But I'm curious."

"What did you like at FEI?"

"Besides the GED, I lifted a lot of iron. Gained twenty-four pounds in ten months."

"Anything you didn't like?"

"Yes, the staff was racial. When I'd go to the bathroom at night and stick my head in their tent on the way back to peek at the TV, they'd have a fit and run me off. When a white kid would come by on the way from the bathroom, they'd let him sit down and watch."

"That's very subtle. Ask Mr. Foster here about real racial discrimination in prisons. He's got a lot harsher stories to tell."

"Maybe he does, judge. But I know what bothers me."

Lester Burrows may be only a piece of damaged merchandise to the system, but I see some good fabric and he is still salvageable. I looked toward Foster for his reaction. He patted Lester on the back, pointing him to the door. "Let's go. Maybe this one will be better. First things first. We'll get you some clothing, a place to sleep, a job, and see your grandma. You know she's been very sick and wants to see you. We'll get to the GED and electronics later."

They were almost out of the front office when I called Lester back. "What about your little boy? Are you going to visit him?" He waited a moment, started to speak, changed his mind, apparently waiting for my follow-up. "You know, Lester, that we know you made up that story. That girl never wanted any part of you. You are not the father of her child."

Now the moonbeam smile was all over the room. "Judge, it seemed the right thing to say at the time. There's no baby. It just popped into my mind, and I said it. That's all." Does Lester now become one of our "stars"? Foster isn't crowning anybody these days. Tomorrow morning something else may pop into Lester's mind.

Two days back from FEI and problems. Yesterday, Lester came in at 4:00 A.M., upsetting Mrs. Zigler. She can't maintain discipline with the others if he comes and goes as he pleases. He claimed he was stuck in Carol City and had no way home, but Foster believes he was out celebrating with the ninety dollars he had earned at FEI. A ten o'clock curfew has been set, and Foster will find an apartment for him to begin independent living. As soon as his birth certificate is located and a social security number obtained, he will be off to work buying food and paying rent like all other mortals. He will grow up fast, or we'll lose him again.

During lunchtime, I glanced up from my salad and there was Lester's head in the door looking for Foster. He needed a ride. Pointedly ignoring his inquiry, I asked, "What happened last night? You forgot when the last bus leaves?"

Spotting Foster, he left hurriedly without answering my question, shouting as he left. "I'm all right. I'm gonna pass the GED."

Early this morning, Foster transported Lester to DMI to take a

GED pre-test. The results had everyone excited, especially Lester. He scored between the ninth- and tenth-grade level, excellent for a kid who literally grew up in the streets and lacked any formal education. That FEI staffer who convinced him that a GED, the high-school diploma equivalent, was within his grasp, may yet turn out to be our anonymous hero.

Four days back and Lester is gone. Mrs. Zigler isn't sure what happened. No particular problems. No incidents. His clothes and belongings were left behind. Grandmother wasn't surprised. She told Foster, "He just like his daddy. Can't count on him for anything." She knew her boy, but was always ready to forgive him.

Foster, sensitive to their special relationship, had made a point of taking Lester to her home for daily visits. Despite her age, infirmity, and preoccupation with religion, she had a calming effect on Lester. Normally he was always on the move, wanting to go somewhere, other than where he was. With her, he'd listen patiently as she talked incessantly about the Lord. Bemused as she recited all her religious truisms, he would sit there, enjoying her presence, pleased to be back in her company. She was the only person he really cared about. One incident may have bothered him. She described it: "When he came by, he say he need shoes. I give him and his cousin money to go out and buy play shoes. He came back later and steal his cousin's shoes. Everybody mad at Lester. Why he do that? He have his own shoes. He always doing things like that."

Yes, indeed, Lester always does things like that. He's been programmed with a computer code that no "hacker" will ever break. He steals and runs and runs and steals. That's the only message that has ever reached him. He may come back in a day or two. This time, he will not be locked up or sent back to FEI. That didn't work in the past and won't now. We'll stay with the GED and independent living.

Ten days gone. The only sign was a visit to grandma for a meal. She assures Foster that Lester will be all right; the Lord will take care of him. I hope so. We haven't succeeded.

On the eleventh day, the message came. It was grandmother notifying Foster that she had received a phone call from Lester: "He tell me he arrested in Broward County—stealing a car and having drugs. He say 'Don't worry. I be all right.' That's all he say. I give him up to the Lord. I can't do no more for him."

Foster's trip to Broward County produced no Lester. He may be in the adult jail or in the juvenile jail, using an alias. Slippery Lester.

Even in jail, we have trouble holding on to him. Engaging in a manhunt to run him down is useless. He's tricky, but after a while, he'll surface. How long he'll stay or what that will mean is hard to predict. As heavyweight champion Joe Louis once said about an opponent: "He can keep running, but he can't hide forever." Joe Louis never met Lester.

## EVIAN VILARS

More than a year ago, in March 1985, we were uncertain as to the course to follow. Evian Vilars had been labeled a potential Hinckley, after being captured in a 3:00 A.M. school break-in dressed in black, in possession of a gun and knife, stating that he chose the school rather than a home because "someone would be home in a house and I'd have to kill him." In a later episode, he had declared war on drivers of Porsches. His family was in fear, the court was in a quandary, and the medical response was halfhearted. My effort to impose long-term residential placement was unsuccessful. The lawyers, social workers, and doctors suggested various combinations of outpatient treatment and residential placement that were either unacceptable or unavailable. His parents, despite their fears, wanted him home with the family. In the process, everyone had become disillusioned and disappointed.

After Evian spent a month in detention lockup and two months in Jackson Memorial Hospital, child psychiatrist Dr. P. released him for outpatient treatment. Then began a year of weekly sessions with Dr. P. and a hospital clinical social worker. Our mental-health clinic staff monitored the progress, as did specially assigned HRS Counselor Alberto Valdez. Limited as this treatment was, nonetheless it was the best available under the circumstances. Every agency contributed liberally—perhaps because a judge and the local newspaper focused attention on Evian.

Today, more than a year later, a jury would conclude that the youth has made it out of the morass. His behavior is no longer a matter of concern. The family live together in apparent harmony. Only Evian's career choice has remained an issue. He still has the military in mind, a choice I cannot support. Dr. P., the hospital clinical social worker, and Valdez disagree. They believe the military will provide the structure he needs. In addition, the navy recruiter, encouraged by Evian's high entrance scores, can't wait to enlist him.

**257**

My position is adamant. Medical assurances to the contrary, in a crisis situation I don't want weapons readily available to him. So long as he is under my jurisdiction—until nineteen—the military recruiters cannot have him. Other than career choice and Jackson Memorial Hospital's bureaucratic insistence that the Vilars family pay more than $7,000 for Evian's two-month hospitalization, no serious problems exist. The hospital bill collectors keep threatening to file suit despite the fact that Evian was ordered there by the court for the protection of the community.

Is Evian really out of the woods? Talking to Dr. P. and his HRS counselor, it would appear so:

*Dr. P.:* "I never felt he was a threat. He needed treatment, but not to avoid killing anyone. He is not a potential Hinckley. I would be shocked if anything terrible happened in the future. All those death threats were just used to manipulate people. The psychotherapy treatment he gets is helping him considerably."

*Gelber:* "Just what does your psychotherapy entail?"

*Dr. P.:* "We talk once a week. It's problem-solving. What's going on in the family? Future plans? My clinical social worker and I are supportive. The problem we have now is that I am leaving the hospital in June. That will end the treatment. You know that he's not even on the hospital roll as an outpatient. He has no card. No one checks him in. There's no bill. I've been doing it on my own. If I stay in town, I'll treat him at no cost as a private patient. But I'll probably leave Miami."

*Gelber:* "What happens after June, when you leave?"

*Dr. P.:* "With good resources, he can go it alone. That's why placing him in a structured setting like the military, or as a police officer would be good for him. He knows you won't permit him in the navy, and he's resigned to that. Now he's talking about being an air controller."

*Gelber:* "Why this preoccupation with weapons, uniforms, jobs with excitement?"

*Dr. P.:* "It may be the Latin macho. But, the important thing is that in the last year he has learned to accept denial. The community doesn't have to give him what he wants. He now can handle that stress. He's still angry at his father, but now he understands him better."

I was impressed with Dr. P. He's a young psychiatrist beginning his own career, still at a stage of serious caring for his patients. I hope he stays that way. But what about Evian? Did I overreact in the beginning?

I called in HRS Counselor Valdez for his views. He has watched all of us the past two years and may be the most objective. He was cautious about Evian's prospects, but mostly he sided with Dr. P.:

> *Valdez:* "Evian is doing fine. He works as a mail handler at the post office at five dollars an hour and plans to enroll at Miami-Dade Community College. His mother says he's a different person, and his father is proud of him because he's saving to buy an old car. I told him if he causes trouble again, he'll go away for a long time. He says he'll never cause trouble again. I believe him."
> *Gelber:* "How can you be sure his problems are all over?"
> *Valdez:* "It's all over. He wants to have a meeting with you so that you can be convinced."

The last time I saw Evian, a year ago, he was sitting in court, confused, suffering chronic depression, and frightened of everything around him. Today he walked in, neatly dressed, tie carefully made, sporting a trim, layered haircut and a thin mustache. Obviously, he had been to the barber for this meeting. Most kids coming into chambers meekly follow their counselors. Evian entered first, approached me, hand outstretched, like one of those pre-law students who want a letter of recommendation for law school. He didn't wait for my question, going right into an account of his doings: "I have a job and I go to school studying to be a paramedic. I want to go to college. I know you will not allow me to enter the military. The police won't take me because of my arrest and psychotherapy treatment. Maybe I'll become an air traffic controller."

He spoke clearly, grammatically, under control: "The situation is much better at home. I get along with my father and all members of my family. I wanted to be a pilot, but now I'm open to things other than the military. I'll be nineteen before long and I want to get started in the right direction."

I didn't have much to say, mostly listening. I wished him well, told him he had the ability to succeed in anything he tried, and encouraged him to visit me in the future.

## CLARK CARDEN

A sense of unreality characterized Clark Carden's situation. The choice of a military school seemed ill-advised for one who had borne the dictatorial repression of a sadistic father. To make it worse, this was a school attended mostly by Cuban students, who conversed in Spanish, a language he did not understand. Shunted off by the court system to this make-believe setting, somehow the youth was supposed to overcome the degradation of what had happened to him. He couldn't and didn't.

All these questions had been raised a year ago to Dr. H., a psychologist appointed by criminal-court Judge Ed Cowart to examine Clark. Dr. H. had then responded to my concerns: "He's a powder keg, cold as ice. I wouldn't say 'no' to him and feel safe going to bed. But the military school is good for him. He needs structure. They have rules and, if he follows them, he knows things will go well. They are disciplinarians, but they are not unreasonable."

Two months after Dr. H.'s visit, a *Miami Herald* headline told it all: "State Failed to Oversee Killer, 15, at Academy." Clark Carden and three other older cadets were charged with molesting several pre-adolescent children at the private military school. Community reaction was strong. Not only had several other recent child molestation cases occurred in private schools, but this incident was magnified by the presence of a convicted killer who was hiding in the school under an assumed name.

The newspaper quoted "El General," founder of the academy, speaking at a bilingual press conference first in English and then in Spanish: "I only took him in the school after the Judge pleaded with me. He has been getting along well with the others. I told him he would be expelled if he made one mistake. This will never happen again. I am going to put closed circuit television in all the rooms. Even the bathrooms."

Once more back to court for Clark, this time on the sex charges and violation of probation, for which he faced upwards of fifty years of hard time. It was plea bargaining time again. The agreement was for the youth to serve ten years in prison followed by ten years of probation. Reexamining him, the psychologists and psychiatrists found he needed treatment more than ever:

> *Psychologist Dr. R.:* "He is in even greater need of a closed-setting psychiatric placement than last time. This is a seriously disturbed individual who functions marginally. His anti-social behavior is likely to continue unless some modification takes place."
> *Psychiatrist Dr. M.:* "He is an angry young man who displaces blame for his own wrong-doing on others. He would benefit from a residential program of psychiatric treatment."

**260**

## Putting Humpty Dumpty Together

*Psychologist Dr. S.:* "He has fear of being sent to a prison and forced to become a "punk" [homosexual]. Clark suffers from a victim-victimizer syndrome. He sets himself up to be hurt by others, does not adequately protect himself, and then when hurt, reacts by striking out to hurt others."
*Psychiatrist Dr. J.:* "He talked about the victims and stated that perhaps he had committed these acts because of some need for revenge. He qualifies for treatment as a mentally disordered sex offender in a residential program."

It was apparent from all the clinical examination that Clark's situation had seriously worsened. What many had anticipated had come true. But how true? Two years ago, after he was assigned to the military academy, a nurse who had worked with Clark at our mental-health clinic predicted the outcome with remarkable accuracy: "When Clark becomes an upper classman with authority over the younger students, he might well emerge as a 'little Hitler' abusing them as he had been treated."

Significantly, during the interviews Clark had confided to several of the doctors that his father had inflicted anal intercourse on him when he was six years old.

In another on-target prediction, Steve Levine, his public defender, had then expressed concern: "Placing Clark in a military school is an untenable situation. It only sets him up to violate probation. When that happens, the next judge won't know the circumstances or have time to find out. As a matter of course, he'll simply storage him away for a long term of years."

Despite the new offenses, Clark had his supporters. His court-appointed guardian ad-litem, in a plea to the state attorney, wrote: "It was most unfortunate that Clark was placed in an unsupervised, untherapeutic environment. There is still a chance for Clark if he is placed in a treatment facility rather than spending that time incarcerated."

A letter from the Polish count stated that, though further financial assistance would not be provided, he was still supportive: "I know that the Judge felt he was making the right decision. However, as it has developed, the academy was not the proper environment for the boy. From the limited contact I had with the boy, he is a young man in dire need of help who deserves help."

The plea bargain worked out between the prosecutor and the public defender called for a ten-year sentence at a youthful-offender institution. Under Florida law, a defendant is thereafter under the sole control of the Department of Corrections as to his treatment and release date. Clark is likely to serve three to five years. Judge Ed Cowart requested he receive psychiatric treatment as a mentally disturbed sex offender, but the prison system works in its own fashion.

Nine months later, when Clark was imprisoned at the Sumter Correctional Institution, a note from his public defender cryptically described his status: "According to the Classification Officer, Clark is an exemplary inmate. He has earned his way into the honor dormitory and has an individual cell. The Classification Officer indicated that Clark was in some sort of vocational training, but was not sure which vocational trade. Unfortunately and perhaps significantly, Clark is not receiving any regular psychiatric treatment. A psychologist sees Clark occasionally on an 'as needed' basis, whatever that means."

Under the typed note was a handwritten addendum: "The local Department of Corrections won't release the post-sentence investigation to me or anyone for that matter. Some friends in Tallahassee are getting it for me."

Clark Carden's future is clouded, to say the least. Linda Berkowitz, district administrator for HRS, was quoted as follows at the time of Clark's arrest on the sex offenses: "I've got a gnawing feeling that this is a kid who fell through the proverbial crack."

Responded Clark's public defender: "He didn't fall in the crack . . . he was pushed in."

## RUDY LANDER
## MARLON JAMESON

My last court contact with Rudy Lander and Marlon Jameson had taken place about eighteen months ago. Both maintained my interest mainly because of the perseverance of their mothers. Rudy, a black ghetto kid who demonstrated a propensity for not getting along with anyone, had a record of assaults that seemed endless. His mother distrusted the criminal-justice system from top to bottom. Marlon, from a white middle-class family, had a battery of lawyers and psychologists in court and a family ready to provide whatever resources were necessary to protect their name and his record. He had been accused of engineering a series of neighborhood burglaries.

## Putting Humpty Dumpty Together

Neither one of the boys made it to the Master Counselor Program. For two years, I had followed their activities, observing these two protective mothers whose backgrounds and approaches were different. What could they do for their troubled children that we couldn't do?

Rudy's mother despised the system, viewing it as racist and inept. She resisted any effort to either punish or assist her son, preferring to carry the burden alone. In our last encounter, she had dramatically contended: "Black kids don't have a chance in your court." This occurred after I had her son locked up prior to his transfer to adult court. There, his troubles continued because of several more arrests. Each time, the entreaties of his mother sufficiently impressed adult-court judges to avoid incarceration. She tried and tried. His luck ran out in December 1985 when he was charged with aggravated assault for threatening a bus passenger with a gun. The judge revoked his probation, sentencing him to 364 days in the county stockade. Three months later, he was out. How is he doing? He's a menace according to his probation officer: "This kid is now seventeen and dangerous. He does what he wants to do. He'll kill someone some day or get killed."

Based on earlier court duels with her, I was uncertain how Mrs. Lander would respond to my message that she telephone me at 8:30 A.M. On the dot, the phone rang and her pleasant, relaxed voice caught me off guard: "Rudy is doing fine. He's served only three months and has now been out two months. He works in a restaurant, talks about going back to school, and acts like a responsible person."

I never had to ask the first question. It was an outpouring as if she had been waiting a long time to say these things to me: "I always remembered the day you told me that sometimes a parent can be a child's worst enemy by loving him too much—overprotecting him. I learned a lot through all of this. I think he's seen the light too. He told me he remembers all the things you told him. He started downhill when his father left home. I don't have to cry myself to sleep anymore. I had to quit every job I had because I was so busy in court with him. He said he'd like to come visit with you. Will you talk to him?"

She thanked me repeatedly as I offered to help her in return. What else could I say? I was glad it had been on the telephone. In person, it would have been a teary exchange. She made my day. I hope Rudy doesn't disappoint her.

Marlon Jameson has avoided contact with the law. When last heard from, his mother had successfully guided him through a variety of programs, finally enrolling him in junior college. A check with Broward County arrest records showed no new arrests. The juvenile police officer who had handled Marlon's case before me confirmed the no-arrest status. He did have some concerns: "There are still break-ins in that neighborhood. Some residents think Marlon is sending younger kids to do the job and he is disposing of the stolen merchandise. There's no proof of that though."

His mother, always cooperative and more than willing to talk in the past, seemed surprised at my interest in her son. "You are aware that we won our appeal and the case was dismissed?"

I told her I was aware of the reversal. "How is he doing?" I continued. Restraining her annoyance, she stated, without elaboration, "Marlon is married, is a father, I'm a grandmother. He works and goes to school. He has no problems."

Two mothers, both doing their jobs, the best they can.

## THE SULTAN BOYS

Becoming involved with Troy and Travis Sultan was mere happenstance. Before me many times, both were remembered mostly for the contempt they showed for the court. Nothing obvious, but it was there. Although they appeared at different times, the attitude was the same. Each sat rigidly at the counsel table, indifferent to his lawyer, barely acknowledging what was going on. Neither one had been before me when candidates for the Master Counselor Program were considered. Neither one would have been selected. They were hardened beyond any ministration of a caring Master Counselor.

I ran into Troy at FEI's Last Chance Ranch, where he was the inmate guide for our visiting group. Everyone was impressed with the new Troy. Smiling, friendly, he added "yes, sir" to all his statements. Back in Miami, I found brother Travis in court again on another serious charge. Still menacing, he was coiled to strike at the slightest provocation, security guards standing alert alongside him.

Two brothers, both at one time seemingly beyond redemption, yet one at FEI, now a model of behavior. Why not follow them through the next year of their lives? Has FEI really made an impact on Troy? Is Travis doomed, bouncing from one jail to another? It turned out that they are first cousins, not brothers, but were close to each other

**264**

and grew up together. The questions remain the same. Are some of these kids lost forever, no matter what the effort?

When seventeen-year-old Travis left my courtroom, snarling at me, he was on the way to criminal court to be tried as an adult, charged with grand theft. He received a sentence of one year in the county stockade plus three years of probation. Three months later, out early, he was back roaming the streets. Minor arrests followed: loitering, malicious destruction of property, battery. All were processed through the adult court. None brought jail time or a violation of probation charge. Shortly thereafter, charged with five counts of robbery by force, he was convicted by a jury. In March of this year, he began a four-year sentence in a state correctional institution as a youthful offender. When he is released in a few years, watch out!

Cousin Troy's return from FEI presented problems from the beginning. What little existed of his family was hard to find and harder to get involved. FEI After Care Counselor Rose Regins took him under her wing, making up for the lack of family. Back in school, he soon dropped out. He quit a job. Returned to FEI, he was again the "yes, sir" boy, doing well. There, Rose made him an offer.

"Would you like to settle in Venus, outside the Last Chance Ranch?"

"No, I want to go home."

Back in Miami, Rose tried again. "School?"

"No."

"Job?"

"No." He had one answer to everything, Rose said: "I ain't gonna do nothing."

A defeated Rose was back before the adult-court judge with a shambling Troy alongside her. The judge asked him: "What are you planning to do?" Troy responded: "Nothing."

"Then you go to jail for thirty days to think about it. Let me know when you are ready to come out."

Troy came out ready to listen. Rose described his new attitude: "He realized that he had to follow the rules. This time, his mother came forward to help. He has a job. Troy has made a commitment to himself. He's responsible now."

The latest report brought Troy's situation up-to-date: "Troy has been employed the past six months by a construction company. He earns $7.50 an hour operating an asphalt machine. His supervisor finds him to be an excellent employee."

Still on maternity leave, Rose, his FEI After Care counselor, is proud of Troy. He made it the hard way, but he made it. Did FEI make the difference? Was it Rose? There was no simple answer for Troy. He didn't know. He only knew things were better. I asked him. "When I first came back from FEI, I was confused. Didn't know what to do. Rose helped me, but I was still confused. Missed some days at school  Then looked for a job. Couldn't fill out applications. Got discouraged. Rose had me a job cooking in a restaurant. They only pay $3 35 an hour. Tried working on a garbage truck. Didn't like it. Got sent back to FEI. Worked there stacking hay in the fields. Liked it, but don't want to live there. This time I came back and decided it's time to get my life together."

I halted him right there. The phrase "time to get my life together" is a stock line used by delinquent kids to impress their elders. "C'mon, Troy. I've heard that line too many times. What really made you change?"

"Judge, I really mean it this time. Learned a lot at FEI. Rose was good to me. My mom needs me. I'm making money running an asphalt machine. I'm gonna be all right."

There it was again, that other stock phrase used by every kid coming out of a program: "I'm gonna be all right."

Maybe it was FEI. Maybe Rose. Maybe Mom. Maybe even the thirty days. "What about your cousin Travis?" I asked.

A touch of concern was in his voice: "I try to know what he do. Call him. Help him. Give him advice. Travis messed up. Too hard-headed. Won't listen to anyone."

When I asked Foster the same questions, he thought a few seconds before replying: "It may have been Troy's time. He was ready. It may never be Travis' time. We just have to be there when they are ready."

# Afterthoughts:
# Knowing What
# Makes the Difference
# Is the Secret of Life

One year? Two years? How about three or four? How much time is needed for rehabilitation? For sure, the Master Counselor Program demonstrated that offering everything available is no guarantee of success. It's mind-boggling to think that, no matter what is done, hard-core delinquents may only be barely touched. What did we leave out? Did we lack enough community resources? Were the families of our charges too far gone and their bad ways too ensconced? Was our game plan too unstructured?

If nothing works, as some people suggest, why not give up on the sixteen- and seventeen-year-old toughs? Let them do what they will and face whatever penalties their crimes warrant. Instead, concentrate on the early teenagers and nip their deviant behavior at the onset. That's called "early intervention," a response professionals in the field always use when the hard questions start coming. Regrettably, no matter how many of these youths are helped, too many slip through the net, still leaving large numbers of older toughs to handle.

Kids with ten arrests are walking cannons, ready to explode. Lock them up and what do you have when they are freed to roam the streets again? How would you like to meet Travis Sultan a few years hence, at age twenty-one, when your car breaks down on a lonely road? I thought of these questions as I sat there listening to Lester Burrows. My perpetual Runner was back. Several months later, another arrest, the same Lester. It's always only a matter of time before he ends up in a police station. Selected first in our experiment, he never for a moment wavered in rejecting our overtures, and we never discovered why. Uncork that secret. Bottle it. You will have America's best-seller.

*The police officer, responding to a burglary-in-progress call, came upon Lester a short distance from the scene, leaning against a store window. Stickers and burrs on his shorts, out of breath, casually drinking from a carton of Jungle Juice, he looked the perfect picture of a juvenile suspect feigning innocence. He also fit the physical description provided by the victim, who had encountered Lester emerging from his house in the middle of the afternoon carrying the stolen stereo.*

*Today, handcuffed, he apparently recognized the futility of it all. I, too, had little to offer. Finally, I asked, "Lester, for a kid as smart as you are, how come you are so bad at being a thief?"*

*Lester sat there quietly, no moonbeam smile, no responses. He had occupied the same chair several times before while discussing plans for the future. He didn't have much to say. As in the past, he steadfastly denied any involvement in the crime. I continued: "Explain this to me, Lester. I understand you have been going to a welding class. Every time you run, you enroll in a welding class, on your own. Would you go to a welding class if we sent you?"*

*"Only if I can pick the school."*

*"Why did you run this time, even though we carefully explained to you that, as soon as you start a job, you can rent your own apartment and be on your own?"*

*"I just want to do it myself. Don't need any help. It's not that I don't appreciate it. I can do it my way."*

*At this point, Foster leaned toward him and said, "Go ahead, tell him what you told me. You can't get in any more trouble than you have."*

*The small smile came out again and quickly faded. "Judge, I got me a job. Always had one. I sell drugs on the street. Whenever I come back, that's where I go. Make a hundred dollars a day. Work mostly at night. That's why I could never stay at Mrs. Zigler's place. The hours didn't work out."*

*To think that all the psychologists had cautioned us not to place*

*Lester in a home without first consulting with him! This was to win his friendship and sway him to our side. Good tactic. Unfortunately, Lester only wanted a placement that didn't interfere with his drug-dealing. Mrs. Zigler's curfew and his job hours just didn't jibe.*

He hesitated for a moment, as if confession was difficult for him, and then stated, "The dope people, they get me an apartment in a HUD project. Pay only twenty dollars a month. Gave me a stash. I got a girl. Plenty money. That's better than Mrs. Zigler's. I guess it all blew my head."

*Foster and I looked at each other in silent understanding. Finally, Foster asked the obvious question:* "If you make out so good, why do you have to do burglaries?"

"I dunno why. They just happen. Maybe I can't wait for payday. I saved me five hundred dollars in two months. I want to do it my way."

*He is a totally confused boy. How do you reach someone so determined to reject any values other than his own? I didn't want to end the discussion, hoping some sudden flow of words would reveal what makes Lester run. After a few moments of silence, suddenly the old moonbeam smile came out in full force.* "Judge, I'm gonna be a father. This girl name Georgia is pregnant and I'm the daddy."

*His proud announcement drew no reaction. We had traveled that ground before. Last time, we had gone along with his "father" scenario. Now there were no takers. Lester as the family man was a game neither Cornelius nor I cared to play. Somewhere in the recesses of his mind, he equated fatherhood with family, without the slightest concept of what either entailed. He left in custody of the bailiff, mumbling the same phrase several times:* "I do it my way."

*Foster, watching him walk out of the room, shook his head in wonderment.* "I don't know if anything he said is true. About the dope, the girl, the job, anything. He don't know where he is."

*Lester doesn't know where he is. Unfortunately, neither do we. Perverse, intransigent, unmovable—all characteristics that don't lend themselves to rational approaches. Keeping in touch with Lester and the others since the experiment ended has been mainly the result of rearrests. A few months after this latest arrest, he was convicted in adult court on the burglary charge and sentenced to four years. At sentencing, he asked for a week's liberty before beginning to serve, claiming he was about to become a father. No one had bothered to advise the sentencing judge of his propensity to disappear. By chance, I learned of his ploy and alerted my col-*

*league. Lester is now serving four years at the Indiantown Correctional Center.*

*When we started this project, I felt confident. For two years, my confidence level wavered: an occasional rise but mostly decline. One crutch was always available to fall back on: although the immediate results may be disheartening, the residual, long-term benefits of the close Master Counselor relationship would pay off in later years. Now, another year later, my reflections are more tempered. All except Dwight Anderson (The Migrant) are about nineteen years of age, and things are not likely to change very much for any of them. During the intervening year since the end of the experiment, four of the six are in the adult prison system. Two seem to have survived and are no longer high-risks out in the street. Win some or lose some—the system changes, but at its own pace.*

The juvenile-justice structure is complex, fragile, controversial, and passing through a change of life. For years, it consisted of the avuncular, kindly old judge preaching virtue and Sunday school tenets. Then, in the 1970s, lawyers came into the picture demanding the full panoply of rights for their clients. In the eighties, victims of violence became the key actors. At that time, the concept of "just desserts" began to gain a foothold. Simply described, it eliminates treatment as the primary consideration and instead focuses on punishment. Some of the proponents of this approach prefer the total elimination of juvenile court. Others would alter the court's century-old philosophy by establishing sentencing guidelines and generally making juvenile courts more like criminal courts. These hard-line, antijuvenile court voices are not new, but this time they are strongly supported not only in the precincts, but also in high government office.

This 1987 philosophy, embodied in a new model juvenile-justice code that features sentencing guidelines, is the product of the U.S. Justice Department's Office of Juvenile Justice and Delinquency Prevention (OJJDP). Thus, the old debate is resurrected, but with a new sense of urgency: "Do we hold youths strictly accountable for their criminal conduct, or do we treat the symptoms of social alienation?" The OJJDP plan of actions opts for the former and calls for intense lobbying of state legislatures to adopt this drastic change. The time for such a movement is fortuitous. Daily reports in the press detail gory crimes committed by juveniles who have recently been released from rehabilitation programs. Part of everyday police lore is

**270**

the little punk who scowls at the arresting officer and says, "You can't do anything to me. I'm a juvenile."

Despite the unimpressive results, I am still supportive of the original concept. Admittedly, providing close, individual attention to only half a dozen clients met rebuff after rebuff. It was disappointing that our experiment was no more effective than the effort among most ordinary programs that deal with larger numbers. Six clients or thirty, the results may not make much difference. Nonetheless, one thought lingers. Would a Master Counselor working exclusively with only one client for two years accomplish what Cornelius Foster couldn't do with a caseload of six? Certainly the pressure of a Foster's daily presence would inhibit criminal activity. Crucial decision-making moments occurred for each of our charges when a steady head was necessary but wasn't there. Although most counseling efforts claim a close counselor-client relationship, the reality of overloaded caseloads makes it impossible. Did we have the right idea, but the wrong number?

Even the best of today's rehabilitation programs employ a short-term, quick-fix approach. Progress is only for the moment, involving a kind of group hypnosis. The few agencies that are successful, like DMI, infuse a revitalizing spirit. For a short time after, a new light shines ahead. Then, the reality of the street corner sets in, and it's back to the old ways. Nobody's there for the long haul when the inspirational message wears off. By what stretch of the imagination can three to six months of daily virtue redo all those early years spent in a moral vacuum? These kids, who are brought up in an atmosphere where the norm is cheating, lying, and stealing, are suddenly exposed to massive doses of goodness. It's a lot easier to perform a heart transplant than to transpose a set of moral values. Had our six individuals all shown positive results, the next great rehabilitation vogue would have been a one-Master-Counselor-to-six formula. Can one-on-one be an additional tool in the total arsenal? How many Lesters can be reached, no matter what we do? As time distances us from the end of the experiment, the early, sure premises become obscure and uncertain.

On its face, the prevailing evidence supports the "just desserts" advocates rather than the supporters of the old rehabilitation model. Clearly, had mandatory sentencing guidelines been imposed from which the court could not deviate, The Runner, The Charmer, The Fighter, and The Migrant would surely have been incarcerated earlier, saving many who became their victims during the last three

**271**

years. Were it only that simple! No matter what the length of stay, punishment is only temporary. More properly framed, the issue is not punishment versus treatment, but for how long can the citizen in the street be placed at risk while we experiment?

As a matter of fact, the issue itself is described inaccurately. It is not treatment versus punishment. "Treatment" suggests some kind of antidote for an illness. Juvenile courts are not hospitals providing prescriptive care. Delinquents have not contracted a disease by virtue of their environment, and no magic medical potions are offered guaranteeing a cure. The term "rehabilitation" better describes this condition, suggesting that attitudes can be altered within a fixed period of time, followed by changes. Rehabilitation is a slowly developing process within the youth, rather than one forced by rote indoctrination.

Punishment is important, but it is only one facet of the equation. Incarceration, by dispatching the violent, repetitive offender to adult prison or even keeping the more malleable delinquent under juvenile lock and key, only marks time. To rely primarily upon punishment creates a negative atmosphere, an admission that imprisonment is the best we can do. More likely to make an impression is a combination of short-term lockup, plus long-term rehabilitation. Unless the crime is shocking or the criminal record extensive, six months to a year maximum incarceration sends the clear message to youths that they must pay a price. This is long enough for healthy reflection. The true test is not how well juveniles adjust to strict conditions of incarceration, but rather their performance in the community upon release. Meeting this test requires an approach that features rehabilitation from the onset.

Unlike the adult system's concern for citizen safety, the juvenile-court philosophy is cloaked in more humane, even patriotic, terms. Concepts establishing the needs of the individual over the demands of the state are aimed at making damaged children whole again. This almost romantic attitude toward youth distinguishes us from nondemocratic regimes throughout the world. Since the early part of this century, we have tolerated and, in fact, encouraged benevolence toward children in distress. Have we run out of patience? Has the cost become too high? Will the juvenile-court bashers win out? Change is definitely in the wind, but solutions are not self-evident. The Master Counselor concept may be only a fragment of the answer, but the OJJDP approach certainly does not herald a new beginning.

## Knowing What Makes the Difference

Actually, sentencing guidelines are not necessary because the tougher approach has, in fact, been employed for some time. It, too, has not passed the test. Most states already send serious repeat offenders to the adult court. Many of them employ preventive detention. The old counseling techniques to instill moral values have been supplemented in most jurisdictions by providing work programs, teaching survival skills, and using a host of other approaches to equip a youngster to cope in the harsh world outside. Juvenile residential institutions are brimming over with detainees who face tougher sanctions than the probation usually imposed when sent to adult court. Juvenile-court sessions do not constitute a group of social workers sitting around exploring family relationships in order to excuse the behavior of the delinquent. The question is not whether we must choose between an offender-oriented system and an offense-oriented system. What exists now is a system devoted to both. Each case continues to be individualized, and, in the process, punishment is meted where warranted, and rehabilitation where it seems a likely disposition.

Despite their misstatement of the problem, are the bashers right? The adult system, offering only superficial pretense at rehabilitation and never having succeeded in finding an appropriate formula for punishment, is hardly the model to replicate. Adopting adult-court measures or simply becoming part of that court will only redesign the problem. The bashers are wrong, but not entirely so. Major surgery is required, but not on their terms. The problem is not our philosophy, but the failure to carry it out properly.

It must be recognized that juvenile courts are capable of playing a supportive, but lesser, role in the child-saving business. Many troubled youth reject court-imposed help. Some live in an unreachable world. Others need more complex assistance than the court is able to provide. Its capabilities are limited. Family and school offer a more intimate interaction with the child. Nurturing must, in great part, come from these institutions. In today's climate of weak family ties, the public school is the likely candidate, perhaps the only one.

Although schools are now accepting greater responsibility for unruly students, dropouts, and drug users, their posture is mainly defensive, intended more to expel than to convert the troublemaker. Their underlying goal to achieve a learning environment, free of disturbing elements, may be unrealistic. It is shortsighted to divorce the school from the child's day-to-day struggle in the street. Family planning, parenting skills, birth-control information, all need to be-

**273**

come part of the education process, in and out of the schools. Drug counselors and family guidance centers can no longer be low-priority school budget items. Channels for the regular exchange of information between the schools and the courts need to be forged. Delinquents returning to school after court confinement must receive extra attention during the transition period rather than be ignored. The juvenile court of the future should be an integral part of the school system, probably housed in the same complex along with social-service agencies to address together the problems of each child.

The holistic approach dealing with the entire family is the only avenue to lower delinquency. The cry is not for less rehabilitation, but for more. Punishment alone is antithetical to sensitivity. Courts dealing with alienated youth, severed families, and life-threatening illnesses such as AIDS need the time and patience to be responsive. The problem is compounded by the influx of large numbers of immigrants into our major population centers, many of whom have nonconforming cultural attitudes toward children. The sensitivity needed to bridge this assimilation period can only come in a less punitive setting.

The establishment of a new juvenile-court structure is long overdue. Because adolescents are now maturing earlier, using age eighteen as the year for adulthood is an anachronism. Realistically, a clientele topped off at age fifteen, made up of minor criminal offenders as well as neglected and abused children, best fits the model. Serving fewer in number, a limited juvenile court can focus where prospects are most encouraging. The new proposed court, now housed together with the school and the caretaker agencies, can rise above the traditional role of assessing guilt or innocence. Bringing all the community social and welfare resources to bear on the problems of the family in its totality will be the major objective. This will require an expansion of the judge's role to directing and monitoring service agencies, as well as seeking legislative and public support for the social needs of youth. Advisory boards will be an important arm to provide expertise for the court.

Broadening the role of the juvenile-court judge will be difficult. Just as social workers are at the bottom of the salary scale and legislative appropriations for child-care budgets are the first to be cut, so the position of juvenile-court judge does not rank high in the legal hierarchy. To attract strong leadership for the position, its status and recognition need to be enhanced dramatically. Serious

**274**

changes will take place when the community begins to comprehend fully that crime and other evidence of social failure are rooted in the public's refusal to address adequately the needs of disadvantaged children. Improvement will occur when legislatures start to invest in long-term responses rather than stopgap reactions to shocking incidents. A malaise, a defeatist attitude, exists in both the community and among professionals in the field. Upgrading the juvenile-justice system requires a renaissance of spirit.

To win public support, disclosure is essential. In some situations, publicly revealing facts of a case may be damaging to a child, but in too many instances secrecy is used only to shield bureaucratic ineptness. The courts cannot bemoan the public's lack of interest while maintaining a shield over what occurs. Not only should juvenile-case information be available for public examination, but accountability must be a key factor. Monitoring social-service providers and reporting on the quality of their performance must be an added role for the juvenile-court judge. Judges in their proposed new roles as managers and public spokesmen may need some additional statutory authority, but the law need not be changed significantly because the inherent powers of the court are extensive and creative judges can find ways to make their voices heard. The juvenile court needs to come out of the closet, revealing all and being accountable. This can be accomplished through strong centralized leadership.

Championing rehabilitation is a lot easier than producing effective programs. The cause has a convincing ring, but not the results. In large part, this is directly attributable to the short-term nature—three to six months—of today's rehabilitation programs as well as the failure to provide adequate follow-up care upon completion of the program. It is axiomatic in the juvenile system that any style program can work, no matter what the content, so long as the staff has the time, zeal, and motivation to reach out to the kids. There are, therefore, no great programs—only great relationships.

Every few years, a particular type program becomes trendy. Several years ago, it was the "scared straight" concept. Show youngsters the harsh, tough jail life and they'll be too frightened to break into a pizza parlor. Recently, wilderness programs have been in vogue. Send the errant boy through the Florida swamps or on a covered-wagon caravan, and he'll be a better man for it. All these approaches work when a program provides long-term dedicated attention. Unfortunately, few programs today allow time for intimate care or for long-term focus. Further exacerbating the problem is the "miracle drug" approach the community has learned to expect. Imprinted in the public mind is the theory that, once a court obtains jurisdiction, the healing process begins immediately and a born-again youth emerges in ninety days.

Unrealistic expectations are generated by a frustrated public demanding a cure and by program operators certain they alone have the answer. Each feeds on the other, producing exaggerated claims and unfulfilled hopes. Almost every program claims a high success rate, some in the range of 75 to 85 percent. For the most part, the figures are accurate, but the definition of success is fuzzy at best. Funds from public or private sources are apportioned according to the skewed success picture painted by the professionals. Most of them admit privately that three or four out of ten hard-cores avoiding arrest for the next three years warrants a special celebration. Yet, this kind of public declaration would markedly lessen refunding from public sources or be the subject of a pronouncement at a gala fund-raiser. Assuring the public that ready answers are just around the corner may be a morale booster, but failure to emphasize the never-ending nature of the struggle can be more costly.

Good programs working with novice delinquents sometimes produce quick results, but kids who have two-page rap sheets didn't get that way overnight. Most juvenile-court clients are tough cookies, who are not amenable to sudden alteration. The total information picture is unreliable: agency heads puff results, the public never learns the truth, and the media stress dramatic individual events. Government-funded social-service agencies are examined with uncritical eyes, unless public scandal erupts. Data are scarce, studies are ignored, and few if any of the experts know what works and for whom. The likelihood for immediate change in any of these factors is limited, but for a new realistic philosophy to emerge, community expectations need to be lowered sharply and a more accurate flow of information provided.

It was no great surprise that the youths in the Master Counselor Program did not respond as anticipated. We were going to do it the old-fashioned way: communicating, guiding, persuading, individualizing each case. Too many things can go wrong—and did. Any modern hard-liner could have told us that. The true surprise was that the lock-'em-up approach fared little better. Eckerd's State School, at Okeechobee, proved to be no more than a way station. FEI's Last Chance Ranch, in the wilds of the Everglades, designed to rehabilitate hard-cores step-by-step through emphasizing hard labor, didn't succeed either. Soft and gentle, or hard and demanding—penetrating the wall doesn't happen easily.

*Perhaps the truest and hardest test was Dwight Anderson (The Migrant). All the negative elements in his case served as a challenge: almost retarded, from an aimless family, and living under subpoverty standards. He possessed no visible talents, lacked ambition or direction, and resisted everything we offered. Our mission was not to match his impossible dream of learning about computers. All that needed to be done was to fit him into some decent pigeonhole to help him function without harming others. The route to take seemed obvious. Provide survival skills: reading, writing, working, communicating, distinguishing right from wrong, and turning the family into a supportive unit.*

*It was never clear whether piercing one more veil would have opened another world for Dwight or whether we never had a chance. For two years, we nursed this family along: catering, cajoling, waiting for improvement. Did growing up in a primitive home setting, as did Dwight, mean he was forever foreclosed from making up the lost ground? As it turns out, hopes were too high. Foster was a stabilizing factor, but even more was needed. The special accelerated school programs for slow learners never reached Dwight. None of the clinical recommendations added much to our knowledge. The boy was of little assistance in the process, not willing to be part of a group he called "retards." Now, three years after we began with the Anderson family, he and the others are back where they started, picking potatoes in the fields. They have moved from the housing project to a one-bedroom apartment, overcrowded and dirty. Mrs. Anderson takes it all in stride. Foster puts it this way: "She lives one day at a time. Living bad. Living good. It ain't no different to her. She's just as happy with Dwight out in the fields."*

*It was a triumph for Mrs. Anderson over the system. Her life-style prevailed because she was there long before we arrived. Like everything else, she brushed off being asked to leave the housing project: "I never did like that place anyway, and those people there didn't like us. My boys didn't do all the bad things they said about them."*

*Dwight, arrested on two burglary charges, has been transferred to the adult court. He's now seventeen, filled out physically, grown from the little boy who first followed Cornelius Foster to my cham-*

*bers into a rangy six-footer. The results of his trials won't make much difference. It's only a matter of time before he is back. One way or another, he'll be a burden to his community.*

Kids like Dwight need to be assigned to a basic-skills program and literally forced to absorb this learning. Not in the casual, volunteer way it's done now, but total immersion in the manner the U.S. Army taught foreign languages during World War II. Pulling palmettos may be tough therapy, but it doesn't come close to a staff of special tutors force-feeding reading and writing. That's real punishment. Perhaps we need to reconstitute the Civilian Conservation Corps (CCC) of the 1930s, this time for delinquent youth and focusing on basic education rather than the work ethic. Probably more significant than the effort to find a track for Dwight was the failure at some early stage to remove him from his home as a dependent child. It is difficult for the system to respond suddenly to criminal behavior after having ignored the early years of family neglect.

The juvenile-justice apparatus is engaged in a constant struggle to convert young, hard-core, violent offenders. It is open warfare. Victories are few, but the conflict goes on. Not so with dependent, neglected, abused children, who attract little attention. Their conduct is not of a criminal nature, and they are not perceived as a threat to the community. Because they are from poor and uneducated families, their cause lacks any political base of support. A tacit understanding seems to prevail among legislators, professionals in the field, and the general public that stricken dependent children require attention only to the extent that community embarrassment can be avoided. If Lester Burrows (The Runner) had found a stable and responsive home among the twenty-odd foster homes that had accommodated him, he would not now be in the Indiantown Correctional Center. Had our dependency program been minimally effective with Dwight Anderson's migrant family before he came to our attention as a young criminal, his chances today would be a lot more promising. Somehow, the public avoids connections between the troubled dependent child and acts of criminal behavior. A page-one scandalous event temporarily spotlights the plight of these children, then quickly fades from public interest.

Most communities have a shadow structure of dependence services: some emergency shelters, a network of foster homes, adoption programs, parent training, and other specialties—far too little of each. When a catastrophic event occurs, the breakdown is attributed to lax supervision or inept management, but in fact only a skeletal social-welfare organization exists, which is barely able to respond to routine matters. Some people question government intervention in the lives of families where no criminal law has been violated, but this is often simply an excuse for inattention.

The federal government has made an effort to impose standards upon the states. Public Law 96-272, the Adoption Assistance and Child Welfare Act, requires states to provide for appropriate child care in order to be eligible for federal funding. This is helpful, but it cannot overcome inertia and indifference at the local government level. A 1986 report by the National Council of Juvenile and Family Court Judges catalogs the failure. Titled "Deprived Children: A Judicial Response," the four-year study outlines seventy-three recommendations. One can only conclude from them that current responses to the problem nationwide are in complete disarray. Adequate funding is sought for a coordinated system of family intervention, and a swifter process is prescribed for out-of-home placement. To assure compliance, the judges ask for judicial and citizen review panels and call for increases in judicial authority to address this out-of-control condition.

Both the federal law and the seventy-three recommendations of the juvenile-court judges support the underlying theme that the court, through a vital, energetic, fully empowered judge, can make the difference. True as this premise may be, more than a charismatic character is needed. The dependency area is a lot more complex than the delinquency forum. Dependency cases are often time-consuming, never-ending bitter quarrels that crowded court calendars are not structured to handle. Judges trained in criminal-law procedure are more at home with delinquency cases. For the most part, they are uncomfortable in the social setting of family disorder.

Delinquencies have a built-in cooling-off period during which legal issues of guilt and pre-trial detention are considered. Lawyers file their motions, counselors have the opportunity to search out behavioral causes, and families can reflect on the events. Not so with dependencies, where immediate responses are crucial. Cases involving the dependent, neglected, and abused child usually require services far more extensive than those offered a delinquent child. In most instances, it is a crisis situation. Time is an important factor; everything needs to be done at once. The abused dependent child and family usually need psychological services, parent training, counseling, welfare assistance, vocational training, and perhaps

**279**

other forms of assistance. The bureaucracy in each case becomes monumental, involving many disciplines, different agencies, and diverse chains of authority.

Too often court-structure planning assumes a judicial omnipotence, whereas often very ordinary, low-level performance is available. The tradition of the black judicial robe presumes more than is underneath. Usually, help is needed. In the federal court, many complicated multi-defendant cases employ case managers to sort out the issues of each day and plan the court agenda. Similarly, the dependency caseload needs this kind of support. Although it may appear to be excessive layering of the court, each judge probably needs a social worker who is specially employed by the court to manage the judge's dependency caseload. This person would monitor selected cases, make certain no cases are lost in the process, and assure maximum efficiency at the judicial level.

Almost every dependency case should also be assigned a citizen-volunteer who is able to guide the child through the maze to make certain that whatever is needed and prescribed is carried out. The presence of an outside force participating in the decision-making immediately alters the balance. Serving as guardians for the children, the volunteers would constantly be evaluating service providers, making them more accountable and providing totally impartial, up-to-the-minute progress reports for the court. Such assistance is available in many communities, but the role has not yet developed to its full potential. By their efforts, these citizen-volunteers become an effective constituency for children, able to influence the media and the legislature. A large citizen-volunteer force could change the face of the dependency situation.

An alternative to the dependency judge is a special master, properly trained to preside over these cases. Judges are miscast as decision-makers in this role. The resolution of family conflict is not an area in which they can claim expertise. They can be more effective in their political persona as an elected judge, assuming the role of spokesman in behalf of the cause of dependent children.

Unlike delinquent cases, where the child's unlawful act is featured, dependencies revolve around the behavior of parents. Servicing the family as a unit requires further extension of the court's authority over parents. Situations involving latch-key children, runaways, unwed teenage pregnancies, and other child-care problems call for the court to assert authority over all parties. Limiting it to control over the child without being able to impose other performance and penalties on the parents is an ineffective, halfway measure. Aspects of the same problem often require separate hearings: in adult criminal court for abuse by the parent; in divorce court for the custody of the child; in probate court for extra-special matters. Legislative effort should turn toward permitting greater family control within the juvenile-court forum.

Dependency vis-à-vis the community is a wrenching situation. Five of the six Master Counselor clients had dependency referrals early in their youth. None except Lester Burrows (The Runner) received even minimal attention. The "foster-care drift" used in his situation involved having a bed in which to sleep, moving from foster home to foster home, and never being part of a family. Foster-care drift is typical for the Lesters of the world. An occasional outpouring of public sympathy results from a highly publicized incident of neglect, yet outright rejection is often the response to any effort at organized reform. The community simply shuns accepting responsibility for what is characterized as an unwillingness of individual families to bear their own burden. With delinquents, the situation differs somewhat; the element of fear is added. In this instance, self-protection forces some community response, but in the case of dependents no impelling motive to assist prevails.

Some trends shine brightly for the moment, flicker a bit, and then fade. For a while, deinstitutionalization—taking the mentally ill child out of a large treatment center for placement in a small community setting—seemed a wholesome approach until neighbors began to overrun zoning boards protesting placement in their neighborhood. Then a flood of child-abuse cases in the press seemed to open the door for government-funded care centers, but that enthusiasm soon abated. Nobody seems certain as to the course to follow.

Whether troubled dependent children flow from societal or family failure or from a faulty welfare system begs the issue. Most of them are victims whose only offense may be disobedience, self-destructiveness, or absence of parents. Somewhere in the collective recess of the public mind is an attitude that spurs rejection. Added to this are prohibitive costs. To provide networks for mental health, child care, parenting skills, and a host of costly residential centers for those children needing major care would require an effort worthy of national campaigns that are mounted to address catastrophic illnesses. The sense of guilt over failure to respond adequately to this class of dependents, added to the frustration and anger over the destructiveness of delinquents, produces a confused populace. It is not likely that a sudden community turnaround will emerge.

Out of fear of crime, the public is somewhat willing to at least tinker with the delinquency system. Piecemeal engineering and often some serious restructuring may be acceptable. It is different with the neglected child: a little help but mostly hands-off. The public accepts dealing with delinquency as a crime-fighting need, but views helping deprived children as do-gooder work by social reformers. Only when the public recognizes that the two are intertwined, feeding on each other, will the full import of the needs of the dependent, neglected, abused child be adequately addressed.

*Why does a youth persist in criminal activity despite all effort at diversion? Lester Burrows (The Runner), living on the street, bouncing from one shelter to another, learned to distrust acceptable standards. For him, crime came with the parcel; he made adjustments. Where abiding by the law didn't fill his need, acting outside the law naturally followed. Most of his crimes, though felonies, were not of an assaultive nature. He was a chronic offender, but more passive than violent.*

*Laurence Samuel (The Fighter) was different. Compulsive in behavior and indifferent in attitude, he was a threat to anyone in his way. Remorse was not an emotion he possessed. He was a tragedy that was almost avoided. The arrival of Mrs. Appel on the scene at the State School clinic was another miracle never fulfilled. Just like Andy's near-miracle with the fanciful tale of a trip around the world so the presence of a fairy godmother didn't convert Laurence.*

*Obviously, his problems were deeper than all our psychologists and psychiatrists were able to fathom. We learned later that the police had uncovered two additional robbery cases, implicating Laurence in the smashing of car windows as well as beating and robbing the occupants. These events occurred within several weeks of his return from State School and during the very time Mrs. Appel was visiting him. No matter what the circumstances, somehow violence was ingrained in him.*

*Although Laurence has been sitting in county jail for almost a year, he has been lucky in the disposition of his cases. As often happens in adult court, his robbery cases have been dropped because of the failure of the state to prosecute. The witnesses either*

**282**

*disappeared or refused to press charges. He's still in county jail, however, waiting trial on an arson charge rising from an aborted attempt to burn down the jail. Laurence likes to leave a calling card wherever he goes. Can he ever straighten out? Mrs. Appel still believes in him. She calls regularly. Foster thinks otherwise: "The only thing he has learned is how to do time. When he gets out he'll be a terror in the streets. You'll read about him."*

The puzzle of how to approach youngsters committing violent acts has never been more difficult. At one end of the spectrum are those calling for removal of these predators from the streets. One researcher has calculated that doubling sentences would increase the jail population about 6 percent and simultaneously lower the amount of crime in the street by 5 percent. The 5-percent reduction is an appreciable gain, but the impact would not address the full scope of the crime problem. What would prospects be for Laurence and Lester a couple of years from now, assuming the prison terms in store for them were doubled? Probably the same.

Imprisonment presents other problems. Recommending an extended stay for a fifteen-year-old thug does not always mean a long incarceration. Correctional authorities pay scant attention to judicial recommendations because they, not the judge, usually make the determination as to length of stay. Their standard for release is based on the youngster's adjustment to the institution. When the individual conforms to the rules and is not disruptive, release is accelerated. Several of our boys became absolute magicians at doing time.

Another factor to consider is the ability of the subculture to replace lost leaders. Somehow, no sooner is one member of the corner crowd lost than a replacement appears. Regardless of a surge in police arrests, the supply seems inexhaustible. Sometimes succession comes from within the family, younger brothers accelerating their criminal activity when an older brother is arrested; other times, from a gang structure that apparently has a waiting list. Arrest does not deter. Among chronic offenders, it is only a condition to which one must accommodate. Hard-liners can find little solace in incarceration. It neither stems the tide nor creates a sense of security. A few individuals are put out of commission temporarily, but the real issues are never faced.

At the opposite end of the scale is early intervention. In this approach, which also has its legion of supporters, those children likely to be involved in criminal behavior are selected and provided the social ingredients to turn them toward normal behavior. At the earliest age, the program consists of the government providing prenatal care, nursery schools, adequate housing, and other social benefits. For the pre-teenager who shows signs of potential criminality, early intervention requires counseling and family assistance. The high cost and the apparent lack of positive results have produced growing public disenchantment with both approaches. In addition, families resent having their children labeled as potential criminals. Perhaps most damaging to the cause of early intervention is the difficulty of proving that the program effort expended many years before is the direct cause of the child's subsequent good citizenship. In choosing between incarceration and early intervention, the angry citizen will opt for the immediate satisfaction provided by the former. Neither one totally fills the bill.

No discussion of hard-core delinquents can avoid the role of gangs. Visions of youth gangs terrorizing neighborhoods and assaulting the elderly have been portrayed in a sensational manner in the media and have been carefully analyzed by sociologists as well. Gangs are viewed as an aberrant phenomenon that is foisted upon a defenseless community. In reality, they are a natural outgrowth. It is almost as if the disaffected have established a parallel learning system. Having failed in the public-school system, they learn their manners and attitudes in the gang. All the attributes expected in the family and at school are evidenced among gang members, who see no evil in their loyalty and obedience to the code. They know no other. Some youth gangs evolve into highly structured, criminal operations, particularly in the drug field. With those groups, little can be done. Theirs is strictly a business venture with which the state cannot compete.

However, a golden opportunity is presented during the early stages of gang development. This is true early intervention. No labeling problem occurs here. Gang membership involves self-selection, movement toward criminal activity, and alienation from family as well as community standards. The at-risk population proclaims its identity and is readily available, but the community reacts almost with indifference. More active missionary work is called for rather than the token effort seen in most cities. We need an inundation of inner-city street workers, reformed drug addicts, retired athletes, and a whole galaxy of people and programs to win over the minds and souls of the gang members.

Researchers in the field have examined innumerable programs to discover some common base from which standards can be set for improving the behavior of chronic juvenile offenders. None is optimistic. Marvin Wolfgang, pre-eminent in the field, studied birth cohorts of 10,000 boys who were born in Philadelphia in 1945; then, in Cohort II, he followed almost 16,000 boys and girls born in 1958. His conclusion that about 6 percent of the entire cohort study commit more than 50 percent of the crime is generally accepted in the field. In terms of violent crime, the Wolfgang study found that this 6 percent committed 71 percent of the homicides, 73 percent of the rapes, 82 percent of the robberies, and 67 percent of the aggravated assaults. Dr. Wolfgang's study showed that a small cadre of Cohort II serious, chronic offenders committed more violent acts than their earlier Cohort I counterparts. To avoid a continued increase in the yet-to-be-done Cohort III study, he recommends stronger sanctions, including incarceration at the first or second felony conviction. Wolfgang's work suggests that little needs to be done with the very minor offender and little can be done for the hard-core offender who has committed five to ten serious offenses. Wolfgang, instead, advocates a special focus on the second and third offender, not yet hard-core.

Another often-quoted report, by researcher Robert Martinson, issued after a comprehensive examination of all existing programs up to 1974, drew this conclusion: "With few and isolated exceptions, the rehabilitative efforts that have been reported so far had no appreciable effect on recidivism." This report, produced at a time when citizens' fear of crime was becoming a national concern, quickly emerged as the basis for the antirehabilitation rhetoric of the late 1970s and the early 1980s.

A more recent, 1985, assessment of intervention strategies for chronic offenders by Peter Greenwood and his associates at Rand Corporation finds some hope. Dr. Greenwood reexamined the work of early researchers as well as more current approaches and found evidence of some effective programs: wilderness-setting programs, such as FEI; small secure units housing no more than fifteen violent or acting-out youth; and group homes for reentry to the community upon returning from incarceration. During the decade between Martinson (1974) and Greenwood (1985), a sharp rise occurred in support of the "nothing works, get-tough" approach, and then a slow imperceptible turn toward rehabilitation, though with a somewhat more pragmatic approach. During this period, virtually total attention was devoted to the violent repetitive offender on the premise that, once Dr. Wolfgang's 6 percent could be identified, diagnosed, and corralled, the mission would be complete. When it became painfully clear that the supply was never-ending and that stronger punishment via transfer to the adult court was not particularly effective, new, less-punitive modes became acceptable.

We are probably passing into still another era in our attitudes toward the juvenile-justice system. Once the sole domain of the government, it is now being infiltrated with private entrepreneur, non–social worker types who carry computers and slide rules. This has happened not only in the juvenile field, but also in the total criminal-justice establishment, where adult prisons have been taken over by corporations that promise to run them better and cheaper. Considering the difficulty governments have experienced with these institutions, some states have gladly contracted for these services. Programs of rehabilitation, particularly for chronic juvenile delinquents, abound under private-sector control. Most are operated through a combination of state contracts and philanthropic endeavors. First to enter the field were the philanthropists, who were able to infuse money, spirit, and new concepts.

In Florida the Dade Marine Institute and eight other marine institutes, as well as FEI, were organized by Robert Rosof, a venture capitalist who began the project as a result of having half a dozen delinquent kids assigned to work on his boat. This came about as a favor to an old college classmate who was serving as a juvenile-court judge. The Boys' Club After Care Program, in Miami, that struggled with Dwight Anderson (The Migrant), was totally funded by millionaire businessman Clifford Perlman through contributions from Caesars World Casino, in Las Vegas, which he owned at one time. He formerly practiced law in Miami, and the After Care Program was his pay-back gift to the city. The State School, in Okeechobee, long the subject of unfavorable criticism, was taken over by the Jack Eckerd Foundation and now has made great strides in ridding itself of the "warehouse" image. Eckerd, owner of a chain of drugstores, has also sponsored several Florida wilderness camps for troubled dependent children.

The gap filled by these captains of industry has instilled confidence in the system and bettered the quality of programming. It also has encouraged entrepreneurs to enter the field for profit. Stronger advocates for juvenile causes in the community and in state legislatures are bound to emerge from this development.

No matter how much interest surges in the hard-core delinquent, it is unrealistic to expect startling results. The private sector will probably introduce greater efficiency, and the expectations of the public may become more realistic. The clamor for better techniques to control the hard-cores will not abate, nor will the demand for harsher punishment. Through it all, so long as advocates remain who support realistic rehabilitation efforts among even the most difficult offenders, the American characteristic to give the child one more chance will probably remain in force.

One small caveat: success in this endeavor sometimes results from selecting less formidable participants. Many private-sector programs offering more sophisticated approaches cater to a better-quality delinquent by excluding hard-cores. Unfortunately, most serious crime is committed by low-IQ individuals who lack the ability to perform on exotic wilderness treks or boating expeditions. Large numbers of individuals in the low intellectual range drift through the delinquency system from crime to crime, almost immune to any assistance. They are on the borderline, not quite eligible for treatment as retarded, but nonetheless out of the mainstream because they lack the ability to be trained. Without constant supervision and daily medication, they are a threat to all in their path. Too often they are ignored. The politics of rehabilitation sometimes results in the selection of clients based primarily on the prospect of success. Admitting only the malleable client produces a higher rate of success and ensures further funding. The test of an effective program needs to be determined, not only on the recidivism rate, but perhaps more significantly on the risk factor in dealing with less manageable clients.

*What happened with Jamie Forest (The Nuisance) tells a lot about the system at its best. Coming in, he had nothing going for him. He was trouble all along the way, but at the end, something turned him. Probably the key was the accumulation of attention he received. Somewhere in the depth of his psyche, he realized and appreciated that no one gave up on him. It may have been Rose, his old FEI counselor, Cornelius Foster, or one of the others he met.*

*A year ago, back from FEI, he was in their After Care Program, a more likely prospect for jail than anything else. He was a real handful, still looking for ways to beat the system. On a job, the supervisor threatened to fire him regularly. Visiting in my chambers, he projected one fantasy after another. Foster, always to the rescue, provided one more chance along with an occasional weekend in*

**287**

*lockup. The Jamie types can't wake in the morning on schedule, can't meet an appointment on time, can't work at a task for a fixed period, and can't follow the simplest instruction. In addition, they are not able to read a newspaper, fill out a job application, or make change. Presumably Jamie's slowness resulted from an early bout with meningitis. That's doctor speculation, perhaps accurate, but not certain. The reservoir of innate ability that I sensed in him never materialized.*

*Jamie was also a perfect candidate for the "falling through the crack" category. Amiable and friendly as a puppy dog, he did nothing to display the red flag signaling serious trouble ahead. He was an amusing nuisance. No one had the time to notice the rising number of arrests. Unlike the Marcos and the Laurences, whose violence attracted attention, Jamie and his kind, who far outnumber the others, are too often overlooked.*

*Where is Jamie today? He's at the head of the class. His new FEI After Care counselor, assisted by Foster, stayed with him, nurturing him through job disappointments, listening to his tales, convincing him he could succeed. Jamie has a job as a driver's helper with a milk-delivery company. He works five days a week, 7:00 A.M. to 4:00 P.M. earning $150 weekly. He's been at it for ten months, working with a driver named Mack who has taken an interest in him. The one thing that has worked for him is having someone special available. Cornelius, Rose, and now Mack provide that helping hand.*

The politics of juvenile court—who inhabit it, how they function, and what they focus on—tell a lot about the court. Unlike the adult court, where harsh legal battle lines are clearly drawn to ensure an adversary relationship between opposing counsel, the juvenile court constitutes a configuration of individuals and groups who have a common goal: the well-being of the troubled child. A gentility and sensitivity is pretended, but it is hard to maintain. Intended to be a systemic search for solutions, the juvenile court has instead been dominated by the adversary court process. The actors dance to their own tune while attempting to conform to the requirements of court procedures. Concern for the child becomes almost incidental to the needs for each discipline to assert itself while the integrity of the court process is also maintained. The variety of disciplines in the juvenile court, which have differing premises, ensures conflict. Experts all, they provide strong opinions, weak solutions, and too

**288**

many unanswered questions—notwithstanding the avowed purpose to offer a profile of the youngster so complete that a responsive program will follow. Structured confusion is the more likely result.

It is difficult to achieve the essence of the juvenile philosophy, namely individualization, in today's courtroom setting. Time is the controlling factor. Among lawyers, the priority is keeping the case afloat. They need to locate witnesses, take depositions, obtain continuances, and do what members of their profession do. Rarely is enough time available. The judges' never-ending pursuit is to move the calendar. Cases need to be managed so that the number entering the system do not outnumber those presently awaiting consideration. The trial calendar for each day is limited by the hours available. Time dictates what happens in the courtroom.

The lawyer-judge courtroom team displays concern for the child, but each element has overriding roles governing its conduct. Legal arenas in any situation are not designed for reflective pursuits; juvenile court is no exception. Some few offenders are appropriately punished. A few others are sufficiently impressed so that they never return. A handful finds solutions to difficult problems. Most pass through unnoticed and untouched. The dynamics of the process and the politics governing crime control keep it that way. Thus, case management becomes almost a mathematical formula governed by the time available.

As time is the key factor in the courts, so is space the important constraint among agencies providing social services. Rehabilitation programs invariably are in short number. Uncertainty prevails about which programs work and for whom. Placement is often in programs that are available, rather than in those that are the most beneficial. The length of stay is determined by the demand for space. The lack of space is insidious, going far beyond the number of slots available in programs. Any social worker's office is easily identifiable by the presence of three or four sharing desks. Clients wait in the anteroom or in the hallway. One secretary serves several social workers, assuring a delay in preparing reports. Space is always short for file cabinets. Records are somewhere, usually in a warehouse. The tendency is for social agencies to grow larger while space decreases. Although low salary scales are blamed for frequent staff turnover, much of this can be charged to the lowered morale arising from the lack of space to perform.

Child-care experts testifying in court add an element of mystique to the courtroom setting. Theirs is a jargon that, blended with the legal language, must present a frightening spectacle to the poor, semiliterate juveniles and their families. Neither time nor patience permits educating or even informing the confused defendant. Although a psychologist alerting the court to the fragile psyche of an errant child performs a valued function, many of the expert opinions are based on a quick interview, which produces a boiler-plate opinion. Rarely are time, space, or staff available to fully examine or understand the client. Full-service clinics are needed on the court premises to examine and treat a host of medical and mental-health problems that afflict children in trouble.

Each discipline has a set of standards established in its own bureaucratic image. The goal first is to satisfy the internal aims of one's own discipline, and then somehow mesh together with others to be a positive influence on the child. Further complicating the relationships are the sources of power governing the doctors, lawyers, police officers, and social-service delivery agencies. Each of their lines of authority springs from different levels, both governmental and from the private sector. Connecting these disciplines at every level is one mass of paper-flow. To add to the incongruity, inevitably too few resources are available to match even the well-thought-out recommendations. Surprisingly, despite the apparent cross purposes and shortcomings, adjustments are ultimately made and all the disparate voices somehow make valid contributions.

Selecting areas of concentration does not arise from a series of carefully planned research papers. It is more happenstance. Political policy at other levels of government can sharply influence options. When a president of the United States declares war on drugs, then the drug scene becomes important, not because of the moral weight of the message but because such a declaration or one by Congress usually means a funding flow will soon drip down. An epidemic of young offenders committing mayhem in a New York City subway may lead the way to extensive action programs against hard-core violent delinquents. A TV special showing dyslexic children as prone to crime will inevitably bring action in the learning-disabled field. The juvenile-justice apparatus is a reactive instrumentality; whatever is the vogue becomes the practice. The constant search for one-fell-swoop answers causes the community virtually to reject long-term approaches for the mentally disturbed children who may be a threat to the public safety. These hard-to-treat cases are costly endeavors and afford only minimal likelihood of progress.

## Knowing What Makes the Difference

The uncertainty of the juvenile philosophy is in great measure the result of having to make do with the little that is offered. Although the procedural process may be somewhat flawed, more disturbing is the political process that treats child care as a second-class community venture. The politics of child care is best exemplified in the periodic national anti-drug-use crusades. Every level of government, the media, and the private sector join full force to impress upon our citizenry, particularly teenagers, the need to strike down this evil. The effort invariably involves destroying a coca crop in foreign lands, closing down parts of our border, and initiating intensive educational programs in our schools.

Despite these aggressive campaigns, only a few resources for actually treating adolescents with drug problems are ever available: treatment centers continue to have long waiting lists, and residential facilities cater only to those having adequate insurance, which in great part eliminates juveniles. Monthly costs of hospital drug programs now run to $16,000 per individual, more than five times the costs of a decade ago. These extravagent fees can only be borne by the very wealthy. In addition, adolescents are not sought because they are the least amenable to treatment. Older addicts, able to recognize their plight, are more responsive and less destructive than the volatile Marco types. Despite the oft-sounded national alert, treatment of youthful offenders continues to rank at the bottom. A recent study in Florida of adolescents needing drug treatment showed only 4 percent were receiving it. The evening news TV shot of the Coast Guard intercepting a drug-runner at sea captures the public imagination a lot more than the sight of a teenager being treated in a drug rehabilitation center.

*"He's a bucket of water," laughed Foster, referring to Andy Sills (The Drinker), who was sitting in my chambers and obviously an unhappy young man. It's been close to two years since he was scheduled for that ill-fated boat trip around the world. Now he was back as a result of a police officer stopping a car for a minor vehicle infraction. Andy was a passenger, and the officer routinely checking identification found an old juvenile court pickup order. The one thing the youth dreaded had happened. He was in lockup again. "He hasn't changed," chortled Foster. "He's still scared to death of being in jail. He's almost twenty and he cried all night."*

*I assured Andy he would be released because the juvenile court no longer had jurisdiction over him. Tight-lipped, he answered my questions with one- or two-word responses. Fear still in his eyes, he resented being subjected to my probing. "Where have you been? What have you been doing? Have you seen Captain Bill? How's Abbie?"*

*He didn't want to talk about the past. A few months in Boston with his father hadn't worked out. Back in Miami, he took odd jobs, staying with friends. Presently he is a stock boy in a retail toy store and plans to return to school. He sees his old girl friend and no longer has an alcohol problem. Captain Bill called him several months ago, but Andy refused to talk to him. He also answered all my questions reluctantly. I finally nodded to Foster that the discussion was over, and he signaled Andy, "Let's go." Both walked to the door, and Andy turned back to me, smiling for the first time. It was clear he wanted to shake hands, but without making the first overture. I took his hand, patted him on the back, and wished him well.*

*A half hour later, his mother came in to see me, wanting to make certain he was released. She confirmed most of what he had said, except for his alcohol problem: "He's not living at home, but I know he still has an alcohol problem, even though he denies it. He comes to visit us and is a good boy. He sees Abbie once in a while. He has other girl friends."*

*When she left, I asked Foster what he thought about his prize student. "Judge, no matter what you say about him, remember that it's more than two years since he was last arrested. Who do we know doing better than that? He deserves an 'A' for effort."*

*He does. Do we? For the moment, he seems to be working out his problems. If he stays straight, we probably deserve a share of the credit. He's a kid who never was a serious criminal. He drifted into criminal behavior and, somehow, the number of his arrests multiplied. A couple of beers, a little stealing—it was all part of the day. He had little to motivate him in another direction, so he did his thing. No one had ever been there to show him another way.*

### Miami Herald 2/23/87

*A seventeen-year-old boy was arrested Monday and charged with stabbing his fifty-year-old roommate to death in the bedroom of their rented Cricket Club apartment. Metro-Dade police arrested the youth as he drove a late model BMW in the garage of their condominium complex. The car's owner, the boy's roommate, was upstairs in bed dead. The teenager and the man were arguing shortly before midnight. The juvenile joined the man in bed, then twenty minutes later stabbed him to death. Police did not release the dead man's name [Captain Bill] pending notification of his next of kin.*

*It could easily have been Andy. Captain Bill is part of his forgettable past. Andy may yet make it.*

*The boy involved in the murder was a runaway who had all kinds of problems. Out of a broken family, living with a tough Marine Corps father, it had been one crisis after another. Since age ten, his life has been a series of drug problems, mental hospitals, and juvenile court. Described as clever and manipulative by our psychologist, he stole from whoever trusted him, and ran from every program. He bore wrist scars from an early suicide attempt, and cocaine was his favorite drug. Captain Bill was always waiting in the wings, ready to share the comforts of his bed.*

*The boy had been only another case number on my court docket, until one day Captain Bill asked to see me on a personal matter. He had the temerity to ask for custody of the boy. The captain was never short of gall. He smiled when I threatened to put him not in, but under the jail if he ever had any contact with the child, well knowing there was little I could do to him. Last week, the boy ran away from a drug program straight to the Cricket Club. The dispute and the resultant murder rose from money stolen from Captain Bill. Stabbed several times with a butcher knife, the body had been in the apartment several days before it was discovered. The boy had invited his friends to the apartment for some partying and a view of the corpse. It was a gruesome way for Captain Bill to go, but it involved some grim poetic justice. The mourners will be few.*

*This could have happened to any one of our six kids. Surviving in the street is a harsh way of life. Many Andys are out there, easy prey for the Captain Bills. Andy was lucky.*

As the juvenile-court philosophy changes, so must the structure itself be altered. Time and space problems flow from more serious structural flaws. Too many of the parts no longer fit comfortably. Andy and the many others like him need a finely tuned system able to react responsively and precisely. A sluggish out-of-step system never quite catches up to the problem.

Not often discussed is the low performance level of personnel employed by the state. At the bottom rung of the pay scale, social-service agencies obviously attract less competent applicants. Those able to perform attain the experience necessary to reach a better job market and depart. Even more telling is the weakness of middle-to-top level management performance. Agencies that have poor success records and lack any prospects of improvement are not attractive to aspiring young executives. An atmosphere of marking time, of keeping the lid on, permeates the operation. Everyone cautiously and fearfully waits for the next case involving the death of an abused child, inappropriately returned to the abuser by the social worker. All these personnel dread picking up the morning paper that contains a fresh account of a new crime committed by one of their charges. It is a cumulative and wearing-down process. Social-delivery systems spawned by the state lack the creativity to reach and stay with Marco and Laurence. Government auditors simply cannot contemplate a Cornelius Foster driving Marco several hundred miles to State School so that they can talk together en route—that's a travel voucher surely rejected.

On the occasion when a program characterized by innovative design and high-quality staff emerges, the state with its institutionalized dogma will inevitably and predictably grind it down. Low-budget, short-term, high-failure endeavors become the rule. The system makes the adjustment to mediocrity. The system becomes institutionalized, too comfortable to be replaced by an unknown quantity. The antidote is obvious: limit the role of the state to that of routine referral and bookkeeping; let the more motivated private-service vendors offer the zeal and fire necessary to make things happen.

Difficulties extend far beyond the condition of field services. They prevail throughout, including the selection of judges. Other than those elected directly to the juvenile court, most are administratively assigned to the juvenile division. No matter what the formal selection procedure, the better trial judges serve in the criminal, civil, or probate divisions. Judges do not consider juvenile court to be an assignment of high standing in the legal community, nor a stepping stone for advancement to higher courts. On occasion, the most inept judges are assigned to juvenile court, where it is assumed the least harm can be done.

In the rare instance where an exceptionally qualified jurist is available for long-term placement in the juvenile court, then the bugaboo of judicial rotation enters the picture. This is a theory that the community is better served by generalist judges rather than by specialists. The concept suggests that judges can be expert in every field of law, always ready to fill the gap where needed. Unfortunately, many assigned to juvenile court are not temperamentally or intellectually suited for the work and some actually resent the assignment. Nothing can be more devastating than a judge going through the motions, putting in time, waiting to complete a one-year stint. The inordinate complexity and the frail condition of the juvenile court require motivated individuals who are able to provide long-term leadership at the helm.

Amidst it all, the juvenile court maintains its purist posture, mainly through nomenclature. Early designers of the system struck down the usage of terminology associated with the adult criminal court. There are no defendants in juvenile court; they are called respondents. The accusatory charging document lacks inflammatory language; it is called a "Petition" and is styled in friendly tones: "In the interest of John Doe." Juveniles are not jailed; they are "detained." It is an "Adjudicatory Hearing," not a trial. No one is sentenced in juvenile court; the more delicate term is "Disposition." This phraseology sets the tone for an idyllic setting, never reached and no longer realistic.

The 1973 U.S. Supreme Court Gault decision forever terminated the judge's kindly grandparent role, where personal morality standards were the rule. Instead, lawyers were required for both sides and a true adversary court situation was imposed. Although now patterned after the adult court, two major differences still remain. In 1984 the U.S. Supreme Court affirmed that juvenile-court judges may impose pre-trial detention almost at will, a luxury not available in the adult court. This is premised on the theory that the tender years of juveniles make them more vulnerable and in need of judicial restraints. In addition, except for a handful of states, juveniles are not afforded a jury trial. Somewhere along the line, in the not too distant future, both these distinctions will be eliminated. When this occurs, virtually all operational differences between the two court systems will be erased. What will be called for then will be a hybrid judge, sensitive to the needs of the child, yet at home in the harsher world of the adult court.

Earlier recommended was lowering the jurisdiction of the court to the child's fifteenth birthday, enabling the court to concentrate upon the group best suited for rehabilitation. Lowering the juvenile age need not place the fifteen- to eighteen-year-old in the nether land of being too old to be offered juvenile court programs and too young to be subjected to longer sentencing where warranted. A second tier of the juvenile court can be established among the age fifteen to eighteen group, giving the judge authority to sentence these juveniles to the same length of servitude as adult-court judges may order. This additional sentencing power would immediately enhance the image of the juvenile court. No longer would it be viewed by the public as an ineffective, weak court. Its esteem in the legal profession would rise. Because of the likelihood of longer-term sentences, more able defense lawyers would be retained and competent jurists would feel more comfortable on the juvenile-court bench. Despite the prospect of longer sentences in juvenile court, the child would be in a better situation, avoiding the vagaries of adult-court sentencing. A judge familiar with the child and his family can maintain a continuity and a consistency currently nonexistent when repeat offenders are transferred to the adult court. This two-tier juvenile court will be able to maintain the original concept of the juvenile court and yet provide for the changing conditions of the times. The legal requirements for these changes are not bureaucratically onerous. The ripples flowing from it will markedly change the power-base of juvenile judges from one of weakness to one of strength.

*"Cool, calculating, and tough" summed up Marco Zargula (The Charmer). He was a product of his home and neighborhood. Larchmont Gardens was the executioner. It hurt watching him go down the drain. Once hard-core offenders jump on the crime merry-go-round, neither school, counselors, nor rehabilitation programs can make a difference. For a while, Greg Bridges, his adult probation officer, kept Marco in line. He arranged for him to have a clean slate with Judge Adams and worked out all his probation problems. Marco was free of drugs, attending school, working, and ready finally to pass the GED. On a few occasions after the program ended, he visited me, talked about his future, looked healthy, but somehow I sensed it wouldn't last. Foster kept an eye on him and his family; it was unofficial, but Marco knew he had a friend if needed. The Calcon brothers continued to be arrested, usually on stolen-motor-vehicle charges. No sooner was one sent away than another was back before me. In response to my questioning, each one always maintained that he and Marco no longer ran together. Although probably inevitable, the downfall began the day Greg Bridges left. As so often happens with field counselors, his assignment had been changed. The new adult probation officer never materialized.*

*Meanwhile, back at home steady deterioration and constant turmoil prevailed. Marco's stepfather, home from New Jersey State*

*Prison, immediately returned to burglary to support his heroin hab-it. He stole the food money in the house, threatened to kill Marco's mother, and finally was arrested for a gas-station robbery. Presently, he is a fugitive being sought by both the local authorities and the FBI. Both sisters have given birth in the last year, and no one in the household is employed.*

*Amidst all this, Marco struggled. The possession-of-marijuana case was dropped, but he finally succumbed to an auto-theft con-viction. After serving a six months' term in the Dade County stock-ade for the theft, he was shipped to the Indian Town Correctional Center for probation violation. Time made it painfully clear that we could not compete with either the family or Larchmont Gar-dens. Growing up with the deficits of a broken, crime-ridden family and a neighborhood of junkies and car thieves, Marco is now a hard-core adult criminal, capable of committing violence, no longer viewed as a "piece of cake."*

The "child savers" had no idea what was in store for the future when they began stirring up the juvenile-justice pot during the early part of this century. They took a set of wonderful ideals relating to the care of our most precious commodity, mixed them, shook gent-ly, and expected harmonious results to result automatically. The failure has been in cementing the components together. Were all the parts of the juvenile-justice system, as it functions today, packaged for a computer model, the results would undeniably call for firing the programmer. The wrong messages keep emerging. The system needs to be rewired so that it extends outward to the community, broadening relationships, rather than being tightened inwardly.

Perhaps most significant is the school-court relationship or lack of it. The delinquent in court is the same child only on a different turf. The one common thread among all the Master Counselor Program clients and most delinquents is failure in school. Yet, the school and the juvenile-justice systems are two entities that are barely civil to each other, more often sparring than sharing. Joint research efforts need to be instituted for early warning detection of potential delin-quents and for the problems of the learning disabled as they relate to crime.

Another court-school concern is the criminal misbehavior of stu-dents outside the school. School administrators face so many disci-pline problems within the classroom that they lack the tolerance, patience, and resources to cope with off-campus concerns. Their image of the proper role of the educator precludes taking on the burden of the crime-prone youngster. Dwight Anderson (The Migrant) is a perfect example. When he was fourteen, both the school and the courts made a genuine effort. Separately, it wasn't enough. Perhaps together it might have been different. A school-court marriage or at least a liaison can evolve only through a willingness on the part of the schools plus a large increase in the number of school counselors, a more pliant court system, and a less bureaucratic social-service system.

Not often discussed freely are subjects that cross over into race relations. These are always sensitive areas that need to be treated gingerly. They, too, fall in the mixer and come out askew. Too often data on the incidence of crime take on, or appear to take on, tones of racism. This is apparent in reporting the disproportionate number of black youths who are involved in violent crime, the high teenage pregnancy rate among black unwed mothers, and the failure to find sufficient number of black adoptive parents. Other data find similar excesses among ethnic groups, such as the high crime rate among both Puerto Ricans in New York and the Cuban refugees in the Mariel boatlift a decade ago. Often, discussions on these data bring angry reactions from black and Latin leaders, some of it warranted by the manner of presentation. The sensitivity of groups to the manner in which data are used only touches the surface.

Suspicion and mistrust run deep in many specific areas. Do authorities single out black offenders for harsher punishment because a mind-set exists that rehabilitation is less likely for them? Are some juvenile programs selectively excluding minority clients? Do our rehabilitation programs employ upper- and middle-management personnel in numbers far below their racial and ethnic population? Some evidence exists to support these propositions. Is the rising black middle class not assuming enough community responsibility as reflected by the small number of black children adopted? Are Latin families failing to maintain the traditional close control over the well-being of their children, who thereby become more involved in crime?

Much of what is done in the name of delinquency control founders because of the silent specter of racial inequality, real or otherwise. Facing these issues head-on cannot be avoided despite the emotion engendered. Racial conflicts usually arise from explosive street incidents that discourage rational responses. Distrust is due, not only to a lack of accurate information, but also to the unwillingness of community leaders to engage in serious dialogue. Gathering sound data, offering forums for discussion, and fostering inner-city outreach programs are essential segments of both community relations and delinquency control. Addressing racial tensions and crime takes more than goodwill. Many untapped reservoirs need to be reached, one of which is the university.

The university as a component of the community should shine brightly, but rarely does. For example, it makes no great rush to participate in the great social experiment called the juvenile court—a boon for the creative researcher. Although university specialists frequently respond to government needs by providing expertise in national and international fields, rarely are they involved in community relations or in the juvenile-justice field. Occasionally a well-funded grant will bear university auspices, but for the most part academic personnel watch from the sidelines.

This arm's-length attitude is not based on a desire to be cloistered among the ivy. Many expounders of theory would cherish the opportunity to test themselves in the field. Does a town versus gown conflict then exist? Do the practitioners reject the theorists out of hand? Mistrust or fear them? None of these. The answer lies in the unwillingness of university leaders to make cooperation with the juvenile courts a status endeavor. They prefer projects that enhance university prestige or encourage benefactors. Involvement in non-profit community ventures, such as juvenile delinquency, will be fostered only when the message to faculty clearly states that professional standing at the university is enhanced by virtue of participation. A public and professional commitment must be made so that citizens know the importance the institution attaches to these concerns, and the faculty are assured that the work they produce will be properly credited as academic achievement.

As in the case of the university, an elitist attitude also exists among the press. Both look down upon what they perceive to be a hapless juvenile-justice process. This image is in great part established by the media. They are carriers, not creators of the message, but their interpretation in great part determines the perception of the observer. Bad things are likely to happen to some children in the system, and occasionally do. In reporting these incidents, the press plays a major role in making the system accountable to the public. Agencies dealing with human services become a fertile hunting ground for the alert reporter. Sometimes the uncovering of a deplorable situation results in long-term gains, but a down-side is evident in constant press supervision. Finding soft spots becomes an easy task and thereby a newsroom staple. Almost any story reporting a tragedy or near-tragedy has within it some point where a different decision might have produced another result: a social worker chooses the wrong custodian for a dependent child or a judge releases a juvenile who thereupon commits another serious offense. Both are newsworthy events, properly to be reported.

As the number of similar stories is repeated, an agency image of ineptness is created, implanted not only in the public mind, but in the mind of reporters and their editors. Without complementary treatment describing the complexities of the total system and the lack of resources, the press establishes standards for performance that are literally unattainable. In essence, the system is declared to be an ensurer for the well-being and safety of those in its charge. It is not that excessive coverage demeans the system, but rather that the coverage is too shallow and fails to educate.

Critics need to forestall shortcomings by showing patience and understanding. Dealing with troubled youngsters is, at best, an at-risk effort. Once the rehabilitation process begins—selecting among uncertain choices and experimenting with new approaches—then unanticipated results are likely to follow. There are too many diverse elements for it to be otherwise. The more venturesome the plan, the greater the error factor. So long as the goal is to turn around the plight of troubled children, a condition of disarray may well persist. There must be a reaching out to respond to the special needs of each child, which often requires rising far above the demands of the system.

*George LaMont, Cornelius Foster, and I were examining the daily court calendar when my secretary advised that Mrs. Lander wanted to see me. Foster, no longer with HRS, is now employed in the Court Administrator's Office working for LaMont. He followed Frank Manning out of HRS several months ago. Manning had departed to head an agency for the Catholic Services Bureau. At least my prediction on Manning's success had been fulfilled.*

*When last we talked, Mrs. Lander had exuded happiness over son Rudy's turnaround, no longer castigating the police and the courts. We had become her allies. Yesterday's phone call told the sad tale: "Rudy's behavior has gone downhill. He's traveling with bad friends again, getting arrested. Can I talk to you in the morning?"*

*I knew it would be a difficult meeting. It was. Before I could even* ask about Rudy, she began a monologue, jumping from one incident to another, needing no prompting from me: "He was going into the army . . . Then he got arrested for stealing . . . Then he got arrested again for selling drugs . . . He's a good kid . . . He was an honor student before all this started . . . I should have told him his father was in prison . . . His half-brother was also in prison . . . His father got out of prison and ran off with a gal . . . Rudy is angry because his father keeps leaving . . . Sometimes I want to kill him . . . Sometimes he acts like he wants to kill me . . . I put him in a white school because I know they have better teachers . . . I've tried everything. . . ."

I listened patiently. She obviously was suffering as the tears welled up, and she couldn't talk anymore. After she left, I asked Foster if he could have helped this kid three years ago when we were considering him as a possible client. "Judge, this boy's mind is gone. Crack has got it. I talked to his mama and she tells me he walks around the house buck-naked. She is scared to death of him. A couple of years ago we had a chance. I could have helped him then. It all depends when you get at them. Finding their right time is what we got to know and being there at that time is what counts."

# Epilogue

## July 14, 1988

**Dwight Anderson (The Migrant):** In April of last year, Dwight, now sixteen, was convicted of Burglary in the adult court and sentenced to serve two years at the Apalachicola Youthful Offender Institution. He should be eligible for release in December 1988. Foster interviewed his mother, who stated she had not heard from him and did not know his whereabouts. According to Foster, she appeared very unconcerned. The interview took place at Jackson Memorial Hospital where Mrs. Anderson had just given birth to a set of twins, giving her a total of twelve children.

**Laurence Samuel (The Fighter):** Laurence is also serving his time in Apalachicola. He was sentenced to five years for Armed Robbery and three years probation for Arson. His mother says he is doing well, and she expects he will be returned home later this year on a work release program. Maureen Appel, the director of health services at State School, continues to keep in touch with him by mail and telephone. "I haven't given up. I still expect good things from him," she says.

**Marco Zargula (The Charmer):** It's hard to believe that little Marco is almost twenty years of age. He is also in Apalachicola, as a result of a thirty-month sentence, and should be returning to Miami shortly. His release date would have been earlier, but he has been a trouble-maker in prison, causing an extended stay. Marco will come home to a household of two sisters and a brother, each with a new child. His mother, Mrs. Roman, now lives somewhere else with a lover. Her husband, Marco's stepfather, is a fugitive from justice

**302**

with several federal criminal charges awaiting him. The Calcon brothers are still around.

**Lester Burrows (The Runner):** Lester is nowhere to be found. Nothing has changed from childhood to age twenty. Several convictions in the adult court resulted in Lester's placement on probation. He failed, however, to report to his probation officer, and currently a warrant for his arrest is outstanding. Lester no longer visits his grandmother, but she and other members of the family occasionally see him in Liberty City walking the streets alone.

**Jamie Forest (The Nuisance):** Jamie is still as feisty as ever. He hasn't had any bouts with the law, but he continues to be difficult with everyone else. Mack, the milk driver, tried to be a big brother, but after three months, Jamie's penchant for challenging people lost him the job as Mack's helper. From there he joined the Job Corps, immediately earning a ten-day suspension for fighting. He's now back in the Job Corps, stationed in Brunswick, Georgia, studying masonry and preparing for his GED. If he can last the year in the Job Corps, Jamie may yet fool a lot of us.

**Andy Sills (The Drinker):** Andy and his father share an efficiency apartment in Miami Beach. Andy had spent several months in Boston with his father before they returned. Both work in a pizza parlor; father is the chef, and Andy delivers. Andy claims to have his drinking problem under control, but Foster on a visit to his apartment observed, "It was hard to take a step without tripping over a beer can." Andy has been arrest-free, no longer sees Abbie, and has no plans to return to school. In my chambers he was a respectful and mature young man, even inquiring about my health. There was almost an air of confidence about him. "I am working, doing the best I can. There's not much more I can ask for. Cornelius had a lot to do with me getting my shit together."

# Index

# Index

# Index

# Index

# Index

3, 37, 52; assessment by, of Lester Burrows, 3, 57, 78–79, 97, 135, 179; role of, 25–26, 49, 63; assessment by, of Dwight Anderson, 32–33, 42, 49–52, 71, 80, 86, 89, 93–94, 102, 119, 138, 179; assessment by, of Marco Zargula, 35, 37, 56–57, 77–78, 89, 135, 150, 162, 179, 204–5; assessment by, of Laurence Samuel, 37, 69–70, 72–73, 88, 179, 184; assessment by, of Andy Sills, 52–55, 69, 71–72, 102, 119, 179, 205; assessment by, of Cornelius Foster, 52, 54, 57, 59–61, 69, 98, 124, 178; employment of, 62–63, 75–76, 79, 300; assessment by, of Jamie Forest, 101, 120, 139, 180, 184, 205

Marco. *See* Zargula, Marco

Marianna State School, 230–31

Martinson, Robert, 285

Master Counselor Program: goals of, 1, 9–10, 13–14, 19, 21–22, 35, 57–58, 61, 68–69, 89, 119, 144, 169; selection for, 2–5, 8–10, 14, 17–20, 22–23, 25, 47–48, 61, 65, 74, 263–64; reaction to, 9, 13, 15, 28, 33, 36, 38, 51, 56–58, 62, 68, 72, 75–76, 98–100, 108, 112–14, 119–20, 133, 138, 140–41, 155, 178, 180–82, 196, 223, 225–26, 239, 267, 270–72, 276, 281, 297; progress of, 9, 28, 35, 37, 52–54, 57–58, 62, 75, 87–88, 90, 97, 107, 119, 122–25, 140–41, 144–45, 178–82, 202, 204–6, 242, 270–71

Mental Health Clinic. *See* Juvenile Court Mental Health Clinic

Mervin, Keith. *See* Lester Burrows

Miami Lakes Technical Institute, 35

Millar, Nick, 148, 161–62, 168–69

Mooney, Pat, 159

Morrison's Cafeteria, 36

Nassau Start Center, 223, 226

National Council of Juvenile Court Judges, 279

Office of Juvenile Justice Delinquency Program (OJJDP), 81–83, 144, 270, 272

Palm Bay Club, 241

Pedro, 207–8, 224

Perlman, Clifford, 286

Perry, Herman, 17, 41, 68

Polish count, 44, 46–47, 261

Raiford State Prison, 28, 40, 59, 65, 119, 125, 133, 149, 193, 200, 202, 215, 229, 231, 233

Regins, Rose, 243–44, 265–66, 287–88

Regnery, Alfred, 81–84, 110, 144

Roman, Frederick (Marco's stepfather), 23, 77–78, 90, 231, 296–97

Roman, Mrs. (Marco's mother), 22, 29, 34, 56, 77, 90–91, 98, 121, 123–24, 127, 130–31, 137, 140, 143, 170, 173, 183, 217, 219–20, 231, 297

Rosof, Robert, 286

Rosselle, Janet, 210, 249, 253, 300

Russell, Rusty, 253

Samuel, Laurence (The Fighter): selection of, 25; arrests of, 25, 29, 36, 55, 70, 73, 93, 101–2, 106, 115–16, 120, 174–75, 201, 247–53, 282–83; school problems of, 25, 29, 36, 55–56, 69–70, 73, 80, 85–86, 88, 92, 101–2, 106, 149, 168, 210, 214, 247–49, 252; family of, 25, 36–37, 70, 73, 92–93, 106, 120, 136, 193, 198, 201–2, 213–14, 247, 250, 253; reaction to, 25, 37, 55–56, 69–70, 72–73, 88, 92–93, 97, 101–3, 106, 113, 115–16, 120, 125–28, 130, 136, 149, 167–68, 171, 173–76, 179–80, 182–84, 192–93, 195–98, 202–4, 206–7, 210–14, 223–24, 230, 247–53, 271, 282–83, 295; reports on, 25, 92–93, 101, 128, 212, 214, 247; clinical evaluations of, 55–56, 70, 86, 88, 92–93, 101, 126, 136, 171, 174–76, 182, 192–93, 195–98, 202–3, 206–7, 211–13, 247, 282; early youth of, 55, 70, 201, 213; remedial efforts for, 69–70, 73, 86, 92–93, 101, 113, 116, 122, 125–28, 136, 149, 166, 169, 171, 174–75, 180, 182–83, 194, 196, 203, 206–7, 211, 213, 247; substance abuse by, 206

Samuel, Walter (Laurence's father), 25, 55, 70, 201–2, 247

**310**

# Index

**311**

# Index